Social and Cognitive Perspectives on the Sermon on the Mount

Studies in Ancient Religion and Culture

Series Editors:

Philip L. Tite, University of Washington

Michael Ng, Seattle University

Studies in Ancient Religion and Culture (SARC) is concerned with religious and cultural aspects of the ancient world, with a special emphasis on studies that utilize social scientific methods of analysis. By "ancient world," the series is not limited to Greco-Roman and ancient Near Eastern cultures, though that is the primary regional focus. The underlying presupposition is that the study of religion in antiquity needs to be located within cultural and social analysis, situating religious traditions within the broader cultural and geopolitical dynamics within which those traditions are located.

This series also encourages cross-disciplinary research in the study of the ancient world. Due to the historical development of various academic disciplines, there has arisen a set of largely isolated and competing fields of study of the ancient world. Often this fragmentation in academia results in outdated or caricatured scholarly products when one discipline does use research from another discipline. A key goal of this series is to help facilitate greater cross- and inter-disciplinary work, bringing together those who study ancient history (especially social history), archaeology (of various methods and geographic focuses, as well as theorists in archaeology), ancient philosophy, biblical studies, early patristics/church history, Second Temple and formative Judaism, and Greek and Roman classics, as well as philologists.

Given the focus on the social and cultural context within which religion functions, the series also publishes studies which explore the various social locations in which real people in antiquity practiced or interacted with their religious traditions. Examples include the domestic cult, food production and consumption, temple worship, funerary practices/monuments, development of social networks, military cult, and ancient medicine.

Finally, the series encourages a broader application of theoretical and methodological tools to the study of the ancient world. While the main perspective is social-scientific (understood broadly), specific analyses from the reservoir of critical theory, narrative theories, economic theory, bio-archaeology, gender analysis, anthropology of religion, and cognitive theory are welcome.

Social and Cognitive Perspectives on the Sermon on the Mount

Edited by
Rikard Roitto, Colleen Shantz, and Petri Luomanen

SHEFFIELD UK   BRISTOL CT

Published by Equinox Publishing Ltd.

UK: Office 415, The Workstation, 15 Paternoster Row, Sheffield, South Yorkshire S1 2BX

USA: ISD, 70 Enterprise Drive, Bristol, CT 06010

www.equinoxpub.com

First published 2021

© Rikard Roitto, Colleen Shantz, Petri Luomanen and contributors 2021

All rights reserved. No part of this publication may be reproduced or transmitted in any form or by any means, electronic or mechanical, including photocopying, recording or any information storage or retrieval system, without prior permission in writing from the publishers.

British Library Cataloguing-in-Publication Data

A catalogue record for this book is available from the British Library.

ISBN-13 978 1 78179 421 0   (hardback)   978 1 78179 422 7   (paperback)
         978 1 78179 999 4   (ePDF)

Library of Congress Cataloging-in-Publication Data

Names: Roitto, Rikard, editor. | Shantz, Colleen, editor. | Luomanen, Petri, 1961- editor.
Title: Social and cognitive perspectives on the Sermon on the Mount / edited by Rikard Roitto, Colleen Shantz and Petri Luomanen.
Description: Sheffield, UK ; Bristol, CT : Equinox Publishing Ltd, 2021. | Series: Studies in ancient religion and culture | Includes bibliographical references and index. | Summary: "Social and Cognitive Perspectives on the Sermon on the Mount offers fresh readings of themes and individual sayings in the Sermon on the Mount using socio-cognitive approaches"-- Provided by publisher.
Identifiers: LCCN 2019058219 (print) | LCCN 2019058220 (ebook) | ISBN 9781781794210 (hardback) | ISBN 9781781794227 (paperback) | ISBN 9781781799994 (ebook)
Subjects: LCSH: Sermon on the mount--Criticism, interpretation, etc. | Sermon on the mount--Socio-rhetorical criticism. | Psychology, Religious.
Classification: LCC BT380.3 .S655 2020 (print) | LCC BT380.3 (ebook) | DDC 226.9/06--dc23
LC record available at https://lccn.loc.gov/2019058219
LC ebook record available at https://lccn.loc.gov/2019058220

Typeset by ISB Typesetting, Sheffield, UK

Contents

	Foreword	vii
1.	Social and Cognitive Perspectives on the Sermon on the Mount: Introduction Rikard Roitto, Colleen Shantz, and Petri Luomanen	1

PART I: INDIVIDUAL COGNITION

2.	It's All in How You Look at It: The Eyes and Morality in Matthew 6.22-23 Colleen Shantz	37
3.	Perception of Risk in the Sermon on the Mount Rikard Roitto	60
4.	Altruism and Prosocial Ideals in the Sermon: Between Human Nature and Divine Potential Thomas Kazen	82
5.	Ritual Acts in the Sermon on the Mount Rodney A. Werline	110

PART II: TEXT AND COGNITION

6.	Emotional Repression and Physical Mutilation? The Cognitive and Behavioral Impact of Exaggeration in the Sermon on the Mount Thomas Kazen	133
7.	Parables in the Sermon on the Mount—a Cognitive and Rhetorical Perspective Lauri Thurén	174
8.	Is There a Reason to Worry? A Pragma-Dialectical Analysis of Matthew 6.25-34 Niilo Lahti	205

PART III: SOCIAL DYNAMICS

9.	Hypocrites and the Pure in Heart: Religion as an Evolved Strategy for In-Group Formation John Teehan	239

10. "Whoever is kind to the poor lends to Yahweh, and will be repaid in full" (Proverbs 19.17): Patterns of Indirect Reciprocity in the Book of Proverbs and in the Sermon on the Mount   264
Anne Katrine de Hemmer Gudme

11. Macarisms and Identity Formation: Insights from the Comparison of 4Q525 and the Sermon on the Mount   286
Elisa Uusimäki

12. Remembering the Sermon in the Mountains of France   307
Alicia J. Batten

Index of References   333
Index of Modern Authors   339
Index of Subjects   347

Foreword

The work of a number of people and institutions have helped to make this project possible. First of all, as editors we would like to extend our heartfelt thanks to all the authors in this volume, who together have created a unique contribution to the study of the Sermon on the Mount. Although a multitude of studies have been devoted to the Sermon, the contributors to this volume share the conviction that developments in the study of human cognition offer new insights to analyze the Sermon's astonishing ability to address audiences throughout the centuries.

This volume began as the fruit of a workshop on social-scientific and cognitive perspectives on the Sermon on the Mount, held in Helsinki, in 2014. The workshop concluded a series of nine workshops in the NordForsk Network on Socio-Cognitive Perspectives on Early Judaism and Early Christianity. The funding from NordForsk enabled scholars from the Nordic countries, together with invited guests, to meet in different Nordic universities for period of three years and develop their research in the broad methodological field of social-scientific and cognitive interpretation of biblical texts. We are grateful for the NordForsk funding but also, more generally, for the support that Nordic countries offer for research in the humanities among other disciplines.

After the workshop, additional authors were invited to contribute to the volume, which has broadened the analytical perspectives of the volume at hand. We are also indebted to Ann Taves and Eric Barreto, whose valuable comments on our approach in the Society of Biblical Literature Annual Meeting (Denver, 2018) have been incorporated into the introduction of the volume, and express our gratitude.

We thank Samuel Auler for his careful work on the manuscript and its bibliography. We are also grateful to Philip Tite, editor of the Studies in Ancient Religion and Culture series, and Sarah Lee, book production manager at Equinox Publishing for their advice and patience as the volume incubated. Finally, special thanks are due to Audrey Mann, project manager, who solved problems with creativity, monitored details both large and small, and generously dug into the work of production during the turmoil of the pandemic year.

Rikard Roitto, Stockholm School of Theology
Colleen Shantz, St. Michael's College, University of Toronto
Petri Luomanen, University of Helsinki

Chapter One

Social and Cognitive Perspectives on the Sermon on the Mount: Introduction

Rikard Roitto, Colleen Shantz, and Petri Luomanen

A Sermon That Has Moved Its Audiences throughout the Centuries

Innumerable readers of the Sermon on the Mount have been deeply moved by it. Some have been provoked to despair, others have been inspired to take action—sometimes even to form communities devoted to its vision of the kingdom. Medieval Christians decided that the Sermon shows the path of celibacy; Lutherans viewed it as a preamble to the gospel of grace, meant to show us our sinful inadequacy; Anabaptists claimed it as the rule of true Christian faith.[1] Throughout history, the Sermon has exercised an influence that perhaps no other biblical text or sermon can parallel.[2]

Scholarly contributions and methodological approaches to the Sermon are also innumerable—so, why still another book on the Sermon on the Mount? What is the new that "social and cognitive perspectives" in this volume offer to its readers? Contributions in this volume grow from developments in the study of human cognition. These, we believe, can cast some new light on one of the astonishing features of the Sermon on the Mount: its ability to influence its audiences throughout the centuries. What innate cognitive capacities and functions of the human mind may help to explain the

---

1. Dale C. Allison, *The Sermon on the Mount: Inspiring the Moral Imagination* (New York: Crossroad, 1999), 1–7.
2. For histories of interpretation, see for example Hans Dieter Betz, *The Sermon on the Mount: A Commentary on the Sermon on the Mount, including the Sermon on the Plain (Matthew 5:3–7:27 and Luke 6:20–49)* (Minneapolis, MN: Fortress Press, 1995); Warren Carter, *What Are They Saying about Matthew's Sermon on the Mount?* (Mahwah, NJ: Paulist Press, 1994); Jeffrey P. Greenman, Timothy Larsen, and Stephen R. Spencer, eds., *The Sermon on the Mount through the Centuries* (Grand Rapids, MI: Brazos Press, 2007); Warren S. Kissinger, *The Sermon on the Mount: A History of Interpretation and Bibliography* (ATLA Bibliography Series; Lanham, MD: Scarecrow Press, 1998); Ulrich Luz, *Matthew 1–7: A Commentary* (Hermeneia; Edinburgh: T&T Clark, 1990); and Jaroslav Pelikan, *Divine Rhetoric: The Sermon on the Mount as Message and as Model in Augustine, Chrysostom, and Luther* (Crestwood, NY: St. Vladimir's Seminary Press, 2000).

Sermon's persistent influence? What patterns of human understanding does it appeal to? What kind of group dynamics does it inspire?

The contributors to this volume use different kinds of behavioral sciences heuristically to understand the Sermon's content and force.[3] Here, the term "behavioral sciences" applies broadly to encompass all disciplines that analyze how humans perceive and behave—for example anthropology, sociology, social identity theory, cognitive psychology, embodied cognition, psychology of emotions, evolutionary psychology, risk perception, ritual theory, and rhetoric. As is commonly recognized in contemporary hermeneutics, in choosing a particular method, one also chooses what kinds of results one will produce. We do, however, believe that our choice of behavioral methods is important precisely because it helps us understand the directive force of the Sermon. The most basic hermeneutical assumption of this volume is that the Sermon, just like any text, is formed by both *innate* and *cultural* cognitive constraints and capacities, and that the Sermon, in turn, informs cognition and culture. In order to understand these processes, we need to understand the human condition.

The Sermon on the Mount in Earlier Scholarship

Our approach shares with the "new" approaches of preceding generations the feature that they also have been children of their time. Earlier scholarship has even partly addressed some of the features in the Sermon that are discussed in this volume. Therefore, and in order to provide an appropriate context for the present volume, it will be helpful to briefly introduce some of the prominent approaches to the Sermon in the history of scholarship. The aim of the following is not to provide an exhaustive description of the earlier scholarship, for which there are other volumes to consult.[4] The purpose is simply to note some influential examples that illustrate how themes related to the three main parts of this volume have been addressed before: individuals as responsive recipients of the Sermon's message (Part I), detailed formal and literary study of the Sermon's text (Part II), and social contexts suggested for the Sermon (Part III).

---

3. On the heuristic use of behavioral sciences, see for example Philip. F. Esler, "Social-Scientific Models in Biblical Interpretation," in *Ancient Israel: The Old Testament in its Social Context*, ed. Philip. F. Esler (London: SCM, 2005), 3–14; Gerd Theissen, *Erleben und Verhalten der ersten Christen: Eine Psychologie des Urchristentums* (Gütersloh: Gütersloher Verlags-Haus, 2007), 20–32.

4. See above n. 2.

The Sermon, Its Ethics, and Individual Recipients

Numerous scholars have been puzzled by the Sermon's high norms and ethical ideals, trying to find interpretations that would make sense as responses required from individual recipients of its message. Eduard Schweizer's comment summarizes much of the twentieth-century scholarship on the Sermon: "The most difficult question posed by the Sermon on the Mount is whether its demands can be fulfilled."[5]

Hans Windisch's book *Der Sinn der Bergpredigt* (1928) marks in many ways a turning point in the twentieth-century German study of the Sermon on the Mount.[6] Windisch targeted two theological lines of interpretation of his time: interpretations that applied either imperative or dogmatic formulations. He claimed both alternatives to be wrong in assuming that literal fulfilment of Jesus' commandments in the Sermon is not possible. The interpretations that followed the imperative line understood Jesus' commandments as aiming at the ethics of mentality or attitude (*Gesinnungsethik*; Wilhelm Herrmann), total denial of law and ethics (H. Hartmann), correct being and ethos instead of doing and ethics (Martin Dibelius), or at total obedience and correct mentality and attitude (Rudolf Bultmann). The dogmatic solutions, for their part, engaged the traditional law versus grace dichotomy, according to which Jesus' commandments were to make people realize their guilt and to effect repentance, conversion, and life in close relationship with God.[7] Windisch's own thesis was that the Sermon provides concrete *terms for entering the kingdom of heaven*, which is a counterpart to the Mosaic law. Jesus is a new lawgiver and the Sermon is the new law. Its commandments are meant to be obeyed and they can be fulfilled.[8] In Windisch's view, the only thing that distinguished Jesus from the rabbis of his time was the role of the Golden Rule, which Jesus used to displace all the "inhuman, cultic and ceremonial parts of the Torah."[9] Obviously Windisch, who was writing in the 1920s, was marred by the inappropriate legalistic

---

5. Eduard Schweizer, *The Good News according to Matthew*, trans. David E. Green (Atlanta, GA: John Knox Press, 1975), 193.
6. The following overview of the history of research from Windisch to post-Sanders covenantal nomistic interpretations is based on Petri Luomanen, *Entering the Kingdom of Heaven: A Study on the Structure of Matthew's View of Salvation* (WUNT, 2/101; Tübingen: Mohr Siebeck, 1998), 3–34.
7. Hans Windisch identifies the early generation of theological interpreters like Carl Stange and Rudolf Kittel as examples. See Windisch, *Der Sinn der Bergpredigt: Ein Beitrag zum Problem der richtigen Exegese* (UNT; Leipzig: Hinrichs, 1929), 22–43.
8. Windisch, *Der Sinn der Bergpredigt*, 10–1, 46–51.
9. Windisch, *Der Sinn der Bergpredigt*, 47–8, 106.

picture of ancient Judaism, which was corrected in New Testament studies only during the last quarter of the twentieth century.[10]

In the English-speaking scholarly world, Benjamin W. Bacon's *Studies in Matthew* (1930) gained a position that was comparable in many respects to Windisch's book in Germany. According to Bacon, Matthew wanted to imitate the five books of Moses and arranged his materials in five sections, all containing a narrative part and a discourse. The Sermon forms the discourse of the first book, following the narrative in chapters 3–4. Bacon pictured Matthew as a converted rabbi who fought against Hellenization and antinomianism but ended up being a "neo-legalist" himself.[11]

The legalistic line of interpretation of the Gospel of Matthew, with the Sermon as its core, reached its culmination point in 1970s and 1980s with ultra-Protestant interpretations of Siegfrid Schulz and Willi Marxsen. In Schultz's view, Matthew espouses the justification of the pious and thus expresses early Catholicism.[12] For his part, Marxsen argued that Matthew's thinking is not Christian at all. Marxsen supported Windisch's characterization of the Sermon on the Mount as a discourse containing the entrance requirements to the kingdom of heaven. For Marxsen people who tried to fulfill the requirements probably thought along the lines of (what Marxsen understood to be) the prevalent Jewish expectation that in the last judgment the fulfilled and unfulfilled commandments were to be weighed.[13] Thus Marxsen drew a provocative conclusion for his time: the Sermon that is often considered as the landmark of Jesus' proclamation is not amenable to Christian interpretation.

More favorable assessments of the "greater righteousness" of the Sermon appeared again in the last quarter of the twentieth century when an understanding of the character of Judaism as covenantal religion became largely accepted among New Testament scholars, thanks to the work of Ed Sanders and others.[14] According to this line of interpretation, Jesus' proclamation of a righteousness that exceeds that of the Pharisees and scribes is taken as a

---

10. It is to be noted, however, that Windisch already realized there being a discrepancy between Matthew's description of the Jews and the testimony of their own sources, Windisch, *Der Sinn der Bergpredigt*, 103–4.

11. Benjamin W. Bacon, *Studies in Matthew* (London: Constable, 1930), xvii, 47, 81.

12. Siegfried Schulz, *Die Mitte der Schrift: Der Frühkatholizismus im Neuen Testament als Herausforderung an den Protestantismus* (Stuttgart: Kreuz Verlag, 1976), 173–8, 84–7.

13. Willi Marxsen, *"Christliche" und christliche Ethik im Neuen Testament* (Gütersloh: Mohn, 1989), 207–16.

14. Ed P. Sanders, *Paul and Palestinian Judaism: A Comparison of Patterns of Religion* (London: SCM, 1977).

variation of traditional covenantal religion where righteousness belongs to the sphere of "staying in."[15]

What is it that makes our focus on individual cognition different from the above described approaches where an individual's response to the message of the Sermon also plays a key role? For those who deemed the norms and ideals as unfulfillable (Dibelius, Bultmann), the logical conclusion was that the Sermon must be aiming at right *ethos or attitude*. Alternatively, the Sermon was seen as aiming at creating an individual *emotional response* of despair in the face of realizing one's sinfulness (Lutheran orthodoxy, Kittel) or in legalistic interpretations simply to an endless struggle of trying to balance one's deeds and misdeeds.

Although these theological interpretations involved individual, even emotional responses, typically what they imagined is part of a more abstract theological system, which is not directly accessible or effective in the text of the Sermon. For these approaches, correct interpretation requires an understanding of a wider theological framework. Our approach does not call forth more abstract theological frameworks; rather, we focus on the ways that the Sermon may appeal more directly to various innate cognitive mechanisms and may even trigger action—without any more sophisticated mediating theological reflection.

In this regard, our approach can be contrasted by one of the most well recognized analyses of the purpose of the Sermon, namely Hans Dieter Betz's suggestion that the Sermon is an "epitome."[16] That is, the Sermon is, according to Betz, a systematic summary of the most important "doctrines" of Jesus's teaching, similar to the handbooks of ancient philosophers. Although Betz recognizes that what Jesus "taught" (5.2) should not only lead the disciple to "hear" but also to "do" (7.24), he still insists that the goal of the Sermon is "enabling the disciples to theologize."[17] Betz, a scholar of impressive learning in theology, has chosen the method of theological

---

15. Benno Przybylski, *Righteousness in Matthew and his World of Thought* (SNTSMS, 41; Cambridge: Cambridge University Press, 1980), 77–107; Roger Mohrlang, *Matthew and Paul: A Comparison of Ethical Perspectives* (SNTSMS, 48; Cambridge: Cambridge University Press, 1984), 17–9; K. Syreeni, *The Making of the Sermon on the Mount: A Procedural Analysis of Matthew's Redactoral Activity* (Annales Scientiarum Fennicae: Dissertationes Humanum Litterarum, 44; Helsinki: Academia Scientiarum Fennica, 1987), 207–26; Luomanen, *Entering the Kingdom of Heaven*, 281–4. Notably a covenantal interpretation of Matthew, though without Sanders's idea about "covenantal nomism," was already provided by W. Trilling, *Das Wahre Israel: Studien zur Theologie des Matthäusevangeliums* (München: Kösel, 1964).

16. Hans Dieter Betz, *Essays on the Sermon on the Mount* (Philadelphia, PA: Fortress Press, 1985), 1–16; Betz, *The Sermon on the Mount,* 70–88.

17. Betz, *The Sermon on the Mount,* 85.

analysis to understand the text, which inevitably produces a didactic understanding of the purpose of the Sermon. The ideal Betzian hearer, just like a trained theologian, is meant to ponder the doctrines of the Sermon carefully. By contrast, the behavioral methods presented here sensitize us to see the action-inducing properties that are already inherent in the text. Thus, for example, we recognize that the Sermon not only evokes intellectual reflection but also affective responses that give impulse to action. That is, a combination of intellectual, perceptual, and emotional stimuli invokes action. The Sermon better resembles a campaign rally speech than an information brochure or a catechism to be memorized.

The early twentieth-century German interpretations where the Sermon is expected to evoke a new kind of mentality or attitude also have their modern counterparts. Charles Talbert has suggested that "character formation" and "decision making" are the purposes of the Sermon on the Mount.[18] That is, the Sermon inspires momentary moral decisions in certain situations, but also has long-term effects on the virtue of its readers. However, while the older interpretations were linked with highly developed theological systems, in the present state of research, and especially in our goal for this volume, individual moral behavior and development can also be analyzed and explained in a psychological framework. Since contemporary psychology agrees with Aristotle's analysis of virtue (character traits) as being composed of both intellectual and emotional properties (*Nic. Eth.* 6.2.1–4), Talbert's suggestion about character formation is to the point.[19] Several contributions of this volume analyze how the Sermon can have both short-term and long-term effects on both perceptual and emotional dispositions.

Text and Cognition

The Sermon's linguistic, structural, and rhetorical features—the focus of Part II of this volume—have also intrigued scholars throughout centuries. In fact, its status as a separate rhetorical and literary unit was elevated when St. Augustine wrote a commentary on Matthew 5–7 with the title *De sermone domini in monte*, thus making the Sermon a special object of study. As Kari Syreeni has aptly noted, the Sermon on the Mount corresponds with

---

18. Charles H. Talbert, *Reading the Sermon on the Mount: Character Formation and Decision Making in Matthew 5–7* (Columbia, SC: University of South Carolina Press, 2004), 27–31. Similarly, Dale Allison whose thesis is expressed in the subtitle of his book: The Sermon is *"Inspiring Moral Imagination."*

19. For example, Jonathan Haidt, "The Moral Emotions," in *Handbook of Affective Sciences*, eds. R. J. Davidson, K. R. Scherer, and H. H. Goldsmith (Oxford: Oxford University Press, 2003), 852–70.

Aristotelian ideals about artistic unity: it has a "beginning, a middle and an end" (Aristotle, *Poetics* VII). This makes the Sermon a unified speech, which may be one reason for its success.[20]

Further, according to Aristotle, the beauty of an object also depends on a proper proportions (*Poetics* VII). The object must not be too small or too large. In the case of a plot (of a tragedy) this means that it must be of a length that can be memorized easily. On the other hand, the plot must be long enough to allow changes in fortune, from good fortune to bad, or from bad to good. Although the Sermon is not a continuous narrative but a sequence of Jesus' teachings, it is interesting to notice that its opening section, the beatitudes, proclaim the turning of bad fortunes to good, while (in keeping with the traditional Two-Ways wisdom teaching) the speech is closed with parables that threaten to turn good fortunes into bad if Jesus' teachings are not followed. Thus, we may say that in terms of Aristotle's criteria for artistic beauty (of a tragedy) the Sermon displays an appropriate structure and length, with attention grabbing examples of twists of fortune.

Although the Sermon with its attention grabbing rhetoric is often presented in public discourse as a prime example of Jesus' proclamation, redaction-critical research has revealed that the structure of the Sermon, its concentric opening and closing formulas (5.1-2; 7.28) and the frames of the middle section ("the law and the prophets" in 5.17 and 7.12) derive from the editor of the Gospel.[21] All the central terms and ideas of the Sermon are also well distributed throughout the Gospel of Matthew.[22] For these reasons, although the Sermon gives the impression of a sermon delivered in a partic-

---

20. Kari Syreeni, "The Sermon on the Mount: Christian or Universal Ethics?," in *Christianity and the Roots of Morality: Philosophical, Early Christian, and Empirical Perspectives,* eds. Petri Luomanen, Anne Birgitta Pessi, and Ilkka Pyysiäinen (Philosophical Studies in Science and Religion, 8; Leiden: Brill, 2017), 140–1. To be sure, in this passage Aristotle actually discusses the plot of a tragedy but as Syreeni points out the principle can be applied to textual units in general.

21. See, for instance, Ulrich Luz, *Das Evangelium nach Matthäus, Mt 1–7* (EKKNT I/1; Zürich: Benzinger Verlag; Neukirchen-Vluyn: Neukirchener Verlag, 1989), 185–8, who finds the center of the Sermon in the Lord's Prayer (6.7-15). For a methodologically sophisticated compositional and redactional analysis of the Sermon, see Syreeni, *The Making of the Sermon on the Mount.*

22. This was already noted by William D. Davies, *The Setting of the Sermon on the Mount* (Cambridge: Cambridge University Press, 1964), 14. This clearly speaks against Betz's hypothesis about the pre-Matthean composition of the Sermon on the Mount. For a detailed criticism of Betz's position, see Graham N. Stanton, *A Gospel for a New People: Studies in Matthew* (Edinburgh: T&T Clark, 1992), 310–25. Betz's idea about a particularistic pre-Matthean Sermon being in tension with the universalistic traits in the other parts of the gospel is also challenged in the narrative analysis of the Sermon by Boris Paschke, *Particularism and Universalism in the Sermon on the Mount:*

ular time and place by Jesus, it is, first and foremost, a literary product that imitates reality.[23]

While earlier historical-critically oriented scholars studied the characteristics of the text of the Sermon by paying attention to the genre and tradition-historical parallels of the smaller units of the Sermon, more recent linguistic approaches have sought to highlight more general cognitive and structural elements in the text. The essays in this volume (particularly those in Part II) share these goals but in marked distinction to some earlier studies. Anna Wierzbicka's *What Did Jesus Mean? Explaining the Sermon on the Mount and the Parables in Simple and Universal Human Concepts* can be classified as one of the first experiments to apply cognitive linguistics in the study of the Sermon on the Mount.[24] Wierzbicka, professor emerita in linguistics at Australian National University, is famous for developing the Natural Semantic Metalanguage (NSM) approach, and her book is an experiment in applying that approach to the Sermon and parables of Jesus. NSM is inspired by Leibniz's idea of self-explanatory core concepts that are required to make less clear concepts comprehensible. NSM is further based on the assumption that there is a core of innate "semantic primes," basic universal meanings that can be expressed in all languages. These include concepts like BAD, SOMEONE, SOMETHING, YOU, I, DO HAPPEN, KNOW, THINK, THIS, and OTHER. Consequently, it is assumed that more complex and culture-specific words and expressions can be analyzed and expressed with the help of these kinds of universal semantic primes.[25]

Wierzbicka's analysis of the beatitude of the weeping results in the following translation into metalanguage:

> sometimes very bad things happen to people
> because these things happen, these people feel something very bad
> like a person feels something very bad when someone dies.[26]

Wierzbicka, who approaches the Sermon as a linguist, is to be credited for making the effort to learn the basics of historical-critical study of the Bible. She is not reading the Sermon simply as a piece of instruction from Jesus,

---

A Narrative-Critical Analysis of Matthew 5–7 in the Light of Matthew's View on Mission (NTAbh, 56; Münster: Aschendorff, 2012).

23. Syreeni, "The Sermon on the Mount: Christian or Universal Ethics?," 141, especially n. 5. Cf., for instance, Aristotle, *Poetics* I.

24. Anna Wierzbicka, *What Did Jesus Mean? Explaining the Sermon on the Mount and the Parables in Simple and Universal Human Concepts* (Oxford: Oxford University Press, 2001), 6–9.

25. Wierzbicka, *What Did Jesus Mean?*, 6–9.

26. Wierzbicka, *What Did Jesus Mean?*, 32.

but engages the tradition history of the passages.[27] Nevertheless, her "translation" of the message of the Sermon into NSM has not been received with enthusiasm among scholars, mainly because the result from this explanatory process gives the impression of being only a pale reflection of the Sermon.[28] When expressed in terms of the irreducible semantic primes the text seems to lose all its aesthetic and emotional power.

Wierzbicka's analysis is built on a set of presuppositions about the character of language that differs markedly from the theory adopted in this volume. The bone of contention lies in the understanding of the role of metaphors in human communication. For Wierzbicka, metaphors are only decoration that might have some artistic value but that need to be explained by explicit and perfectly clear concepts:

> The principle is clear: a metaphorical definition is not a real definition, because it stands itself in need of an explanation. Definitions are—by definition—verbal explications. It doesn't make sense to try to make the meaning of a word or an expression EXPLICIT by means of a linguistic device (metaphor) which by definition can't convey meaning in a fully explicit manner. But that's precisely what definitions are meant to achieve: to "translate" obscure concepts into clear ones, complex concepts into simple ones, not fully explicit concepts into fully explicit ones.[29]

In contrast to Wierzbicka, the present volume is more in line with the understanding of metaphors developed by George Lakoff and Mark Johnson.[30] Chapters here fully acknowledge the fundamental role of metaphors in language and the embodied character of language that cannot be detached

---

27. In contrast to Andrej Kodjak, *A Structural Analysis of the Sermon on the Mount* (Religion and Reason: Method and Theory in the Study and Interpretation of Religion; New York: Mouton de Gruyter, 1986).

28. See, for instance, Maurice Casey, review of *What Did Jesus Mean? Explaining the Sermon on the Mount and the Parables in Simple and Universal Human Concepts*, by Anna Wierzbicka, *Theology* 106 (2003): 193–4. Alan S. Kaye, review of *What Did Jesus Mean? Explaining the Sermon on the Mount and the Parables in Simple and Universal Human Concepts*, by Anna Wierzbicka, *Language* 79 (2003): 226–7.

29. Anna Wierzbicka, "Metaphors Linguists Live By: Lakoff and Johnson contra Aristotle," *Paper in Linguistics* 19 (1986): 294–5. Consequently, Wiertzbicka also assumes emotions to have psychological non-bodily character (p. 299): "Rather, when we see tears, or a drooping posture, in somebody else we tend to interpret it as a sign of an emotion which we can identify (sub-consciously) in psychological, non-bodily terms, of the kind spelled out in the definitions given above. And what applies to experience applies also to conceptualization: the claim that we conceptualize emotions via their external symptoms is totally unsubstantiated."

30. George Lakoff and Mark Johnson, *Metaphors We Live By* (London: University of Chicago Press, 1980). Lakoff and Johnson, *Philosophy in the Flesh: The Embodied Mind and its Challenge to Western Thought* (New York, NY: Basic Books, 1999).

from the meaning of words. Thomas Kazen's chapter on exaggeration in the Sermon (Chapter 6) is an example of the benefits of taking the fundamental metaphorical character of language seriously by analyzing its modifications through blending theory and showing how new blends, if successful, may enhance understanding. That is, we understand better by developing metaphorical language, not by explaining metaphors by simpler cognitive primes. Colleen Shantz's chapter (Chapter 2) and Kazen's other contribution (Chapter 4), for their part, show how fundamental the embodied character of language is in human communication.[31]

Stephen Toulmin's approach to argumentation, applied in two articles of this volume (Thuren, Chapter 7, and Lahti, Chapter 8), shares with Wierzbicka's theory the idea of analyzing texts in terms of underlying implicit concepts and structure. However, there is a clear difference between these approaches, too. While the NSM theorizes universal meaning and core grammar, Toulmin's approach is—as the name "pragma-dialectical" indicates—more pragmatic in character. At its heart lies the distinction between "field-dependent" and "field-invariant" arguments. This implies that it is not possible to create a list of universally valid arguments that would be applicable in all cases; rather, there is a stable set of argument types that can be selected according to the circumstances in which the argumentation takes place. What is decisive in the analysis is the argumentative field and the position of a concept in the argumentative structure, not its specific, possibly universally attested, contents and validity.[32]

Social Dynamics

Part III of this volume addresses social dynamics and, thus, may find its closest scholarly forebear in redaction criticism. Redaction-critical analysis focuses on the final form of the gospels (or any text) as the product of editorial efforts. It further assumes that such editing took place for particular purposes and, for that reason, redaction criticism also entails consideration

---

31. Lakoff even refuses to see the NSM as a part of cognitive linguistics, see Roberta Pires de Oliveira, "Cognitive Semantics: In the Heart of Language, an Interview with Georg Lakoff," *Fórum Lingüístico* 1 (1998): 83–119. For less extremist critique and mediating positions, see Joseph Hilferty, "Mothers, Lies, and Bachelors: A Brief Reply to Wierzbicka (1990)," *Word* 48 (1997): 51–9, and Marija M. Brala, "NSM within the Cognitive Linguistics Movement: Bridging Some Gaps," *Jezikoslovlje* 4 (2003): 161–86. Wierzbicka is supported by Cliff Goddard, "Bad Arguments against Semantic Primitives," *Theoretical Linguistics* 24 (1998): 129–56, who has developed the approach with her.

32. Cf. Stephen Edelston Toulmin, *The Uses of Argument* (Cambridge: Cambridge University Press, 2003), 11–40.

of the setting where the editing took place. For many early redaction critics, the setting was primarily pictured in theological terms. However, as an heir of *form criticism* with its idea about *Sitz im Leben*—that, in turn, was partly inspired by the rise of social sciences in the beginning of the twentieth century—redaction-critical analysis also raises questions about the social setting in which the final forms of the gospels were produced.

In one influential study of this sort, W. D. Davies's *Setting of the Sermon on the Mount* found the social context for Matthew's Sermon in the post-70 CE period, when Judaism was recovering and reorganizing its functions after the tragic loss of its center, the Jerusalem temple. In Davies's view, the Sermon on the Mount could be fruitfully regarded as a Christian answer to the deliberations at Jamnia, which Davies pictured as the center of post-70 Judaism under the leadership of Johanan ben Zakkai.[33] Later scholarship has shown this picture to be too simplistic.[34] Indeed, by the end of the first century CE, different Jewish movements and factions were still struggling and competing for power—though also tolerating and living in peace with each other—reflecting the general "sectarian" character of the Second Temple Judaism even before 70 CE.[35] After Davies, the picture of Matthew's relation to contemporary Judaism has become more nuanced, and the discussion has been balanced by paying more attention to Matthew's place in the Graeco-Roman world at large, especially its imperial aspects.[36] However, scholarship on the Gospel of Matthew still largely shares Davies's basic assumption that the final editing of the gospel and the Sermon cannot be understood without explicating its relation to (other) Jewish movements of its time.[37]

---

33. Davies, *The Setting of the Sermon on the Mount*, 256–315, esp. 315.

34. The process of consolidation and "parting of the ways" between Judaism and Christianity was much more complex and took several centuries. See Daniel Boyarin, *Dying for God: Martyrdom and the Making of Christianity and Judaism* (Stanford, CA: Stanford University Press, 1999); Boyarin, *Border Lines: The Partition of Judaeo-Christianity* (Philadelphia, PA: The University of Pennsylvania Press, 2004); Adam H. Becker and Annette Yoshiko Reed, eds., *The Ways that Never Parted: Jews and Christians in Late Antiquity and Early Middle Ages* (Minneapolis, MN: Fortress, 2007).

35. Albert I. Baumgarten, *The Flourishing of Jewish Sects in the Maccabean Era* (JSJSup, 55; Atlanta, GA: Society of Biblical Literature, 1997).

36. For this perspective, see especially Warren Carter, *Matthew and the Margins: A Socio-Political and Religious Reading* (JSNTSup, 204; Sheffield: Sheffield Academic Press, 2000), 128–95; Carter, *Matthew and Empire: Initial Explorations* (Harrisburg, PA: Trinity Press International, 2001).

37. For instance, Hans-Jürgen Becker and Serge Ruzer, eds, *The Sermon on the Mount and its Jewish Setting* (CahRB, 60; Paris: J. Gabalda, 2005). For an overview of more recent studies on Matthew, see Eve-Marie Becker and Anders Runesson, eds., *Mark and Matthew I: Comparative Readings, Understanding the Earliest Gospels in*

The development of social-scientific analysis of the Bible has also provided tools for better understanding the social dynamics that characterized the setting where the Gospel of Matthew and the Sermon received their final editorial touch. On the one hand, social-historical analysis has added details to the picture of the social setting where the Sermon was transmitted.[38] On the other hand, theories and models adopted from social sciences have further clarified the social dynamics between the Sermon and its social setting. Berger and Luckmann's sociology of knowledge with legitimation as its key concept provided a smooth transition from purely theological exposition towards recognition of the multiple ways that a social context can instigate justification of new practices and ideas.[39] In the case of Matthew, the idea of legitimation provides means to clarify continuity and tension between an emerging Christian/Jewish-Christian identity and more traditional Jewish convictions and practices.[40] Furthermore, the advent of sectarian studies moved the discussion even more squarely to the arena of social interaction between Matthew's community and other groups and institutions, with social-scientific theories and models paving the way.[41]

Social psychological perspectives, especially the social identity approach, have further clarified the group processes implied in the Gospel of Matthew and the Sermon.[42] Social identity theory has strong cognitive foundations

---

their First Century Settings (WUNT, 271; Tübingen: Mohr Siebeck, 2011); Becker and Runesson, *Mark and Matthew II: Comparative Readings, Reception History, Cultural Hermeneutics, and Theology* (WUNT, 304; Tübingen: Mohr Siebeck, 2013).

38. David L. Balch, ed., *Social History of the Matthean Community: Cross-Disicplinary Approaches* (Minneapolis, MN: Fortress, 1991) paved the way for such undertakings.

39. Petri Luomanen, "The Sociology of Knowledge, the Social Identity Approach, and the Cognitive Study of Religion," in *Explaining Christian Origins and Early Judaism: Contributions from Cognitive and Social Science,* ed. Petri Luomanen, Risto Uro, and Ilkka Pyysiäinen (BibInt, 89; Leiden: Brill, 2007), 201–8.

40.   J. Andrew Overman, *Matthew's Gospels and Formative Judaism: The Social World of the Matthean Community* (Minneapolis, MN: Fortress, 1990) provides an example of the first applications of the sociology of knowledge to Matthew's gospel.

41.   Among the first to apply sectarian perspective to Matthew's gospel were Stanton, *A Gospel for a New People*, 85–107 and Anthony J. Saldarini, *Matthew's Christian-Jewish Community* (CSHJ; Chicago. IL: University of Chicago Press, 1994). For an overview and evaluation of this branch of studies, see Petri Luomanen, "The 'Sociology of Sectarianism' in Matthew: Modeling the Genesis of Early Jewish and Christian Communities," in *Fair Play: Diversity and Conflicts in Early Christianity, Essays in Honour of Heikki Räisänen,* ed. Ismo Dunderberg, Christopher Tuckett, and Kari Syreeni (Leiden: Brill, 2002).

42.   The social identity approach is an umbrella concept that refers to two closely related theories: social identity theory that was developed in the 1970s by Henri Tajfel and John Turner, and to Turner's self-categorization theory. For an overview of these

since Henry Tajfel developed its core ideas on the basis of experiments of perception and categorization he made in the field of cognitive psychology in the 1950s and 1960s.[43] Because human cognition has remained practically the same during the last millennia, the study of group processes provides a means to bridge the hermeneutical gap between our present reality and the original historical context of the Sermon.[44] Group processes inherent in the text of the Sermon with their innate and universal cognitive basis may also partly explain the community forming potential of the Sermon.

Philip Esler's analysis of the beatitudes is a fine example of the benefits of applying a social identity approach in the analysis of the Sermon.[45] Esler's argument in his study on the beatitudes (which actually has bearing on the whole Sermon) is that the beatitudes are best understood as a way to describe the identity of the Matthean community. The beatitudes contain group norms (e.g., "poor in the spirit," 5.3), narratives about the group's aspirations (e.g., "they will inherit the land," 5.5), and descriptions of the group's current reality (e.g., persecution, 5.10-11). Later in the Sermon, the audience is contrasted with outgroups, such as "the scribes and the Pharisees" (5.20), "the hypocrites" (6.5), and "the Gentiles" (6.7). The ethics of the group is a means to advertise the group to the world (5.13-16). These are typical features of a discourse that formulates the identity of a group in relation to other groups. The simple observation that large portions of the Sermon address its audience in the plural precludes purely individualistic interpretations. The last section of chapters in this volume emphasize the

---

theories, see Naomi Ellemers and Alexander Haslam, "Social Identity Theory," in *Handbook of Theories of Social Psychology*, ed. Paul A. M. van Lange, Arie W. Kruglanski, and E. Tory Higgins (London: Sage, 2012), 379–98; John Turner and Katherine J. Reynolds, "Self-Categorization Theory," in *Handbook of Theories of Social Psychology*, ed. Paul A. M. van Lange, Arie W. Kruglanski, and E. Tory Higgins (London: Sage, 2012), 399–417.

43. Dominic Abrams and Michael A. Hogg, "An Introduction to the Social Identity Approach," in *Social Identity Theory: Constructive and Critical Advances*, ed. Dominic Abrams and Michael A. Hogg (New York: Harvester Wheatsheaf, 1990), 19–20.

44. Petri Luomanen, Risto Uro, and Ilkka Pyysiäinen, "Introduction: Social and Cognitive Perspectives in the Study of Christian Origins and Early Judaism," in *Explaining Christian Origins and Early Judaism: Contributions from Cognitive and Social Science*, ed. Petri Luomanen, Risto Uro, and Ilkka Pyysiäinen (BibInt, 89; Leiden: Brill, 2007).

45. Philip F. Esler, "Group Norms and Prototypes in Matthew 5.3–12: A Social Identity Interpretation of the Matthean Beatitudes," in *T&T Clark Handbook to Social Identity in the New Testament*, ed. J. Brian Tucker and Coleman A. Baker (London: T&T Clark, 2013). Esler also had a key role in introducing the sociology of knowledge to biblical studies and he has been one of the scholars to develop sectarian studies. For the application of the social identity analysis to the Sermon see also Elisa Uusimäki's contribution to this volume (Chapter 1).

community forming aspects of the Sermon and analyze the group dynamic effects that the Sermon might have on a community of readers.

What Can Social and Cognitive Sciences Add?

Given the interest of this volume in the *action-inducing* potentials of the text, it may seem surprising to apply *cognitive approaches* to the Sermon, for "cognition" is frequently used as a synonym for "thought" and understood as only subsidiary to action. But the technical, scientific understanding of cognition differs in significant ways from common understandings of the term. For example, if we surveyed a sample of our friends, asking them what cognition is, chances are good that the majority would describe it as somehow representational or perhaps as computational—even if they didn't use those words. In its naïve form, representationalism suggests that we carry around mental images or symbols in our minds that correspond to external reality.[46] Thinking, in this view, exists in the process of aligning those internal representations to external stimuli, like a matching exercise with mental flash cards. This everyday sense of cognition assumes a high level of correspondence between mental states and the external world and, indeed, much of the time this is what thinking *feels* like to us.

There are many more sophisticated expressions of representationalism, including those advocated by philosophers of mind.[47] For example, representationalism accounts for the fact that beliefs and desires can affect which stimuli we notice as well as the variations in what we apprehend about them. It has also been popular in part because of the dominance of computational models and the attractiveness of comparing the mind to a computer. However, even in its most refined form representationalism is limited in its explanatory power. For example, it does not adequately account for the body, not merely as the conduit through which representations are enacted, but as an actual contributing aspect of cognition.[48] The associated

---

46. This brief definition is a significantly simplified account of more sophisticated accounts.

47. Representational views have been in circulation at least since Thomas Hobbes, who was among the first to give this sort of account. For a useful summary of the range of views, see Jonathan S. Spackman and Stephen C. Yanchar, "Embodied Cognition, Representationalism, and Mechanism: A Review and Analysis," *Journal for the Theory of Social Behaviour* 44.1 (2013): 46–79.

48. One of the landmark descriptions of the way that knowledge depends on the physical properties of our embodiment is the description of the perception and phenomenology of color (originally published in 1991) by Francisco J. Valera, Evan Thompson, and Eleanor Rosch, *The Embodied Mind: Cognitive Science and Human Experience* (rev. edn; Cambridge, MA: MIT Press, 2016), 157–71.

conversations are complex and multidisciplinary, but for the purposes of this introduction, two sets of concepts can distinguish the popular understanding of representationalism from more rigorous views of cognition as it is employed in this volume.

Two Ways to Reconsider Cognition

The first set of concepts concerns how much of our cognition takes place without conscious attention. Part of the reason we imagine a close correspondence between our mental states and the external world is because so much mental activity is not consciously available to us. Jonathan Haidt describes the conscious/unconscious distinction through the image of a rider and an elephant. The relatively tiny rider signifies conscious, effortful thinking—the sort that we are aware of because it feels like it is under our control. But as Haidt clarifies, control pertains "only when the elephant doesn't have desires of his own. When the elephant really wants to do something, I'm no match for him."[49] It is a vivid analogy. In turn, the elephant signifies feelings, social contexts, biological drives, and the like; in short, factors that exert their influence without our intention and sometimes even contrary to it. Yes, the rider and the elephant work together but one of them does much more of that work. Cognitive studies include explorations of non-conscious contributions to human knowing and action.

The Nobel laureate Daniel Kahneman has increased attention to this division of mental labor, in part, by studying patterns in decision-making and action. He (and others)[50] examined biases in thinking that seemed to be repeated, even in situations where they proved to be wrong. Those studies resulted in his delineation of two kinds of thinking, *System 1* and *System 2*, in order to distinguish a division in our mentation. System 2 involves attention to "effortful mental activities ... often associated with the subjective experience of agency, choice, and concentration."[51] This kind of thinking needs no further description since it corresponds to what we typically understand as cognition. System 2 corresponds to the *rider* that we imagine to be in control of our thought processes. By contrast, System 1 (corresponding roughly to Haidt's elephant) "operates automatically and quickly,

---

49. Jonathan Haidt, *The Happiness Hypothesis: Finding Modern Truth in Ancient Wisdom* (New York: Basic Books, 2006), 4.

50. Particularly Amos Tversky with whom he co-authored a number of works, including *Judgment under Uncertainty: Heuristics and Biases* (New York: Cambridge University Press, 1982).

51. Daniel Kahneman, *Thinking, Fast and Slow* (Toronto: Doubleday Canada, 2011), 21.

with…no sense of voluntary control."[52] This mode also includes tasks like riding a bike, detecting when an object is close enough to reach, or conducting single-digit addition—in short, cognitive functions that may have involved learning but take place without conscious effort. Further, System 1 includes a range of *cognitive heuristics*, which are "simple procedure[s] that help find adequate, though often imperfect, answers to difficult questions."[53] It is the attention to System 1 and its effects—both successful and unsuccessful—that, in part, distinguishes cognitive science from everyday understandings of cognition. In this volume, John Teehan (Chapter 9) deals explicitly with Kahneman's paradigm, but other chapters also address some of the innate patterns of thinking that appear across cultures (especially Thurén, Chapter 7, and Lahti, Chapter 8, on rhetoric).

A second set of concepts that distinguishes contemporary cognitive theory from naïve definitions is *4E cognition*—that is, cognition is embodied, embedded, enactive, and extended. Consider this example: a person cycles to work every day and likes to take a narrow shortcut between a dumpster and a brick wall, with about seven centimeters of leeway on either side. In order to ride through successfully, this cyclist simply looks straight ahead and pedals because her body (muscles, central nervous system, brain), interacting with the bicycle, in that physical space, *knows* how to do it. It is not simply that the physical circumstances are *represented* in the mind of the cyclist; rather, the particularity of the human body and its capacities for motion and perception constitute the knowing. Furthermore, this particular knowledge exists only in that combination of factors of body-place-tool-experience. Note further that relying on System 2 thinking in these circumstances usually impedes success (as well as reducing the fun), resulting in wobbles or scrapes with the wall. This example nicely illustrates two of the Es. It is obviously an *embodied* form of knowing that is constituted by neural and sensory information. But it also illustrates the *enactive* character of cognition. In this case, "knowledge emerges through the primary agent's bodily engagement with the environment, rather than being simply determined by and dependent upon either pre-existent situations or personal construals."[54] In other words, the cyclist does not rely on representations, but on emergence that comes into being

---

52. Kahneman, *Thinking*, 20.
53. Kahneman, *Thinking*, 98. A common example is the unconscious use of the "gaze heuristic," which works remarkably well for catching a ball: simply fix the moving ball in your gaze and adjust your speed and position so that the angle of ball remains constant. You and the ball will meet in an excellent position for catching. See Michael K. McBeath, Dennis M. Schaffer, and Mary K. Kaiser, "How Baseball Outfielders Determine Where to Run to Catch Fly Balls," *Science* 268 (1995): 569–73.
54. Robert A. Wilson and Lucia Foglia, "Embodied Cognition," *The Stanford*

only within the moment. This example illustrates a much more dynamic understanding of cognition than traditional representational concepts allow. Knowing is *enactive* and arises in the interaction of the human agent and their social, material, and conditioned context.

With regard to *embodied* cognition, what is true of an obviously physical/embodied act like biking also holds for less physical behaviors as well. As suggested in the preceding section, even something as culturally elaborated as language is firmly anchored in bodily experience. For example, if you have found yourself gesturing while speaking or even while searching for a word you cannot remember, you have experienced something of the embodied character of words. George Lakoff and Mark Johnson have led the way in exploring the embodied character of language. Their book, *Metaphors We Live By*, traces recurrent figures of speech whose abstract concepts depend immutably on the experience "of our bodies and the shared ways that we all function in the everyday world."[55] They have identified a set of image schemas that pervade language and depend on bodily experience. For instance, we describe many abstract concepts using *containment schemas* of "in" and "out": those two are *in* love; that person is *out of* control; I am *in* a good mood. Likewise, we use *path schemas* to efficiently convey abstract ideas of change or progress: we have a long way to go before the end of this presidency; our conversation was sidetracked by an anecdote; this movie has had plenty of twists and turns. Each of these schemas communicates effectively because of its evocation of our bodies interacting with the environment.

Turning to the concepts of embedded and extended cognition, the former will likely seem more intuitively obvious to historians and biblical scholars who are used to considering the social, cultural, and material circumstances in which texts are formed. However, the claim that cognition is *embedded* is a little more robust and more particular than general attention to historical context. The synonym "situated" may better capture the meaning. Any event, including the physical conditions, within which an agent perceives and acts is constitutive of cognition. The category of *extended* cognition captures the fact that cognition is distributed beyond the mind of any individual. In the case of our cyclist, the bicycle itself contributes to the act of cognition undertaken. But cognition may also be extended across a group. Consider, for instance, the different experience of watching a movie with a group in a theatre and watching it alone. Embeddedness and extension are relevant to the

---

Encyclopedia of Philosophy (Spring 2017 Edition), ed. Edward N. Zalta. At https://plato.stanford.edu/archives/spr2017/entries/embodied-cognition/.

55. Lakoff and Johnson, *Metaphors We Live By*, 245.

final section of essays in this volume. For instance, Anne Gudme's chapter (Chapter 10) shows how irresistibly particular patterns of relationships generate corresponding impulses for exchange and Alicia Batten's essay (Chapter 12) illustrates something of distributed or extended cognition among the communities of post-WWII France, whose insights into the Sermon were affected by their shared attention to it. Indeed, the printed form of the Sermon in itself can serve as a continued extension of cognition for those who take it up and read it again, thereby reactivating a set of associations.

Cognition and Evolution

By this point, readers may already be anticipating the fact that the cognitive science of religion draws significantly on evolutionary theory. Cognitive studies presuppose that human knowing is guided by these sorts of innate capacities or patterns or thinking precisely because they have provided an adaptive (survival) advantage to human beings. We do not need to choose these patterns consciously; rather, they are bequeathed to us through the evolutionary conditioning of our earliest genetic forebears.

One case of such genetic inheritance is the range of behaviors related to identifying other agents (human, animal, or indeed superhuman) in our vicinity. For example, no matter how familiar we may be with the creaking sounds of our own homes on a winter's evening, it remains difficult to block a faint reflex of alarm (*What was that?!*) when we hear them. You can imagine how such over-attribution of agency would have provided a survival advantage to our distant forebears who lived in unpredictable settings with fairly high levels of danger. It was much better for them to falsely imagine another agent in their vicinity than to calmly wait for fuller evidence. Those who picked up a weapon or ran for cover survived at higher rates than their wait-and-see companions. It is not the case that the over-attributors were always correct in their reactions. However, the cost of their false positives would be paid back in a single instance of advanced warning of a real predator or juicy bit of prey. Their resulting survival advantage ensured that this genetic trait could be passed along.

In fact, like these hypothesized forebears, we routinely over-attribute such agency. We tend to see faces in inanimate objects—in the clouds, in the windows and doors of a building façade, in the grill and headlights of a car, in toast.[56] We also instinctively attribute agency or goal motivations to patterns of movement or natural sounds. For example, in one of the earliest

---

56. See Stewart Guthrie's book-length discussion of the contribution of anthropomorphism to religious phenomena; Stewart E. Guthrie, *Faces in the Clouds: A New*

experiments of this sort, participants were shown a short film of inanimate shapes moving in predetermined patterns.[57] Rather than neutrally describing the squares forming an ever contracting ring around the triangle (for example), participants inevitably attributed intentions and desires to the shapes: the squares were bullying the triangle. The shapes were automatically seen as enemies and friends, bullies and heroes. It proves nearly impossible for observers to resist interpretations that read these inanimate objects as if they were agents with intentions.

To a certain degree we are stuck with the evolved apparatus that was better suited to an earlier geological era and, given the exceedingly slow rate of biological evolution, we will be stuck with it for a long time. However, that apparatus includes numerous characteristics that also make us sensitive to social learning and, thereby, open the door to cultural influence working alongside our biological inheritance. Through this second avenue, cultures compensate for the lag-time in genetic evolution, developing and passing on practices that respond more quickly to changing circumstances. The term *dual inheritance* describes the coextensive tracks of these two forces as they have continued through the history of homo sapiens. Some of the tension between enduring genetic inheritance, on the one hand, and new or changing contexts, on the other, works itself out through cultures as they develop ways of sometimes exploiting our cognitive habits and sometimes subverting them. For instance, among the many advantages of rituals is their capacity to focus a group's attention on cultural norms and to do so by means that are innately appealing to their human participants. So, it is not surprising that virtually every culture has rituals and, at the same time, that those rituals differ in content. Likewise, even though two societies may have distinct portraits of their deities, both sets of superhuman beings share a subset of underlying patterns. As Pascal Boyer puts it, "given the general properties of human minds, certain types of representations are more likely than others to be acquired and transmitted."[58]

By studying the Sermon from a cognitive perspective, we are able to highlight both the points at which it sometimes draws on natural tendencies in its audience (indeed in its many audiences through the centuries) *and*

Theory of Religion (New York: Oxford University Press, 1993). For a less rigorous treatment, follow the Twitter feed of "Faces in Things."

57. Fritz Heider and Marianne Simmel, "An Experimental Study of Apparent Behavior," *The American Journal of Psychology* 57 (1944): 243–59.

58. Pascal Boyer, "Cognitive Constraints on Cultural Representations: Natural Ontologies and Religious Ideas," in *Mapping the Mind: Domain Specificity in Cognition and Culture*, ed. Lawrence A. Hirschfeld and Susan A. Gelman (Cambridge: Cambridge University Press, 1994), 391–411.

the places in which it sometimes contends with those tendencies in order to move beyond them. Some of the Sermon's most difficult teachings invite their audience to override natural tendencies. For example, a number of the chapters deal with the difficulty of altruism—whether through self-sacrifice within the group (see Chapter 3 by Rikard Roitto and Chapter 9 by John Teehan), or by resisting the urge for competition with outgroup individuals (see Colleen Shantz, Chapter 2), and even extending to non-retaliation and love toward active opponents (see Thomas Kazen, Chapter 4). Cultural products like the Sermon draw on natural cognitive and social capacities in order to overcome other innate drives. Thus, attention to the findings of cognitive science increases our sense of the more remarkable demands of the Sermon, as well as deepening our sense of the ways in which the teachings are embedded in the richness of culture. Finally, the profoundly and immutably embodied character of cognition helps us to retrieve this aspect of Christian origins—a feature that has often been drowned out by our attention to logocentric interpretations.

We want to round out this discussion of innateness and universality with a couple of caveats about such theorizing. The cognitive sciences do, of course, also recognize individual variation and the potential of culture to form cognition, but nevertheless claim a certain degree of universality and innateness that is biological rather than cultural. The caveats concern the bases for the "universal" partner in the biology-culture interplay. The first caution has to do with the evidence on which cognitive theory is based. A disproportionate number of experimental studies on human behavior have relied on American and European students as test subjects. While there is a growing body of cross-cultural research on human cognition, by no means can it match the volume of experiments conducted on a rather narrow sampling of young-adult, Western students. Therefore, the most reliable studies are those conducted with subjects from multiple age groups and cultural backgrounds. Furthermore, combinations of laboratory and real-world studies are highly valued, as are studies that have been repeated—and whose results have been replicated—by a second group of researchers. Historians must become more discerning users of behavioral research that claims universality, in part by assessing the degree to which it has been cross-culturally tested and verified.

The second caveat goes beyond unjustified use of behavioral sciences to consider the effects that might be generated by claims of universal capacities. Eric Barreto has drawn on queer hermeneutics and disability studies to reflect on the possible hermeneutical by-products of such research.[59] He

---

59. Eric D. Barreto, "Response to the Panel on 'The Sermon on the Mount (Matt

asks us to consider the political and ideological implications that the use of claims of innateness and cross-cultural universality—even empirically well-grounded ones—may have on those with, for instance, autism or other cognitive expressions. Neuro-typical or average cognition easily becomes another norm against which variations in cognition are constructed as deviations that fall outside of the margins of our concern. Furthermore, since much research is based on Western subjects, that is, internationally the most politically powerful population, unreflecting use of cognitive sciences can unwittingly become a way to oppress theological interpretations from other cultures by implicitly making stronger epistemological claims than is warranted. In light of those possibilities, Barreto argues that scholars who use cognitive "universals" as hermeneutical tools need to reflect on and explicitly name the limitations of such an approach. We would do well also to attend to multiple minority cognitions of a phenomenon as heuristic tools to understand the meaning of texts. Using the cognitive biases that are most likely shared by contemporary humans and their ancestors as a hermeneutical bridge across time and culture is by all means a valuable contribution to historical-critical research, but it must be accompanied by careful evaluation of what kind of knowledge is produced by the method.

Emotion, Reason, and Action

Research on emotions in the Bible is currently an expanding field of inquiry.[60] Emotions are essential to our motivation to act, perhaps even more so than rational deliberation.[61] The complex question of how much our emotions are formed by culture and biology respectively is still not solved, but humanist scholars who emphasize cultural factors without even taking innate human factors into consideration do not mirror the growing body of research on the evolution of human emotions and studies of children's maturation.[62] Several chapters in this volume use research on emotions to explore how the Sermon elicits emotions and thereby action.

5–7): Cognitive and Social Scientific Theories'" (presented at the Annual Meeting of the Society of Biblical Literature, Denver, CO, 2018).

60. F. Scott Spencer, ed., *Mixed Feelings and Vexed Passions: Exploring Emotions in Biblical Literature* (Atlanta, GA: Society of Biblical Literature Press, 2017) is an excellent sample of current research.

61. Bryce Huebner, Susan Dwyer, and Marc Hauser, "The role of Emotion in Moral Psychology," *Trends in Cognitive Sciences* 13 (2009): 1–6.

62. Lance Workman and Will Reader, *Evolutionary Psychology: An Introduction* (3rd edn; Cambridge: Cambridge University Press, 2014), especially ch. 11 on emotions. Recently, Lisa Feldman Barrett has sought to refine the discussion by distinguishing between innate mechanism that underpin emotion, which she calls "affect," and

The moral exhortations of the Sermon on the Mount appear extreme to many readers and its message elicits a range of emotions. When the Sermon commands non-retaliation and love of enemies (5.38-48) an intuitive sense of justice connected to anger clashes with the impulses to feel empathy, restore relations and forgive. Thomas Kazen's discussion in Chapter 4 examines how the Sermon encourages the reader to negotiate this clash in favor of non-retaliation and love. The challenges in the Sermon to live morally even if that choice endangers you (e.g., 5.10-12, 27-30, 38-48; 6.25-42) might evoke fear as well as awe. Rikard Roitto, in Chapter 3, surveys what we can learn from a range of scholarly fields to understand why the Sermon is experienced as convincing by some and unrealistically demanding by some.

Rhetoric explores how words convince by affecting intellect and emotion. Many biblical scholars have chosen to analyze New Testament texts through the lens of ancient rhetorics, while others—confident that rhetoric moves us in ways that persist across cultures—have used analytical categories from contemporary rhetoric and the psychology of language.[63] Both groups agree that modern rhetorical theory has bearing on ancient texts, since rhetorical studies scrutinize how speech engages emotion, thought patterns, and social relations, which to a large extent rest on innate human cognitive capacities. Two contributions in this volume use a contemporary theory, pragma-dialectics, to evaluate the rhetorical efficacy—particularly the argumentative structure—of certain passages of the Sermon. Niilo Lahti, Chapter 8, helps us understand the strengths and weaknesses of Jesus argumentation for a worry-free attitude (6.25-42) and Lauri Thuren, Chapter 7, discusses how parables contribute to the argument of the Sermon and what rhetorical qualities they have.

Emotion and conceptualization are, not surprisingly, discussed in linguistics too, since language can communicate both. Linguistics has converged with cognitive science through cognitive linguistics, blending theory, neurolinguistics and other theories that analyze how language relates to human thinking and feeling.[64] This research sees language as evolving together with

---

the conscious construction of emotions that is influenced by both affect and culturally learned cognition, Lisa Feldman Barrett, *How Emotions Are Made: The Secret Life of the Brain* (Boston, MA: Houghton Mifflin Harcourt, 2017).

63. For a recent overview of the debate on the relevance of ancient and modern rhetoric, see Stanley E. Porter and Bryan R. Dye, eds., *Paul and Ancient Rhetoric: Theory and Practice in the Hellenistic Context* (Cambridge: Cambridge University Press, 2014), especially the contributions by Lauri Thuren (ch. 7) and L. Gregory Bloom (ch. 13).

64. Several helpful Oxford Handbooks overview the cognitive turn in linguistics; e.g., Bernd Heine and Heiko Narrog, eds., *The Oxford Handbook of Linguistic Analysis* (2nd edn; Oxford: Oxford University Press, 2015); Dirk Geeraerts and Hubert Cuyckens, eds., *The Oxford Handbook of Cognitive Linguistics* (New York: Oxford University

our embodied experiences of the world, as we discussed in the preceding section. A fascinating rhetorical problem in the Sermon is why its hyperboles provoke and fascinate. How literally should a reader take the many apparently absurd demands of the Sermon (e.g., 5.22, 28-30, 38-48)? Are they meant to be humorous? Thomas Kazen, Chapter 6, shows how recent advances in research on the linguistic function of exaggeration can help us understand how the seemingly absurd imagery and exhortation can evoke a moral response by the comic effect of hyperbole.

Social Dynamics

Within the Gospel of Matthew, the message of the Sermon on the Mount is aimed largely at a community, even while it sometimes also addresses individual behavior. It paints a vision of the social identity of those who participate in the shared endeavor to realize the kingdom of heaven. This identity is, on the one hand, characterized by being different—different from the Pharisees and different from the Gentiles—but on the other hand also by continued interaction with people outside the community of believers (cf. discussion above).

Social identity theory and self-categorization theory, together often called the social identity approach, have grown in popularity among biblical scholars ever since Philip Esler's pioneering use of the approach to understand Paul.[65] The social identity approach analyzes the shared imagination of a group's identity among its members and its group dynamic effects.[66] For example, the self-esteem hypothesis states that groups strive to formulate an identity that maximizes the self-esteem and value of the group. The meta-contrast principle claims that social self-categorization, just like other cognitive processes of categorization, tend to optimize distinctions in social

---

Press, 2010). For an introduction to linguistic research on emotions, see Ulrike Lüdtke, ed., *Emotion in Language: Theory – Research – Application* (Consciousness & Emotion Book Series, 10; Amsterdam: John Benjamins, 2015).

65. A recent example is J. Brian Tucker and Coleman A. Baker, eds., *T&T Clark Handbook to Social Identity in the New Testament* (London: Bloomsbury T&T Clark, 2014). Philip Esler introduced the theory to New Testament studies in *Galatians* (New Testament Readings; New York: Routledge, 1998) and *Conflict and Identity in Romans: The Social Setting of Paul's Letter* (Minneapolis, MN: Fortress, 2003).

66. For a recent overview of the social identity approach, see Shelley McKeown, Reeshma Haji, and Neil Ferguson, eds., *Understanding Peace and Conflict through Social Identity Theory: Contemporary Global Perspectives* (Cham: Springer International Publishing, 2016), especially Part I where different aspects of the research field are presented. For an introduction to the social identity approach for biblical scholars, see Rikard Roitto, *Behaving as a Christ-Believer: A Cognitive Perspective on Identity and Behavior Norms in Ephesians* (ConBNT, 46; Grand Rapids, MI: Eisenbrauns, 2011), chs. 5–11.

identity relative to other relevant social categories in order to maximize the experienced meaningfulness of the group. In the case of Matthew, the most relevant social categories are the Pharisees and scribes (5.20; 7.29), and the Gentiles (5.47; 6.7, 32), which the Sermon portrays in marked contrast to the ideal Matthean believer. The social identity approach also suggests that social groups share an identity prototype, that is, a shared construct of the ideal group member. This identity prototype not only functions in contrast to outgroups, but also functions as a normative ideal within the community. Members who resemble the identity prototype are appreciated as good group members while those who deviate from the prototype are more likely to be reprimanded or even excluded. The appeal to a shared ingroup prototype can account for the rhetorical force of a number of sayings in the Sermon. For example, the audience is not merely asked to do good in the antitheses; they are asked to fulfil their identity as "children of your Father in heaven" (5.45). Elisa Uusimäki, Chapter 11, elaborates how the beatitudes (5.1-12) portray the prototypical community member and compares their community-building function to 4QBeatitude in the Dead Sea Scrolls. Rikard Roitto, Chapter 3, argues that one of the Sermon's strategies to encourage risk-taking is to portray willingness to take risk as prototypical.

Scholars who research the function of religion from an evolutionary perspective agree that religion increases individual and group fitness, but they debate whether this advantage should be considered a by-product or an adaptation. Humans are skilled at complex forms of cooperation in large groups compared to other species. Those who argue that religion is an adaptation typically suggest that religious beliefs in morally interested gods and religious rituals contribute to the willingness to cooperate within a community.[67] The Supernatural Punishment Hypothesis suggests that the idea of an all-knowing god who punishes evil and rewards good contributed to the cohesiveness of groups, particularly large societies in which it was difficult to monitor each other's behavior. Other scholars point to costly religious rituals and other costly behavior, as a way to signal one's commitment to the community and thus also to deter less committed members from free riding on the resources of the group. John Teehan, Chapter 9, argues that the promises and threats of divine intervention in the Sermon fits the Supernatural

---

67. See especially the work by Ara Norenzayan, *Big Gods: How Religion Transformed Cooperation and Conflict* (Princeton, NJ: Princeton University Press, 2013). John Teehan has argued more modestly that gods do not necessarily have to be *big*, but only "morally relevant." See Teehan, "Religion and Morality: The Evolution of the Cognitive Nexus," in *The Oxford Handbook of Evolutionary Psychology and Religion*, eds. James R. Liddle and Todd K. Shackelford (Oxford Handbooks Online, October 2016; publication forthcoming 2021).

Punishment Hypothesis well and that the message of the Sermon probably fostered cooperation, and that the costly ethics of the Sermon could function as displays of group commitment.

The social dynamics of sharing and reciprocation have been the center of attention to many branches of behavioral sciences.[68] The expectation to reciprocate gifts is present in most, perhaps all, cultures. Yet, the reciprocation need not be immediate and symmetrical, but is often deferred and different. Moreover, not all reciprocity is direct. Often it is indirect, that is, A gives to B who gives to C and so on with the sense that eventually A will be given something from, for example, F. In the ancient world, the gods were both recipients and givers of gifts.[69] From an evolutionary perspective, indirect reciprocity can be seen as a cultural evolution that strengthens groups and thus increases inclusive fitness—and including gods in the exchange seems to improve the willingness to give.[70] Anne Gudme uses these insights in Chapter 10 to explore how the ethics of secret alms giving in the Sermon can be experienced as reasonable if God is conceived to be included in the chain of givers in the indirect exchange of gifts.

Social groups share memories, which form their interaction. Such collective memory is studied in the field of social memory research.[71] Within New Testament studies, social memory theory has often been used (and, according to several scholars, abused) to discuss how the early Christ-movement remembered Jesus.[72] Social memories reside not only in the minds of a population, but are also stored in ritual celebrations and artifacts such as texts and buildings. The external representations of social memory contribute to durability over time, although we must of course recognize that social memories are flexible and constantly contested and reformulated in response to

---

68. For an overview, see for example Gadi Algazi, "Introduction: Doing Things with Gifts," in *Negotiating the Gift: Pre-Modern Figurations of Exchange*, ed. G. Algazi, V. Groebner, and B. Jussen (Göttingen: Vandenhoeck & Ruprecht, 2003), 9–27 and Anne Gudme, Chapter 10 in this volume.

69. Daniel Ullucci, "Sacrifice and Votives," in *Oxford Handbook of Early Christian Rituals*, ed. R. Uro, R. DeMaris, J. Day, and R. Roitto (Oxford: Oxford University Press, 2018), 282–301.

70. Ara Norenzayan and Azim F. Shariff, "The Origin and Evolution of Religious Prosociality," *Science* 322 (2008): 58–62.

71. For example, Eviatar Zerubavel, "Social Memories: Steps towards a Sociology of the Past," in *The Collective Memory Reader*, ed. Jeffrey K. Olick, Vered Vinitzky-Seroussi, and Daniel Levy (Oxford: Oxford University Press, 2011). See also Alicia Batten, Chapter 12, in this volume.

72. For a summary of the debate, see Thomas Kazen, *Scripture, Interpretation, or Authority? Motives and Arguments in Jesus' Halakic Conflicts* (WUNT, 320; Tübingen: Mohr Siebeck, 2013), 13–22.

new contexts. The Matthean community created a written artifact of social memory when certain members of the community composed the Gospel of Matthew. It was an artifact that could be replicated by scribes and shared throughout the Christ-believing movement. The Sermon on the Mount can be seen, therefore, as a social memory with potential to guide social behavior in groups in which the Sermon is repeated and honored. Being an especially beloved text unit in the Christian canon, the Sermon has continued to influence all kinds of Christian groups throughout history. Alicia Batten (Chapter 12) shares an excellent example from northern France during World War II of the Sermon's impact as social memory.

Ritual

Ritual theory is an actively developing field of study and it is regularly applied in the interpretation of biblical texts.[73] Anthropologists like Roy Rappaport emphasize that ritual is a mode of communication, not only with gods but also among the participants.[74] Rituals strengthen the group's shared worldview and social order and the participants, in part by signaling their status and commitment to each other. Costly signaling theory proposes that rituals increase cooperation by testing and reliably communicating each group member's commitment to the group.[75] Signaling theory is another example of the way that cultures draw on evolved tendencies to turn them to new ends. Only a highly committed member would be prepared to undergo long, painful and in other ways costly rituals. This approach to rituals pinpoints the controversial nature of Jesus's command that one should perform prayers and fasting in secret (6.1-19). Such a practice seemingly destroys the social value of the rituals.

An analysis of ritual that only describes its social function and does not capture the participants' *experience* of ritual efficacy is incomplete, and to this end, as one of the latest additions to ritual studies, cognitive science of religion

---

73. For an introduction to the rich field of ritual studies and its use in biblical Studies, see Risto Uro, *Ritual and Christian Beginnings: A Socio-Cognitive Analysis* (Oxford: Oxford University Press, 2016), especially ch. 1; Risto Uro, Juliette Day, Richard DeMaris, and Rikard Roitto, eds., *The Oxford Handbook of Early Christian Rituals* (Oxford: Oxford University Press, 2018); Richard DeMaris, Jason T. Lamoreaux, and Steven C. Muir, eds., *Early Christian Ritual Life* (London: Routledge, 2017).

74. Roy Rappaport, *Ritual and Religion in the Making of Humanity* (Cambridge: Cambridge University Press, 1999), ch. 3.

75. Richard Sosis,"Religious Behaviors, Badges, and Bans: Signaling Theory and the Evolution of Religion," in *Where God and Science Meet: How Brain and Evolutionary Studies Alter our Understanding of Religion*. Vol. 1: *Evolution, Genes, and the Religious Brain*, ed. Patrick McNamara (Westport, CT: Praeger, 2006), 61–86.

is helpful. For instance, ritual form theory, suggested by Robert McCauley and Thomas Lawson, analyzes the "grammar" rituals that are experienced as effective.[76] They argue that we interpret rituals the same way we interpret ordinary action, with the difference that we imagine that the divine, in one way or another, participates in the ritual action and causes some kind of supernatural efficacy. This capacity among us humans to blend ordinary actions with imaginations of divine action is further analyzed by Jesper Sørensen, who argues that our minds experience efficacy through cognitive blends of the performed action and its believed efficacy.[77] Rodney Werline (Chapter 5) uses these insights to discuss the ritual instructions of the Sermon (6.1-19).

Conclusion: On the Use of Social and Cognitive Sciences

As we hope the preceding sections demonstrate, this volume provides both new insights into elements of the Sermon on the Mount and draws on a rich range of empirical and theoretical studies in the process. The primary theoretical investment of the volume offers a friendly rejoinder to cultural constructivism. In agreement with contructivists, these chapters acknowledge the significance of culture in shaping artefacts like the Sermon. In addition, most of the arguments here are invested in claims about the (evolutionarily derived) innateness of certain patterns of thinking and acting that interact with culture. Thus, the theory of dual (biology and culture) inheritance informs the whole volume to varying degrees. However, on the whole we have perhaps been less explicit about our *methods in applying* the social and cognitive models that have been employed here and might govern new work that will rely on these approaches. For that reason, we give the last words to Ann Taves, who has been both an early adopter of cognitive science for the study of religion and who has long been thoughtful about methodology in historical work.

In a formal response to some of the papers presented in this volume, Taves outlined three sets of decisions about our research questions and the ways that they can be supported by the use of social and cognitive sciences.[78]

---

76. Robert N. McCauley and E. Thomas Lawson, *Bringing Ritual to Mind: Psychological Foundations of Cultural Forms* (Cambridge: Cambridge University Press, 2002).

77. Jesper Sørensen, *A Cognitive Theory of Magic* (Cognitive Science of Religion Series; Lanham, MD: Altamira, 2007).

78. The four options outlined in this section are summarized from comments by Taves in response to some of the papers represented in this volume: Ann Taves, "Response to the Panel on 'The Sermon on the Mount (Matt 5-7): Cognitive and Social Scientific Theories'," Annual Meeting of the Society of Biblical Literature (Denver, CO, 2018). Taves has long reflected on method in the study of religion and we felt that her thoughts on our methodology deserved wider circulation.

The first and most basic distinction is whether the *starting-point* is based in theory or historical phenomenon. A researcher can begin by noticing a *phenomenon* in historical artefacts (for instance, private ritual or repeated rhetorical structures) and then interpret that phenomenon with the aid of behavioral research that can facilitate our understanding. Such a research procedure is *phenomenon-driven*. The counterpart to that method is the *theory-driven* approach. In this case a researcher may begin with a behavioral theory (for instance, a robust view of embodied cognition or a theory of gift-giving) and decide to see what happens if that theory is used as a lens to interpret a certain historical artefact, such as the Sermon on the Mount.

The second type of categorization identified by Taves is the distinction between three different kinds of *investments in history*. The first kind is *interpretative*: What does this phenomenon in the text mean, either for the original recipients or for later recipients of the text? Social and cognitive sciences can serve to discern how the phenomenon was experienced by its audiences. The second kind is e*xplanatory*: Why does this historical or textual phenomenon exist? To what extent can our knowledge about human cognition and social dynamics help us explain how this phenomenon came into being? The third kind is *predictive*: What effects could this phenomenon in a certain historical artefact produce? Again, behavioral sciences can facilitate the discussion of how people might have reacted to a historical text, for instance the Sermon, and even formulate hypotheses about its reception in different sorts of settings, for example.

Finally, Taves offers perhaps the broadest distinction: that between research that attempts to understand history and research that attempts to evaluate a theory. In the first case, *the theory provides heuristic resources* to understand history. Most of the alternatives in the preceding three sections would fit in this category since the hermeneutical work of interpreting historical artefact is guided by insights from behavioral research. In the second case, *history provides empirical material* to test theory. This use is more tenuous because no single historical case is sufficient to prove or disprove a theory and because the empirical material from historical artefacts is often anecdotal/subjective and not open to external verification. Still, historical examples provide a significant source of natural data that complements controlled scientific study. Collectively we need to attend to the evidence of history to either confirm a theory or provide a case that challenges the theory and thus inspires further research that could refine the theory. Taves's distinctions provide the basic blueprints for a whole range of future studies that incorporate models and theories from cognitive and social sciences. We hope that the essays that follow might help to inspire some of them.

Biographical Note

Docent Rikard Roitto is a University Lecturer at the Stockholm School of Theology at University College Stockholm. Roitto specializes in using behavioral sciences to interpret the New Testament and other historical texts. He is one of the editors of *The Oxford Handbook of Early Christian Rituals* (Oxford University Press, 2018).

Colleen Shantz is Associate Professor of New Testament and Christian origins at St. Michael's College in the University of Toronto. She explores the significance of experiential aspects (practices of ecstatic experience, ritual, and emotion) in the first generations of the Christ movement. Currently, she is also the Graduate Director of the Toronto School of Theology.

Petri Luomanen is Professor of New Testament and Early Christian Culture and Literature at the Faculty of Theology, University of Helsinki. Luomanen has published widely on early Jewish Christianity and he is an active developer of multidisciplinary, especially socio-cognitive, approaches to early Christianity. His recent publications include P. Luomanen, A. B. Pessi, and I. Pyysiäinen, eds., *Christianity and the Roots of Morality: Philosophical, Early Christian, and Empirical Perspectives* (Philosophical Studies in Science and Religion, 8; Leiden: Brill, 2017).

Bibliography

Abrams, Dominic, and Michael A. Hogg. "An Introduction to the Social Identity Approach," 1–9 in *Social Identity Theory: Constructive and Critical Advances*. Edited by Dominic Abrams and Michael A. Hogg. New York: Harvester Wheatsheaf, 1990.

Algazi, Gadi. "Introduction: Doing Things with Gifts," 9–27 in *Negotiating the Gift: Pre-Modern Figurations of Exchange*. Edited by G. Algazi, V. Groebner, and B. Jussen. Göttingen: Vandenhoeck & Ruprecht, 2003.

Allison, Dale C. *The Sermon on the Mount: Inspiring the Moral Imagination*. New York: Crossroad, 1999.

Bacon, Benjamin W. *Studies in Matthew.* London: Constable, 1930.

Balch, David L., ed. *Social History of the Matthean Community: Cross-Disciplinary Approaches*. Minneapolis, MN: Fortress, 1991.

Barrett, Lisa Feldman. *How Emotions Are Made: The Secret Life of the Brain*. Boston, MA: Houghton Mifflin Harcourt, 2017.

Barreto, Eric D. "Response to the Panel on 'The Sermon on the Mount (Matt 5–7): Cognitive and Social Scientific Theories'." Presented at the Annual Meeting of the Society of Biblical Literature, Denver, CO, 2018.

Baumgarten, Albert I. *The Flourishing of Jewish Sects in the Maccabean Era.* Supplements to the Journal for the Study of Judaism, 55. Atlanta, GA: Society of Biblical Literature, 1997.

Becker, Adam H., and Annette Yoshiko Reed, eds. *The Ways that Never Parted: Jews and Christians in Late Antiquity and Early Middle Ages*. Minneapolis, MN: Fortress, 2007.

Becker, Eve-Marie, and Anders Runesson, eds. *Mark and Matthew I: Comparative Readings, Understanding the Earliest Gospels in their First Century Settings*. Wissenschaftliche Untersuchungen zum Neuen Testament, 271. Tübingen: Mohr Siebeck, 2011. https://doi.org/10.1628/978-3-16-151560-6

—*Mark and Matthew II: Comparative Readings, Reception History, Cultural Hermeneutics, and Theology*. Wissenschaftliche Untersuchungen zum Neuen Testament, 304. Tübingen: Mohr Siebeck, 2013. https://doi.org/10.1628/978-3-16-152546-9

Becker, Hans-Jürgen, and Serge Ruzer, eds. *The Sermon on the Mount and its Jewish Setting*. Cahiers de la Revue Biblique, 60. Paris: J. Gabalda, 2005.

Betz, Hans Dieter. *Essays on the Sermon on the Mount*. Translated by L. L. Welborn. Philadelphia, PA: Fortress, 1985.

—*The Sermon on the Mount: A Commentary on the Sermon on the Mount, including the Sermon on the Plain (Matthew 5:3–7:27 and Luke 6:20–49)*. Edited by Adela Y. Collins. Hermeneia. Minneapolis, MN: Fortress, 1995.

Boyarin, Daniel. *Dying for God: Martyrdom and the Making of Christianity and Judaism*. Stanford, CA: Stanford University Press, 1999.

—*Border Lines: The Partition of Judaeo-Christianity*. Philadelphia, PA: The University of Pennsylvania Press, 2004. https://doi.org/10.9783/9780812203844

Boyer, Pascal. "Cognitive Constraints on Cultural Representations: Natural Ontologies and Religious Ideas," 391–411 in *Mapping the Mind: Domain Specificity in Cognition and Culture*. Edited by Susan A. Gelman and Lawrence A. Hirschfeld. Cambridge: Cambridge University Press, 1994. https://doi.org/10.1017/CBO9780511752902.016

Brala, Marija M. "NSM within the Cognitive Linguistics Movement: Bridging Some Gaps," *Jezikoslovlje* 4 (2003): 161–86.

Carter, Warren. *What Are They Saying about Matthew's Sermon on the Mount?* Mahwah, NJ: Paulist Press, 1994.

—*Matthew and the Margins: A Socio-Political and Religious Reading*. Journal for the Study of the New Testament Supplement Series, 204. Sheffield: Sheffield Academic Press, 2000.

—*Matthew and Empire: Initial Explorations*. Harrisburg, PA: Trinity Press International, 2001.

Casey, Maurice. Review of *What Did Jesus Mean? Explaining the Sermon on the Mount and the Parables in Simple and Universal Human Concepts* by Anna Wierzbicka, *Theology* 106 (2003): 193–4. https://doi.org/10.1177/0040571X0310600307

Davies, William D. *The Setting of the Sermon on the Mount*. Cambridge: Cambridge University Press, 1964.

DeMaris, Richard, Jason T. Lamoreaux, and Steven C. Muir, eds. *Early Christian Ritual Life*. London: Routledge, 2017. https://doi.org/10.4324/9781315623832

Ellemers, Naomi, and Alexander Haslam. "Social Identity Theory," 379–98 in *Handbook of Theories of Social Psychology*. Edited by Paul A. M. van Lange, Arie W. Kruglanski, and E. Tory Higgins. London: Sage, 2012. https://doi.org/10.4135/9781446249222.n45

Esler, Philip F. *Galatians*. New Testament Readings. New York: Routledge, 1998.

—*Conflict and Identity in Romans: The Social Setting of Paul's Letter*. Minneapolis, MN: Fortress, 2003.

—"Social-Scientific Models in Biblical Interpretation," 3–14 in *Ancient Israel: The Old Testament in its Social Context*. Edited by Philip F. Esler. London: SCM, 2005.
—"Group Norms and Prototypes in Matthew 5.3-12: A Social Identity Interpretation of the Matthean Beatitudes," 147–72 in *T&T Clark Handbook to Social Identity in the New Testament*. Edited by Coleman A. Baker and J. Brian Tucker. London: Bloomsbury/T&T Clark, 2013.
Geeraerts, Dirk, and Hubert Cuyckens, eds. *The Oxford Handbook of Cognitive Linguistics*. New York: Oxford University Press, 2010. https://doi.org/10.1093/oxfordhb/9780199738632.001.0001
Goddard, Cliff. "Bad Arguments against Semantic Primitives," *Theoretical Linguistics* 24 (1998): 129–56. https://doi.org/10.1515/thli.1998.24.2-3.129
Greenman, Jeffrey P., Timothy Larsen, and Stephen R. Spencer, eds. *The Sermon on the Mount through the Centuries*. Grand Rapids, MI: Brazos Press, 2007.
Guthrie, Stewart E. *Faces in the Clouds: A New Theory of Religion*. New York: Oxford University Press, 1993.
Haidt, Jonathan. "The Moral Emotions," 852–70 in *Handbook of Affective Sciences*. Edited by R. J. Davidson, Klaus R. Sherer, and H. Hill Goldsmith. Oxford: Oxford University Press, 2003.
—*The Happiness Hypothesis: Finding Modern Truth in Ancient Wisdom*. New York: Basic Books, 2006.
Heider, Fritz, and Marianne Simmel, "An Experimental Study of Apparent Behavior," *The American Journal of Psychology* 57 (1944): 243–59. https://doi.org/10.2307/1416950
Heine, Bernd, and Heiko Narrog, eds. *The Oxford Handbook of Linguistic Analysis*, 2nd edn. Oxford: Oxford University Press, 2015. https://doi.org/10.1093/oxfordhb/9780199677078.013.0019
Hilferty, Joseph. "Mothers, Lies, and Bachelors: A Brief Reply to Wierzbicka (1990)," *Word* 48 (1997): 51–9. https://doi.org/10.1080/00437956.1997.11432462
Huebner, Bryce, Susan Dwyer, and Marc Hauser. "The Role of Emotion in Moral Psychology," *Trends in Cognitive Science* 13 (2009): 1–6. https://doi.org/10.1016/j.tics.2008.09.006
Kahneman, Daniel. *Thinking, Fast and Slow*. New York: Farrar, Straus & Giroux, 2011.
Kazen, Thomas. *Scripture, Interpretation, or Authority: Motives and Arguments in Jesus' Halakic Conflicts*. Wissenschaftliche Untersuchungen zum Neuen Testament, 320. Tübingen: Mohr Siebeck, 2013. https://doi.org/10.1628/978-3-16-152894-1
Kaye, Alan S. Review of *What Did Jesus Mean? Explaining the Sermon on the Mount and the Parables in Simple and Universal Human Concepts* by Anna Wierzbicka, *Language* 79 (2003): 226–7. https://doi.org/10.1353/lan.2003.0088
Kissinger, Warren S. *The Sermon on the Mount: A History of Interpretation and Bibliography*. ATLA Bibliography Series. Lanham, MD: Scarecrow Press, 1998.
Kodjak, Andrej. *A Structural Analysis of the Sermon on the Mount*. Religion and Reason: Method and Theory in the Study and Interpretation of Religion. New York: Mouton de Gruyter, 1986. https://doi.org/10.1515/9783110890556
Lakoff, George, and Mark Johnson. *Metaphors We Live By* (London: University of Chicago Press, 1980).
—*Philosophy in the Flesh: The Embodied Mind and its Challenge to Western Thought*. New York: Basic Books, 1999.
Lüdtke, Ulrike, ed. *Emotion in Language*. Theory – Research – Application, Consciousness

& Emotion Book Series, 10. Amsterdam: John Benjamins, 2015. https://doi.org/10.1075/ceb.10

Luomanen, Petri. *Entering the Kingdom of Heaven: A Study on the Structure of Matthew's View of Salvation.* Wissenschaftliche Untersuchungen zum Neuen Testament, 2/101. Tübingen: Mohr Siebeck, 1998.

—"The 'Sociology of Sectarianism' in Matthew: Modeling the Genesis of Early Jewish and Christian Communities," 107–30 in *Fair Play: Diversity and Conflicts in Early Christianity: Essays in Honour of Heikki Räisänen.* Edited by Ismo Dunderberg, Christopher Tuckett, and Kari Syreeni. Leiden: Brill, 2002.

—"The Sociology of Knowledge, the Social Identity Approach, and the Cognitive Study of Religion," 199–229 in *Explaining Christian Origins and Early Judaism: Contributions from Cognitive and Social Science.* Edited by Petri Luomanen, Ilkka Pyysiäinen, and Risto Uro. Biblical Interpretation Series, 89. Leiden: E. J. Brill, 2007.

Luomanen, Petri, Risto Uro, and Ilkka Pyysiäinen. "Introduction: Social and Cognitive Perspectives in the Study of Christian Origins and Early Judaism," 1–33 in *Explaining Christian Origins and Early Judaism: Contributions from Cognitive and Social Science.* Edited by Petri Luomanen, Risto Uro, and Ilkka Pyysiäinen. Biblical Interpretation Series, 89. Leiden: Brill, 2007.

Luz, Ulrich. *Das Evangelium nach Matthäus, Mt 1–7.* Evangelisch Katholischer Kommentar zum Neuen Testament, 1/1. Zürich: Benzinger Verlag; Neukirchen-Vluyn: Neukirchener Verlag, 1989.

—*Matthew 1–7: A Commentary.* Hermeneia. Edinburgh: T&T Clark, 1990.

Marxsen, Willi. *"Christliche" und christliche Ethik im Neuen Testament.* Gütersloh: Mohn, 1989.

McBeath, Michael K., Dennis M. Shaffer, and Mary K. Kaiser. "How Baseball Outfielders Determine Where to Run to Catch Fly Balls," *Science* 268.5210 (1995): 569–73. https://doi.org/10.1126/science.7725104

McCauley, Robert N., and E. Thomas Lawson. *Bringing Ritual to Mind: Psychological Foundations of Cultural Forms.* Cambridge: Cambridge University Press, 2002. https://doi.org/10.1017/CBO9780511606410

McKeown, Shelley, Reeshma Haji, and Neil Ferguson, eds. *Understanding Peace and Conflict through Social Identity Theory: Contemporary Global Perspectives.* Cham: Springer International Publishing, 2016. https://doi.org/10.1007/978-3-319-29869-6

Mohrlang, Roger. *Matthew and Paul: A Comparison of Ethical Perspectives.* Society for New Testament Studies Monograph Series 48. Cambridge: Cambridge University Press, 1984. https://doi.org/10.1017/CBO9780511520426

Norenzayan, Ara. *Big Gods: How Religion Transformed Cooperation and Conflict.* Princeton, NJ: Princeton University Press, 2013. https://doi.org/10.1515/9781400848324

Norenzayan, Ara, and Azim Shariff. "The Origin and Evolution of Religious Prosociality," *Science* 322 (2008): 58–62. https://doi.org/10.1126/science.1158757

de Oliveira, Roberta Pires. "Cognitive Semantics: In the Heart of Language, an Interview with Georg Lakoff," *Fórum Lingüístico* 1 (1998): 83–119.

Overman, J. Andrew. *Matthew's Gospels and Formative Judaism: The Social World of the Matthean Community.* Minneapolis, MN: Fortress, 1990.

Paschke, Boris. *Particularism and Universalism in the Sermon on the Mount: A Narrative-Critical Analysis of Matthew 5–7 in the Light of Matthew's View on Mission.* Neutestamentliche Abhandlungen, Neue Folge, 56. Münster: Aschendorff, 2012.

Pelikan, Jaroslav. *Divine Rhetoric: The Sermon on the Mount as Message and as Model*

in Augustine, Chrysostom, and Luther. Crestwood, NY: St. Vladimir's Seminary Press, 2000.
Porter, Stanley E., and Bryan R. Dye, eds. *Paul and Ancient Rhetoric: Theory and Practice in the Hellenistic Context.* Cambridge: Cambridge University Press, 2014. https://doi.org/10.1017/CBO9781139683647
Przybylski, Benno. *Righteousness in Matthew and his World of Thought.* Society for New Testament Studies Monograph Series, 41. Cambridge: Cambridge University Press, 1980.
Rappaport, Roy A. *Ritual and Religion in the Making of Humanity.* Cambridge Studies in Social and Cultural Anthropology, 110. Cambridge: Cambridge University Press, 1999.
Roitto, Rikard. *Behaving as a Christ-Believer: A Cognitive Perspective on Identity and Behavior Norms in Ephesians.* Coniectanae Biblica: New Testament Series, 46. Grand Rapids, MI: Eisenbrauns, 2011.
Saldarini, Antonio J. *Matthew's Christian-Jewish Community.* Chicago Studies in the History of Judaism. Chicago, IL: The University of Chicago Press, 1994.
Sanders, Ed P. *Paul and Palestinian Judaism: A Comparison of Patterns of Religion.* London: SCM, 1977.
Schulz, Siegfried. *Die Mitte der Schrift: Der Frühkatholizismus im Neuen Testament als Herausforderung an den Protestantismus.* Stuttgart: Kreuz Verlag, 1976.
Schweizer, Eduard. *The Good News according to Matthew.* Translated by David E. Green. Atlanta, GA: John Knox Press, 1975.
Sørensen, Jesper. *A Cognitive Theory of Magic.* Cognitive Science of Religion Series. Lanham, MD: Altamira, 2007.
Sosis, Richard, and Eric R. Bressler. "Cooperation and Commune Longevity: A Test of the Costly Signaling Theory of Religion," *Cross-Cultural Research* 37 (2003): 211–39. https://doi.org/10.1177/1069397103037002003
Spackman, Jonathan S., and Stephen C. Yanchar, "Embodied Cognition, Representationalism, and Mechanism: A Review and Analysis," *Journal for the Theory of Social Behaviour* 44.1 (2013): 46–79. https://doi.org/10.1111/jtsb.12028
Spencer, F. Scott, ed. *Mixed Feelings and Vexed Passions: Exploring Emotions in Biblical Literature.* Atlanta, GA: SBL Press, 2017. https://doi.org/10.2307/j.ctt-1w1vm30
Stanton, Graham N. *A Gospel for a New People: Studies in Matthew.* Edinburgh: T&T Clark, 1992.
Syreeni, Kari. *The Making of the Sermon on the Mount: A Procedural Analysis of Matthew's Redactoral Activity.* Annales Academiae Scientiarum Fennicae: Dissertationes Humanum Litterarum, 44. Helsinki: Academia Scientiarum Fennica, 1987. https://doi.org/10.1163/9789004343535_010
—"The Sermon on the Mount: Christian or Universal Ethics?," 140–61 in *Christianity and the Roots of Morality: Philosophical, Early Christian, and Empirical Perspectives.* Edited by Petri Luomanen, Anne Birgitta Pessi, and Ilkka Pyysiäinen. Philosophical Studies in Science and Religion, 8. Leiden: Brill, 2017.
Talbert, Charles H. *Reading the Sermon on the Mount: Character Formation and Decision Making in Matthew 5–7.* Columbia, SC: University of South Carolina Press, 2004.
Taves, Ann. "Response to the Panel on 'The Sermon on the Mount (Matt 5-7): Cognitive and Social Scientific Theories'." Annual Meeting of the Society of Biblical Literature. Denver, CO, 2018.

Teehan, John. "Religion and Morality: The Evolved Cognitive Nexus," in *The Oxford Handbook of Evolutionary Psychology and Religion.* Edited by J. Liddle and T. K. Shackelford. Oxford: Oxford University Press, 2016. Currently available online, https://doi.org/10.1093/oxfordhb/9780199397747.013.11. Publication forthcoming 2021.

Theissen, Gerd. *Erleben und Verhalten der ersten Christen: Eine Psychologie des Urchristentums.* Gütersloh: Gütersloher Verlags-Haus, 2007.

Toulmin, Stephen Edelston. *The Uses of Argument.* Cambridge: Cambridge University Press, 2003. https://doi.org/10.1017/CBO9780511840005

Trilling, Wolfgang. *Das Wahre Israel: Studien zur Theologie des Matthäusevangeliums.* München: Kösel, 1964.

Tucker, J. Brian and Coleman A. Baker, eds. *T&T Clark Handbook to Social Identity in the New Testament.* London: Bloomsbury T&T Clark, 2014.

Turner, John, and Katherine J. Raynolds. "Self-Categorization Theory," 399–417 in *Handbook of Theories of Social Psychology.* Edited by Paul A. M. van Lange, Arie W. Kruglanski, and E. Tory Higgins. London: Sage, 2012.

Tversky, Amos, and Daniel Kahneman. *Judgment under Uncertainty: Heuristics and Biases.* New York: Cambridge University Press, 1982. https://doi.org/10.1017/CBO9780511809477.002

Ullucci, Daniel C. "Sacrifice and Votives," 282–301 in *Oxford Handbook of Early Christian Rituals.* Edited by R. Uro, R. DeMaris, J. Day, and R. Roitto. Oxford: Oxford University Press, 2018. https://doi.org/10.1093/oxfordhb/9780198747871.013.16

Uro, Risto. *Ritual and Christian Beginnings: A Socio-Cognitive Analysis.* Oxford: Oxford University Press, 2016. https://doi.org/10.1093/acprof:oso/9780199661176.001.0001

Uro, Risto, Juliette Day, Richard DeMaris, and Rikard Roitto, eds. *The Oxford Handbook of Early Christian Rituals.* Oxford: Oxford University Press, 2018. https://doi.org/10.1093/oxfordhb/9780198747871.001.0001

Valera, Francisco J., Evan Thompson, and Eleanor Rosch, *The Embodied Mind: Cognitive Science and Human Experience,* revised edn. Cambridge, MA: MIT Press, 2016 [1991], 157–71.

Wierzbicka, Anna. "Metaphors Linguists Live By," *Paper in Linguistics* 19 (1986): 287–313. https://doi.org/10.1080/08351818609389260

—*What Did Jesus Mean? Explaining the Sermon on the Mount and the Parables in Simple and Universal Human Concepts.* Oxford: Oxford University Press, 2001.

Wilson, Robert A., and Lucia Foglia, "Embodied Cognition," in *The Stanford Encyclopedia of Philosophy* (Spring 2017 Edition), ed. Edward N. Zalta. https://plato.stanford.edu/archives/spr2017/entries/embodied-cognition/

Windisch, Hans. *Der Sinn der Bergpredigt: Ein Beitrag zum Problem der richtigen Exegese.* Untersuchungen zum Neuen Testament. Leipzig: Hinrichs, 1929.

Workman, Lance, and Will Reader, *Evolutionary Psychology: An Introduction,* 3rd edn. Cambridge: Cambridge University Press, 2014. https://doi.org/10.1017/CBO9781107045187

Zerubavel, Eviatar. "Social Memories: Steps towards a Sociology of the Past," 221–4 in *The Collective Memory Reader.* Edited by Jeffrey K. Olick, Vered Vinitzky-Seroussi, and Daniel Levy. Oxford: Oxford University Press, 2011.

PART I
INDIVIDUAL COGNITION

Chapter Two

It's All in How You Look at It:
The Eyes and Morality in Matthew 6.22-23

Colleen Shantz

The lamp of the body is the eye. Therefore, if your eye is whole/singular, your entire body will be full of light; but if your eye is miserable, your whole body will be full of darkness. If then the light in you is darkness, how great the darkness is. (Matt. 6.22-23)

Introduction

The focus of this chapter, the saying in Matthew 6.22-23 about the eye and morality, is an apt test case for cognitive approaches. In fact, this chapter was born of just such a curiosity: could the so-called 4E theory of cognition help to explain the preservation of a saying that finds hardly any purchase in contemporary imagination? By way of illustration, when I have quoted the saying with no context to theology students, only a minority recognize it as even vaguely familiar, let alone meaningful or instructive. This response is in sharp contrast to their awareness of most of the other sayings in the Sermon on the Mount. The saying's lack of resonance with contemporary WEIRD[1] readers makes its presence in the Sermon all the more intriguing. How *does* an extended aphorism like this one come into being and what makes it worth preserving in a discourse like the Sermon? As mentioned in the introduction to this volume,[2] cognition is often described as (i) embodied, (ii) embedded, (iii) enactive, and (iv) extended. As such it integrates both what is understood to be universal or at least broadly generalizable—especially biological and inherited psychological characteristics—with what is deemed particular and distinctive—especially cultural developments and contextual particularities.

---

1. WEIRD is an acronym for white, educated, industrial, rich, democratic people—whose responses to and views of the world do not exhaust the available options for human behaviour. As an example of the lack of interpretive resonance, Daniel Harrington places the saying under the conveniently amorphous heading "Other Teachings (6:19–7:20)." Daniel J. Harrington, *The Gospel of Matthew* (Sacra Pagina; Collegeville, MN: Michael Glazier, 2007).
2. See p. 16.

Its peculiarity is among the features that make this saying an interesting test case for the heuristic power of cognitive theory. Though brief, the saying makes explicit appeal to at least two of the Es of the formula: embedded and embodied. The first section that follows explores the geographic and historical character of the Mediterranean basin as a shaper of culture, in particular some of the factors that heighten suspicion among inhabitants. Indeed, culture provides context for the values in the saying; however, it does not explain how the eye came to express the focus of the concern. In other words, while the aphorism is grounded undeniably in first-century Mediterranean norms, the rhetorical effectiveness of this saying also appeals explicitly to biological embodiment—especially *the experience of sight*. The centrality of the eyes is the second characteristic that makes it an interesting test case. Is this more universal experience of eye contact and seeing part of what gives this saying the stickiness that helps cultural elaboration succeed and a foundation from which to interpret its significance? In the second and longest section that follows I will outline the role of vision in the social character of cognition, showing how the eye, and, hence, embodied cognition, provides an apt locus for interpersonal morality.

But briefly, before beginning this analysis, it is worth noting that others have wondered about the (now) unfamiliar ideas in this unit. Even a generous assessment would conclude that Matthew 6.22-23 is an odd construction. There is no way around that fact. That the eye should be a lamp or light seems unlikely enough. But the parallel composition that aligns asymmetrical elements—"singular" (*haplous*) versus "evil" (*ponēros*)—only increases its awkwardness. Furthermore, how is the whole of the body contingent on the eye? By the time we read that the light in you can be darkness we seem to be in the territory of absurdist theatre. How might we reason our way backwards from the finished unit to the factors that impelled its construction? How do we explain its existence as a precursor to its interpretation? Interpreters who have been curious about the appeal to the eye have tended to search the history of ideas for a solution. Indeed, it turns out that some other ancient writers also thought of the eye as a source or a receiver of light. Hans Dieter Betz has led the way, identifying a number of comments in Greek literature, from archaic to Hellenistic, about the functioning of the eye and its relationship to light.[3] He further shows that two proto-scientific

---

3. Hans Dieter Betz, *The Sermon on the Mount: A Commentary on the Sermon on the Mount, including the Sermon on the Plain (Matthew 5:3–7:27 and Luke 6:20–49)* (Minneapolis, MN: Fortress Press, 1995), 442–8. Betz offers parallels from the Pythagoreans, pre-Socratics (exemplified by Heraclitus), Parmenides, Empedocles, Theophrastus, and Democritus (who posited the intriguing proto-scientific explanation that objects send out atoms that create air-imprints that, with the help of the sun, are carried to the eye).

theories exist among ancient authors: either that light is carried to the eye by other particles (intromission) or that the eye emits light, which then illumines objects (extramission), a view that most later philosophers, including Aristotle, rejected.

Betz works backward from these ancient comments to posit an explanatory context for Matthew 6.22-23. He begins with the two options facing the interpreter in cutting through the opacity of the saying: "Is the SM with its images and concepts primarily a collection of individual wisdom sayings, prephilosophical in nature, or are the sayings assembled in the SM succinct statements of theological arguments involving philosophical ideas of a more developed nature?"[4] The question is mostly rhetorical since Betz, himself, offers the conclusion that Greek ideas are responsible.[5]

> One cannot understand the argument about the human eye and its functioning … without some knowledge concerning ancient theories of sense perception and cognition. If one assumes this point, one must also conclude that the debate about such theories was widespread in the circles of philosophers and theologians at the time of the New Testament and that this debate had entered into Jewish circles.[6]

He concludes that the passage comes down on the side of Empedocles's and Plato's understandings of the eye and discounts early, atomistic theories.[7] So, for Betz, the saying arises from a philosophical debate about the mechanics of sight. Of course, he had not been exposed to studies showing that children and "naïve adults" even today describe the functioning of the eye with elements of extramission.[8] At the very least, exposure to philosophical accounts is not necessary to generate such ideas; they appear naturally. Following this interpretative trail, Ulrich Luz considers what effect the saying would have had on its early audiences. He claims matter-of-factly that the mention of lamp "makes the readers immediately think of

---

Dale Allison and Candida Moss supplement Betz's attention to Greek sources with relevant Jewish parallels. See Dale C. Allison, "The Eye Is the Lamp of the Body (Matthew 6.22–23=Luke 11.34–36)," *New Testament Studies* 33 (2009): 61–83; and Candida R. Moss, "Blurred Vision and Ethical Confusion: The Rhetorical Function of Matthew 6:22–23," *Catholic Biblical Quarterly* 73 (2011): 757–76.

4. Betz, *The Sermon on the Mount*, 438.
5. Betz, *The Sermon on the Mount*, 438–9: "One can hardly have any doubt that Hellenistic-Jewish literature was influenced by Greek ideas early on, although explicit references to Platonic (i.e., Middle-Platonic) doctrines do not occur until Philo of Alexandria."
6. Betz, *The Sermon on the Mount*, 442.
7. Betz, *The Sermon on the Mount*, 445.
8. See Charles G. Gross, "The Fire that Comes from the Eye," *The Neuroscientist* 5 (1999): 58–64.

the widely held ancient conviction that the human eye has its own light that shines on the dark surroundings."⁹ This observation is rooted squarely in representationalism (as described in the introduction to this volume) and it makes sense as a possible contribution to the intelligibility of the saying.

The rest of this chapter explores what else might contribute to the saying and how 4E cognition might help us to see these other contributions and possibly even why the saying seems no longer effective. The rise of cognitive perspectives has, at least in part, been fueled by attention to the interplay of the cultural and the bio-psychological. The final section that follows considers the effect of the saying as it is placed within the Sermon. When cognitive readings are successful one of their primary contributions is integration of these otherwise diverse sets of data, providing a much richer sense of how human beings make and receive meaning. Thus, rather than replacing or merely offering an alternative approach to those already in use, cognitive readings have potential to integrate levels of information in multi-level explanations.[10]

Embedded: The Evil Eye in Mediterranean Context

To say that cognition is *embedded* is to recognize the power of physical and social contexts in constraining and fostering the ways we come to know, and in shaping the content of that knowledge. But the contexts in which our thinking is embedded also encompass the embodied experiences of factors like climate and geography. The term embedded suggests the reciprocal relationship between our inherited psycho-biological character as human beings and the material world in which we function. There is no intelligence apart from the embodied-embedded system in part because thinking that is free of context is also without meaning.

While social contexts are more routinely examined, it is worth beginning with the broad view of geographical terrain as a relevant aspect of context. The Canadian novelist Margaret Atwood has made some brief anthropological reflections along these lines, although she was engaged in literary criticism at the time. Canadians often reflect on the differences between their culture and that of the United States—a difference that seems all the more intriguing given their many similarities, including the common origin of both countries primarily as British settler colonies.[11] Atwood, a voracious

---

9. Ulrich Luz, *Matthew 1–7: A Commentary*, trans. James E. Crouch, rev. edn. (Hermeneia; Minneapolis, MN: Fortress Press, 2007).

10. Edward Slingerland, *What Science Offers the Humanities: Integrating Body and Culture* (New York: Cambridge, 2008).

11. These nationalist sensibilities were of course largely antagonistic to the nations

reader, looked to early literature of both colonies as her data for analysis and on that basis concluded in part that:

> Possibly the symbol for America is The Frontier, a flexible idea that contains many elements dear to the American heart: it suggests a place that is new, where the old order can be discarded (as it was when America was instituted by a crop of disaffected Protestants, and later at the time of the Revolution); a line that is always expanding, taking in or "conquering" ever-fresh virgin territory (be it The West, the rest of the world, outer space, Poverty or The Regions of the Mind); it holds out a hope, never fulfilled but always promised, of Utopia, the perfect human society.[12]

By contrast, her review of Canadian settler literature showed that the theme of *survival* (including its means and alternatives) has characterized the early and classic works of Canadian fiction because it also reflects the character of the nation state. She summarizes it thus: "Much Canadian writing suggests that failure is required because it is felt—consciously or unconsciously—to be the only 'right' ending, the only thing that will support the characters' (or their authors') view of the universe."[13] The typology is not perfect for every expression of the two cultures; indeed, no typology could claim such sufficiency. But it does help to illustrate the way geography, climate, and historical happenstance generates and sustains cultural features (more about that in a moment).

The Mediterranean context that encompassed the period of the Gospels can also be placed within this typology. The comparison, including an expansion of the Atwood-Frye observations, appears in Table 1. For those living in Canada, the challenges of geography, climate, and landlocked isolation fostered an orientation toward a particular kind of collective in which a small band of likeminded people cling to the vestiges of "civilization" as the best hope of life or the place from which it is lost. Contemporary Canadian habits of orderly queues, universal healthcare, tolerance of difference, and relative politeness are, arguably, of a kind with that early sensibility. In

---

and cultures that had long lived on the continent before it became known as North America.

12. Margaret Atwood, *Survival: A Thematic Guide to Canadian Literature* (Toronto: Anansi, 1972), 31. Atwood's use of "Canadian," as typical of that time, does not encompass the First Peoples of Canada or their narratives, who, before the arrival of Europeans, didn't worry overmuch about survival.

13. Atwood, *Survival*, 44. Atwood's schema was based in part on Northrup Frye's notion of the "garrison mentality" in Canadian literature. See Northrup Frye, "Conclusion to a Literary History of Canada," in *The Bush Garden: Essays on the Canadian Imagination* (Toronto: Anansi, 1975), 215–53. While Atwood credits the cultural threat posed by the USA, Frye identified the vastness of land and severity of climate as the source of the peculiar Canadian disposition.

contrast, American themes were cast in a context where individual effort and resolve were far more likely to be successful; if one was determined and capable then more land and resources were there for the taking. As Atwood argued, the frontier, as an ever-moving edge, captures this idea nicely.

As for the larger context of the Mediterranean basin, it was shaped by a deeper history of contact between clans, settlements, and ethnic groups embedded in topography that created microregions. Historians Peregrine Horden and Nicholas Purcell have accumulated evidence from antiquity to show that there were nonetheless strong connections, by turns harmonious and conflictual, among these localities.[14] In that historical and geographical context the household—a more expansive concept in antiquity than today[15]—served as an organizing structure and eventually a central metaphor. The metaphor captures both the idea of a central locus (the male head) and the diminishing degrees of benefit and attachment that radiated from that point. The emperor Augustus strategically capitalized on the currency of this image, positioning himself as the *pater familias* of the entire empire. For example, he commissioned, with support of the Senate, relief images of the imperial family to decorate the *Ara Pacis Agustae*, an altar dedicated to the goddess of peace and celebrating Augustus's return from a series of military campaigns. While the altar ostensibly celebrates the goddess, it also functioned effectively as propaganda for Augustus as head of his own family and source of all good things—including peace—flowing to the empire.[16]

Table 1: Cultural Themes

	Central metaphor	*Cultural dynamic*
United States	Frontier	Conquest
Canada	Outpost/Garrison	Survival
Mediterranean basin	Oikos (household)	Competition

---

14. Peregrine Horden and Nicholas Purcell, *The Corrupting Sea: A Study of Mediterranean History* (Oxford: Basil Blackwell, 2000).

15. For example, Book I of *Economics*, attributed to Aristotle, lays out structure of an ideal household (characterized by dominion over both people and possessions) as the pattern for all forms of governance. Of course the English word "economy" comes directly from the Greek word for household management, οἰκονομία.

16. John Dominic Crossan and Jonathan Reed offer a vigorous interpretation of this monument as imperial propaganda of household. See *In Search of Paul: How Jesus's Apostle Opposed Rome's Empire with God's Kingdom* (New York: HarperCollins, 2004), 90–4. Even a tempered version of their argument gives significant insight into the power of the household as a cultural dynamic.

The idea of a collective culture for the whole Mediterranean basin has been debated in recent decades; however, there is less reason to question it in antiquity.[17] A persistent feature of ancient Mediterranean culture was its agonistic character. In other words, its social interactions were colored by struggle and competition. Struggle could tinge interactions from official political forms, where debate was the primary means of conducting business and elite men were trained in its practices, to the valuing of athletic contests, to many everyday interactions in public. A second characteristic of the Mediterranean region of this period is the concept of *limited good*. Bruce Malina describes the perspective as "the socially shared conviction that the resources enabling a community to realize its range of needs are in finite supply and that any disruption of the social equilibrium can only be detrimental to community survival."[18] Such a view begins in a lived reality of periods of drought, of competition for land, and of periods of general scarcity. But once established, it is elaborated in distinctive ways that appear to bear little relation to these material circumstances. For example, one of the primary goods for which people might contend was honor.

This pervasive dynamic of competition fuels the logic of the evil eye and brings us back to our text: "if your eye is evil(/miserable) your whole body will be full of darkness." When someone sees that you have something valuable, they are likely to look at it and you with envy; and equally when someone else receives an extraordinary benefit, there is reason to wonder how they came by it. The cultural construct of the evil eye gives structure to this anxiety about the power of envy. For example, because of the sudden and pronounced change in the tally of goods that it entails, the birth of a child tends to arouse evil eye concerns even today. Young children,

---

17. A useful overview by Albera Dionigi traces the rise, fall, and renewal of the category of Mediterranean anthropology, outlining some of the historical and epistemological currents that pushed along. While he identifies some undue emphasis on "exoticized" themes and the need to recognize regional differences (e.g., the Levant) along with general trends, none of these critiques are fatal to the thesis. See Albera Dionigi, "Anthropology of the Mediterranean: Between Crisis and Renewal," *History and Anthropology* 17 (2006): 109–33.

18. Bruce Malina, *The New Testament World: Insights from Cultural Anthropology*, 3rd edn. (Louisville, KY: Westminster John Knox, 2001), 112–3. The term "limited good" was originally coined by George M. Foster, "Peasant Society and the Image of Limited Good," *American Anthropologist* 67 (1965): 293–315. He proposed that it was a feature of many, if not most, traditional societies. To identify it as part of Mediterranean culture is not to say that the perception does not arise elsewhere (viz. common views of refugees as a threat to the limited good of European and North American cities that receive them); rather it is to say that it is embedded more thoroughly in institutions and norms of a culture.

especially if they are considered beautiful or otherwise special, are protected with charms against the malevolent gaze of others. (Indeed, evil eye bracelets for children are currently for sale through Etsy and Amazon, with the added innovation of gendered color options.)

The evil eye is a fascinating example of the embeddedness of cognition. The philosopher and anthropologist Evard Westermarck conducted much of his ethnographic work in North Africa, especially Morocco, where he spent a total of seven years. While there he noted the strength of evil eye sensitivities and a variety of practices that were invested in efforts to avoid attracting an envious gaze.[19] Interactions around food were especially dangerous: "To take food in the presence of some hungry looker-on is like taking poison … the evil then actually enters into the body with the food." That poison is transmitted by the eyes of the hungry onlooker.[20] Because of the heightened risk in such moments the culture maintained a number of prophylactic conventions. For example, "To avoid the danger of eating in the presence of somebody else the latter is asked to partake of the food or is at any rate offered a morsel. If he refuses the invitation there is little danger of eating in case he is a friend, but a stranger is hardly allowed to refuse."[21] To avoid any unintended glimpse of food, people who were carrying it were careful to keep it covered from sight and, Westermarck reports the general view that "only insane people" eat in public, the street or marketplace, because of the risk of being seen possessing something in the face of someone else's need.

Westermarck's work encompassed the early decades of the twentieth century, but allusions to the evil eye also pervade the periods and regions in which biblical literature was produced.[22] John Elliot has devoted much of his career to documenting the occurrences. He defines the evil eye construct as "a web of ideas, beliefs, attitudes, emotions, symbols, and actions that … appears to have remained relatively stable over time."[23] Indeed, that stability is evidenced in the fact that, well before the Sermon on the Mount was compiled, Hebrew texts were replete with examples of the moral functioning of the eye and its gaze, and after it the Mishnah and Talmud continued

---

19. Edvard Westermarck discusses the evil eye in *Ritual and Belief in Morocco*. Vol. 1 (London: Macmillan, 1926), 422–6.

20. Westermarck, *Ritual and Belief*, 422.

21. Westermarck, *Ritual and Belief*, 426.

22. Rivka Ulmer suggests that the view spread especially rapidly in the Hellenistic period. See Rivka Ulmer, *The Evil Eye in the Bible and in Rabbinic Literature* (Hoboken, NJ: KTAV, 1994), 5. She discusses examples from Greek literature, including Plutarch and *The Illiad* on p. 137.

23. See John Elliott, *Beware the Evil Eye: The Evil Eye in the Bible and the Ancient World*. Vol. 2: *Greece and Rome* (Eugene, OR: Cascade Books, 2016), 18.

the pattern. Elliot's examples include ancient scientific explanations about the functioning of the eye and the understanding that some substance or force emanates from it. Regarding the former category, he observes that ancient scientific minds, it is essential to keep in mind, regarded the evil eye and its operation as a physical reality working in accord with natural properties and potencies as then understood. The plausibility of this belief rested on the prevalent notion that the eye was an active agent whose emissions were comparable to the sun projecting rays of light or to a lamp emitting beams of light.[24] Because the eye was understood to exert physical force it also had physical effects. Whether or not one knew the source, the evil eye could be blamed for many misfortunes (illness, death, loss, injury).

However, significantly, these explanations of the mechanisms of the eye are by no means prevalent; nor are they necessary to the meaningful use of the construct. As the preceding discussion suggests, most common is the association of the eye with either generosity or stinginess and this theme appears in both wisdom literature and legal material. The "good eye," is identified in those who share their bread with the poor (Prov. 22.9), while greedy people regard others with an evil eye (Prov. 28.22). Texts that extol and define good character frequently warn against people who live with an evil eye (e.g., Prov. 23.6; Tob. 4.7, 16; Sir. 14.3, 10). In the Torah, reference to a good or bad eye illustrates correspondingly good or bad social morality. So reviled is selfishness in Israelite law that the threat of divine punishment can include being cursed with an evil eye of neglect for even loved ones (e.g., Deut. 28.5-57).[25] In those texts, indifference to the needs of others can be described as dispersed throughout the body, such that an evil eye (*ayin hara*) often accompanies a hard heart and a clenched hand (e.g., Deut. 15.7-11). I might continue to pile up examples, including those in contemporaneous cultures, but I'll trust that these suffice to show the ubiquity of the evil eye construct.

Embeddedness in Mediterranean culture goes a long way toward accounting for the persistence of the sensitivities about abundance and lack; however, it does less to explain why the eye should represent those scruples and why the evil eye complex persisted so successfully. In fact, this same literature imagines other effects of the eye as well. The eye can also be used to express

---

24. Elliott, *The Evil Eye*, 63. Among the ancient scientific views, Elliott cites Aristotle's theory—perhaps more Freudian than Newtonian—that menstruating women could ruin the surface of new mirrors by the bloody red emanations from their eyes (*On Dreams*, 459b 27-32).

25. Elliott lists these and other examples, *The Evil Eye*, 158. Ulmer treats many examples of midrash that introduce evil eye concepts in order to explain biblical texts. For example, in the Talmud (b. Bava Mezi'a 87a), Abraham and Sarah are treated as examples of the two kinds of eyes in their treatment of their unexpected guests at Mamre (Gen. 18).

the general state of regard of one person for another. The idiom of finding grace or evil in someone's eyes is common. The frequent phrase "the eyes of the Lord" is used to express general divine disposition (e.g., Deut. 11.12; Ps. 34.16, 33.18-19; Prov. 5.21, 15.3; 2 Chr. 16.9; Jer. 16.17). Also common is the idiom of finding grace or evil in someone's eyes. One's eye can mourn (Ps. 88.9). In the Saul-David saga, the moment that Saul's jealousy is kindled toward David is similarly and ominously marked: "So Saul eyed David from that day on" (1 Sam. 18.9). To account for the eye as the marker in these and other cultural constructs we need to consider embodied cognition.

Embodied: Eyes and the Person

One obvious place to begin the effort to reverse-engineer this saying is the eye and embodied cognition. On the surface, this saying is invested in ideas about vision and its relationship to interior moral dispositions. The reference, in verse 23a, to the "evil eye" is the clearest indication of that association. This section shows how examination of the phenomenology of sight and, more specifically, the social psychological significance of sight deepens this surface meaning and roots it in embodiment. Two kinds of data—the behavior of infants and cross-cultural similarity—are especially relevant to this point because they help to distinguish cultural elaborations from more innate, and hence universal, human capacities. A variety of experimental designs have helped to identify and describe the significant relationship between vision, human development, and a range of contingent social behaviors. I trace some of these studies here.

I See What You See: Eyes and Shared Attention

The first phase of visual-cognitive development in humans consists of shared attention with others. Given all the things that newborn humans cannot do, their ability, within days of birth, to imitate the facial behaviors of others seems surprising. And yet babies do, in fact, consistently open their mouths, stick out their tongues (even replicating a side as opposed to forward thrust), and purse their lips in correspondence to the actions of an adult exemplar. Then, within weeks of these early, nearly reflexive behaviors, infants begin to more closely share attention with their caregivers. Both of these capacities are essential to psychological wellbeing throughout life[26] and are the first steps toward the indispensible human capacity for mentalizing.

---

26. Attachment theory suggests that physical and affective closeness to a caregiver is vital to wellbeing throughout life. The term was proposed by John Bowlby, *Clinical Applications of Attachment Theory* (London: Routledge, 1988). The theory proposes

A variety of experiments have been designed to test the extent and character of innate orientation to the ocular. Collectively they demonstrate that babies show clear signs of affective awareness of the gaze of others and are thoroughly predisposed to the eyes as the key point of social knowledge. In one set of experiments, infants who were no more than five days old were presented with paired photographs of a face; one photo of the face was gazing directly at the camera, and the second of the same face with a diverted gaze. The results showed that even newborns looked at the direct-gaze face both longer and more frequently than its averted-gaze partner. As the experimenters note, the findings seem even more significant given the scant psychophysiological difference between direct and averted gaze with no verbal communication and no other changes in expression accompanying it.[27] In other words, eye contact is the only generalizable mental mechanism that could account for the newborns' fine distinctions between the two faces and, thus, eye contact alone is sufficient to generate statistically significant variations. Experiments of this sort offer support for the hypothesis that we possess a neural network "dedicated to find socially relevant stimuli for further processing,"[28] and that others' eyes are the most salient cue in exercising this skill. In another set of studies, this time with two-month-old babies, caregivers alternated between looking directly at infants and averting their gaze—even by merely shifting vision to the child's ear rather than the eyes. Consistently, the babies changed their behavior in coordination with the adult gaze. They smiled more and were more physically responsive during the periods of eye contact.[29]

Concomitant with this attraction to and interest in the eyes of other people, infants also display sensitivity to being looked at. Early childhood psychologist, Vasudevi Reddy, has collected a range of evidence that infants

---

further that healthy attachment provides both for comfort when stressed and for the security to take risks. A number of studies have established the significance for attachment of eye contact in infancy.

27. Teresa Farroni, et al., "Eye Contact Detection in Humans from Birth," *Proceedings of the National Academy of Sciences of the United States of America* 99/14 (2002): 9602–5.

28. Farroni, et al., "Eye Contact Detection," 9604.

29. D. Muir and S. Hains, "Young Infants' Perception of Adult Intentionality," in *Early Social Cognition*, ed. P. Rochat (Mahwah, NJ: Erlbaum, 1999), 176–7. See also the early studies by Colwyn Trevarthen, "Communication and Cooperation in Early Infancy: A Description of Primary Intersubjectivity," in *Before Speech*, ed. M. Bullowa (Cambridge: Cambridge University Press, 1979), 321–47; and Beatrice Beebe, Daniel Stern, and Joseph Jaffe, "The Kinesic Rhythm of Mother-Infant Interaction," in *Of Speech and Time: Temporal Speech Patterns in Interpersonal Contexts*, ed. A. W. Siegman and S. Feldstein (Mahwah, NJ: Erlbaum, 1979), 23–34.

also behave coyly in response to attention from others.[30] Even before they have developed a full mental representation of self, the perception of another's gaze, or even their own reflection in a mirror, results in coy smiles or alternation between returning the gaze and gaze aversion with smiling. By seven to twelve months of age many babies will avoid significant eye contact with strangers. Given the developmental stage of the children, the term "shy" is not quite applicable in these cases, but the behavior is nonetheless affective and sensory and triggered by eye contact.

Perhaps only the love of a parent or the professionalism of a psychologist can account for excitement about the next stage, but a subsequent and related element of intersubjective capacities (and one that is immediately relevant to the saying on the eye) is *gaze-following*. Typically, at around eight months of age, children progress from an interest in eyes to perception of the significance of the movements of others' eyes. In other words, they now display the sensitivity to a wider range of visual behavior in others and are able to pick up where someone is looking and to look there too.[31]

Psychologists debate the degree to which looking-where-the-other-looks is merely imitation or actually demonstrates slightly more sophisticated mechanisms. The minimalist, or "lean view," proposes that when babies mimic the movement of the other's head, their gaze inevitably falls on the same object as the adult. In other words, at this point in development there is no shared intention in looking, only an imitative reflex. The competing "rich view" proposes that the action is driven by "particular cognitive operations or second-order representational competencies"[32] and it accents the role of the eyes in these parallel acts rather than merely the motion of the head. Experimenters continue to collect evidence about which explanation is accurate at this earliest stage, but even in the lean view the process is on a trajectory to shared attention. Weighing in on the rich side, Reddy points out that representation is not the only measure of cognition. Rather, she suggests that affective and somatic cognition are foundational to representation. In her own words, "early infant engagement with others' attention does indeed show awareness of others as

---

30. Vasudevi Reddy, "On Being the Object of Attention: Implications for Self-Other Consciousness," *Trends in Cognitive Sciences* 7 (2003): 397–402.

31. Some of the foundational work in this area was conducted by Simon Baron-Cohen and colleagues and reported in his landmark monograph, *Mindblindness: An Essay on Autism and Theory of Mind* (Cambridge, MA: MIT Press, 1995).

32. Timothy P. Racine, "Getting beyond Rich and Lean Views of Joint Attention," in *Joint Attention: New Developments in Psychology, Philosophy of Mind, and Social Neuroscience*, ed. Axel Seemann (Cambridge, MA: MIT Press, 2011), 23. See also Stephen R. H. Langton, Roger J. Watt, and Vicki Bruce. "Do the Eyes Have it? Cues to the Direction of Social Attention," *Trends in Cognitive Sciences* 4 (2000): 50–9.

attending beings" but it is "a qualitatively different kind of awareness, which provides an emotional, nonrepresentational, link between self and other."[33] In Reddy's estimation, infant studies have been overly invested in identifying the beginning of representational thinking and as a result have neglected the foundational role of affective cognition. As she emphasizes, affective and embodied awareness of the other "must lead to, rather than result from, representations of self and other as psychological entities."[34]

The third development in this visual-cognitive trajectory is *protodeclarative pointing*. As the term suggests, babies, somewhere between ten to twelve months of age, are now able to look at something to which another person is pointing, and even to point in order to indicate their own object of interest. Thus, the locus of attention has now shifted markedly beyond the direct engagement self and other to more distal objects of shared attention. Furthermore, the gesture of pointing extends and emphasizes the action of looking. The child is now able to coordinate other behaviors (e.g., pointing, crossing the room to retrieve something) more fully with their own mental state (attention) with another person's. You can also see how this behavior moves closer to what we typically think of as communication. Information is conveyed between subjects by simple sign language. With this step, a sense of intention becomes possible.

I See What You Mean

The abilities outlined so far are all maturationally natural[35] and so too is the final development in early childhood that we will discuss—theory of mind, or ToM. Compared to the other developments, ToM is more widely known and studied in part because of its significance in understanding differences in cognition in autism.[36] It is also an ability that is essential to empathy,

---

33. Reddy, "Object of Attention," 397.
34. Reddy, "Object of Attention," 397. Reddy's work is strongly and helpfully invested in enactive cognition.
35. The term was coined by Robert McCauley. He uses it to distinguish *practiced naturalness*—skills that often vary across cultures and require special artifacts and/or a period of special instruction to learn (like riding a bike or playing piano)—from those cognitive capacities that arise at about the same age across cultures without any special effort or apparatus to train them. For a detailed discussion, see ch. 2, "Maturational Naturalness" in McCauley, *Why Religion Is Natural and Science Is Not* (Oxford: Oxford University Press, 2011).
36. Again the work of Simon Baron-Cohen has been foundational in identifying this capacity and its role in neuro-typical development. It has often been suggested that although people with autism can learn to attend to other's subjectivity, they are lacking natural ToM.

as well as to deception and to fullness of intersubjectivity. Intersubjectivity enables agents to mutually influence one another and thus facilitates a whole range of prosocial behaviors. However, it is so ubiquitous in our lives that it is easy to take it for granted. Sociologist, Tim Dant, amplifies some of its extraordinary character:

> There is something exclusive about one's own mind; it is one's innermost part, something intimate and private, a hidden element of one's personality, at the very core of one's being. It is the seat of feelings, ideas, thoughts, sensations, and experiences that are one's own alone and on it is based our sense of self. And yet our understanding of other people as individuals, and of the collective social world around us, depends on knowing what is in their minds. We draw on information about their expressive body and our own previous experiences to impute a feeling or infer a response to another person. We might ask them what led to their smile or raised eyebrow and their answers might confirm our informed guesses or tell us that we got it wrong. The capacity to know someone else's mind seems to be part of being human.[37]

Although Dant describes a conscious process of trying to understand another person's thoughts, such intuitions about what others are thinking are often automatic, rapid and nonconscious and arise naturally at about 36–48 months of age.

The experiment that best illustrates this capacity is called the Sally and Anne Test, developed by Baron-Cohen and colleagues.[38] In the landmark study, 61 children (14 with Down Syndrome, 20 with autism, and 27 who were neurotypical)[39] watched a puppet show whose plot is illustrated in Figure 1. Puppet Sally places a marble in her basket. When Sally leaves the scene, puppet Anne moves the marble to a box where it is hidden from sight. When Sally returns to the scene the experimenter asks the children three different questions: the Belief Question (Where will Sally look for her marble?), the Reality Question (Where is the marble really?), and the Memory Question (Where was the marble in the beginning?). Of course, the Belief Question assesses the difference between reality and what Sally expects based on her prior knowledge. While all but one of the children responded correctly to the Memory and Reality questions there was a marked difference in responses on the Belief question. About 85% of the Down Syndrome and neurotypical children responded correctly that Sally

---

37. Tim Dant, "In Two Minds: Theory of Mind, Intersubjectivity, and Autism," *Theory & Psychology* 25 (2015): 45–62, 45.

38. Simon Baron-Cohen, Alan M. Leslie, and Uta Firth, "Does the Autistic Child Have a 'Theory of Mind'?" *Cognition* 21 (1985): 37–46.

39. The ages of the three groups of children varied quite widely because they were screened for their ability to meet the communicative demands of the test. The original study describes the comparable "mental age" of the subjects (p. 40).

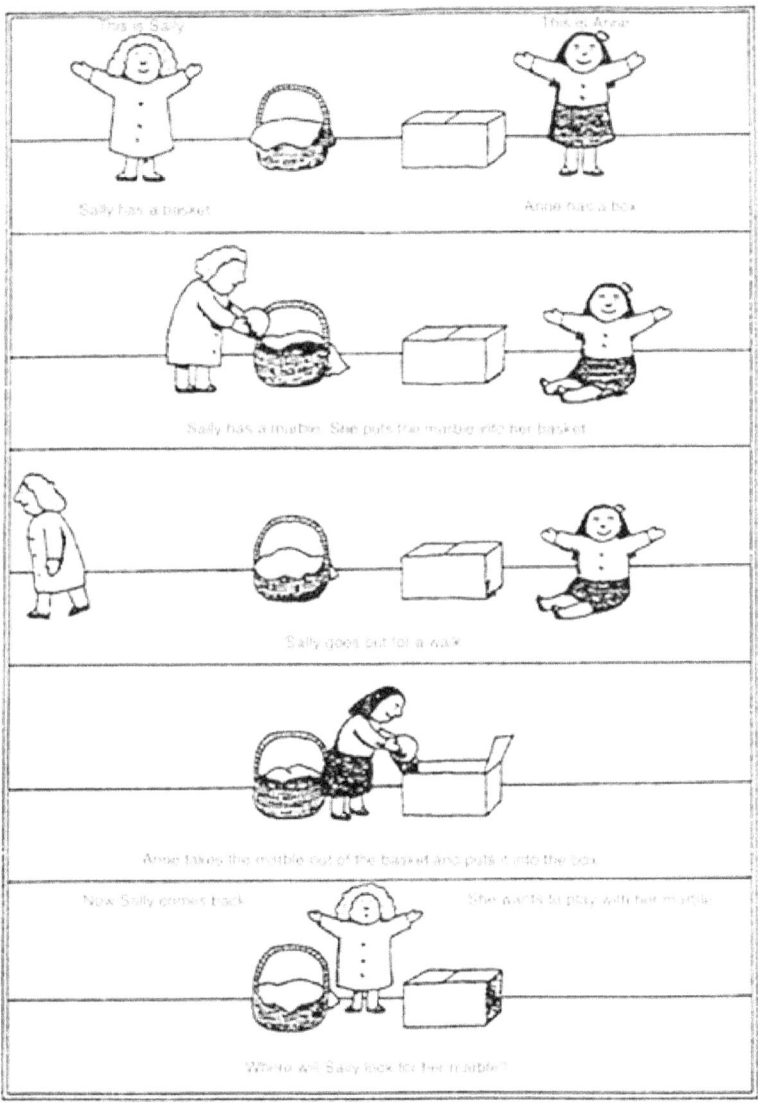

Figure 1. Sally-Anne test. Fair use, https://en.wikipedia.org/wiki/Sally%E2%80%93-Anne_test.

would look in the basket for the marble, while only 20% of the autistic children perceived this correctly. The watershed study describes the source of the incorrect answers as "an inability to represent mental states. As a result of this the autistic subjects are unable to impute beliefs to others and are thus at a grave disadvantage when having to predict the behaviour of other people."⁴⁰ The test is a brilliant example of the natural onset of the ability to *mentalize*, or to know the content of another person's perspective.

Table 2: Maturationally natural visual-cognitive abilities

Behavior	Age of onset	Cognitive capacity
Shared attention	from birth	Mimicry
Gaze following	8 months	Affective engagement and responsiveness
Proto-declarative pointing	12 months	Shared attention
Perspective taking	36–48 months	Theory of mind

ToM sits on a continuum with the other phenomena discussed here. The very early—and, hence, untrained—appearance of capacities like shared gaze (summarized in Table 2) suggests that these features of vision and mirroring are evolved rather than learned. The relationship between gaze and the ability to read someone else's desire has been measured in children as young as two years of age[41] and initial PET studies show the neurological overlap in the mental activity of a child engaged in ToM tasks or in discernment of eye gaze.[42] Furthermore, the neurological difference between subjects with autism and those without also suggests that the centrality of eyes in attachment and social behavior has a genetic basis. One is hard-pressed to exaggerate the adaptive value of these early developments, especially their value for social interaction.[43] The adaptive value extends beyond the information provided by vision; rather, early childhood sightedness helps to establish fundamental social skills that serve the individual throughout life. The naturalness of these capacities (for most types of minds) should not distract from how profound they are to so much that is human. The attachment formed through eye contact and shared attention is foundational to human sociality. Similarly, to distinguish between what I see and what another person sees makes possible both empathy and deception. The point I want to emphasize here is the key role played by all things ocular in tasks

---

40. Baron-Cohen, et al., "Does the Autistic Child Have a 'Theory of Mind'?" 43.
41. K. Lee, et al., "Children's Use of Triadic Eye Gaze Information for 'Mind Reading'," *Developmental Psychology* 34 (1998): 525–39.
42. Andrew J. Calder, et al., "Reading the Mind from Eye Gaze," *Neuropsychologia* 40 (2002): 1129–38.
43. Indeed, studies from earlier generations explored the difficulties that congenitally blind children had with attachment and social adaptation throughout life, difficulties that are not experienced by those who become blind after early childhood. See for example Vincent, B. von Hasselt, "Social Adaptation in the Blind," *Clinical Psychology Review* 3 (1983): 87–102.

so key to human sociality. No wonder, then, that various forms of embodied cognition draw on these visual capacities.

Recognizing: Seeing Makes It So

George Lakoff and Mark Turner have famously identified "understanding as seeing" as a ubiquitous metaphor (in English). A number of studies have since probed the more precise character of the metaphor, but its significance is undeniable in a number of languages. Often the verb for seeing is a regular substitute for verbs of knowing. Every native English speaker would know instinctively that "I see what you mean" is not meant to be taken literally and that "as I see it ..." refers to ideological perspectives rather than one's line of sight. Though short of being a universal expression,[44] the world's languages are peppered with indications of the connection between seeing and knowing or understanding. By way of illustration, Table 2 illustrates a partial and unsystematically opportunistic (i.e., I asked my bilingual friends for examples) sampling of idioms that connect seeing and knowing.

Some linguistic links between vision and cognition are very old indeed— so old as to become obscured as language evolved as, for example, the word "wise" illustrates. In several languages (e.g., German, Old Norse, and Dutch) the word for wise has a common root *weid-*, which originally meant *seeing* or *vision*. In the English word "wit" grew from the same root. More relevant for the current discussion, the ordinary verb for knowing in the Greek of the New Testament, *oida*, likewise has its etymology in the word for sight. The same is true of the Sanskrit word *veda*.

But, as the heading of this subsection suggests, sometimes the metaphor of sight moves beyond the abstract realm of knowledge to express more enactive connotations.[45] This use of sight is more immediately phenomenological than neurological; however, it is a short step from seeing-leads-to-knowing to seeing-makes-it-so. In other words, we experience an overlap between seeing what something is and bringing something into effect by looking at it in a particular way. Phenomenologically, the moment of my conscious observation is also the point at which the information comes into being for me. Of course, in thoughtful analysis I can extend that reality back

---

44. See John Chernoff, "'Hearing' in West African Idioms," *The World of Music* 39 (1997): 19–25. Similarly, in French, entendre is more commonly associated with understanding.

45. Interestingly, a study of naturally occurring sayings that employ seeing-as-understanding in English show that they typically communicate the *process of attaining* knowledge. In that regard they already express active connotations. See Alice Deignan and Lynne Cameron, "A Re-Examination of UNDERSTANDING IS SEEING," *Cognitive Semiotics* 5 (2014): 220–43.

in time to before I saw it, but interrupting these felt conditions requires a kind of detached effort that is expensive, so to speak, in terms of the cognitive energy it requires. Likewise, I can remind myself, as the day progresses that the earth is turning relative to the sun, but I will still mostly *experience* the sun as rising and setting and use language that reflects that feeling.

Table 3: Idioms of Seeing-as-Knowledge

Language	Original	Literal meaning	Usage
Akan (spoken in Ghana)	*muhu dɛm*	I see like that (on its own muhu means "I see")	To understand or agree with another
Tamil	கண்ணோட்டம் (*kaṇṇōṭṭam*)	Eye-look	Connoting perspective or opinion
French	*Tu vois ç'que j'veux dire?*	You see what I want to say?	A phrase to seek confirmation of understanding
Spanish	*ya veo*	I see	To understand
Portuguese	*estou a ver* or *estou vendo*	I'm seeing	Normally the progressive form of the verb is used to indicate that one is following an argument.
	Ele não se enxerga	he doesn't see himself	To lack self-awareness
Romanian	*Încep să văd*	I'm starting to see	To indicate that one is following another's meaning
	O, acum văd	Oh, now I see	To indicate insight
Russian	Я вижу / *Ya vizhu*	I see	To understand
Finnish	*minä näen*	I see	To express one's own opinion or interpretation
Vietnamese	*tôi thấy*	I see	To understand
German	*erblicken*	to catch sight of	To understand

The Sermon on the Mount has a number of ethical injunctions that relate the eye or vision not only to particular knowledge/perspectives, but also to the actions that might follow from such ways of thinking. Probably the most striking is the claim that "whoever looks at a woman in order to desire her has already committed adultery in his heart. Therefore, if your right eye causes you to stumble, pluck it out and throw it away" (5.28-29). Similarly, Matthew 7.3-5 equates moral-ethical status with the state of the eyes. In this case, the saying ridicules the fastidiousness of the saying about the chip of wood in your brother's eye while there is a whole log sticking out of your own. Thus, clarity of sight substitutes for soundness of character, with a subtext against moral smugness thrown in for good measure.

These examples of linguistic expressions of an embodied perception illustrate again the natural dependence of culture and biology. As mentioned, sayings of seeing-as-knowing are not universal. Indeed, such idioms are not present in Urdu, Hindi, Gujarati, Polish, or Italian, and many West African cultures even employ hearing—not seeing—for a wide range of perceptual acts that overlap with understanding. These examples epitomize how embodied dispositions help to shape and are, in turn, constrained by the settings in which those humans live. And with that observation (pardon the embodied metaphor) we turn to consideration of the (now somewhat less strange) saying about the eye as a lamp.

Conclusion: Enacting the Meaning of the Saying

Let's return for a moment to the questions—and the sorts of answers—that we began with. Interpretation of this passage has been significantly invested in the history of ideas. Recall the interpretative framework set out by Betz: "Is the SM with its images and concepts primarily a collection of individual wisdom sayings, prephilosophical in nature, or are the sayings assembled in the SM succinct statements of theological arguments involving philosophical ideas of a more developed nature?" This way of framing the problem assumes that cognition is predominantly representational. To put it in exaggerated form, this sort of representational cognition depends on a presumption of prepackaged concepts that are stored in the brain and deployed into situations. That sort of theory of cognition fits Ulrich Luz's sense that the saying would make ancient audience "immediately think of the widely held ancient conviction that the human eye has its own light that shines on the dark surroundings." Such arguments can be deepened and nuanced by the insights of embodied cognition and affect.

Certainly the saying coheres with other concepts in the Sermon; but that fact, while not irrelevant, is weak justification for its presence in the collection. One theme it shares with other parts of the discourse is the association of light with goodness or positive value. That theme appears most strongly in the claim that the disciples are the light of the world and should shine accordingly (Matt. 5.14-16). Like this saying, several units in the collection aimed at tying together intention and behavior, creating singularity of purpose. The most explicit examples may be the so-called antithesis, each of which refers to a legal requirement (no murder, 5.21; no adultery, 5.27; no false vows, 5.33; retaliation must be in exact proportion, 5.38; and love your neighbor, 5.43) and then adds a corresponding affective/attitudinal requirement. Likewise, in 7.1-5 as in the unit under discussion, the general health and functioning of the eye serves as a metric for the integrity of the person. The former makes that claim explicitly and humorously with the comparison between a speck and a log.[46] Finally, the sermon includes several kinds of exhortations to generosity and against greed or even worry about possessions (e.g., 5.42; 6.3-4, 25-33; 7.7-11). The warnings against avarice include the two sayings that flank our passage, namely 6.19-21 and 6.24. So, the saying fits with much of the other material in the Sermon and, as Betz would have it, it participates in its theo-philosophical thrust: "According to the theology of Jesus, then, the decisive point in dealing with material goods is that of perspective. If one envisions one's life in the perspective of the treasures in heaven, this perspective will inform and guide the human heart ..."[47] Because it fits the general thrust this conceptually eccentric saying comes along for the ride, carried by its more propositionally lucid neighbors.

Enactivism describes an alternative to this sort of representationalist understanding of cognition. In this case it also provides a more compelling role for the saying about the eye. As described in the introduction to this volume, enactivism posits that cognition is generated in the interaction of fully embodied, autonomous human beings with their situation, broadly construed. (The dependence of enactivism on the principles of embeddedness and embodiment should be obvious.) Hence cognition arises within that interaction rather than relying on preexisting representations, stored in an abstracted mind, and selectively applied to externalities. To use a straightforward example, the color red is not a present in the mind as a representation that can be connected to its external reality; instead, red is known in the momentary confluence of light, object, and a particular kind of animal body with specific visual apparatus.[48] Correspondingly, cognition does not progress (as per Betz's quote above) from the perspective of heavenly treasures, but something more immediate and tangible is at play.

An enactivist framework offers a more robust sense of the power of the saying about the eye and what it contributes to the set of three aphorisms about wealth. It enhances the triad in part by connecting selfishness to specific bodily acts of perception and to bodily danger or contamination. The two sayings that flank it draw contrasting parallels between human and divine/earthly and heavenly/temporal and eternal realities: you cannot serve God and mammon; store up treasures in heaven. These are principles

46. See Kazen's discussion in this volume, p. 166
47. Betz, *The Sermon on the Mount*, 435.
48. Evan Thompson has devoted an entire monograph to the question of color and its perception. Evan Thompson, *Colour Vision: A Study in Cognitive Science and the Philosophy of Perception* (London: Routledge, 1995).

to which Matthew's audience of insiders might assent. But assenting to a concept is not the same thing as acting on it. And even *internalizing* a concept does not ensure that it will be enacted. The metaphor of the eye as a lamp lodges selfishness within bodily functions—in this case vision with its deep embeddedness in social wellbeing and empathy. Furthermore, it does this with a phrase (*ho ophthalmos ponēros*; the evil eye) that evokes cultural norms. Finally, the unit contains an implied threat to bodily integrity: If you look on others parsimoniously you contaminate the whole of your body with darkness. The affective arousal that accompanies potential danger also heightens the possible ways that the saying might be activated. In short, it is not because audiences "immediately think of the widely held ancient conviction that the human eye has its own light that shines on the dark surroundings" that the saying would have been effective; rather, Matthew 6.22-23 is rich with embodied links and targeted to a culturally conditioned set of values. Representational thinking plays a part in formal study[49]—the kind of thing academics do when we analyze a text; however, in the flow of "on-line" cognition it has much more to do with the interplay of the multiple potentials available within the situation. Each of the embodied and social connections present in the saying furnishes another potential link within a lived moment. The sum total of these features helps to explain why such a saying may have been successful enough for inclusion in the Sermon. And the social virtues it helped to stimulate likely also contributed to the survival of first communities that received the teaching.

Biographical Note

Colleen Shantz is Associate Professor of New Testament and Christian origins at St. Michael's College in the University of Toronto. She explores the significance of experiential aspects (practices of ecstatic experience, ritual, and emotion) in the first generations of the Christ movement. Currently, she is also the Graduate Director of the Toronto School of Theology.

Bibliography

Allison, Dale C. "The Eye Is the Lamp of the Body (Matthew 6.22–23=Luke 11.34–36)," *New Testament Studies* 33 (2009): 61–83. https://doi.org/10.1017/S0028688500016052

---

49. Notwithstanding my allowance for representational thinking, see the discussion of scientific reasoning by Ezequiel Di Paolo and Evan Thompson, "The Enactive Approach," *The Routledge Handbook of Embodied Cognition*, ed. Lawrence Shapiro (London: Routledge, 2014), 68–78, 69–71.

Atwood, Margaret. *Survival: A Thematic Guide to Canadian Literature*. Toronto: Anansi, 1972.
Baron-Cohen, Simon. *Mindblindness: An Essay on Autism and Theory of Mind*. Cambridge, MA: MIT Press, 1995. https://doi.org/10.7551/mitpress/4635.001.0001
Baron-Cohen, Simon, Alan M. Leslie, and Uta Firth. "Does the Autistic Child Have a 'Theory of Mind'?" *Cognition* 21 (1985): 37–46. https://doi.org/10.1016/0010-0277(85)90022-8
Beebe, Beatrice, Daniel Stern, and Joseph Jaffe. "The Kinesic Rhythm of Mother-Infant Interaction," 23–34 in *Of Speech and Time: Temporal Speech Patterns in Interpersonal Contexts*. Edited by A. W. Siegman and S. Feldstein. Mahwah, NJ: Erlbaum, 1979.
Betz, Hans Dieter. *The Sermon on the Mount: A Commentary on the Sermon on the Mount, including the Sermon on the Plain (Matthew 5:3–7:27 and Luke 6:20–49)*. Edited by Adela Y. Collins. Hermeneia. Minneapolis, MN: Fortress, 1995.
Bowlby, John. *Clinical Applications of Attachment Theory*. London: Routledge, 1988.
Calder, Andrew J., Andrew D. Lawrence, Jill Keane, Sophie K. Scott, Adrian M. Owen, Ingrid Christoffels, and Andrew W. Young. "Reading the Mind from Eye Gaze," *Neuropsychologia* 40 (2002): 1129–38. https://doi.org/10.1016/S0028-3932(02)00008-8
Chernoff, John. "'Hearing' in West African Idioms," *The World of Music* 39 (1997): 19–25.
Crossan, John Dominic, and Jonathan Reed. *In Search of Paul: How Jesus's Apostle Opposed Rome's Empire with God's Kingdom*. New York: HarperCollins, 2004.
Dant, Tim. "In Two Minds: Theory of Mind, Intersubjectivity, and Autism," *Theory & Psychology* 25 (2015): 45–62. https://doi.org/10.1177/0959354314556526
Deignan, Alice, and Lynne Cameron. "A Re-Examination of UNDERSTANDING IS SEEING," *Cognitive Semiotics* 5 (2014): 220–43.
Di Paolo, Ezequiel, and Evan Thompson. "The Enactive Approach," 69–71 in *The Routledge Handbook of Embodied Cognition*. Edited by Lawrence Shapiro. London: Routledge, 2014.
Dionigi, Alberta. "Anthropology of the Mediterranean: Between Crisis and Renewal," *History and Anthropology* 17 (2006): 109–33. https://doi.org/10.1080/02757200600633272
Elliott, John H. *Beware the Evil Eye*. Vol. 2: *The Evil Eye in the Bible and the Ancient World*. Eugene, OR: Cascade Books, 2016. https://doi.org/10.2307/j.ctv1131hck
Farroni, Teresa, Gergely Csibra, Francesca Simion, and Mark H. Johnson. "Eye Contact Detection in Humans from Birth," *Proceedings of the National Academy of Sciences of the United States of America* 99 (2002): 9602–5. https://doi.org/10.1073/pnas.152159999
Foster, George M. "Peasant Society and the Image of Limited Good," *American Anthropologist* 67 (1965): 293–315. https://doi.org/10.1525/aa.1965.67.2.02a00010
Frye, Northrop. "Conclusion to a Literary History of Canada," 215–53 in *The Bush Garden: Essays on the Canadian Imagination*. Toronto: Anansi, 1975.
Gross, Charles G. "The Fire that Comes from the Eye," *The Neuroscientist* 5 (1999): 58–64. https://doi.org/10.1177/107385849900500108
Harrington, Daniel J. *The Gospel of Matthew*. Sacra Pagina. Collegeville, MN: Michael Glazier, 2007.
von Hasselt, Vincent B. "Social Adaptation in the Blind," *Clinical Psychology Review* 3 (1983): 87–102. https://doi.org/10.1016/0272-7358(83)90007-7

Horden, Peregrine, and Nicholas Purcell. *The Corrupting Sea: A Study of Mediterranean History*. Oxford: Basil Blackwell, 2000.
Langton, Stephen R. H., Roger J. Watt, and Vicki Bruce. "Do the Eyes Have it? Cues to the Direction of Social Attention," *Trends in Cognitive Sciences* 4 (2000): 50–9. https://doi.org/10.1016/S1364-6613(99)01436-9
Lee, K., M. Eskritt, L. A. Symons, and D. Muir. "Children's Use of Triadic Eye Gaze Information for 'Mind Reading,'" *Developmental Psychology* 34 (1998): 525–39. https://doi.org/10.1037/0012-1649.34.3.525
Malina, Bruce J. *The New Testament World: Insights from Cultural Anthropology*. 3rd rev. and exp. edn. Louisville, KY: Westminster John Knox Press, 2001.
McCauley, Robert N. *Why Religion Is Natural and Science Is Not*. Oxford: Oxford University Press, 2011.
Moss, Candida R. "Blurred Vision and Ethical Confusion: The Rhetorical Function of Matthew 6:22–23," *Catholic Biblical Quarterly* 73 (2011): 757–76.
Muir, Darwin, and Sylvia Hains. "Young Infants' Perception of Adult Intentionality: Adult Contingency and Eye Direction," 155–88 in *Early Social Cognition*. Edited by P. Rochat. Mahwah, NJ: Erlbaum, 1999.
Racine, Timothy P. "Getting beyond Rich and Lean Views of Joint Attention," 21–42 in *Joint Attention: New Developments in Psychology, Philosophy of Mind, and Social Neuroscience*. Edited by Axel Seemann. Cambridge, MA: MIT Press, 2011.
Reddy, Vasudevi. "On Being the Object of Attention: Implications for Self-Other Consciousness," *Trends in Cognitive Sciences* 7 (2003): 397–402. https://doi.org/10.1016/S1364-6613(03)00191-8
Slingerland, Edward. *What Science Offers the Humanities: Integrating Body and Culture*. New York: Cambridge, 2008. https://doi.org/10.1017/CBO9780511841163
Thompson, Evan. *Colour Vision: A Study in Cognitive Science and the Philosophy of Perception*. London: Routledge, 1995.
Trevarthen, Colwyn. "Communication and Cooperation in Early Infancy: A Description of Primary Intersubjectivity," 321–47 in *Before Speech*. Edited by M. Bullowa. Cambridge: Cambridge University Press, 1979.
Ulmer, Rivka. *The Evil Eye in the Bible and in Rabbinic Literature*. Hoboken, NJ: KTAV, 1994.
Westermarck, Edvard. *Ritual and Belief in Morocco*. Vol. 1. Routledge Revivals, 1926.

Chapter Three

Perception of Risk in the Sermon on the Mount

Rikard Roitto

Introduction

I have always been moved by the way the Sermon on the Mount demands that its audience adheres to a risky ethics for the sake of a greater good. The Matthean Jesus (henceforth just "Jesus") commands the disciples to rejoice in the face of persecution (5.11-12), turn the other cheek (5.39), forgive and give without limitation (5.40-42; 6.12, 14-15), stop worrying about food and clothes (6.24-26), and so on. In short, Jesus demands nothing less than from the disciples than that they take "the narrow gate" and "the hard road" (7.13-14) which is to "do the will of my Father in heaven" (7.21), no matter how dangerous it might be. Different kinds of risks are pitted against each other in the Sermon. Material and economic risks (e.g., 5.40-42), risks of bodily harm (e.g., 5.27-30; 6.25-34), and risks of social stigmatization (e.g., 5.10-12, 39), are weighed against risking one's good standing with God and the risk of rejection in the final judgment (e.g., 6.1-8, 17-20; 7.15-28). Jesus wants the audience to understand that it is the road of economic, bodily, and social risk that manifests the kingdom of heaven.

Throughout history, some who read the Sermon on the Mount have become worried and provoked by its ethos, but others have become inspired to try to do what the Sermon demands.[1] This brings us to the two problems of this essay: First, how does the Sermon of the Mount convince its audience that these risks are worth taking? Second, to the extent that the Sermon actually convinced its audience in the Matthean community, what group dynamic effects might it have had? In order to reflect on these problems, I use research on perception of risk heuristically to explore the rhetoric of the Sermon.[2] Both cross-culturally recurring human behavior and culture-specific patterns of the first-century Mediterranean will be considered.

---

1. For histories of interpretation, see note 2 in the introduction.
2. On the heuristic use of behavioral sciences in biblical studies, see note 3 in the introduction.

The Social Situation of the Matthean Community

In order to discuss the communication strategy of the Sermon, we must first sketch a picture of the social situation of the Matthean community, which is the most immediate audience of the Sermon. Even if Richard Bauckham is right that the Gospel of Matthew was written for an audience beyond the Matthean community,[3] it does not follow that the social situation of the Matthean community has not formed the interests and worries of the Matthean redaction.[4]

There is much uncertainty about several aspects of the Matthean community, and I will not attempt to rehearse the scholarly debate here. Most scholars, however, would agree that the Gospel reflects a Jewish-Christian community in tension with Pharisaic/Proto-Rabbinic groups.[5] This situation is also apparent in the Sermon on the Mount, where Jesus' teachings are presented as a superior interpretation of the Torah (5.17-48).

More controversial is the social location of the community. Although Eduard Schweizer once argued that the Matthean community was a radical community of itinerant charismatics,[6] recent research points towards a non-itinerant community in a city, with several of its members living firmly above subsistence level. As Robert McIver points out, there is no special M material (traditions occurring only in Matthew) about itinerancy.[7] Aaron Gale demonstrates that Matthew contains more references to money and cities than the other Synoptic Gospels, and that the redactional activity of Matthew points towards a degree of Rabbinic education, all of which makes it difficult to claim that the Matthean community as a whole was very poor or itinerant.[8] It must be said about Gale's reconstruction, though, that although he demonstrates the education of the Matthean authors, he does not fully appreciate that the intended Gospel audience might be more heterogenous than the authorial group is. The variety of followers of Jesus in the Gospel seems to reflect a community consisting of both the retainer class and the non-elite, as Evert-Jan Vledder and Andries van Aarde have

---

3. Richard Bauckham, "For Whom Were the Gospels Written?," in *The Gospels for All Christians: Rethinking the Gospel Audiences,* ed. Richard Bauckham (Grand Rapids, MI: Eerdmans, 1998), 9–48.
4. Robert K. McIver, *Mainstream or Marginal?: The Matthean Community in Early Christianity* (Frankfurt: Peter Lang, 2012), 41–50.
5. McIver, *Mainstream or Marginal?*, 19–23.
6. Eduard Schweizer, *Matthäus und seine Gemeinde* (Stuttgart: KWB, 1974).
7. McIver, *Mainstream or Marginal*, 69.
8. Aaron M. Gale, *Redefining Ancient Borders: The Jewish Scribal Framework of Matthew's Gospel* (New York: T&T Clark, 2005), 64–161.

argued.[9] Even if the authors were well educated and fairly wealthy, we need to assume a certain amount of social stratification within the Matthean community. Nevertheless, if evidence points toward a non-itinerant and at least partially wealthy community, what do we make of all the exhortations to accept bodily and economic risks?

Most of the radical exhortations to take risky action in the Sermon on the Mount is Q-material:[10] rejoicing in persecution (Luke 6.22-23/Matt. 5.11-12), relentless giving and turning the other cheek (Luke 6.27-36/ Matt. 5.9-42, 44-48), forgiveness of debt (Luke 11.4/Matt. 6.12, 14-15), and exhortations not to worry about food and clothes (Luke 12.22-31/Matt. 6.25-33). Several researchers, most famously Gerd Theissen, have suggested that the tradents of the sayings in Q were itinerant preachers who travelled between the villages of Galilee, very much like Jesus did, and therefore were exposed to dangers such as violent assaults and starvation.[11] This assumption has been questioned, however. Risto Uro, for example, has suggested that although many of the sayings in Q seem to reflect a community of itinerants, the "final" form of Q (the form that can be reconstructed from Matthew and Luke) betrays a situation where the transmission of Q is in the hands of resident community members. Q 10.2 (Luke 10.2/Matt. 9.38), for instance, is formulated from the perspective of those who send out the missionaries.[12] Richard Horsley and William Arnal go even further and claim that in its current form, all references to itinerancy in Q function metaphorically to express the vulnerability of the people living in local communities. For Horsley, Q reflects a situation of poverty and struggle to survive.[13] Arnal reconstructs a situation where local village scribes transmit

---

9. Evert-Jan Vledder and Andries van Aarde, "The Social Stratification of the Matthean Community," *Neotestamentica* 28 (1994), 511–22.

10. Q is a hypothetical text source, which many scholars assume Matthew and Luke had access to. According to the two-source hypothesis, Matthew and Luke were written independently of each other, but they both had access to Mark and several sources that are unknown to us. Among the unknown sources, one of them must have been common to Matthew and Luke, since several almost identical sayings of Jesus appear in both Matthew and Luke even though the saying is not present in Mark. This hypothetical common source is called Q (from German "Quelle").

11. E.g., Gerd Theissen, "Wanderradikalismus Literatursoziologische Aspekte der Überlieferung von Worten Jesu im Urchristentum," *Zeitschrift für Theologie und Kirche* 70 (1973): 245–71.

12. Risto Uro, *Sheep among the Wolves: A Study on the Mission Instructions of Q* (Annales Academiae Scientiarum Fennicae: Dissertationes Humanum Litterarum, 47; Helsinki: Suomalainen Tiedeakatemia, 1987), 114, 204.

13. Richard A. Horsley, *Sociology and the Jesus Movement* (New York: Crossroad, 1989).

Q in a situation of social marginalization, when the central administrations of Tiberias and Sepphoris robbed the local scribes of their professions.[14]

While scholarship on the social location of Q cannot be said to have reached a consensus, I think it has been demonstrated that the community composing the final version of the text was no longer itinerant and poor, even if they had been at some stage in their history. Rather, the most important risk for this community was social. This gives us reason think that discourse about taking bodily and economic risks can function metaphorically to encourage people to take social risks. This insight is also relevant for our understanding of how the sayings about bodily risk might have functioned in the Matthean community. According to the reconstruction above of the social situation of the Matthean community, the community was not that poor and did not have to endure literal bodily and economic danger on a daily basis. Rather, their most acutely experienced danger was the danger of social marginalization. A salient example from the Sermon on the Mount of a metaphorical understanding of Q-material in the Matthean community is the makarisms, where "poor" (Luke 6.20) is interpreted as "poor in Spirit" (Matt. 5.3) and "hungry" (Luke 6.21) interpreted as "hungry for righteousness" (Matt. 5.6).

A closer inspection of the risks of the Sermon on the Mount shows that they are quite easily interpreted as more social than material—a matter of enduring marginalization and shame. Persecution in the Sermon does not involve death and severe beating but insults and false slander (5.11). Being slapped without defending oneself (5.39) is more a matter of enduring shaming humiliation than of getting hurt.[15] For a person who is not on the edge of starvation, accepting that other people take advantage of you (5.40-42) is more a matter of enduring denigration and a reputation of being a fool than a matter of risking actual malnourishment.[16] The vivid illustrations of risky real-life situations in 5.40-42 function rhetorically as "verbal icons,"[17] that is, illustrations which evoked reflection on what the general principles of not resisting evil (v. 39) and loving ones enemies (v. 44) might mean. The exhortation not to worry about food and clothes in 6.25-34 is headed by the general principle that one cannot serve two masters (6.24), which makes

---

14. William E. Arnal, *Jesus and the Village Scribes: Galilean Conflicts and the Setting of Q* (Minneapolis, MN: Fortress Press, 2001).

15. Jerome Neyrey, *Honor and Shame in the Gospel of Matthew* (Louisville, KY: Westminster John Knox, 1998), 204–5.

16. Neyrey, *Honor and Shame*, 205–8.

17. Term suggested by Charles H. Talbert, *Reading the Sermon on the Mount: Character Formation and Decision Making in Matthew 5–7* (Columbia, SC: University of South Carolina Press, 2004), 91, 100.

the passage a matter of social loyalty expressed through the willingness to prioritize the kingdom of heaven over material welfare. We do not need to imagine that Matthean community members risked actual starvation for the exhortations to trust God's material care to be meaningful, only that they might have been in a social situation where their loyalty to the kingdom resulted in lost business opportunities, since they were sometimes viewed with suspicion by potential business partners.

How the Sermon on the Mount Influences Perception of Risk

Now that we have sketched the social situation of the Matthean community, we are ready to engage with research on risk-perception to understand the rhetoric of risk in the Sermon on the Mount.

Emotion and Risk

In economic risk models, risk can be mathematically described as the probability of loss multiplied by the magnitude of loss.[18] However, when we decide how risky something is in everyday life it is usually impossible for us to calculate the magnitude and probability of harm mathematically. We usually do not have the time and energy to consider all factors, and even when we try, we often end up with an unmanageable pile of variables to take into consideration, so complex and unquantifiable that we simply cannot calculate the risk correctly.

Rather, as Melissa Finucane and others have shown in their research on risk perception, in real life situations we usually make quite intuitive estimates of risk based on emotional associations with the situation.[19] If the positive emotions win, we find the risk acceptable; if the negative emotions take the upper hand, we experience danger. This heuristic strategy is fast, does not take much cognitive effort, and often works quite well. However, this also means that we tend to underestimate the risk of things we like and overestimate the risk of things we do not like. If you enjoy parkour or freeride skiing you are likely to underestimate the risk of injury involved in

---

18. For an introduction to mathematical calculations of risk and reward in economics, see Jakša Cvitanić and Fernando Zapatero, *Introduction to the Economics and Mathematics of Financial Markets* (Cambridge, MA: MIT Press, 2004), ch. 5.

19. Melissa L. Finucane, et al.,"The Affect Heuristic in Judgment of Risks and Benefits," *Journal of Behavioral Decision Making* 13 (2000): 1–17; Melissa L. Finucane, "The Role of Feelings in Perceived Risk," in *Handbook of Risk Theory: Epistemology, Decision Theory, Ethics, and Social Implications of Risk*, ed. Sabine Roeser, et al. (Dordrecht: Springer Netherlands, 2012), 677–91.

the activity. Fully edible food that looks disgusting to you will sound your inner risk alarm, even if you know that it is actually healthy.

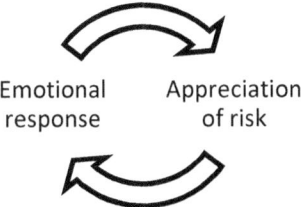

Emotional response   Appreciation of risk

Dread. One of the most well established results in research on how emotions affect our perception of risk is that when we humans are overwhelmed with "dread," that is, a strongly emotional experience that something is dangerous, rational reasoning about probabilities becomes blocked, and we estimate the risk as very high.[20] For instance, it does not help to inform someone who dreads airplanes that flying is actually safer than driving.

This insight is interesting for our understanding of the rhetoric of the Sermon on the Mount. The Sermon consistently avoids spelling out the possible horrifying consequences for someone who is persecuted (5.10-12), does not defend him-/herself against evildoers (5.39), and gives until s/he is bankrupt (5.42). Most readers would probably infer these potential dangers spontaneously anyway, but the Sermon avoids imagery which might evoke more dread than is necessary. The fearful consequences of not practicing the ethics of the Sermon, on the other hand, are elaborated with dread-invoking imagery. Such people will not be let into the kingdom of heaven (5.20) but harshly rejected (7.21-23), they will be thrown into prison (5.25-26), into Gehenna (5.29-30) and into the fire (7.29); and their "fall will be great" just like a badly built house in a storm (7.27).

In short, the Sermon on the Mount avoids evoking dread for behavior that it wants to promote, and instead impresses the reader with dreadful imagery for what will happen to those who behave differently. This rhetorical strategy can lessen the listener's emotional experience that pursuing the ethics of the Sermon is dangerous and instead amplify the perceived risk of continuing with a more conventional lifestyle.

---

20. Paul Slovic and Elke U. Weber, "Perception of Risk Posed by Extreme Events," (Paper prepared for discussion at the conference "Risk Management Strategies in an Uncertain World," Palisades, New York, 12–13 April, 2002; https://www.ldeo.columbia.edu/chrr/documents/meetings/roundtable/white_papers/slovic_wp.pdf).

Benefit and Risk

Finucane, et al., show that if we believe that something is rewarding, we underestimate the risk involved, since the promise of benefit evokes positive emotions.[21] This goes in the other direction, too. If we are convinced that something is dangerous, we will underestimate the potential reward. In one experiment, Finucane, et al., asked participants in an experiment to estimate the benefit of various items (smoking, pesticides, surfing, eating beef, etc.) under time pressure. The participants showed a strong tendency to judge items as either safe and beneficial or as dangerous and unbeneficial. That is, the judgment of risk and benefit tended to be either uniformly negative or uniformly positive. Objectively, certain actions may be both dangerous and rewarding simultaneously, but we tend to appreciate situations as either safe and rewarding or unsafe and unrewarding due to our emotional appraisal of the situation. We prefer a uniform emotional appraisal of situations so that we can decide how to act. Finucane, et al., calls this tendency of affective consistency "the halo effect."[22]

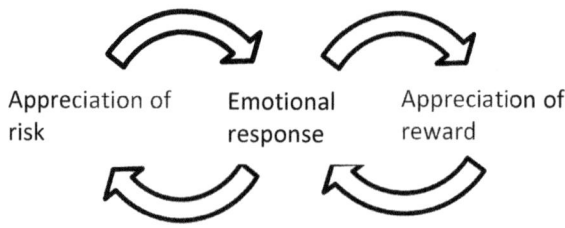

	Risk is experienced as low ⇔ positive emotions	Risk is experienced as high ⇔ negative emotions
Reward is experienced as high ⇔ positive emotions	Uniformly positive emotions → Do it!	Mixed emotions → Rewarding but risky, what to do?
Reward is experienced as low ⇔ negative emotions	Mixed emotions → Safe but pointless, why do it?	Uniformly negative emotions → Do not do it!

These insights are valuable for our understanding of how the Sermon alters the perception of risk. Already at the beginning of the Sermon, the last two of the beatitudes inform the listener that those who are persecuted for the sake of "righteousness" (5.10) and "me [i.e., Jesus]" (5.11) are to be congratulated (*makarioi*) since the "reward/wage (*misthos*) is great" (5.12). The promise of great reward is reinforced later on by the negative contrasting

---

21. Finucane, et al., "Affect Heuristics."
22. Finucane, et al., "Affect Heuristics," 13.

claim that ordinary ethical and ritual conduct does not merit any special "reward" (5.46; 6.1, 2, 5, 6). This theme is then reinforced towards the conclusion of the Sermon, where we are told that "the narrow gate and the hard road" lead to life (7.14), and that only a person who acts (*ho poiōn*, 7.21) according to the radical ethics of Jesus will enter the kingdom of heaven, but others will not. The above-mentioned promises of reward are of extra-worldly nature, but basic this-worldly benefits are promised, too, like food, clothes, and protection from danger (6.24-34; 7.7-11).

Effectively, this kind of rhetoric can affect the audience to underestimate the dangers of the ethics in the Sermon. According to Finucane's studies, if you give someone information about reward, the perception of risk changes. Likewise, if you give information about risk, the perception of reward changes. The reason for this is that the emotional response to information about reward spills over to the perception of risk, and the other way around.

Information: The reward of following the ethics of the Sermon is great → Positive emotional appraisal → Lowered perception of risk → Increased willingness to act according to the ethics of the Sermon.

Information: The reward of ordinary ethical behavior is limited. It is even dangerous for you on judgment day. → Negative emotional appraisal → Increased perception of risk → Decreased willingness to act according to ordinary ethics.

That is, if the Sermon convinces, the positive emotional appraisal of the reward effectively repels the negative emotions needed to experience the ethics of the Sermon as dangerous. (Of course, a listener who is not convinced by the Sermon may downplay the reward and instead focus on the negative emotions evoked by what s/he experiences as a reckless ethics.)

We might protest that promises of this-worldly benefits in the Sermon are very basic, just enough food and clothing (6.24-34), but nothing more. On the contrary, dreams of becoming rich and honored in society are explicitly rejected as illegitimate goals (6.1-8, 16-24). However, I think that we, as rich, individualistic Westerners, might interpret what is dangerous and what is beneficial differently from the Matthean community. We need to ask what a community of the Matthean kind typically fears and desires.

One of the most well-known theories of how we perceive risk is the so called "cultural theory of risk," suggested by Mary Douglas and Aaron Wildavsky.[23] Their claim is that different kinds of societies find different things

---

23. Mary Douglas and Aaron Wildavsky, *Risk and Culture: An Essay on the Selection of Technological and Environmental Dangers* (Berkeley, CA: University of California Press, 1982). Cf. Aaron Wildavsky and Karl Dake, "Theories of Risk Perception: Who Fears What and Why?," *Daedalus* 119 (1990): 41–60. Lennart Sjöberg criticizes

dangerous. They divide societies into four groups, depending on two variables, which they call "group" and "grid." The variable *group* measures how strongly bonded people feel to each other and the variable *grid* measures how strictly regulated the roles in society are.

Individualistic societies, like many modern Western societies, are low on both group and grid. According the analysis of Douglas and Wildavsky, such societies fear anything that threatens the individual's integrity and freedom. The relevance of this insight for our discussion is that an individualist reader, for instance a typical Western scholar, is especially provoked by how the ethics of the Sermon threatens the safety of the individual. We do, therefore, perhaps intuitively overestimate the provocation of, for instance, the last two antitheses (5.38-48) to the Matthean audience.

Hierarchical societies, like large portions of the ancient Mediterranean societies, are high on both group and grid. What such societies fear is disruption of social order. We can therefore suggest that a person in power in antiquity would not have been as provoked by the riskiness of the ethics of the Sermon as by how the Sermon breaks with conventional social roles and patterns of interaction and threatens social order.

The Matthean community, however, is best characterized as an "egalitarian" community, as Leland White suggests (e.g., Matt. 20.25-28; 23.1-12).[24] By "egalitarian" I do not mean a group where everyone is absolutely equal and where there no power structures whatsoever. Rather, it means a group which is critical towards power hierarchies in its surrounding society and has a relatively flat organization. In biblical scholarship, John Elliott has rightly criticized scholars for using the term "egalitarian" in a way that imposes modern ideals of equality on Jesus.[25] Mary Douglas appreciates that recent research on her theory of group and grid has refuted the idea that a completely egalitarian group totally void of power structures could even function.[26] Rather, Douglas argues, an egalitarian group is primarily critical towards unfair power structures in their surrounding society, and skeptical but not entirely hostile to all power structures within the community. Perhaps

---

their theory for its fairly low predictive value on the individual level, but recognizes its value as a tool in qualitative research to understand communities. Lennart Sjöberg, "Risk Perception and Societal Response," in *Handbook of Risk Theory: Epistemology, Decision Theory, Ethics, and Social Implications of Risk*, ed. Sabine Roeser, et al. (Dordrecht: Springer Netherlands, 2012): 661–75.

24. Leland J. White, "Grid and Group in Matthew's Community: The Righteousness/Honor Code in the Sermon on the Mount," *Semeia* 35 (1986), 61–90.

25. John H. Elliott, "Jesus Was Not an Egalitarian: A Critique of an Anachronistic and Idealist Theory," *Biblical Theology Bulletin* 32 (2002): 75–91.

26. Mary Douglas, "A History of Grid and Group Cultural Theory," http://projects.chass.utoronto.ca/semiotics/cyber/douglas1.pdf (2006).

a more fitting term would be "communitarian," but we stick to the terminology of Douglas and Wildavsky's theory.

Such a community is high on group but low on grid. Such groups fear increased inequality and distrust authorities, according to the analysis of Douglas and Wildavsky. This means that where an individualist might focus on the dangers of being persecuted in the last two beatitudes (5.10-12), an egalitarian group is likely to focus more on the vision in the beatitudes of a future where current injustices and shaming will cease and where happiness and honor belongs to the just. Where an individualist might focus on the bodily danger involved in the ethics of the last two antitheses (5.38-48), an egalitarian community is likely to focus more on how the ethics there have potential to question oppressive hierarchical power structures. In short, the balance between benefits and dangers was probably perceived as much more positive by the Matthean community (and other egalitarian Christian communities who have endeavored to live by the Sermon throughout history) than it would by an average individualist reader of the Sermon.

Moral Appraisal and Risk

When we read "No harm happens to the righteous, but the wicked are filled with trouble," (Prov. 12.21) it feels true, even though we (just like Job and Ecclesiastes) know it is not really the case. Why does the causal connection between morality and well-being feel so intuitively right?

An important factor in the emotional appraisal of a situation is morality. Our everyday appraisal of the moral quality of actions is intuitive and ends up in an emotional appraisal. Several researchers during the last decade have argued that all rational moral reasoning depends on post-hoc constructs to justify the immediate emotionally-based moral judgment.[27] Bryce Huebner, Susan Dwyer, and Marc Hauser, however, have argued that the evidence for this conclusion is weak, and that the emotional response usually comes after a quick, often unconscious, analysis of causal effects and intentionality.[28] The emotions then function to motivate action. No matter what comes first, however, there is a broad consensus that we tend to have positive emotions about things that we consider morally good and negative emotions about what we find morally bad.

---

27. E.g., Jonathan Haidt, "The Emotional Dog and its Rational Tail: A Social Intuitionist Approach to Moral Judgment," *Psychological Review* 108 (2001): 814–34; Jesse J. Prinz, "The Emotional Basis of Moral Judgments," *Philosophical Explorations* 9 (2006): 29–43.

28. Bryce Huebner, Susan Dwyer, and Marc Hauser, "The Role of Emotion in Moral Psychology," *Trends in Cognitive Science* 13 (2009): 1–6.

Studies which directly assess the correlation between risk perception and moral appraisal are rare, but Mariette Berndsen and Joop van der Pligt have conducted a study on the perceived risk of eating meat, where both emotional and moral appraisal correlate with perceived risk.[29] Since both moral appraisal and risk perception correlate with emotional states, it is reasonable to assume a correlation between moral appraisal and risk similar to the above mentioned correlation between perceived benefit and risk. Either the positive emotions associated with high morality dominate, so that the negative emotions associated with risk are suppressed, or the negative emotions associated with risk dominate, so that the positive emotions associated with morality are suppressed.

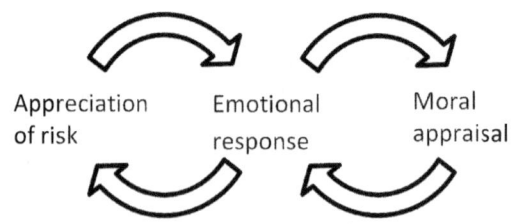

Appreciation of risk — Emotional response — Moral appraisal

	Risk is experienced as low ⇔ positive emotions	Risk is experienced as high ⇔ negative emotions
The action is appraised as moral ⇔ positive emotions	Uniformly positive emotions → Do it!	Mixed emotions → What to do?
The action is perceived as immoral ⇔ negative emotions	Mixed emotions → What to do?	Uniformly negative emotions → Do not do it!

This insight is quite important for our understanding of why the Sermon on the Mount sometimes creates a willingness to accept risk, but sometimes indignation over how unreasonable the ethics are. When the audience is challenged to turn the other cheek, give without distinction, and so on, in the two last antitheses in 5.38-48, these ethics are presented as superior ethics, just like the four preceding antitheses. Here, the emotional appraisal can take one of two routes. Either the positive emotional appraisal of the superior morality dominates, or the negative emotional appraisal of the danger dominates. Jerome Neyrey has shown that many people in antiquity would in fact not have perceived the ethics of the last two antitheses as superior morality, but rather as shameful folly.[30] Nevertheless, the Sermon

---

29. Mariette Berndsen and Joop van der Pligt, "Risks of Meat: The Relative Impact of Cognitive, Affective and Moral Concerns," *Appetite* 44 (2005): 195–205.

30. Neyrey, *Honor and Shame*, 190–211.

itself presents its dangerous ethics as superior morality, and many listeners probably bought into the argument of the Sermon.[31] If so, they would have found the danger involved in this ethics acceptable, since the fear evoked by danger was suppressed by positive emotions of moral superiority.

Prototypicality and Risk

In extreme sports, the heroes are those who fearlessly throw themselves into dangerous situations and handle the danger competently. They are the ones who have the highest status within their subculture. In terms of social psychology, bravery is considered a prototypical character trait for members of some groups, and those who display these characteristics will be seen as embodying the identity of the group. Prototypical group members are therefore usually the most highly appreciated group members and have more influence over the group than other group members.[32] Deviant members, on the other hand, are marginalized in different ways, and do not have much influence over the other group members.[33] That is, being prototypical elicits all kinds of positive emotions and social benefits, while being deviant elicits all kinds of negative emotions and social detriments.[34]

The ethics of the Sermon on the Mount is not just a general ethics, even if its rhetoric is decidedly universal, but an ethics for the kingdom of heaven. That is, it was considered prototypical for Matthean community members to act according to its ethics, and those who had the courage to do so would feel better about themselves and be more admired than other community members. Philip Esler has shown that the beatitudes at the beginning of

---

31. Cf. my analysis in Rikard Roitto, "Forgiveness and Social Identity in Matthew: Obliging Forgiveness," in *Social Memory and Social Identity in the Study of Early Judaism and Early Christianity*, ed. Jutta Jokiranta, Samuel Byrskog, and Raimo Hakola (Vandenhoeck & Ruprecht, 2016), 187–210.

32. John C. Turner, "Explaining the Nature of Power: A Three-Process Theory," *European Journal of Social Psychology* 35 (2005): 1–22. The concept of prototypicality in social identities was first presented in John C. Turner, et al., *Rediscovering the Social Group: A Self-Categorization Theory* (Oxford: Blackwell, 1987).

33. Jose M. Marques, "The Black-Sheep Effect: Out-Group Homogeneity in Social Comparison Settings," in *Social Identity Theory: Constructive and Critical Advances*, ed. D. Abrams and M. A. Hogg (London: Harvester Wheatsheaf, 1990), 131–51; Jose M. Marques, et al., "Social Categorization, Social Identification, and Rejection of Deviant Group Members," in *Blackwell Handbook of Social Psychology: Group Processes*, ed. Michael A. Hogg and Scott Tindale (Malden, MA: Blackwell, 2001), 400–24.

34. For a more complete review of the relevance of social identity theory for New Testament scholarship, see Rikard Roitto, *Behaving as a Christ-Believer: A Cognitive Perspective on Identity and Behavior Norms in Ephesians* (Grand Rapids, MI: Eisenbrauns, 2011).

the Sermon are neither just general ethical maxims, nor just words of consolation, but prototypical attitudes for the Matthean community.[35] Both the first and the last beatitude state that "theirs is the kingdom of heaven" (5.3, 10). Esler's interpretation resolves the long-held debate about whether the makarisms are exhortations or consolations since as descriptions of a prototypical member of the kingdom of heaven, they function as both an ideal to strive for and an identity narrative of hope. The last beatitude in particular is important for our discussion because it claims that the kingdom belongs to the persecuted. In the last two antitheses, where Jesus demands risky behavior, he does not promise rewards, but rather claims that "you will be your heavenly Father's sons, for he makes his sun rise on the evil and on the good, and sends rain on the righteous and on the unrighteous" (5.45). Such a person is "perfect, as your heavenly Father is perfect" (5.48). That is, whoever acts according to the risky ethics of the Sermon is a prototypical group member, a child of God.

The positive psychological and social effects of being a prototypical member thus had the capacity to overcome the negative emotions associated with danger, just like in any group where bravery is considered prototypical. We will get back to the group-dynamic effects of this conclusion below, but here we concentrate on the positive emotion of feeling honorable, which comes from feeling prototypical. These positive emotions can reduce the perceived risk and thus inspire moral action.

Ordinary ethics, on the other hand, are not just portrayed as inferior ethics in the Sermon, but as the ethics of various contrasting outgroups. Caring only for your next of kin and worrying about material safety is typical of the Gentiles (5.46-47; 6.31-32). This contrasting rhetoric creates a meta-contrast between the ingroup and the outgroup.[36] Ordinary ethics thus amount to being like the morally inferior outgroup, which is something you want to avoid when you identify strongly with a group. Ordinary ethics are thus loaded with negative emotional associations in the Sermon, which in

---

35. Philip F. Esler, "Group Norms and Prototypes in Matthew 5.3–12: A Social Identity Interpretation of the Matthean Beatitudes," in *T&T Clark Handbook to Social Identity in the New Testament*, ed. J. Brian Tucker and Coleman A. Baker (London: T&T Clark, 2013), 147–71.

36. The "meta-contrast principle" is a well-tested hypothesis suggesting that groups tend to maximize the experience that their group is meaningful by defining their identity in a way that maximizes the perceived contrast with relevant outgroups. See, e.g., Penelope J. Oakes, "The Categorization Process: Cognition of the Group in the Social Psychology of Stereotyping," in *Social Identity Theory: Constructive and Critical Advances*, ed. Dominic Abrams, and Michael A. Hogg (London: Harvester Wheatsheaf, 1990), 28–47; S. Alexander Haslam, et al., "The Group as a Basis for Emergent Stereotype Consensus," *European Review of Social Psychology* 8 (1998): 203–39.

turn make the Sermon's statements about how risky it is in an eschatological perspective to act like that (5.20; 7.21-27) believable.

Trust in the Messenger and Risk

Roger Kasperson and others have developed the insight that people's perception of risk is modified by how risk is communicated in the community.[37] One of their key insights is that people only believe the message that something is safe if they trust the messenger. The messenger can be either a person or an institution. For instance, whether people feel safe about nuclear power or genetically modified crops is partly a matter of whether experts and authorities are experienced as trustworthy in their judgment that the technology is safe.

This is a key factor when someone who listens to the Sermon on the Mount is to decide whether the risks of the lifestyle promoted by the Sermon are acceptable. The Sermon promises that those who take the risk will be protected by God. "Do not worry" is the theme of a long section in the Sermon (6.24-34), which promises that God, like a good "father", will intervene on behalf of his "children" and give them food and clothes. But why should the audience trust this assurance?

Within the narrative world of the Gospel, Jesus is trustworthy because he demonstrates with his own behavior that one can successfully live like this, and that God is indeed on the side of those who do. As Charles Talbert points out, a trustworthy speaker was supposed to live what he taught according to ancient ideals, and this is exactly what Jesus does in the Gospel of Matthew.[38] Already at his birth, he is miraculously protected by God (2.1-18). At his temptation in the desert, he rejects worldly goods and honor when tested by the Devil (4.1–11). He is itinerant and has nowhere to live (8.19-22), sleeping calmly in the midst of a storm that symbolizes forces of chaos (8.23-27). Throughout the Gospel, he continues his activity fearlessly in spite of recurring hostilities from religious leaders and sends his disciples to do the same (e.g., 10.1-39). Finally, he even meets his own death voluntarily, trusting that it is God's plan to resurrect him (16.21; 17.22-23; 20.18-19). In terms of social identity theory, Jesus is a prototypical exemplar of the lifestyle he promotes, and as such experienced as trustworthy. Jesus is also

---

37. Their model is called "SARF," which means "Social Amplification of Risk Framework." Roger E. Kasperson, et al., "The Social Amplification of Risk: A Conceptual Framework," *Risk Analysis* 8 (1988): 177–87; Jeanne X. Kasperson and Roger E. Kasperson, eds., *The Social Contours of Risk.* Vol. 1: *Publics, Risk Communication and the Social Amplification of Risk* (London: Earthscan, 2005).

38. Talbert, *Reading the Sermon on the Mount*, 18–20.

described as someone who teaches with authority, which amazes his audience (7.29). If the audience of the Sermon accepted the worldview of the Gospel, they would have experienced Jesus as exceptionally trustworthy. Not only that, this audience would find the promises of God's fatherly care plausible, since Matthew is full of narrative examples of God's intervention for the sake of those who participate in the kingdom of heaven.

Many readers of Matthew might have problems accepting the worldview of the text, but when the Sermon on the Mount was read in the Matthean community, we can reasonably assume that this particular community was an audience that did not hear the Sermon with a lens of suspicion, but rather with predisposition to accept the message of the text. It was a community of people who had decided that Jesus is their Lord, and the text was the trustworthy primary witness to the activities of their trustworthy Lord. This means that when Jesus ensures that they will be all right because of God's fatherly care, they probably found the risk analysis of Jesus plausible. That is, the Matthean community, with its regular reading of its authoritative text about their authoritative founder, had created an institution which was able to communicate with trustworthiness that the risk is acceptable.

The Group Dynamic Effects of the Discourse about Risk in the Sermon on the Mount

In the first section of this chapter, I argued that it is reasonable to assume that the most acutely experienced risks in the Matthean community were social more than bodily or economic, and that they therefore interpreted the exhortations in the Sermon to endure risk as a challenge to be prepared to take social risk. Assuming that this is correct, the sermon would have (a) insulated the community from the pressure to assimilate to the more dominant Pharisaic versions of Jewish piety, and (b) encouraged continued risky interaction with society, which might have resulted in what we may call "self-stigmatizing leadership":

Insulation from social pressure to assimilate. If the Matthean community was slandered (5.11) and accused of illegitimate interpretations of the Torah by Pharisaic Jews (e.g., 5.17; 9.10-17; 12.1-15; 15.1-20; 19.3-9; 23.1-26), this must have been experienced as a serious accusation for a community that prided themselves on practicing the Torah with utmost zeal (5.17-48; 7.12-27). As David DeSilva has suggested, such communities must find strategies to insulate themselves from the social shaming of the surrounding society.[39]

---

39. David A. DeSilva, *Honor, Patronage, Kinship & Purity: Unlocking New Testament*

A devout community member must be not be dependent on approval by "the humans" (6.1), that is, non-Matthean groups of Jews such as "the scribes and the Pharisees" (5.20). For a person living in the first-century Mediterranean, the risk of social shame was as real as any bodily or economic risk.[40] When the Sermon creates an imagination where it is morally heroic, prototypical, and beneficial for your status before God (see analysis above) to take social risks in relation to the rest of society, it basically says it does not matter what other groups in your society say, since you can know that you are honorable before God as long as you remain loyal to Jesus and do his will. This positive imagination had the capacity to triumph over the experienced social danger of losing honor. Thus, this imagination might have been able to help the community to resist the impulse to assimilate to more dominant groups.

Continued risky interaction with society. More important than the resistance against assimilation, however, is that the encouragement to take social risks had the potential to stop the community from becoming an isolationist community and instead inspired it to remain a conversionist community.[41] There is no attitude of withdrawal from the rest of society in the Sermon on the Mount (or in the Gospel of Matthew as a whole). Rather, enduring persecution and slander seems instrumental to the Matthean effort to spread its conviction to other Jews. The last macarism changes the address from "happy are those who ..." in the first eight macarisms (5.3-10) to "happy are you ..." (5.11-12). The direct address to "you" then continues in the following verses: "you are the salt of the earth ... you are the light of the world ... let your light shine before others, so that they may see your good works and give glory to your Father in heaven" (5.13-16). That is, the author juxtaposes the need to endure persecution and slander with their calling to demonstrate the goodness of their convictions to outgroups. Enduring persecution and spreading the message goes hand in hand, just like in the mission speech (10.16-23).

The provocatively risky behaviors in the last two antitheses (5.38-48) most reasonably had an advertising effect, too. Jerome Neyrey has argued

---

Culture (Downers Grove, IL: Inter-Varsity, 2000a), 78–84; David A. DeSilva, *Perseverance in Gratitude: A Socio-Rhetorical Commentary on the Epistle "to the Hebrews"* (Grand Rapids, MI: Eerdmans, 2000b).

40. Cf. Bruce J. Malina, *The New Testament World: Insights from Cultural Anthropology*. 3rd revised and expanded edn. (Louisville, KY: Westminster John Knox Press, 2001), 58–67.

41. The terms "introversionist sect" and "conversionist sect" are suggested by R. Bryan Wilson, *Religious Sects: A Sociological Study* (New York: McGraw-Hill, 1970). I prefer the word "community" over "sect" here, to avoid confusion about the many different definitions of "sect" among scholars.

that many of the behaviors in this passage would have been conceived as weak and foolish—that is, shameful—by others. Neyrey ends up concluding that "This disciple, then, will be considered a weakling, a wimp, a worthless no-account who cannot defend his honor, a person of whom one takes advantage, a man to be ashamed of. This, we maintain, is the 'cross' of following Jesus: the loss of honor."[42] Although Neyrey definitely has a point, I think his analysis misses how people can become fascinated when others consciously do something out of the norm. Therefore, I would like to lean on Helmut Mödritzer's analysis of Jesus' self-stigmatizing leadership.[43] His analysis is an application of Wolfgang Lipp's study of self-stigmatizing leadership.[44]

Lipp regards deviant behavior, which he calls "borderline behavior," as essential both for the stigma and the charisma phenomena. Borderline behavior is experienced as being deviant because it pushes its carrier towards the edge or out of the group. Borderline behavior could, however, also make a group begin to doubt the validity of the practice it assumes to be normal. Consciously applied, borderline behavior could therefore create the possibility of initiating social changes and of making oneself the centre of events, or even of occupying a morally highly valued position. In this sociological context Lipp also talks about "self-stigmatization." Through the process of self-stigmatization, people could be capable of giving the situation of the establishment negative connotations and the situation of the "oppressed" positive connotations.[45]

Mödritzer applies this idea to several of the habits of the historical Jesus: 1) provoking purity taboos, and 2) making himself vulnerable by (a) having nowhere to live, (b) preaching non-self-defense, and (c) seeking his own death. The phenomenon that Mödritzer indicates applies to the ethics of the last two antitheses in the Sermon, "do not resist an evildoer" (5.39), "love your enemies" (5.42). In the light of Lipp's theory of self-stigmatizing leadership, it is likely that the behavior prescribed by Jesus could lead not only to condemnation, but also to fascination. First, being merciful and avoiding retaliation was sometimes considered morally superior, even divine, in antiquity.[46] At the time when Christianity began, mercy was considered the number

---

42. Neyrey, *Honor and Shame*, 211.
43. Helmut Mödritzer, *Stigma und Charisma im Neuen Testament und seiner Umwelt: Zur Soziologie des Urchristentums* (Freiburg: Universitäts Verlag, 1994).
44. Wolfgang Lipp, *Stigma und Charisma: Über soziales Grenzverhalten* (Berlin: Reimer, 1985).
45. Johannes Steyrer, "Charisma and the Archetypes of Leadership," *Organization Studies* 19 (1998): 807–28, 812–3.
46. Cf. Maurius Reiser, "Love of Enemies in the Context of Antiquity," *New Testament Studies* 48 (2001): 411–27.

one quality of (the) God(s), both by Jews[47] and Romans.[48] Second, we can imagine how the suffering that could follow from being taken advantage of and not protesting could grab the attention of people, who would then have problems understanding why someone would choose to suffer voluntarily. Gerd Theissen argues that the purpose of surprising non-retaliatory behavior in the Jesus-movement was to cause reflection and awareness of guilt.[49] Third, we can imagine how acts of unwarranted generosity and non-retaliation could cause intuitive emotions of admiration and affection, even in a culture preoccupied with challenge and riposte. When victims practice non-retaliation, it often creates emotions of affection and empathy in those who hear about it.[50] Jonathan Haidt, who has done the most extensive work on admiration for good deeds, shows that when people do unmotivated good deeds, such as giving to aggressors and those who cannot pay back, those who hear about it are filled with gratitude and become inspired to do the same.[51] Haidt's research suggests that this is not a Western phenomenon, but a phenomenon that is even stronger in collectivistic cultures. We should therefore assume that at least sometimes those who practiced the ethics of the last two antitheses were admired by those who saw it. Leviticus instructs that "You shall not hate in your heart anyone of your kin … You shall not take vengeance or bear a grudge against any of your people, but you shall love your neighbor as yourself" (19.17-18). The ethics of non-retaliation and love of enemy in Matthew 5.38-48 could be said to take this covenantal ethics to a shocking, self-stigmatizing, extreme, that could perhaps subvert existing social orders and cause fascination.

---

47. This is one of the main points of Ed P. Sanders, *Paul and Palestinian Judaism: A Comparison of Patterns of Religion* (Philadelphia, PA: Fortress Press, 1977).

48. Melissa Barden Dowling, *Clemency & Cruelty in the Roman World* (Michigan, MI: University of Michigan Press, 2006).

49. Gerd Theissen, *Sociology of Early Palestinian Christianity* (Philadelphia, PA: Fortress Press, 1978), 99–100, 107–8.

50. Suresh Kanekar and Maharukh B. Kolsawalla, "The Nobility of Nonviolence: Person Perception as a Function of Retaliation to Aggression," *Journal of Social Psychology* 102 (1977), 159–60; Andrew. B. Newberg, et al., "The Neuropsychological Correlates of Forgiveness," in *Forgiveness: Theory, Research and Practice*, ed. Michael E. McCullough, Kenneth I. Pargament, and Carl E. Thoresen (New York: Guilford Press, 1999), 91–110.

51. Jonathan Haidt, "Elevation and the Positive Psychology of Morality," in *Flourishing: Positive Psychology and the Life Well-Lived*, ed. C. L. M. Keyes and Jonathan Haidt (Washington DC: American Psychological Association, 2003), 275–89; Sara B. Algoe and Jonathan Haidt, "Witnessing Excellence in Action: The Other-Praising Emotions of Elevation, Admiration, and Gratitude," *Journal of Positive Psychology* 4 (2009): 105–27.

Conclusion

The Sermon on the Mount has the rhetorical power to influence a sympathetic reader to perceive the risks of its ethics as worth taking. Research on how we humans perceive risk shows that our evaluation of whether a risk is worth taking or not is dependent on whether positive or negative emotions dominate. The Sermon does not argue by detailed risk-calculations, but rather by letting positive emotions defeat negative emotions of fear. The discourse avoids provoking negative emotions about possible risky consequences and simultaneously evokes positive emotions about its ethics. One way to evoke positive emotions is to remind the listener of the rewards of doing good. Another way is to emphasize the moral superiority of the ethics. Still another way is to present the ethics as prototypical for those who belong to the kingdom of heaven. Fears are moderated by promises of divine intervention for those who are not afraid to expose themselves to danger, and Jesus is the trustworthy guarantor of this assertion.

To the extent that the Sermon was able to inspire the Matthean community, we can imagine that it helped the community to handle a situation where they were being marginalized by other Jewish groups. The risk of being socially shamed was turned upside down into a sense of moral superiority, which in turn helped them to withstand the pressure to assimilate. To the extent that they practiced the ethics of the Sermon, they avoided becoming isolated from the rest of society and instead interacted with it in ways that might have provoked fascination among their neighbors.

Biographical Note

Docent Rikard Roitto is a University Lecturer at the Stockholm School of Theology at University College Stockholm. Roitto specializes in using behavioral sciences to interpret the New Testament and other historical texts. He is one of the editors of *The Oxford Handbook of Early Christian Rituals* (Oxford University Press, 2018).

Bibliography

Arnal, William E. *Jesus and the Village Scribes: Galilean Conflicts and the Setting of Q*. Minneapolis, MN: Fortress Press, 2001.

Bauckham, Richard. "For Whom Were the Gospels Written?," 9–48 in *The Gospels for All Christians: Rethinking the Gospel Audiences*. Edited by Richard Bauckham. Grand Rapids, MI: Eerdmans, 1998.

Berndsen, Mariette, and Joop van der Pligt. "Risks of Meat: The Relative Impact of Cognitive, Affective and Moral Concerns," *Appetite* 44 (2005): 195–205. https://doi.org/10.1016/j.appet.2004.10.003

Cvitanić, Jakša, and Fernando Zapatero. *Introduction to the Economics and Mathematics of Financial Markets*. Cambridge, MA: MIT Press, 2004.
DeSilva, David A. *Honor, Patronage, Kinship & Purity: Unlocking New Testament Culture*. Downers Grove, IL: InterVarsity, 2000a.
—*Perseverance in Gratitude: A Socio-Rhetorical Commentary on the Epistle "to the Hebrews."* Grand Rapids, MI: Eerdmans, 2000b.
Douglas, Mary. "A History of Grid and Group Cultural Theory," 2006. http://projects.chass.utoronto.ca/semiotics/cyber/douglas1.pdf
Douglas, Mary, and Aaron Wildavsky. *Risk and Culture: An Essay on the Selection of Technological and Environmental Dangers*. Berkeley, CA: University of California Press, 1982. https://doi.org/10.1525/9780520907393
Dowling, Melissa Barden. *Clemency & Cruelty in the Roman World*. Michigan, MI: University of Michigan Press, 2006. https://doi.org/10.3998/mpub.145291
Elliott, John H. "Jesus Was Not an Egalitarian: A Critique of an Anachronistic and Idealist Theory," *Biblical Theology Bulletin* 32 (2002): 75–91. https://doi.org/10.1177/014610790203200206
—"Group Norms and Prototypes in Matthew 5.3-12: A Social Identity Interpretation of the Matthean Beatitudes," 147–72 in *T&T Clark Handbook to Social Identity in the New Testament*. Edited by Coleman A. Baker and J. Brian Tucker. London: Bloomsbury/T&T Clark, 2013.
Finucane, Melissa L. "The Role of Feelings in Perceived Risk," 677–91 in *Handbook of Risk Theory: Epistemology, Decision Theory, Ethics, and Social Implications of Risk*. Edited by Per Sandin, Martin Peterson, Sabine Roeser, and Rafaela Hillerbrand. Dordrecht: Springer Netherlands, 2012. https://doi.org/10.1002/(SICI)1099-0771(200001/03)13:1<1::AID-BDM333>3.0.CO;2-S
Finucane, Melissa L., Ali Alhakami, Paul Slovic, and Stephen M. Johnson. "The Affect Heuristic in Judgment of Risks and Benefits," *Journal of Behavioral Decision Making* 13 (2000): 1–17.
Gale, Aaron M. *Redefining Ancient Borders: The Jewish Scribal Framework of Matthew's Gospel*. New York: T&T Clark, 2005.
Haidt, Jonathan. "The Emotional Dog and its Rational Tail: A Social Intuitionist Approach to Moral Judgment," *Psychological Review* 108 (2001): 814–34. https://doi.org/10.1037/0033-295X.108.4.814
—"Elevation and the Positive Psychology of Morality," 275–89 in *Flourishing: Positive Psychology and the Life Well-Lived*. Edited by Jonathan Haidt and C. L. M. Keyes. Washington, DC: American Psychological Association, 2003. https://doi.org/10.1037/10594-012
Haidt, Jonathan, and Sara B. Algoe. "Witnessing Excellence in Action: The Other-Praising Emotions of Elevation, Admiration, and Gratitude," *Journal of Positive Psychology* 4 (2009): 105–27. https://doi.org/10.1080/17439760802650519
Haslam, S. Alexander, John C. Turner, Penelope J. Oakes, C. McGarty, and K. J. Reynolds. "The Group as a Basis for Emergent Stereotype Consensus," *European Review of Social Psychology* 8 (1998): 203–39. https://doi.org/10.1080/14792779643000128
Horsley, Richard A. *Sociology and the Jesus Movement*. New York: Crossroad, 1989.
Huebner, Bryce, Susan Dwyer, and Marc Hauser. "The Role of Emotion in Moral Psychology," *Trends in Cognitive Science* 13 (2009): 1–6. https://doi.org/10.1016/j.tics.2008.09.006
Kanekar, Suresh, and Maharukh B. Kolsawalla. "The Nobility of Nonviolence: Person

Perception as a Function of Retaliation to Aggression," *Journal of Social Psychology* 102 (1977): 159–60. https://doi.org/10.1080/00224545.1977.9713256

Kasperson, Jeanne X., and Roger E. Kasperson, eds. *The Social Contours of Risk*. Vol. 1: *Publics, Risk Communication and the Social Amplification of Risk*. London: Earthscan, 2005.

Kasperson, Roger E., Ortwin Renn, Paul Slovic, Halina S. Brown, Jacque Emel, Robert Goble, Jeanne X. Kasperson, and Samuel Ratick. "The Social Amplification of Risk: A Conceptual Framework," *Risk Analysis* 8 (1988): 177–87. https://doi.org/10.1111/j.1539-6924.1988.tb01168.x

Lipp, Wolfgang. *Stigma und Charisma: Über soziales Grenzverhalten*. Berlin: Reimer, 1985.

Malina, Bruce J. *The New Testament World: Insights from Cultural Anthropology*. 3rd rev. and exp. edn. Louisville, KY: Westminster John Knox Press, 2001.

Marques, Jose M. "The Black-Sheep Effect: Out-Group Homogeneity in Social Comparison Settings," 131–51 in *Social Identity Theory: Constructive and Critical Advances*. Edited by D. A. Abrams and M. A. Hogg. London: Harvester Wheatsheaf, 1990.

Marques, Jose M., Dominic Abrams, Dario Páez, and Michael A. Hogg. "Social Categorization, Social Identification, and Rejection of Deviant Group Members," 400–24 in *Blackwell Handbook of Social Psychology: Group Processes*. Edited by Michael A. Hogg and Scott Tindale. Malden, MA: Blackwell, 2001. https://doi.org/10.1002/9780470998458.ch17

McIver, Robert K. *Mainstream or Marginal? The Matthean Community in Early Christianity*. Frankfurt: Peter Lang, 2012.

Mödritzer, Helmut. *Stigma und Charisma im Neuen Testament und seiner Umwelt: Zur Soziologie des Urchristentums*. Freiburg: Universitäts Verlag, 1994. https://doi.org/10.13109/9783666539305

Newberg, Andrew B., Eugene G. d'Aquili, Stephanie K. Newberg, and Verushka deMarici. "The Neuropsychological Correlates of Forgiveness," 91–110 in *Forgiveness: Theory, Research, and Practice*. Edited by M. E. McCullough, K. I. Pargament, and Carl E. Thoresen. New York: Guilford, 2000.

Neyrey, Jerome H. *Honor and Shame in the Gospel of Matthew*. Louisville, KY: Westminster John Knox Press, 1998.

Oakes, Penelope J. "The Categorization Process: Cognition of the Group in the Social Psychology of Stereotyping," 28–47 in *Social Identity Theory: Constructive and Critical Advances*. Edited by Dominic Abrams and Michael A. Hogg. London: Harvester Wheatsheaf, 1990.

Prinz, Jesse J. "The Emotional Basis of Moral Judgments," *Philosophical Explorations* 9 (2006): 29–43. https://doi.org/10.1080/13869790500492466

Reiser, Maurius. "Love of Enemies in the Context of Antiquity," *New Testament Studies* 48 (2001): 411–27. https://doi.org/10.1017/S002868850100025X

Roitto, Rikard. *Behaving as a Christ-Believer: A Cognitive Perspective on Identity and Behavior Norms in Ephesians*. Coniectanae Biblica: New Testament Series, 46. Grand Rapids, MI: Eisenbrauns, 2011.

—"Forgiveness and Social Identity in Matthew: Obliging Forgiveness," 175–86 in *Social Memory and Social Identity in the Study of Early Judaism and Early Christianity*. Edited by Samuel Byrskog, Raimo Hakola, and Jutta Jokiranta. Novum Testamentum et Orbis Antiquus/Studien zur Umwelt des Neuen Testaments, 116. Göttingen: Vandenhoeck & Ruprecht, 2016.

Sanders, Ed P. *Paul and Palestinian Judaism: A Comparison of Patterns of Religion.* Philadelphia, PA: Fortress Press, 1977.

Schweizer, Eduard. *Matthaus und seine Gemeinde.* Stuttgart: KWB, 1974.

Sjöberg, Lennart. "Risk Perception and Societal Response," 661–75 in *Handbook of Risk Theory: Epistemology, Decision Theory, Ethics, and Social Implications of Risk.* Edited by Sabine Roeser, Rafaela Hillerbrand, Per Sandin, and Martin Peterson. Dordrecht: Springer Netherlands, 2012.

Slovic, Paul, and Elke U. Weber. "Perception of Risk Posed by Extreme Events." Paper prepared for discussion at the conference "Risk Management Strategies in an Uncertain World," Palisades, New York, 12–13 April, 2002; https://www.ldeo.columbia.edu/chrr/documents/meetings/roundtable/white_papers/slovic_wp.pdf

Steyrer, Johannes. "Charisma and the Archetypes of Leadership," *Organization Studies* 19 (1998): 807–28. https://doi.org/10.1177/017084069801900505

Talbert, Charles H. *Reading the Sermon on the Mount: Character Formation and Decision Making in Matthew 5–7.* Columbia, SC: University of South Carolina Press, 2004.

Theissen, Gerd. "Wanderradikalismus: Literatursoziologische Aspekte der Überlieferung von Worten Jesu im Urchristentum," *Zeitschrift für Theologie und Kirche* 70 (1973): 245–71.

—*Sociology of Early Palestinian Christianity.* Philadelphia, PA: Fortress Press, 1978.

Turner, John C. "Explaining the Nature of Power: A Three-Process Theory," *European Journal of Social Psychology* 35 (2005): 1–22. https://doi.org/10.1002/ejsp.244

Turner, John C., Michael A. Hogg, Penelope J. Oakes, Stephen D. Reicher, and Margaret S. Wetherell. *Rediscovering the Social Group: A Self-Categorization Theory.* Oxford: Blackwell, 1987.

Uro, Risto. *Sheep among the Wolves: A Study on the Mission Instructions of Q.* Annales Academiae Scientiarum Fennicae: Dissertationes Humanum Litterarum, 47. Helsinki: Academiae Scientiarum Fennicae, 1987.

Vledder, Evert-Jan, and Andries van Aarde. "The Social Stratification of the Matthean Community," *Neotestamentica* 28 (1994): 511–22.

White, Leland J. "Grid and Group in Matthew's Community: The Righteousness/Honor Code in the Sermon on the Mount," *Semeia* 35 (1986): 61–90.

Wildavsky, Aaron, and Karl Dake. "Theories of Risk Perception: Who Fears What and Why?" *Daedalus* 119 (1990): 41–60.

Wilson, R. Bryan. *Religious Sects: A Sociological Study.* New York: McGraw-Hill, 1970.

Chapter Four

Altruism and Prosocial Ideals in the Sermon: Between Human Nature and Divine Potential

Thomas Kazen

Introduction

In the Sermon on the Mount, the author (for sake of convenience from now on called "Matthew") collects and systematizes a number of difficult and provoking moral instructions found in the traditions he is using.[1] Much of this is presented in figurative and rhetorically exaggerated language, which has caused considerable problems through the Gospel of Matthew's reception history, although I have elsewhere argued that the figurative level was usually intuitively understood by an early audience.[2] Some of the most problematic statements for later generations to handle are those found in the so-called antitheses, which contrast Jesus' sayings with received tradition of old (Matt. 5.21-22),[3] and of these, the fifth and sixth antitheses have a particularly provocative character.

> [38] You have heard that it was said, "An eye for an eye and a tooth for a tooth." [39] But I say to you, Do not resist an evildoer. But if anyone strikes you on the right cheek, turn the other also; [40] and if anyone wants to sue you and take your coat, give your cloak as well; [41] and if anyone forces you to go one mile, go also the second mile. [42] Give to everyone who begs from you, and do not refuse anyone who wants to borrow from you.

> [43] You have heard that it was said, "You shall love your neighbor and hate your enemy." [44] But I say to you, Love your enemies and pray for those who persecute you, [45] so that you may be children of your Father in heaven; for he

---

1. Much of this material belongs to the double tradition, which for many scholars equals the Q source.
2. Thomas Kazen, "Emotional Repression and Physical Mutilation? The Cognitive and Behavioral Impact of Exaggeration in the Sermon on the Mount," Chapter 6 in this volume.
3. The formula *ēkousate hoti errethē [tois archaiois]... egō de legō hymin ...* has been understood to indicate anything from replacement of the Torah to rabbinic-style exposition. For a discussion, see for example W. D. Davies and Dale C. Allison, *A Critical and Exegetical Commentary on the Gospel according to Saint Matthew*. Vol. 1: *Matthew 1–7* (Edinburgh: T & T Clark, 1988), 505–9.

makes his sun rise on the evil and on the good, and sends rain on the righteous and on the unrighteous. [46] For if you love those who love you, what reward do you have? Do not even the tax collectors do the same? [47] And if you greet only your brothers and sisters, what more are you doing than others? Do not even the Gentiles do the same? [48] Be perfect, therefore, as your heavenly Father is perfect.[4]

These antitheses express prosocial attitudes and behaviors, verging on the extreme, some of which are seemingly impossible to comply with. Are they just unrealistic ideas? Is the altruism they presuppose, or prescribe, reasonable human behavior? Are the actions suggested in these purported words of Jesus in line with human nature? Does the altruism expressed here require the suppression of natural inclinations by the constraints of culture, education, or divine aid? Or are prosocial behaviors and altruism triggered by innate emotions, which evolved because they gave the human species an adaptive advantage?

In the following, I will analyze the fifth and sixth altruistic antitheses of the Sermon on the Mount in the light of biological and psychological research on empathy, prosocial behavior, and altruism. After an initial overview of Matthew and his sources, I will discuss the evolutionary basis for morality, search for a reasonable definition of altruism, and discuss the evolution of empathy, forgiveness, and the need for justice. Against this background I will proceed to interpret the prosocial sayings of the Sermon and ask about the extent to which they work alongside (together with) human nature and cognition (in the sense of human evolved emotions and dispositions), and about the extent to which they run counter to the biological and evolutionary processes.

Matthew and His Sources

Although he has occasionally made use of material from the double tradition in the previous antitheses, in the last two, Matthew builds on virtually the same sayings that we find in the Gospel of Luke's "Sermon on the Plain" (Luke 6.27-36),[5] but differently arranged. The way in which Matthew chooses to sort his material is interesting. In Luke, the material corresponding to Matthew's sixth antithesis actually surrounds the material found in Matthew's fifth antithesis. Although in theory one could think of an earlier source structured like Matthew, and of Luke as scattering the material of his source, this is highly unlikely based on Luke's use of sources elsewhere

---

4. Matt. 5.38-48 (NRSV).
5. The exceptions are introductions (5.38-39a, 43) and the extra mile saying (5.41); all other material is more or less paralleled in Luke.

and his style of writing.⁶ Matthew's six antitheses are evidently his literary creation,⁷ incorporating a wealth of traditions, from the double tradition as well as from Mark, plus his own unique material. Moreover, Matthew's sixth antithesis is tightly argued and it would make little sense to break it up. Hence the opposite is much more likely, that Matthew has thematized his source(s) and thus created a systematic account.⁸

It is interesting to note what Matthew achieves with this move. He separates the two issues of enemy love and non-retaliation, which in Luke (Q?) are held together. This might be a conscious manœuvre, in line with his thematic thinking.⁹ But one of the perhaps unintended results is that all of the difficult and unrealistic *actions* (non-retaliation) are placed in the fifth antithesis, while mental *attitudes and words* (enemy love and prayer for persecutors) find their place in the sixth. This has been shown to cause problems and confusion for later interpreters, since, at surface level, the mental attitudes and words of the sixth antithesis are easier to comply with than the suggested concrete behavior of the fifth. The admonitions of the sixth antithesis are thus possible to take literally, and this disturbs the inclination to understand the fifth as some sort of figurative or loose talk.¹⁰

As a result, the Sermon can easily be read as a demand for a limitless and humanly speaking impossible altruism. In our time, the figurative or hyperbolic dimension has often been lost, or at the most, grudgingly mentioned,

---

6. Luke is usually understood to follow (and redact/rewrite) one source at a time, rather than mixing material from several sources into a single section. For a discussion of Luke's use of sources, see for example François Bovon, *Luke 1: A Commentary on the Gospel of Luke 1:1–9:50* (Hermeneia; Minneapolis, MN: Fortress, 2002), 6.

7. This is the majority view. Cf. Gordon M. Zerbe, *Non-Retaliation in Early Jewish and New Testament Texts: Ethical Themes in Social Contexts* (JSPSS, 13; Sheffield: Sheffield Academic Press, 1993), 177.

8. This is how Matthew is generally seen to work (cf. Ulrich Luz, *Matthew 1–7: A Commentary* [Hermeneia; Minneapolis, MN: Fortress, 2007], 5), although his technique is, of course, more sophisticated than this, as he usually (but not always) follows the Markan order and takes Mark as his springboard, but then inserts Q materials (and special material) regardless of their original order or context, to fit his thematic constructions. For further discussion, see for example Ulrich Luz, *Studies in Matthew* (Grand Rapids, MI: Eerdmans, 2005), chs. 3 and 11 (originally in German in different publications). On the other hand, the way in which Matthew often faithfully reproduces Mark's language, together with the freedom that Luke sometimes displays, makes it possible to suggest that Matthew may at times be closer to Q in wording, too—even if not in order.

9. For a different view, see Zerbe, *Non-Retaliation*, 178–9.

10. For a detailed argument, see Kazen, "Emotional Repression," Chapter 6 in this volume.

but then warned against.[11] Through the history of interpretation, various attempts have been made to handle the altruistic demands. Maybe the Sermon's ethics are apocalyptic interim ethics? Or perhaps they are just there to convince human beings of their utter depravity and need of salvation without works.[12] The theologies reflected by such desperate attempts have little to do with Matthew's own tendencies.

As argued elsewhere in this volume, the author of the fifth and sixth antitheses probably intended a loose, figurative interpretation of their prosocial and altruistic message. Their earliest literal reception is found in the *Didache*, which incorporates some of the material into a section with concrete instructions and modifies some of these commands to make them possible to fulfil literally. Within their context in the Sermon, however, the altruistic demands should be read as loose, figurative, and highly charged challenges to practice generosity, forgiveness, non-revenge, and enemy love.[13]

The Evolutionary Basis for Morality

In our modern era, many have asked themselves whether prosocial behavior, or altruism, has any foothold in human beings, as evolved, biological organisms. Darwin understood morality as a product of evolution, which had evolved from primary emotions of pain and pleasure, to reach its peak in the golden rule. He did not see this development as the result of selfishness, but based on social instincts reinforced or modified by community opinions.[14]

In popular opinion, however, evolution is often equated with human selfishness. The background to this situation involves a long history, beginning with Thomas Huxley (morality is derived from culture and unnatural) and Herbert Spencer (survival of the fittest), continuing with Edward O. Wilson (socio-biology) and Richard Dawkins (the "selfish gene"). The latter have often been charged with the idea that human beings cannot be genuinely altruist, but are inherently selfish and thus evil. The accusation may be partly unjust, but such has been the popular reception of socio-biology and the

---

11. Harvey K. McArthur, *Understanding the Sermon on the Mount* (London: Epworth, 1960), 141. See further Kazen, "Emotional Repression" in this volume.

12. For a list of possible interpretations, see McArthur, *Understanding the Sermon*, 105–27. See also Gerd Theissen and Anette Merz, *The Historical Jesus: A Comprehensive Guide* (Minneapolis, MN: Fortress, 1998), 347–8.

13. See further Kazen, "Emotional Repression."

14. Charles Darwin, *The Descent of Man, and Selection in Relation to Sex, Part 1* (The Works of Charles Darwin, 21; New York: New York University Press, 1989), 101–31, (1877 [1st edn., 1874], 97–127).

"selfish gene" metaphor. In actual fact, selfishness is a mental state, which can only be ascribed to wilful and conscious individuals, not to biological building-blocks. Even genes must cooperate with other genes within an organism in order for it to be functional and replicate.

Dawkins suggested that since human beings have the unique capacity to "rebel against the tyranny of the selfish replicators,"[15] let us *"teach* generosity and altruism because we are born selfish."[16] The religious version of this view is just as pessimistic, although it substitutes genes for original sin and education for salvation.[17] Today, however, many researchers regard this as an unfortunate distortion of evidence. Based on evolutionary biology, developmental psychology, and neuroscience, numerous scholars are eager to repudiate such simplified views. Prosocial tendencies and altruistic behaviors are shown to be just as natural and innate as their opposites.

Although a previous understanding of morality focused on rational deliberations,[18] the last decades have seen a more nuanced understanding of how moral choices and moral behaviors are based on a complex interaction between intuition and rationality. In this process, evolved emotions, such as empathy, fear, and disgust, play an important role.[19] A number of factors

---

15. Richard Dawkins, *The Selfish Gene* (Oxford: Oxford University Press, 1989 [1976]), 201.

16. Dawkins, *Selfish Gene*, 3, italics original.

17. As in some (especially) reformed anthropologies, which regard the human nature as "totally depraved." Cf. Thomas Kazen, "Self-Preserving and Other-Oriented Concerns in the Jesus Tradition," in *Voces Clamantium in Deserto: Essays in Honor of Kari Syreeni*, ed. S.-O. Back and M. Kankaanniemi (Studier i exegetik och judaistik utgivna av Teologiska fakulteten vid Åbo Akademi, 11; Åbo: Åbo Akademi University, Faculty of Theology, 2012), 124–48, 126.

18. As in Lawrence Kohlberg's type of developmental psychology; cf. Lawrence Kohlberg, *The Philosophy of Moral Development: Moral Stages and the Idea of Justice* (San Francisco, CA: Harper & Row, 1981); Lawrence Kohlberg, et al., *Moral Stages: A Current Formulation and a Response to Critics* (Contributions to Moral Development, 10; Basel: Karger, 1983).

19. Jonathan Haidt, "The Emotional Dog and its Rational Tail: A Social Intuitionist Approach to Moral Judgment," *Psychological Review* 108 (2001): 814–34; Jonathan Haidt, "The Moral Emotions," in *Handbook of Affective Sciences*, ed. R. J. Davidson, et al. (Oxford: Oxford University Press, 2003); Jonathan Haidt, *The Righteous Mind: Why Good People Are Divided by Politics and Religion* (London: Allen Lane, 2012); Joshua D. Greene, *Moral Tribes: Emotion, Reason, and the Gap between Us and Them* (New York: Penguin Press, 2013). Note that this evaluation of the role of emotion for morality neither places emotion in opposition to cognition (but rather regards it as part of cognition), nor does such evaluation imply any "oughts."

have contributed to this development, especially within the fields of evolutionary biology, evolutionary psychology,[20] and neuroscience.[21]

In *Descartes' Error* (1994), Antonio Damasio demonstrated how rational thinking ends up in dysfunctional action when emotions are impaired. Emotion and intuition are simply integral parts of human cognition and decision-making.[22] Psychological experiments, such as the "trolley problem" experiments by Joshua Greene and colleagues,[23] as well as the experiments of Jorge Moll and colleagues, comparing the degree of emotional involvement in different types of judgments,[24] provided important evidence. Jonathan Haidt demonstrated how moral decisions relate to rational motivation, resulting in a "social intuitionist model."[25] Frans de Waal and other primatologists and ethologists made experiments which suggested animal "proto-morality."[26]

The conclusion is that much western thinking has been mistaken, based as it is on a dichotomous anthropology, from Plato's and Aristotle's ideals that reason should be the master over the passions,[27] to Immanuel Kant's

---

20. Taking over from the much (and often unjustly) discredited sociobiology; cf. Haidt, *Righteous Mind*, 33–6.

21. Haidt provides an account of this development (with an autobiographical touch) within the overall argument of *Righteous Mind*.

22. Antonio Damasio, *Descartes' Error: Emotion, Reason and the Human Brain* (New York: Grosset/Putnam, 1996).

23. See for example Joshua D. Greene, et al., "An fMRI Investigation of Emotional Engagement in Moral Judgment," *Science* 293 (2001): 2105–8; Greene, *Moral Tribes*.

24. Jorge Moll, et al., "The Neural Basis of Human Moral Cognition," *Nature Reviews. Neuroscience* 6 (2005): 799–809.

25. Haidt, "Emotional Dog." The social intuitionist model suggests that moral judgments are first triggered by intuitions (emotions) and then rationalized (*post hoc* justification). This takes place, however, in contexts of social interaction, creating a sort of feedback loop, in which moral judgments influence others' intuitions and others' judgments influence one's own intuitions.

26. The literature is vast. For a few examples, see Frans B. M. de Waal, *Good Natured: The Origins of Right and Wrong in Humans and Other Animals* (Cambridge, MA: Harvard University Press, 1996); Stephanie D. Preston and Frans B. M. de Waal, "Empathy: Its Ultimate and Proximate Bases," *Behavioral and Brain Sciences* 25 (2002): 1–72; Frans B. M. de Waal, *Primates and Philosophers: How Morality Evolved* (The University Center for Human Values Series; Princeton, NJ: Princeton University Press, 2006); Sarah F. Brosnan, "'Nonhuman Species' Reactions to Inequity and Their Implications for Fairness," *Social Justice Research* 19 (2006): 153–85; Marc Bekoff and Jessica Pierce, *Wild Justice: The Moral Lives of Animals* (Chicago, IL: University of Chicago Press, 2009).

27. Cf. Simo Knuuttila and Juha Sihvola, "How the Philosophical Analysis of Emotions Was Introduced," in *The Emotions in Hellenistic Philosophy*, ed. J. Sihvola and T.

categorical imperative.²⁸ David Hume was basically right that reason is subordinate to the emotions.²⁹ And from an evolutionary perspective, this is why human rationality evolved in the first place.

Against the background of overwhelming evidence for the role emotions play in human morality,³⁰ Jonathan Haidt has sorted emotions into families. Other-condemning emotions, including contempt, anger, and disgust, guard the moral order. Self-conscious emotions, including shame, embarrassment, guilt, and pride, constrain individual behavior in a social context. Other-suffering emotions, including empathy, induce altruism and prosocial action. Other-praising emotions, including awe, elevation, and gratitude, respond to good deeds.³¹ Haidt construed a taxonomy of moral emotions, understood as "emotions that are linked to the interests or welfare either of society as a whole or at least of persons other than the judge or agent."³² Assuming a definition of morality mainly as prosocial attitudes, emotions were ranked, so that those triggered by disinterested elicitors³³ and motivating humanitarian actions were considered more moral than others. As a result, empathy scored high, fear scored low, and disgust came somewhere in between.³⁴ With different definitions, however, more emotions can be understood as crucial for morality.

This is in fact implied by Haidt's more recent publications on "moral foundations theory," which suggests six evolved universal cognitive modules, forming the basis for cultural constructions of morality: care/harm, liberty/oppression, fairness/cheating, loyalty/betrayal, authority/subversion, and sanctity/degradation.³⁵ With a broadened view of welfare, morality can be

---

Engberg-Pedersen (The New Synthese Historical Library, 46; Dordrecht: Kluwer Academic Publishers, 1998), 1–19.

28. Cf. John Teehan, "Kantian Ethics: After Darwin," *Zygon* 38 (2003): 49–60.

29. In contrast to Kant, for whom reason was seen as having no function to preserve the human organism, but only to produce human morality, Hume regarded emotions as primary and reason as secondary, in the sense that reason actually serves the emotions and is subordinate to them.

30. There is no room for details here. For further discussion of some of the evidence mentioned, see Thomas Kazen, *Emotions in Biblical Law: A Cognitive Science Approach* (Sheffield: Sheffield Phoenix, 2011), and for extensive reviews and references, see Haidt, *Righteous Mind* and Greene, *Moral Tribes*.

31. Haidt, "Moral Emotions."

32. Haidt, "Moral Emotions," 853 (original italics removed).

33. I.e., they are not the immediate result of one's own needs or interests.

34. Depending on the extent to which these emotions are understood to be related to one's own interests or the welfare of others.

35. Haidt, *Righteous Mind*, 112–86. Liberty/oppression was added relatively recently, after Haidt realized that the five initial foundations did not capture "conservative notions of fairness, which focused on proportionality, not equality" (*Righteous*

seen as somehow involved in all six modules, with the result that neither fear, nor disgust, would necessarily be less important in the construction of morality than empathy is. We need to understand morality in a broader sense than is common in the western world, which usually regards it from an individualistic perspective, separate from social conventions and community concerns.

Disgust, for example, is involved in evaluations of a range of behaviors and conditions, from taboos and ritual purity concerns to sexual acts and religious practices. Biologically evolved emotional reactions against threatening physical substances and situations, selected for their adaptive advantages, feed into culturally constructed conceptions of things not appropriate, and strongly influence moral systems. Fear, originally selected for similar reasons, motivates various avoidance behaviors and protective measures, depending on the social and cultural framework. Empathy, without which a socially complex species like *homo sapiens* would not have survived, not only underlies our capacity to care for offspring and keep together in groups, but becomes an important basis for the more inclusive and altruistic expressions of morality that arise in various cultures.[36]

Although there is a focus on empathy and its relationship to prosocial behavior in the present article, this does not mean that I consider empathy to be more "moral" than other emotions. However, empathy is good to think with when we try to understand the ways in which altruism results from a combination of ultimate (biologically evolved) and proximate (culturally constructed) factors.

Definitions of Altruism

Whether or not altruism is compatible with human nature depends on what we mean by the term.[37] Those who deny the existence of "genuine" altruism

---

Mind, 169). It should be pointed out that although Haidt's "moral foundations theory" draws in part on cross-cultural anthropological and psychological research, it is construed with a view to the present political landscape in the United States, and employed in order to understand and explain the conflicting values of Democrats and Republicans in particular. The model is open to criticism from a variety of angles; for a critical view from within the same American cultural and political sphere, see Greene, *Moral Tribes*, 334–46.

36. I have elsewhere analyzed these emotions in more detail, and detected and discussed their moral impact in the Pentateuchal legal collections; see Kazen, *Emotions*.

37. For a modern intellectual history of altruism, see Lee Alan Dugatkin, *The Altruism Equation: Seven Scientists Search for the Origins of Goodness* (Princeton, NJ: Princeton University Press, 2006). For a recent defense of altruism, distinguishing between and focusing more on action than intention, thoughts, and feelings, see David Sloan

usually define it in such a way that it is precluded from the start. This thwarts the discussion.

Many expressions of prosocial behavior can be accounted for as kin altruism: we are prepared to forego our own advantages for the sake of individuals genetically related to us. Others qualify as reciprocal altruism, or interaction-based altruism, which expects returns for generous acts, stops if the other defects repeatedly, and resumes cooperation if the other does. Still other expressions may be classified as group altruism or group solidarity, a kind of strategic cooperation, which gives an advantage to all participants. The first is often dismissed as just another sort of selfishness (cf. Dawkins). But as Zwick and Fletcher point out, "[k]inship is the simplest way to get altruism established, not its essence."[38] The second represents a classic "tit-for-tat" behavior and is often dismissed as a studied form of selfishness: individuals engage in generous behaviors as long as they benefit from them. The third type of altruism, sometimes called "mutualism," is often excepted since the cooperation it involves is only strategic, and hence not truly self-sacrificing.[39] In the end nothing much is left.

Evolutionary theory understands behaviors and propensities to evolve naturally because of adaptive advantages. But if every type of prosocial behavior, which also promotes inclusive fitness,[40] is understood more or less as selfishness in disguise, altruism is already ruled out as a meaningless concept from the beginning; the existence of the object for discussion is made impossible by default.[41] It should be obvious that no human being can be entirely selfless, since only a biologically living, feeling, and thinking self will be able to do something for others. This, however, requires a sense

---

Wilson, *Does Altruism Exist? Culture, Genes, and the Welfare of Others* (New Haven, CT: Yale University Press, 2015).

38. Martin Zwick and Jeffrey A. Fletcher, "Levels of Altruism," *Biological Theory* 9 (2014): 100–7, 102.

39. Ironically, the result of this kind of logic is that every attempt to explain altruistic behavior—whether kin altruism, reciprocal altruism, or mutualism—by natural selection would automatically disprove the existence of that which one tries to explain. This suggests underlying definitions that are untenable. Critics would perhaps object that while behavior can be seemingly altruistic, motives cannot. But since every behavior has evolutionary and biological aspects, this is tantamount to denying human beings motives or intentions whatsoever. This is a possible stance, but it would make the discussion meaningless.

40. Inclusive fitness, meaning behavior which promotes one's genetic offspring.

41. Cf. Robert L. Trivers, "The Evolution of Reciprocal Altruism," *The Quarterly Review of Biology* 46 (1971): 35–57, who plainly (and in my view falsely) states: "Models that attempt to explain altruistic behavior in terms of natural selection are models designed to take the altruism out of altruism" (p. 35).

of belonging, so that the self is by definition somehow involved in the larger group which benefits from the behavior. Frans de Waal has argued that the scope of such a sense of group belonging can be extended almost infinitely, depending on the experienced sufficiency of resources.[42] There is no point in limiting the concept of altruism to an absolute selflessness, to the point where the self no longer has any needs and no longer is related to any group. Such selves are only fictional creations of western individualism.

I would thus opt for a broad definition of altruism as a spectrum of prosocial or other-serving attitudes and behaviors that stretch beyond certain given limits (whether self, kin, tribe, nation, or race), into a wider sense of group belonging.[43]

Feeling and Understanding with Others

Altruistic behaviors are based on the capacity to feel with others. Empathy is commonly defined as "an affective response more appropriate to someone else's situation than to one's own."[44] This response can be aroused at various levels, ranging from motor mimicry and emotional contagion, to direct association, mediated association, and cognitive perspective-taking.[45] Two steps in the evolution of *homo sapiens* as a successful social species are crucial for the formation of a multi-levelled empathy: mirror neurons and a Theory of Mind.

Mirror neurons were first found in experiments on monkeys. They are active in performing as well as in observing an action. But although they seem to be suited for action imitation, this capacity belongs to a relatively late stage in evolution, which is hardly present in monkeys and only partially in apes.[46] It is likely that mirror neurons did not originally evolve

---

42. See for example de Waal, *Good Natured*, 212–4; de Waal, *Primates and Philosophers*, 161–5; cf. de Waal, *The Age of Empathy: Nature's Lesson for a Kinder Society* (New York: Broadway Books, 2009).

43. The various ways in which human beings actually acquire such a widened sense is a fascinating topic in itself, for which there is no room here. Relevant issues include the role of awe, meditation, mysticism, and ritual coordination for human cooperation and a widened sense of belonging.

44. Martin L. Hoffman, "The Contribution of Empathy to Justice and Moral Judgment," in *Empathy and Its Development*, ed. N. Eisenberg and J. Strayer (Cambridge Studies in Social and Emotional Development ; Cambridge: Cambridge University Press, 1987), 47–80, 48.

45. Martin L. Hoffman, *Empathy and Moral Development: Implications for Caring and Justice* (Cambridge: Cambridge University Press, 2000), 5; Preston and de Waal, "Empathy," 2–4, Table 2.

46. We are here talking of observing an action and then repeating it afterwards.

for imitation, but for understanding actions performed by others, as well as their emotional states. Studies of humans suggest that mirror mechanisms cause the observer to enact the actions of others inside him/herself and share their emotions, thus transforming what others do and feel into the observer's own experience.[47] It seems that the same neural circuits as those activated by feeling pain are also activated by seeing another person in pain.[48] This would indicate that at the very lowest end of the scale, empathy is (based on) a sort of (analogy to) motor mimicry, which is a prerequisite for emotional contagion.

The other important step in the formation of empathy is Theory of Mind, the ability to recognize the mental state of others.[49] Humans are not completely unique in being able to recognize what others think and thus represent their inner world, but they are by far more advanced at this than apes and elephants. Such access to an *inner* inner world,[50] from which one can observe one's own inner world and make inferences about others, is necessary for the levels of empathy belonging to the upper end of the scale, mediated association and perspective-taking, for which more advanced cognitive capacities are required.

At one end of the scale, empathy is an emotional response which requires little or no reasoning. At the other end of the scale, human rational capacities facilitate empathic feelings and empathy-induced actions without any close match between the empathizer's and the victim's initial affects.[51] The

---

Monkeys do mirror or reflect simple behaviors, i.e., motor mimicry, as is clear from the research on mirror neurons performed on macaques, which perform imitation of facial imagery.

47. Laurie Carr, et al., "Neural Mechanisms of Empathy in Humans: A Relay from Neural Systems for Imitation to Limbic Areas," *Proceedings of the National Academy of Sciences of the USA* 100 (2003): 5497–5502; Marco Iacoboni and Mirella Dapretto, "The Mirror Neuron System and the Consequences of Its Dysfunction," *Nature* 7 (2006): 942–50; Giacomo Rizzolatti and Laila Craighero, "The Mirror-Neuron System," *Annual Review of Neuroscience* 27 (2004): 169–92; Giacomo Rizzolatti and Laila Craighero, "Mirror Neuron: A Neurological Approach to Empathy," in *Neurobiology of Human Values*, ed. J.-P. Changeux, et al. (Research and Perspectives in Neuroscience; Berlin: Springer, 2005), 107–23.

48. Giacomo Rizzolatti and Maddalena Fabbri Destro, "Mirror Neurons," *Scholarpedia* 3 (2008): 2055 (http://www.scholarpedia.org/article/Mirror_neurons), with further references to research by T. Singer, Saarela, et al., and Gallese, et al.

49. De Waal, *Primates and Philosophers*, see especially Appendix B, 69–73; cf. de Waal, *Good Natured*; Peter Gärdenfors, *How Homo Became Sapiens: On the Evolution of Thinking* (Oxford: Oxford University Press, 2003), 83–109.

50. The expression comes from Gärdenfors, *How Homo Became Sapiens*, 113–4 and elsewhere.

51. Hoffman, *Empathy*, 5.

different levels of empathy depend on each other, in a manner for which de Waal uses the image of a Russian doll. Perspective-taking is dependent on acquiring a perspective in the first place, through one's own experiences, through emotional development, and through the capacity to mirror others' affects, including reactive crying and motor mimicry. The outer layers thus build upon the inner ones.[52]

Multileveled empathy contributes greatly to the inclusive fitness of the human species, by paving the ground for prosocial action in general and for altruism in particular. It is functional at all levels: even a small child reacting to another child at the level of emotional contagion contributes to call the attention of parents or other adults.[53] Also for reasoning adults, it takes quite some effort to withstand the pull from the lower levels of empathy and overrule them. For doing that it seems that we need other *emotions* to enter the game.[54]

This means that humanitarian behavior is based on biological evolution and firmly rooted in the neurobiological constitution of human beings. At the same time it is thoroughly shaped by culture.[55] Higher or more cognitive levels of empathy in particular take on expressions that are context-dependent cultural constructs and interact with a number of other evolved/cultural emotional concerns. These may restrain expressions of more immediate, lower levels of empathy. Prosocial agency and altruism is an evolved emotionally-based capacity in constant negotiation with other such capacities, and always subject to cultural constraints.

Justice, Revenge, and Forgiveness

One of these other capacities is a sense of justice, which demands fair treatment and fair distribution. This is a complex phenomenon, including a number of emotions, mainly anger in response to unjustified behavior or

---

52. De Waal, *Primates and Philosophers*, 37–42 (Figure 4). For another overview of various levels, definitions and perspectives, see Jean Decety and William Ickes, eds., *The Social Neuroscience of Empathy* (Cambridge, MA: The MIT Press, 2009).

53. See the examples in Hoffman, *Empathy*, 63–92.

54. For this, see my discussions in Kazen, *Emotions*.

55. Cf. Michael Tomasello, *Why We Cooperate?* (Cambridge, MA: Boston Review, 2009). Even among apes and monkeys, levels of "cultural" shaping of empathic or prosocial behavior can be observed, for example in rhesus monkeys who learn to practice the peace-making skills of stump-tailed macaques after long periods of interaction and acculturation. De Waal, *Good Natured*, 163–208.

unfair treatment of self or others,[56] envy and jealousy,[57] but also to varying degrees pride, contempt, shame, embarrassment, and guilt. Even empathy has a role here, as it contributes to the capacity to feel and identify with others who are unjustly treated. From an evolutionary perspective, our sense of justice and associated reparative mechanisms have developed because of their adaptive value, as a survival strategy which protects the individual by restoring an equilibrium.[58]

A basic sense of fairness can be traced in non-human species, too. It has long been observed that primates like chimpanzees can, similarly to human children, have temper tantrums when frustrated or offended, which at times leads to revenge.[59] Other studies suggest that a number of primates as well as dogs react to unequal distribution.[60] A number of reconciliatory behaviors have been observed in non-human species, including third-party mediators.[61]

---

56. Cf. Dennis L. Krebs, "The Evolution of a Sense of Justice," in *Evolutionary Forensic Psychology: Darwinian Foundations of Crime and Law*, ed. J. D. Duntley and T. K. Shackelford (New York: Oxford University Press, 2008), 229–45, here 235; Leonard Berkowitz, "Anger," in *Handbook of Cognition and Emotion*, ed. T. Dalgleish and M. J. Power (Chichester: John Wiley & Sons, 1999), 411–28; Haidt, "Moral Emotions," 856–7; Mick J. Power and Tim Dalgleish, *Cognition and Emotion: From Order to Disorder* (Hove, UK: Psychology Press, 1997), 304–5.

57. Martin P. East and Fraser N. Watts, "Jealousy and Envy," in *Handbook of Cognition and Emotion*, 569–88.

58. Frans B. M. de Waal and Filippo Aureli, "Shared Principles and Unanswered Questions," in *Natural Conflict Resolution*, ed. F. Aureli and F. B. M. de Waal (Berkeley, CA: University of California Press, 2000), 375–9, 376. Cf. A. B. Newberg, et al., "The Neuropsychological Correlates of Forgiveness," in *Forgiveness: Theory, Research, and Practice*, ed. M. E. McCullough, K. I. Pargament, and C. E. Thoresen (New York: Guilford, 2000), 91–110, here 91–101.

59. Brosnan, "Nonhuman Species' Reactions"; Frans B. M. de Waal, *Chimpanzee Politics: Power and Sex among Apes* (25th Anniversary edn.; Baltimore, MD: John Hopkins University Press, 2007 [1982]), 98–105; Frans B. M. de Waal, *Peacemaking among Primates* (Cambridge, MA: Harvard University Press, 1989), 37–69.

60. Brosnan, "Nonhuman Species' Reactions," 170–9; Sarah F. Brosnan and Frans B. M. de Waal, "Monkeys Reject Unequal Pay," *Nature* 425 (2003): 297–9; Sarah F. Brosnan and Frans B. M. de Waal, "Fair Refusal by Capuchin Monkeys," *Nature* 428 (2004): 140; Megan van Wolkenten, Sarah F. Brosnan, and Frans B. M. de Waal, "Inequity Responses of Monkeys Modified by Effort," *Proceedings of the National Academy of Sciences* 104 (2007): 18854–9; Friederike Range, et al., "The Absence of Reward Induces Inequity Aversion in Dogs," *Proceedings of the National Academy of Sciences* 106 (2009): 340–5.

61. For further discussion with examples and references, see Kazen, *Emotions*, 45–6.

Cross-cultural studies of human reconciliation rituals suggest a number of behaviors that aim at restoring an equilibrium.[62] Talion, compensation, and various types of reconciliation rituals ensure a minimum level of mutual acceptance, necessary for resumed interaction, whether or not forgiveness has taken place.[63] Talion and compensation in fact seem to be foundational to every organized society. Theft, violence and coercion not only compromise personal integrity, but disturb the social balance. In a hierarchical honor-society—which describes most societies through history—justice is not seen as full equality, but individuals are entitled to their assigned status,[64] and unwarranted humiliating treatment should be either avenged or compensated for. If not, the social fabric will be strained to a point where injustice may cause ruptures and threaten the structures.[65]

This, however, is only one part of the equation. The other part is forgiveness,[66] which has its own emotional and evolutionary logic, in which the needs of self and empathy for others play equal roles. Empathy ensures that even a victim can easily imagine how the perpetrator would feel if treated in a similar way. Such imagination makes revenge less satisfactory in cases where a continued or restored relationship is highly prized. According to the valuable relationships hypothesis, quick reconciliation between individuals has evolved among social species to preserve relationships of crucial importance. Group-living organisms that were willing to forgive their kin simply had better chances to survive than those who did not.

---

62. Douglas P. Fry, "Conflict Management in Cross-Cultural Perspective," in *Natural Conflict Resolution*, ed. F. Aureli and F. B. M. de Waal (Berkeley, CA: University of California Press, 2000), 334–51. Cf. William Ian Miller, *Eye for an Eye* (Cambridge: University Press, 2006), 17–30, who discusses talion and compensation from the perspective of restoring an equilibrium, "getting even."

63. For recent discussions of forgiveness in antiquity, see Charles L. Griswold, *Forgiveness: A Philosophical Exploration* (Cambridge: Cambridge University Press, 2007); David Konstan, *Before Forgiveness: The Origins of a Moral Idea* (Cambridge: Cambridge University Press, 2011); see also the essays in *Ancient Forgiveness: Classical, Judaic, and Christian*, ed. Charles L. Griswold and David Konstan (Cambridge: Cambridge University Press, 2012).

64. Cf. Aristotle in *Nicomachean Ethics*, book 5, especially ch. 3.

65. For a fascinating discussion of the role of talion in human history and literature, see Miller, *Eye for an Eye*, 17–69, 197–202.

66. By forgiveness I do not here refer to the full range of emotions and attitudes often assumed in the modern world, including recognition of guilt and regret or remorse on the part of the perpetrator, and giving up anger or resentment on the part of the forgiver, but a rather more basic attitude of non-retaliation and continued cooperation. For a discussion of definitions, see Konstan, *Before Forgiveness*, 1–21.

De Waal and others have proved this to be true for various kinds of primates in a number of studies.[67] One of the most conspicuous experiments shows how long-tailed macaques that were taught to cooperate in order to obtain food experienced a doubling of post-conflict reconciliations.[68] This is not caused by rational consideration, but results from what McCullough calls "the forgiveness instinct," which is part of the human mindset, too. Moreover, forgiveness in close relationships lowers levels of anxious tension. This means that forgiveness, like revenge, is context-sensitive and depends on how we experience our relationship to the perpetrator. Forgiveness, just like revenge, can give emotional satisfaction. When empathy enters the game, it plays on the side of forgiveness, and may seriously disturb the satisfaction gained from revenge.[69]

Non-retaliation in the Sermon

According to the fifth antithesis (Matt. 5.38-42), Jesus contradicts the talion principle (eye for an eye) with a demand not to resist evil (vv. 38-39). This is then exemplified in three ways: turn the other cheek when struck (v. 39), give also your coat to the one who sues you for your tunic (v. 40), and walk two miles with the one who conscripts you for one (v. 41). A fourth saying is added almost as an afterthought: give to the one who asks and do not turn away from the one who wants to borrow from you (v. 42).

These commandments are often understood as "unnatural" and opposite to human nature, and the injunction not to resist evil could even be seen as immoral and irresponsible, leading to passivity and victimization. The interpretation of *mē antistēnai tō ponērō*, usually translated *"do not resist evil,"* is, however, open to discussion. In view of Matthew's reference to talion law in the context, the phrase is best understood as prohibiting retaliation. Turning the other cheek is an even stronger rhetorical way of expressing the same thing: don't hit back.[70] The problem is how to relate such altruistic behavior

---

67. Frans B. M. de Waal and A. van Roosmalen, "Reconciliation and Consolation among Chimpanzees," *Behavioral Ecology and Sociobiology* 5 (1979): 55–66; Filippo Aureli and Colleen Schaffner, "Causes, Consequences and Mechanisms of Reconciliation: The Role of Cooperation," in *Cooperation in Primates and Humans: Mechanisms and Evolution*, ed. P. M. Kappeler and C. P. van Schaik (Berlin: Springer, 2006), 121–35; Michael McCullough, *Beyond Revenge: The Evolution of the Forgiveness Instinct* (San Francisco, CA: Jossey-Bass, 2008), 124–7.
68. Marina Cords and Sylvie Thurnheer, "Reconciling with Valuable Partners by Long-tailed Macaques," *Ethology* 93 (1993): 315–25; McCullough, *Beyond Revenge*, 126.
69. McCullough, *Beyond Revenge*, 147–54.
70. The suggested behavior can also be understood from a pragmatic perspective,

to the function of revenge or compensation for satisfying a sense of justice and protecting personal integrity? Where is the morality in a practice if it leaves moral emotions upset?

Here the valuable relationships hypothesis and the "forgiveness instinct" may provide some explanation. Forgiveness and reconciliation are central concerns in the Sermon as a whole: this is the primary message of the first antithesis (Matt. 5.21-26) and one of the main features in the Lord's Prayer (6.12), the only one which immediately receives a detailed exposition (6.14-15). The exposition clarifies that the brief phrase of the prayer actually means that divine forgiveness is conditional on inter-human forgiveness.

However, the valuable relationships hypothesis will not so easily make sense in view of the commended altruism and non-retaliatory behavior, unless we assume a "family setting" for these sayings. A few indications for this can, in fact, be found in the immediate context of the Sermon. In the first antithesis, the entire exposition of the command not to be angry is phrased in filial language: do not be angry at a brother (Matt. 5.22) and if you remember that your brother has anything against you as you bring your sacrifice, reconcile with him first (vv. 23-24). The warnings against judging consistently assume interaction between brothers (7.1-5). Moreover, the whole Sermon breathes a familial setting by repeatedly referring to God as "your father" (*ho patēr hymōn / sou*).[71] As part of an intra-family ethics, non-retaliation of the type described here is fully compatible with "human nature" and in line with inclusive fitness as understood from an evolutionary perspective. The behavior described would then represent an extended kin altruism, including reciprocal and mutualist traits, working alongside human nature and cognition. Those towards whom such generous attitudes are displayed would be regarded as valuable relations.

But there is a caveat: not all of the language in the fifth antithesis fits this interpretation. The saying about giving up even one's coat assumes if not a courtroom setting at least a situation of debt[72] and the command to walk an extra mile (Matt. 5.41) hardly suggests a "family setting," but

---

as Syreeni suggests in particular for the version of *Didache*, which "shows a tension between the high *ideal* of perfection and the more modest *practical* requirements." The motivation for enemy love is unclear and the reason for not reclaiming one's possessions is explicitly stated: "since you cannot do so anyway" (*Did.* 1.4). See Kari Syreeni, "The Sermon on the Mount and the Two Ways Teaching of the Didache," in *Matthew and the Didache: Two Documents from the Same Jewish-Christian Milieu?*, ed. H. van de Sandt (Assen/Minneapolis, MN: Royal Van Gorcum/Fortress, 2005), 87–104, 96–7.

71. E.g., Matt. 5.16, 45, 48; 6.4, 6, 8, 9 (our father), 14, 15, 18, 26, 32; 7.11.

72. Cf. Zerbe, *Non-Retaliation*, 180–1, on the implications of the differences in order (*chitōn / himation*) between Matthew and Luke.

rather conscription by an enemy soldier (*hostis se angareusei* ...).[73] It is notable, however, that precisely the language reminiscent of legal proceedings (*krithēnai*) and the sentence about an extra mile are not attested in the double tradition.[74] Is it possible that the familial language and "family setting" belongs to Matthew's source, but that Matthew's own redactions and expansions move outside of this framework? As we will see, this suggestion is corroborated in the subsequent antithesis.

Enemy Love in the Sermon

The sixth antithesis (Matt. 5.43-48) posits the Holiness Code's command to love one's neighbor (Lev. 19.18) and hate one's enemy (Matt. 5.43; not in the biblical text)[75] against Jesus' command to love enemies and pray for persecutors (v. 44). The motivation given (v. 45) is *imitatio Dei*; the purpose is to be or become "sons of your heavenly father" (*hopōs genēsthe huioi tou patros hymōn tou en ouranois*), who shines his sun and sends rain on good and evil alike. Then follows an argument in two parallel parts against a limited reciprocal altruism (tit-for-tat): there is nothing deserving reward (*misthon*) in doing good to those who merely reciprocate, as also tax collectors do (v. 46), and there no "surplus" (*perisson*) in greeting brothers (*adelphous*) only, as also Gentiles (*hoi ethnikoi*) do (v. 47). The recipients should thus aim to be perfect (*teleioi*) like their father in heaven (v. 48), again suggesting *imitatio Dei* as the ideal for human behavior.

Here, too, the notion of an intra-family ethics would make the altruistic ideals less utopian and more in line with what biology and psychology say about human dispositions. At first sight, some of the familial language may support such an interpretation. But here, too, there is a caveat. Matthew discards the attitude to greet brothers only (v. 47) as too limited. He expects a "surplus" morality: not just brothers, but also enemies. Doesn't this prove that the Sermon's altruism is not envisaged for a "family setting," and cannot be explained by the valuable relationships hypothesis and the like, within an evolutionary framework? Isn't the prosocial behavior and altruism demanded by Matthew simply against human nature?

Again, a comparison with Luke and asking about Matthew's own redactions of his sources may be helpful. Luke has three parallel arguments instead of Matthew's two, questioning acts of reciprocal altruism (Luke 6.32-34).

---

73. For the military terminology, see Davies and Allison, *Matthew 1–7*, 546–7 and Luz, *Matthew 1–7*, 273–4.

74. Cf. Zerbe, *Non-Retaliation*, 181, with slightly different conclusions.

75. The closest one could come is probably Ps. 139.21-22, but the explicit command to hate one's enemies is not a biblical one.

While the intent is the same, criticizing the limited character of a strictly reciprocal altruism, there is no indication of "family" as an insufficient motivation, as in Matthew. In fact, elsewhere in the double tradition, too, judgment, forgiveness and reconciliation are discussed within the framework of filial language.[76]

We may thus suggest that the "family setting" in a broad sense is assumed in the Sermon's source, just as it is evident in the broader framework of the Sermon, although Matthew's redaction and reshuffling has slightly obscured it. From a different angle, Matthew can be understood to extend prosocial precepts, originally reflecting intra-family ethics, and make them applicable to a wider context, including outgroup adversaries.[77] As we will see, this is a development which has precedents.

Enemies as Ingroup?

Several sections of the Sermon, and especially the two last antitheses, may be read as a commentary on parts of the Holiness Code, in particular Leviticus 19, which also came to play an important role elsewhere in early Christian ethical discourse.[78] Crucial parts of that chapter (19.9-18, 32-37) emphasize justice and prosocial behavior. Non-retaliation and love of neighbor surface especially in vv. 17-18, and to this the passage on immigrants (*gērîm*) (vv. 33-34) must be added.

The central passage for our purpose (vv. 17-18) reads:

> You must not hate your brother (*'āḥîkā*) in your heart. Do reprove your fellow (*'ămîtekā*) and you will not bear sin because of him. You must not retaliate (*tiqqōm*) or bear a grudge against the sons of your people (*běnê 'ammekā*), but you must love your neighbor (*rē 'ăkā*) as yourself. I am YHWH.

Both the fifth (do not retaliate) and the sixth (love your enemies) antitheses find their source here, as well as the filial language which motivates a non-retaliatory and altruist attitude. Although this passage from the Holiness Code

---

76. Cf. Q 6.41-42; 11.2-4; 12.58-59 (?); 17.3-4.

77. This, in turn, can be interpreted as making a virtue out of necessity, as in *Didache* (see n. 70 above), reflecting a context of oppression and marginalization (cf. Zerbe, *Non-Retaliation*, 184–5), or more positively, as aristocratic ethics for lower-class people. Cf. Theissen and Merz, *Historical Jesus*, 347–8.

78. The role and influence of Lev. 19 has been noted with regard to Matthew, James, *Didache*, *Barnabas*, etc. On this issue, see for example Luke Timothy Johnson, "The Use of Leviticus 19 in the Letter of James," *Journal of Biblical Literature* 101 (1982): 391–401; John S. Kloppenborg, "The Transformation of Moral Exhortation in *Didache* 1–5," in *The Didache in Context: Essays on Its Text, History and Transmission*, ed. C. N. Jefford (Leiden: Brill, 1995), 88–109, 97–104; Kari Syreeni, "The Sermon on the Mount," 94–6.

talks of not hating your *brother*, and of loving one's *neighbor*, the "family" which is the object of this kin altruism is conspicuously extended later in the chapter. Leviticus 19.33-34 warns against oppressing the stranger (*gēr*) and envisages such a person as almost fully integrated (v. 34): "the foreigner who resides with you shall be among you as a citizen to you (*kĕ'ezrāḥ mikkem yihyeh lākem haggêr haggār 'ittĕkem*) and you must love him as yourself (*wĕ'āhabtā lô kāmôkā*). For all practical purposes, then, the foreigner is equated with the citizen,[79] and what is said about loving the foreigner (*gēr*) as oneself is first said of the neighbor (*rēa'*). Although "enemy" is not explicitly mentioned, the foreigner is placed on the same level as the brother who should not be hated, the neighbor who should be loved, and the sons of the people who should not be subject to retaliation. It would not have been so far-fetched then, for later interpreters to understand this text as a general command not to retaliate, but to show love to all adversaries, whether citizens or foreigners.

Examples of further reflection are provided by Jesus Sirach in two passages, none of which is extant in Hebrew.

> Like a drop of water from the sea and a grain of sand, so are a few years among the days of eternity. That is why the Lord is patient (*emakrothymēsen*) with them and pours out his mercy (*eleos*) upon them. He sees and recognizes that their end is miserable; therefore he grants them forgiveness (*exilasmon*) all the more. The compassion (*eleos*) of human beings is for their neighbors (*ton plēsion autou*), but the compassion (*eleos*) of the Lord is for every living thing (*epi pasan sarka*). He rebukes and trains and teaches them, and turns them back, as a shepherd his flock.[80]

> The vengeful will face the Lord's vengeance (*ekdikēsin*), for he keeps a strict account of their sins. Forgive your neighbor (*plēsion*) the wrong (*adikēma*) he has done, and then your sins will be pardoned when you pray. Does anyone harbor anger against another, and expect healing from the Lord? If one has no mercy (*eleos*) toward another like himself, can he then seek pardon (*exilasetai*) for his own sins?[81]

---

79. For details and exceptions, see Christophe Nihan, "Resident Aliens and Natives in the Holiness Legislation," in *The Foreigner and the Law: Perspectives from the Hebrew Bible and the Ancient Near East*, ed. R. Achenbach, et al. (Wiesbaden: Harrassowitz, 2011), 111–34. Although the status and definition of the *gēr* changes over time, the foreigner is considered as a recipient of charity already in the Covenant Code and in Deuteronomy. For arguments against the *gēr* in Deuteronomy referring to landless or displaced Israelites, see Carly L. Crouch, *The Making of Israel* (VTS, 162; Leiden: Brill, 2014), 216–23.

80. Sirach 18.10-13, NRSV.

81. Sirach 28.1-4, NRSV.

It is likely that Sirach elaborates on the Holiness Code, at least in part.[82] For Sirach, the vulnerability (short life, miserable death) of human beings induces empathy or mercy (*eleos*) in God, of a kind that is universal, as it is directed to *every human being*—a better translation of *epi pasan sarka* than that of the NRSV, in view of the LXX idiom. This is placed in contrast to human mercy, which is directed only towards one's neighbor or kin (*ton plēsion autou*). So God grants forgiveness (*exilasmon*). Perhaps we could say that the limitations of human kin or group altruism are understood to correspond to the very limitations that surround human life on the whole, while an empathic concern for all creation is envisaged as a divine capacity.

At the same time, Sirach expects human behavior to accommodate to God's (*imitatio Dei*). Divine revenge (*ekdikēsis*) is mostly a response to vengeful humans. To forgive the wrongdoings (*adikēma*) of one's neighbor (*plēsion*) is a prerequisite for obtaining divine forgiveness. Human and divine mercy (*eleos*) are like corresponding vessels.

Although the terminology differs, the Sermon's portrayal of inter-human forgiveness as a condition for divine forgiveness corresponds with that of Sirach. The command in Matthew's fifth antithesis not to retaliate is also fully in line with Sirach's advice and the motivations and arguments of the sixth antithesis are almost identical with Sirach's emphasis on divine compassion for every living being, which humans ought to imitate. The authors seem to agree that from the divine perspective, all human beings are the same: the good and the evil, enemies and brothers.

Altruism as Extended Kinship and Divine Potential

We can detect a trajectory of sorts, from the Holiness Code, through Sirach, to the Sermon, with regard to empathy, altruism, and non-revenge. Intertextual connections are clearly present. These, however, may arguably be viewed as only ripples on the surface of a much more general and pervasive shift, triggered by Israel's increasing interaction with the surrounding world, and with Hellenism in particular. We should be careful not to misconstrue this process as if "primitive selfishness gradually gave way to a more universal and ethical idea of human sympathy."[83] There are, however, certain aspects of this development which relate to social and linguistic

---

82. For arguments that especially Sirach 28 is an exposition of Lev. 19.17-18, see Zerbe, *Non-Retaliation*, 39–44.

83. David Konstan, *Pity Transformed* (London: Duckworth, 2001), 19.

constructions of emotional experience and expression,[84] and others that reflect changes in how the divine was conceptualized.

As David Konstan has pointed out, the classical Greek concept expressed by the term *eleos* depended on two things: whether or not the suffering was deserved and the recognition that one could have been in similar circumstances, but is not.[85] This "did not mean identifying with the experience of another; rather, it was just insofar as one did not share another's misfortune that one was in a position to pity it."[86] Aristotle, among others, provides clear evidence for such views. But in the same breath, Aristotle also talks of *eleos* as an emotion, a feeling of pain (*lypē*).[87] Even though a philosophical ideal saw "evaluation as an essential component of pity," says Konstan, "there was another, less theorized conception of pity as an unmediated response to suffering as such. These senses were not neatly discriminated in ordinary usage."[88]

In fact, Greek terms for empathy or compassion in general are emotional. Françoise Mirguet has argued for a marked shift in the evaluation and understanding of pity taking place with the translation of Hebrew scriptures into Greek and the appearance of new scriptures in Greek. While Hebrew terms for empathy and compassion mostly refer to general attitudes and actions, Greek comparative terms do not exactly match, as they rather convey internal feelings.[89] Although Greek scriptures are full of hebraisms, and some of these may occasionally represent mistranslations,[90] the translation process frequently shifts the meaning of Hebrew terms like *ḥesed*, *raḥûm* and *ḥannûn* towards an emphasis on affective, inner responses, by rendering them with Greek terms, such as *eleos*, *eleēmosynē*, *oiktos*, or *oiktirmos*.[91] Especially *ḥesed*, which expresses benevolence, favor, or grace, and often

---

84. This is not to say that the biological conditions for feeling with others vary with time and context, but categorizations and conceptualizations of emotion complexes and prosocial attitudes definitely do, as they are to a considerable degree cultural constructions.

85. David Konstan, *The Emotions of the Ancient Greeks: Studies in Aristotle and Classical Literature* (Toronto: University of Toronto Press, 2006), 201–2.

86. Konstan, *Emotions*, 213.

87. Aristotle, *Rhetoric* 2.8. Cf. the rich discussions in Konstan, *Pity*, and in Françoise Mirguet, *An Early History of Compassion: Emotion and Imagination in Hellenistic Judaism* (Cambridge: Cambridge University Press, 2017), 24–34.

88. Konstan, *Pity*, 48.

89. Mirguet, *Compassion*, 86. For a discussion of *eleos* in Greek, see Konstan, *Pity*.

90. As a flagrant example, Mirguet mentions Ruth "pitying" Boaz (Ruth 3.10 LXX), *Compassion*, 90.

91. Mirguet, *Compassion*, 64–108.

refers to divine benevolence towards human beings, undergoes this shift, as it is rendered by *eleos*.[92]

As a result of this development, the benevolence and compassion of the Israelite god was interpreted in decidedly emotional terms and pity came to be understood as one of God's main attributes, even as part of the divine essence. While the Homeric gods could show occasional pity, they were quite unreliable, to say the least. More abstract and philosophical gods were even less moved by emotions. According to Aristotle, two categories of people were unaffected by the pain of pity: those who had already lost everything themselves and those who had no reason to fear a similar fate.[93] The latter condition would have applied even more to immortal and impassible gods. With Hellenistic conceptions of the divine as transcendent, universal, and self-sufficient, compassion could hardly be seen as a typically divine trait.[94]

For the Israelite god, Hellenistic influence and hybridity had very opposite results. As the originally tribal god became increasingly transcendent and universal, divine benevolence towards that god's own people seems to have gradually developed into an intensely emotional commitment to the whole inhabited world. Such a god's pity did not limit itself to victims of undeserved suffering, but was extended into mercy in view of wrongdoing and empathy towards all human beings. While Aristotle reserved human *eleos* for the *homoioi* (those who are similar, peers, kin),[95] Jewish texts affected by Hellenistic influence expanded divine empathy towards a wider altruism, based on a widened sense of kin, and made this both into an ideal for human behavior and a characteristic of ingroup identity.[96]

As already mentioned, Frans de Waal argues that empathy, based on a sense of group belonging, can be extended almost infinitely, the limitation being to what extent available resources are experienced as sufficient.[97] A

---

92. For the way in which *eleos* shifts the meaning of *ḥesed* in Greek scriptures, see Jan Joosten, "חסד 'bienveillance' et ἔλεος 'pitié': Réflexions sur une equivalence lexicale dans la Septante," in *"Car c'est l'amour qui me plait, non le sacrifice...": Recherche sur Osée 6:6 et son interpretation juive et chrétienne*, ed. E. Bons (Supplements to the Journal for the Study of Judaism, 88; Leiden: Brill, 2004), 25–42.
93. Aristotle, *Rhetoric* 2.8; Konstan, *Pity*, 130–1.
94. Konstan, *Pity*, 105–24.
95. Aristotle, *Rhetoric* 2.8; Konstan, *Pity*, 111–2. Cf. Sirach's criticism of human *eleos* for only embracing the *plēsion* (neighbor, kin); Sirach 18.13. Note that Aristotle makes an exception for close family, since he thinks we then react as if we were in danger ourselves, rather than with pity. This is in line with Aristotle's understanding of *eleos* as requiring a certain distance.
96. Cf. the discussions about the role of compassion for group identity in Mirguet, *Compassion*, e.g., 182–4, 224–5.
97. See above, n. 42.

divine perspective on human beings, as envisaged by the Sermon and Sirach alike, does not seem to know any limits. Human beings, however, regularly face such limits, and their moral emotions and innate capacities, like empathy and sense of justice, have been shaped and kneaded by evolution and culture, in contexts full of threats, hardships, and severe restrictions. Nevertheless, various types of altruism have overcome obstacles along the way and restricting and protective emotions have been negotiated with the help of multiple levels of empathy. These are the conditions under which human beings and their morality evolved.

The Sermon presents some real challenges with regard to altruistic behavior. But just as kinship could be viewed as an efficient way to "get altruism going" in an evolutionary sense, the extension of kin altruism, by establishing fictive kinship patterns, is a way of expanding the human perspective, which draws on biological underpinnings and cultural development alike.[98] In the fifth and sixth antitheses, Matthew expands the family setting and transcends the fictive kin discourse that characterizes his source and dominates the Sermon at large, in order to incorporate every human being, even adversaries and enemies. Although Matthew is no full-blown universalist, some of his examples suggest an understanding, like that of Sirach, of the other as a human being like oneself (*anthrōpon homoion autō*; Sir. 28.4). This becomes in effect a challenge to extend altruism beyond the borders of kin, clan, and group. The implication of *imitatio Dei* supplies a further challenge to imagine the divine perspective and the divine mind, and somehow identify with it.

It seems, then, that in the evolution of human altruism, culture and cognition coevolve with the biological basis for human behavior, in a sense working alongside human nature and expanding its potential range. One decisive factor in this development, at least in an early Jewish and early Christian context, is how God is envisaged, and to what extent divine empathy and altruism reach beyond the bounds of the ingroup in people's imagination. Altruism, based as it is on biologically evolved empathy, ultimately turns out to be a potentially unrestricted capacity of the divine mind, as it is envisaged by the Jewish-Christian author of the Sermon, in a context and at a time when the Israelite God goes more universal than ever before. Human beings are challenged to follow suit.

---

98. Cf. Zwick and Fletcher, "Levels of Altruism"; Maximilian P. Holland, "Social Bonding and Nurture Kinship: Compatibility between Cultural and Biological Approaches" (Dissertation; University of London: London School of Economic and Political Science: Department of Sociology, 2004); David M. Schneider, *A Critique of the Study of Kinship* (Ann Arbor, MI: The University of Michigan Press, 1984); Edward O. Wilson, *The Social Conquest of Earth* (New York: Liveright, 2012), 49–56.

Biographical Note

Thomas Kazen is Professor of Biblical Studies, Stockholm School of Theology at University College Stockholm. His research interests include biblical law and Jewish halakha, ritual and purity, Jesus traditions and their development, conceptual metaphors, emotions, sociocognitive and psychobiological approaches, power and hierarchy. Recent books include *Impurity in Early Judaism and the Jesus Tradition: Critical Issues and New Directions* (SBL, 2021); *Dirt, Shame, Status: Perspectives on Same-Sex Relationships in the Bible and Antiquity* (in Swedish; Makadam, 2018); *Scripture, Interpretation, or Authority? Motives and Arguments in Jesus' Halakic Conflicts* (Mohr Siebeck, 2013); and *Emotions in Biblical Law: A Cognitive Science Approach* (Sheffield Phoenix, 2011).

Bibliography

Aureli, Filippo, and Colleen Schaffner. "Causes, Consequences and Mechanisms of Reconciliation: The Role of Cooperation," 121–35 in *Cooperation in Primates and Humans: Mechanisms and Evolution*. Edited by P. M. Kappeler and C. P. van Schaik. Berlin: Springer, 2006. https://doi.org/10.1007/3-540-28277-7_7

Bekoff, Marc, and Jessica Pierce. *Wild Justice: The Moral Lives of Animals*. Chicago, IL: University of Chicago Press, 2009. https://doi.org/10.7208/chicago/9780226041667.001.0001

Berkowitz, Leonard. "Anger," 411–28 in *Handbook of Cognition and Emotion*. Edited by T. Dalgleish and Mick J. Power. Chichester: John Wiley, 1999.

Bovon, François. *Luke 1: A Commentary on the Gospel of Luke 1:1–9:50*. Hermeneia. Minneapolis, MN: Fortress, 2002.

Brosnan, Sarah F. "'Nonhuman Species' Reactions to Inequity and Their Implications for Fairness," *Social Justice Research* 19 (2006): 153–85. https://doi.org/10.1007/s11211-006-0002-z

Brosnan, Sarah F., and Frans B. M. de Waal. "Monkeys Reject Unequal Pay," *Nature* 425 (2003): 297–99. https://doi.org/10.1038/nature01963

—"Fair Refusal by Capuchin Monkeys," *Nature* 428 (2004): 140. https://doi.org/10.1038/428140b

Carr, Laurie, Marco Iacoboni, Marie-Charlotte Dubeau, John C. Mazziotta, and Gian Luigi Lenzi. "Neural Mechanisms of Empathy in Humans: A Relay from Neural Systems for Imitation to Limbic Areas," *Proceedings of the National Academy of Sciences* 100 (2003): 5497–502. https://doi.org/10.1073/pnas.0935845100

Cords, Marina, and Sylvie Thurnheer. "Reconciling with Valuable Partners by Long-Tailed Macaques," *Ethology* 93 (1993): 315–25. https://doi.org/10.1111/j.1439-0310.1993.tb01212.x

Crouch, Carly L. *The Making of Israel: Cultural Diversity in the Southern Levant and the Formation of Ethnic Identity in Deuteronomy*. Supplements to Vetus Testamentum, 162. Leiden: Brill, 2014. https://doi.org/10.1163/9789004274693

Damasio, Antonio. *Descartes' Error: Emotion, Reason and the Human Brain*. New York: Grosset/Putnam, 1996.

Davies, W. D., and Dale C. Allison. *Introduction and Commentary on Matthew I-VII*. Vol. 1 of *A Critical and Exegetical Commentary on the Gospel according to Saint Matthew*. International Critical Commentary. Edinburgh: T&T Clark, 1988.

Darwin, Charles. *The Descent of Man, and Selection in Relation to Sex, Part 1*. The Works of Charles Darwin, 21. New York: University Press, 1989 (1877).

Dawkins, Richard. *The Selfish Gene*. Oxford: Oxford University Press, 1989 (1976).

Decety, Jean, and William Ickes, eds. *The Social Neuroscience of Empathy*. Cambridge, MA: The MIT Press, 2009. https://doi.org/10.7551/mitpress/9780262012973.001.0001

Dugatkin, Lee Alan. *The Altruism Equation: Seven Scientists Search for the Origins of Goodness*. Princeton, NJ: Princeton University Press, 2006. https://doi.org/10.1515/9781400841431

East, Martin P., and Fraser N. Watts. "Jealousy and Envy," 569–88 in *Handbook of Cognition and Emotion*. Edited by T. Dalgleish and Mick J. Power. Chichester: John Wiley & Sons, 1999. https://doi.org/10.1002/0470013494.ch27

Fry, Douglas P. "Conflict Management in Cross-Cultural Perspective," 334–51 in *Natural Conflict Resolution*. Edited by F. Aureli and Frans B. M. de Waal. Berkeley, CA: University of California Press, 2000.

Gärdenfors, Peter. *How Homo Became Sapiens: On the Evolution of Thinking*. Oxford: Oxford University Press, 2003.

Greene, Joshua D. *Moral Tribes: Emotion, Reason, and the Gap between Us and Them*. New York: Penguin Press, 2013.

Greene, Joshua D., R. Brian Sommerville, Leigh E. Nystrom, John M. Darley, and Jonathan D. Cohen. "An fMRI Investigation of Emotional Engagement in Moral Judgment," *Science* 293.5537 (2001): 2105–8. https://doi.org/10.1126/science.1062872

Griswold, Charles L. *Forgiveness: A Philosophical Exploration*. Cambridge: Cambridge University Press, 2007. https://doi.org/10.1017/CBO9780511619168

Griswold, Charles L., and David Konstan, eds. *Ancient Forgiveness: Classical, Judaic, and Christian*. Cambridge: Cambridge University Press, 2012. https://doi.org/10.1017/CBO9780511978654

Haidt, Jonathan. "The Emotional Dog and its Rational Tail: A Social Intuitionist Approach to Moral Judgment," *Psychological Review* 108 (2001): 814–34. https://doi.org/10.1037/0033-295X.108.4.814

—"The Moral Emotions," 852–70 in *Handbook of Affective Sciences*. Edited by R. J. Davidson, Klaus R. Sherer, and H. Hill Goldsmith. Oxford: Oxford University Press, 2003.

—*The Righteous Mind: Why Good People Are Divided by Politics and Religion*. London: Allen Lane, 2012.

Hoffman, Martin L. "The Contribution of Empathy to Justice and Moral Judgment," 47–80 in *Empathy and Its Development*. Edited by N. Eisenberg and J. Strayer. Cambridge Studies in Social and Emotional Development. Cambridge: Cambridge University Press, 1987.

—*Empathy and Moral Development: Implications for Caring and Justice*. Cambridge: Cambridge University Press, 2000. https://doi.org/10.1017/CBO9780511805851

Holland, Maximilian P. "Social Bonding and Nurture Kinship: Compatibility between Cultural and Biological Approaches," Dissertation; London School of Economic and Political Science: Department of Sociology, 2004. https://doi.org/10.2139/ssrn.1791365

Iacoboni, Marco, and Mirella Dapretto. "The Mirror Neuron System and the Consequences of Its Dysfunction," *Nature* 7 (2006): 942–50. https://doi.org/10.1038/nrn2024

Johnson, Luke Timothy. "The Use of Leviticus 19 in the Letter of James," *Journal of Biblical Literature* 101 (1982): 391–401. https://doi.org/10.2307/3260351

Joosten, Jan. "חסד 'bienveillance' et ἔλεος 'pitié': Réflexions sur une equivalence lexicale dans la Septante," 25–42 in *"Car c'est l'amour qui me plait, non le sacrifice…": Recherche sur Osée 6:6 et son interpretation juive et chrétienne*. Edited by E. Bons. Journal for the Study of Judaism Supplement Series, 88. Leiden: Brill, 2004.

Kazen, Thomas. *Emotions in Biblical Law: A Cognitive Science Approach*. Hebrew Bible Monographs, 36. Sheffield: Sheffield Phoenix, 2011.

—"Self-Preserving and Other-Oriented Concerns in the Jesus Tradition," 124–48 in *Voces Clamantium in Deserto: Essays in Honor of Kari Syreeni*. Edited by S.-O. Back and M. Kankaanniemi. Studier i exegetik och judaistik utgivna av Teologiska fakulteten vid Åbo Akademi,11. Åbo: Åbo Akademi, 2012.

Kloppenborg, John S. "The Transformation of Moral Exhortation in Didache 1–5," 88–109 in *The Didache in Context: Essays on Its Text, History and Transmission*. Edited by C. N. Jefford. Leiden: Brill, 1995. https://doi.org/10.1163/9789004267237_006

Knuuttila, Simo, and J. Sihvola. "How the Philosophical Analysis of Emotions Was Introduced," 1–19 in *The Emotions in Hellenistic Philosophy*. Edited by J. Sihvola and T. Engberg-Pedersen. The New Synthese Historical Library, 46. Dordrecht: Kluwer Academic Publishers, 1998. https://doi.org/10.1007/978-94-015-9082-2_1

Kohlberg, Lawrence. *The Philosophy of Moral Development: Moral Stages and the Idea of Justice*. San Francisco, CA: Harper & Row, 1981.

Kohlberg, Lawrence, Charles Levine, and Alexandra Hewer. *Moral Stages: A Current Formulation and a Response to Critics*. Contributions to Moral Development, 10. Basel: Karger, 1983.

Konstan, David. *Pity Transformed*. London: Duckworth, 2001.

—*The Emotions of the Ancient Greeks: Studies in Aristotle and Classical Literature*. Toronto: University of Toronto Press, 2006. https://doi.org/10.3138/9781442674370

—*Before Forgiveness: The Origins of a Moral Idea*. Cambridge: Cambridge University Press, 2011.

Krebs, Dennis L. "The Evolution of a Sense of Justice," 230–48 in *Evolutionary Forensic Psychology: Darwinian Foundations of Crime and Law*. Edited by J. D. Duntley and T. K. Shackelford. New York: Oxford University Press, 2008. https://doi.org/10.1093/acprof:oso/9780195325188.003.0012

Luz, Ulrich. *Studies in Matthew*. Grand Rapids, MI: Eerdmans, 2005.

—*Matthew 1–7: A Commentary*. Edited by Helmut Koester. Translated by James E. Crouch. Rev. edn. Hermeneia. Minneapolis, MN: Fortress, 2007.

McArthur, Harvey K. *Understanding the Sermon on the Mount*. London: Epworth, 1960.

McCullough, Michael. *Beyond Revenge: The Evolution of the Forgiveness Instinct*. San Francisco, CA: Jossey-Bass, 2008.

Miller, William Ian. *Eye for an Eye*. Cambridge: Cambridge University Press, 2006.

Mirguet, Françoise. *An Early History of Compassion: Emotion and Imagination in Hellenistic Judaism*. Cambridge: Cambridge University Press, 2017. https://doi.org/10.1017/9781316536520

Moll, Jorge, Roland Zahn, Ricardo de Oliveira-Souza, Frank Krueger, and Jordan Grafman. "The Neural Basis of Human Moral Cognition," *Nature Reviews Neuroscience* 6 (2005): 799–809. https://doi.org/10.1038/nrn1768

Newberg, Andrew B., Eugene G. d'Aquili, Stephanie K. Newberg, and Verushka deMarici. "The Neuropsychological Correlates of Forgiveness," 91–110 in *Forgiveness: Theory, Research, and Practice*. Edited by M. E. McCullough, K. I. Pargament, and Carl E. Thoresen. New York: Guilford, 2000.

Nihan, Christophe. "Resident Aliens and Natives in the Holiness Legislation," 111–34 in *The Foreigner and the Law: Perspectives from the Hebrew Bible and the Ancient Near East*. Edited by R. Achenbach, R. Albertz, and J. Wöhrle. Wiesbaden: Harrassowitz, 2011.

Power, Mick J., and Tim Dalgleish. *Cognition and Emotion: From Order to Disorder*. Hove, UK: Psychology Press, 1997.

Preston, Stephanie D., and Frans B. M. de Waal. "Empathy: Its Ultimate and Proximate Bases," *Behavioral and Brain Sciences* 25 (2002): 1–72. https://doi.org/10.1017/S0140525X02000018

Range, Friederike, Lisa Horn, Zsófia Viranyi, and Ludwig Huber. "The Absence of Reward Induces Inequity Aversion in Dogs," *Proceedings of the National Academy of Sciences* 106 (2009): 340–5. https://doi.org/10.1073/pnas.0810957105

Rizzolatti, Giacomo, and Laila Craighero. "The Mirror-Neuron System," *Annual Review of Neuroscience* 27 (2004): 169–92. https://doi.org/10.1146/annurev.neuro.27.070203.144230

—"Mirror Neuron: A Neurological Approach to Empathy," 107–23 in *Neurobiology of Human Values*. Edited by J.-P. Changeux, Antonio Damasio, and Wolf Singer. Research and Perspectives in Neuroscience. Berlin: Springer, 2005. https://doi.org/10.1007/3-540-29803-7_9

Rizzolatti, Giacomo, and Maddalena Fabbri Destro. "Mirror Neurons," *Scholarpedia* 3 (2008): 2055. https://doi.org/10.4249/scholarpedia.2055

Schneider, David M. *A Critique of the Study of Kinship*. Ann Arbor, MI: The University of Michigan Press, 1984.

Syreeni, Kari. "The Sermon on the Mount and the Two Ways Teaching of the Didache," 87–104 in *Matthew and the Didache: Two Documents from the Same Jewish-Christian Milieu?* Edited by H. van de Sandt. Assen/Minneapolis, MN: Royal Van Gorcum/Fortress, 2005.

Teehan, John. "Kantian Ethics: After Darwin," *Zygon* 38 (2003): 49–60. https://doi.org/10.1111/1467-9744.00476

Theissen, Gerd, and Anette Merz. *The Historical Jesus: A Comprehensive Guide*. Minneapolis, MN: Fortress, 1998.

Tomasello, Michael. *Why We Cooperate?* Cambridge, MA: Boston Review, 2009. https://doi.org/10.7551/mitpress/8470.001.0001

Trivers, Robert L. "The Evolution of Reciprocal Altruism," *The Quarterly Review of Biology* 46 (1971): 35–57. https://doi.org/10.1086/406755

de Waal, Frans B. M. *Peacemaking among Primates*. Cambridge, MA: Harvard University Press, 1989.

—*Good Natured: The Origins of Right and Wrong in Humans and Other Animals*. Cambridge, MA: Harvard University Press, 1996.

—*Primates and Philosophers: How Morality Evolved*. The University Center for Human Values Series. Princeton, NJ: Princeton University Press, 2006. https://doi.org/10.1515/9781400830336

—*Chimpanzee Politics: Power and Sex among Apes*. 25th anniversary edn. Baltimore, MD: John Hopkins University Press, 2007 (1982).

—*The Age of Empathy: Nature's Lesson for a Kinder Society*. New York: Broadway Books, 2009.
de Waal, Frans B. M., and Filippo Aureli. "Shared Principles and Unanswered Questions," 375–82 in *Natural Conflict Resolution*. Edited by Frans B. M. de Waal and F. Aureli. Berkeley, CA: University of California Press, 2000.
de Waal, Frans B. M., and A. van Roosmalen. "Reconciliation and Consolation among Chimpanzees," *Behavioral Ecology and Sociobiology* 5 (1979): 55–66. https://doi.org/10.1007/BF00302695
Wilson, David Sloan. *Does Altruism Exist? Culture, Genes, and the Welfare of Others*. New Haven, CT: Yale University Press, 2015.
Wilson, Edward O. *The Social Conquest of Earth*. New York: Liveright, 2012.
van Wolkenten, Megan, Sarah F. Brosnan, and Frans B. M. de Waal. "Inequity Responses of Monkeys Modified by Effort," *Proceedings of the National Academy of Sciences* 104 (2007): 18854–9. https://doi.org/10.1073/pnas.0707182104
Zerbe, Gordon M. *Non-Retaliation in Early Jewish and New Testament Texts: Ethical Themes in Social Contexts*. Journal for the Study of Pseudepigrapha Supplement Series, 13. Sheffield: Sheffield Academic Press, 1993.
Zwick, Martin, and Jeffrey A. Fletcher. "Levels of Altruism," *Biological Theory* 9 (2014): 100–7. https://doi.org/10.1007/s13752-013-0145-8

Chapter Five

Ritual Acts in the Sermon on the Mount

Rodney A. Werline

Introduction

The Sermon on the Mount includes instructions about the practice of piety—almsgiving, prayer and fasting (Matt. 6.1-18). Such actions fall into the category of ritual. Traditionally, biblical scholarship has generally approached this portion of the text as it has the rest of the Sermon on the Mount—as important for its thoughts, in this case, related to these rituals about privately practicing one's faith without ostentatiousness. This section of the Sermon seemingly invited interpreters to take this approach because the instructions emphasize proper attitudes and motivations; it seems to interiorize the rituals. Interpreters then typically proceeded to treat the passage as part of a history of ideas, or perhaps more specifically, as containing foundational theological and spiritual concepts. Certainly, there are "thoughts" presented in the Matthean text, and these are connected with ritual. However, the discussion about avoiding ostentatiousness does not erase the ongoing *practice* of the rituals, which Jesus affirms, assuming that his disciples will continue to engage in these practices. This fact calls for methods and theories that move beyond the boundaries of analysis of thoughts or ideas. Ritual theory provides tools that can illuminate these neglected aspects of the text. In doing so, ritual theory complements traditional historical critical methodology and does not completely invalidate that project. Within the massive amount of secondary literature on the Sermon on the Mount still lie many insightful examinations of these texts.

Ritual theory has its own complicated history and its own areas of debate.[1] Disagreements among theorists leave some key issues unresolved,

---

1. Easy access to ongoing debates within the area of ritual theory is available in Catherine Bell, *Ritual Theory, Ritual Practice* (New York: Oxford University Press, 1992). See also, Nathan D. Mitchell, *Liturgy and the Social Sciences* (Collegeville, MN: Liturgical, 1999). Also, see Talal Asad's thorough critique of Clifford Geertz's location of ritual in a web of symbolic action and meaning in *Genealogies of Religion: Discipline and Reasons of Power in Christianity and Islam* (Baltimore, MD: The Johns Hopkins University Press, 1993), 27–79.

for example a consensus on a definition of ritual, which will occasionally come to the foreground in this essay. In addition, theories may even generate new problems. Nevertheless, I employ an eclectic methodological approach to ritual, but one which leans most heavily on cultural anthropology, supplemented with theories from the cognitive science of religion. An eclectic approach has an advantage over theorists who argue that ritual can be understood in only one way to the exclusion of all others, or who reduce ritual to one function. Effects of ritual action differ according to the individual, and even a particular ritual may have a different effect on the same person as the person performs the action in different moments in life. Further, ritual can have layers of meanings and effects for a person who performs the act. A public ritual will simultaneously generate many different effects when multiple participants are involved, in part due to their particular social locations and life situations during the production of the ritual.[2] Consequently, those who analyze ritual would do well to refer to a range of possible effects on participants rather than isolating one feature as *the* distinguishing mark of ritual.

Further, an eclectic approach better serves the interpreter given the nature of our ancient sources—that they are generally quite limited and incomplete when speaking about or referring to ritual. The interpreter can only make use of what the text offers, and, thus, apply the method or methods that best suit the available textual data. In proceeding this way, however, one must resist any uncritical and careless rush to find an immediate application of various features of a theory to a text. Theories from cultural anthropology frequently arise from extensive direct observation of and conversation with the people whom the anthropologist is studying. Thus, any correspondences between the context that gave rise to the theory and ancient Mediterranean contexts must be carefully weighed and considered. Nevertheless, ritual theory offers a fresh angle on the text and draws the interpreter to features of

---

2. Cf. Gananath Obeyeskere's discussion about public and private symbols in "Medusa's Hair: An Essay on Personal Symbols and Religious Experience," in *A Reader in the Anthropology of Religion*, ed. Michael Lambek (2nd edn.; Malden, MA: Blackwell, 2008), 356–67. Obeyeskere examines the meaning of matted hair for a Hindu ascetic woman. While his interpretation relies heavily on psychological theory, he concludes that the woman with the matted hair has taken on a public symbol which she has internalized in relationship to her own life; the public symbol acquires a personal meaning. He concludes, "All symbols are cultural and public; but a cultural symbol may exist on many levels—the personal and the social. It can communicate different messages, emotional and cognitive" (p. 366). When Obeyeskere questioned the public about the woman's matted locks, not one person could connect the hair with ascetic celibacy, the intended public meaning of the hair. Instead, the symbol primarily evoked "fear, horror, disgust, revulsion" (p. 365).

the text that traditional methodology has not noticed. Further, ritual theory grounds the text in the real, embodied lives of the members of the community, and is not solely or primarily about disembodied theological concepts.

Ritual theory can also assist in addressing an additional problem that frequently arises when scholars interpret these passages and other New Testament texts related to practice—an incorrect assumption that these texts intentionally establish a sharp boundary between "Christianity" and Judaism. Scholars, especially those writing from a confessional perspective, sometimes read Jesus' discussion about ritual in the Sermon on the Mount as correcting, or perhaps even negating, Jewish practice in order to establish the uniqueness of Jesus and the early church over against Judaism of the time. Emphasis falls on distinction and separation. However, ritual analysis shows that, rather than breaking from Judaism through reshaping ritual, the directives about ritual practice in the Sermon on the Mount assume a competency in particular Jewish practices known to Matthew's community; Matthew's Jesus does not diverge from those practices and certainly does not break from that local expression of Jewish piety. Because of the variety in Second Temple Judaism and the fact that Jewish rituals, including prayer, had not been standardized in that era, any determination of the exact practices of the Judaism in which Matthew's community participated proves impossible

Basic Description of Almsgiving, Prayer and Fasting in Second Temple Judaism

Almsgiving, prayer and fasting are well attested acts of piety in various Jewish circles by the time that Matthew is written. Israelite literature included demands that society attend to the needs of the poor (e.g., Exod. 23.11; Lev. 19.9-10; 23.22; Deut. 14.28-29; 24.19-22; Job 29.12, 16; Prov. 14.31; 19.17; 28.27). This continued into the Second Temple period, as texts such as Sirach (7.10; 12.3; 29.8; 35.4) and Tobit (4.7, 16; 12.8-9; 14.2, 8, 10) taught the importance of supporting the poor. In Tobit, giving alms provided a means of forgiveness of sins: "For almsgiving saves from death and purges away every sin" (Tob. 12.9). The practice occurs in several scenes in the New Testament (e.g., Luke 11.41; 12.33; Acts 3.2-3, 10; 10.2, 4, 31; 24.17).

Israelite literature mentions fasting several times. Israel prepared for and observed the Day of Atonement with fasting (Lev. 16.29). Also, lament and mourning might include fasting. People would fast in order to prevent a horrible disaster from coming upon an individual or the people as a whole, or they might engage in the act as part of an appeal to remove a calamity that the people were already suffering (e.g., Neh. 9.1; Est. 4.3; Joel 1.1-14). Prayer and fasting occur together in several texts (e.g., Dan. 9.3; Tob. 12.8;

Acts 14.23; and the textual variant in Mark 9.29). Further, a Q tradition includes a discussion about fasting in light of the Pharisees' practice (Matt. 9.14-17; Luke 5.33-39). However, the purpose of the practice of fasting referred to in the Sermon on the Mount is somewhat unclear. Weekly fasts are not mentioned in any of the books collected in the New Testament. The *Didache* states that the "hypocrites" fast on Monday and Thursday (*Did.* 8.1). The Dead Sea Scrolls contain no reference to fasting.[3]

Of course, prayer is widely attested in ancient Israelite literature and in Second Temple Jewish literature. While a discussion about prayer in Second Temple Judaism would demand a lengthy treatment, for this examination it is important to note that there were no widely practiced fixed prayers or fixed times for prayers during this period. Daniel prays at the time of the evening *tamid* offering (Dan. 9.21), and Daniel 6 reports that he prayed three times each day while facing Jerusalem (vv. 10-11). However, the Dead Sea Scrolls legislate that the community pray at several times during the day and night. These times sometimes related to the movements and appearances of heavenly bodies. The New Testament mentions hours for prayer in Acts 3.1.[4] Matthew's Jesus' discussion about prayer, then, cannot be a critique of any highly standardized and regulated Jewish institution.

As some have noted, the Lord's Prayer attains a place of prominence because it remains the only instruction about the content of prayer that Jesus gives the disciples, not just in Matthew and Luke, but in all four gospels. Many gospel traditions depict Jesus frequently praying. Jesus directs his disciples to pray about events related to the future destruction of the temple (Matt. 24.20; Mark 13.18). In the Marcan tradition, Jesus also explains that a particular kind of demon can only be cast out if one has engaged in much prayer (Mark 9.29), and Luke depicts Jesus telling a parable that instructs the disciples to persist in prayer (Luke 18.1). When Jesus retires from supper to pray in the garden on the night of his arrest, he encourages the disciples to pray in preparation for the arrival of the moment of trial (Matt. 26.41; Mark 14.38; Luke 22.46). However, none of these passages contains the form of prayer that the disciples are to pray or a suggested model for prayer's content.

It is difficult to argue that the Lord's Prayer becomes memorable because it displays a special poetic beauty. Its sparse language and brevity suggest simplicity in prayer, which stands in contrast to the caricature of the person who prays with many words in order to be heard. However, the brevity may

---

3. For an overview, see Noah Hacham, "Fasting," in *The Eerdmans Dictionary of Early Judaism*, ed. John J. Collins and Daniel C. Harlow (Grand Rapids, MI: Eerdmans, 2010), 634–6.

4. For a full and wonderful treatment of this issue, see Jeremy Penner, *Patterns of Daily Prayer in Second Temple Period Judaism*, (STDJ, 104; Leiden: Brill, 2012).

also, in part, mean that the Lord's Prayer is only an outline of topics that should appear in prayer, or it functions as an outline upon which petitioners improvised. This may be especially true of the shorter version of the prayer in Luke. Evidence for such practices in antiquity can be found in rabbinic literature, as some rabbis encouraged improvisation when reciting the Eighteen Benedictions (*amidah*).[5]

Ritual Action and Cognitive Science

Ritual and Agency

Cognitive science of religion searches for explanations of religious behavior within already existing cognitive systems which have evolved in humans for a variety of adaptive purposes, some of which are only tangentially related to religion. Cognitive theorists begin with the premise that, as human action, ritual will be most stable if it is somehow based within these evolutionarily developed patterns of thinking. Robert N. McCauley and Thomas E. Lawson especially emphasize this throughout their investigation of ritual:

> Our theory of religious ritual competence is rooted in the claim that participants' cognitive representations of their ritual acts result from the same system for the representation of action that we utilize in representing ordinary actions. The representations of rituals arise from a perfectly ordinary cognitive system expressly devoted to the representation of action, not (just) the representation of ritual action.[6]

The implications of this observation are rather significant. There is not a particular action that is uniquely and only religious. While rituals might be innovative, cognitive science argues that the innovations depend upon elements chosen from a limited set of underlying principles. Ritual action is not *sui generis*, a totally unique production.[7] Therefore, context, meaning and purpose must establish one action as religious and another as not. Further,

---

5. See Joseph Heinemann, *Prayer in the Talmud: Forms and Patterns* (SJ, 9; Berlin: De Gruyter, 1977), 42–53.

6. Robert N. McCauley and Thomas E. Lawson, *Bringing Ritual to Mind: Psychological Foundations of Cultural Forms* (Cambridge: Cambridge University Press, 2002), 115.

7. This problem can also arise in cultural anthropological theories about ritual. See, e.g., the discussion in Mitchell, *Liturgy and the Social Sciences,* 70–1, esp. n. 58, in which he discusses Talal Asad's position that he does not see a significant difference between ritual action and ordinary behavior (in *Genealogies of Religion*, 167). A similar problem exists in defining religious experience, see Ann Taves, *Religious Experience Reconsidered: A Building Block Approach to the Study of Religion and Other Special Things* (Princeton, NJ: Princeton University Press, 2009), 3–4, 16–8.

because the impulse for ritual action can be found in typical human behavior, McCauley and Lawson, as well as Pascal Boyer, argue that they have developed an understanding of religion that can be universally applied.[8]

It is important for the interpreter to note, however, that McCauley and Lawson's theory about ritual is somewhat restricted by their definition. They know that within "religious contexts" people "pray, sing, chant and kneel."[9] However,

> [e]ven though such activities may be parts of religious rituals, such activities, in and of themselves, do not qualify as religious rituals in our theory's technical sense. All religious rituals—in our technical sense—are inevitably connected sooner or later with actions in which CPS-agents [culturally postulated superhuman agents] play a role and which bring about some change in the religious world.[10]

CPS-agents are superhuman because they possess some counter-intuitive quality. While a priest may not generally be considered super-human, as ritually approved special agents, they can fulfill this role.

Since humans use ritual in order to achieve some effect in their world, McCauley and Lawson place ritual action within the human fixation on agency and causality. Following Pascal Boyer, they assert that humans begin to understand causality at an early age. Children learn rather quickly that sticks and stones do not move on their own. However, they also begin to discover that they cannot understand what causes every action in their world. This becomes complicated by the fact that, even as adults, humans cannot explain the reason for a hurricane, an illness, a famine, or the collapse of a grain silo. Several cognitive scientists have noticed this human tendency to attribute agency to anything for which the cause is unclear. Harvey Whitehouse, for example, agrees with their assessment.[11] In their quest to control and understand their environment, humans constantly search for the mechanisms that operate the world. Justin Barret identifies one of these mechanisms as a hyperactive agent-detection device (HADD), a naturally developed impulse passed down from the ancestors whose awareness and wariness of their surroundings would have provided essential traits for survival.[12] Through evolutionary development, human ancestors knew

---

8. E.g., see Pascal Boyer, "Explaining Religious Ideas: Elements of a Cognitive Approach," *Numen* 39 (1992): 27–57.
9. McCauley and Lawson, *Bringing Ritual to Mind*, 13.
10. McCauley and Lawson, *Bringing Ritual to Mind*, 13.
11. Harvey Whitehouse, *Modes of Religiosity: A Cognitive Theory of Religious Transmission* (Oxford: Alta Mira, 2004), 30, 32.
12. See Justin L. Barret, *Why Would Anyone Believe in God?* (Lanham, MD: Alta Mira, 2004), 31–44.

that a cracking of a stick could mean that a large animal was hunting them. According to Barret, this cognitive trait intensified the human impulse to over-ascribe the causes of uncertain events to agents, as opposed to natural, unintentional causes.

Rituals, as McCauley and Lawson define them, have three basic components: (1) a Culturally Posited Supernatural agent (CPS-agent), or a ritually appointed intermediary, such as a priest;[13] (2) an Act (by means of an instrument; (3) and a Patient, the person upon whom the ritual is performed.[14] The CPS-agent, or a priest, generally employs some kind of instrument (e.g., water, bones, smoke, or sacrifice) in a ritualized activity with the intention to change the condition of the patient, the person who seeks an alteration of circumstances.[15] The group generally limits this kind of ritual action to religious insiders. The patient may need to engage in certain preparatory actions in order for the ritual to be effective.[16] Further, this kind of ritual has the special quality of sometimes making later rituals possible and effective.[17] For example, a male who becomes a rabbi can only do so if he previously experienced his bar-mitzvah. In such cases, cognitive science speaks of earlier religious rites being "embedded" in a later ritual action.[18] As they note, "rituals are invariably connected with other rituals ... [P]articipating in anything other than entry-level religious rituals turns unwaveringly on having performed earlier religious rituals ..."[19] This statement, however, reinforces McCauley and Lawson's limited definition of ritual, because, as they claim, one may do all the other religious rituals that they list, such as prayer, without having performed the initiatory rite.

While McCauley and Lawson's understanding of ritual, as mentioned, limits it to actions that generally mark a change in a person's status or condition—marriage, initiation into a group, moving from childhood into adulthood, healing—one might be able to extend some of their observations to religious actions that they do not consider ritual, such as prayer. They open their theory to this possibility as they list ritual action's essential features:

> Ritual's structural descriptions portray basic action structures, which: ... presume that at least two of these roles must always be filled (viz., that every action has an agent and that the agent must do something) ... [and which also] reflect the constraints that although any item filling the role of the agent

---

13. McCauley and Lawson, *Bringing Ritual to Mind*, 13–4.
14. McCauley and Lawson, *Bringing Ritual to Mind*, 14.
15. McCauley and Lawson, *Bringing Ritual to Mind*, 16–23.
16. McCauley and Lawson, *Bringing Ritual to Mind*, 17.
17. McCauley and Lawson, *Bringing Ritual to Mind*, 16.
18. McCauley and Lawson, *Bringing Ritual to Mind*, 19.
19. McCauley and Lawson, *Bringing Ritual to Mind*, 15–6.

may also serve as a patient, not all items that serve as patients may also fill the agent role ...[20]

Humans might intercede for others in prayer, but they might also pray for themselves. Thus, a suppliant could act as both a ritually appointed CPS-agent replacement intermediary and the patient. Those praying frequently concern themselves with causality and with the hope of changing their or other's situation. Praying functions as the "Act" required in the theory.

Matthew's comments about ritual practice explain how the disciples may gain the favor of the deity through action. Indeed, proper ritual practice can bring reward from the deity, as the text states:

> Beware of practicing your piety before others in order to be seen by them; for then you have no reward from your Father in heaven. (Matt. 6.1)

> [S]o that your alms may be done in secret; and your Father who sees in secret will reward you. (v. 4)

> But whenever you pray, go into your room and shut the door and pray to your Father who is in secret; and your Father who sees in secret will reward you. (v. 6)

> [S]o that your fasting may be seen not by others but by your Father who is in secret; and your Father who sees in secret will reward you. (v. 18)

Often underemphasized in reading the passage, the text does indeed assert that almsgiving, prayer and fasting are actions that God notices and rewards; thus, humans seek agency that will bring good favor their way. There can be little doubt that the text is interested in finding favor with God and seeking a reward for that behavior. The immediate context does not clarify how this divine favor might be realized in this life or beyond this life. Within the broader context of the Sermon on the Mount, however, those who conform to Jesus' teachings are like the man who built his house upon the rock (7.24-27), and at the day of judgment Jesus will recognize them and they will enter the kingdom (7.21-23).

Ritual and Compulsive Action

Harvey Whitehouse discusses another natural human impulse that may provide a cognitive and behavioral pattern for ritual practice. According to Whitehouse, rituals seem to "activate some rather powerful mechanisms dedicated to protection against contaminants," and "when addressed to supernatural agents, they are capable of triggering tacit intuitive judgments

---

20. McCauley and Lawson, *Bringing Ritual to Mind*, 12–3.

about the appropriate forms that these rituals should take."[21] The repeatability of most rituals and the concern to perform them accurately and under proper conditions, he believes, bear some resemblance to Obsessive Compulsive Disorder, albeit with several significant differences as well.[22]

Although the discussion about ritual practice in the Sermon is especially concerned about the private execution of the rituals, which will assist the practitioner in achieving the proper attitude, rather than careful attention to detailed action, nevertheless only with the proper attitude does one properly enact the practices. For the one who does not practice the rituals in secret, that person receives a reward in the moment of reception of public praise. However, those seeking praise also may be among those who, at the eschatological judgment, will not enter the kingdom, despite claims about their extraordinary actions (Matt. 7.21-23).

Hans Dieter Betz argues that this attention to the proper way to execute ritual resembles a general concern in the Greco-Roman world about how one properly approaches the deity, and he goes so far as to label this aspect of the Sermon on the Mount as "cultic instruction":

> Presenting cultic instruction was no ordinary matter in antiquity … The basic question for such thinking must have been the notion of what is "acceptable to God" (εὐπρόσδεκτον τῷ θεῷ). One should realize that ancient people were, much more than we are,[23] concerned about the ways in which to approach the deity in the appropriate manner. Approaching the deity required particular conditions such as a state of purity, external as well as internal. Other important dispositions were indicated by terms like "devout" (εὐλαβής), "well pleasing" (εὐάρεστος), "acceptable" (εὐπρόσδεκτος), and foremost, "religious" (εὐσεβής).[24]

Fred S. Naiden also provides extensive accounts of various strategies, postures, clothing and statements that a suppliant in Greek or Roman religion might employ when seeking an audience with and favor from a person of power or a deity.[25] The approach is crucial because it is the suppliant's first impression upon the person or deity. An improper attitude conveyed in a

---

21. Whitehouse, *Modes of Religiosity*, 33.
22. Whitehouse, *Modes of Religiosity*, 33–4.
23. Betz's statement that people in antiquity demonstrated more concern about approaching the deity than modern humans reflects a modern bias.
24. Hans Dieter Betz, *The Sermon on the Mount: A Commentary on the Sermon on the Mount, including the Sermon on the Plain (Matthew 5:3–7:27 and Luke 6:20–49)* (Minneapolis, MN: Fortress, 1995), 331–2. Unfortunately, at this juncture in his argument, Betz only cites texts from the New Testament and early Christian literature.
25. Fred S. Naiden, *Ancient Supplication* (New York: Oxford University Press, 2006), 29–69. Cf. also, Jerome H. Neyrey, *Give God the Glory: Ancient Prayer and Worship in Cultural Perspective* (Grand Rapids, MI: Eerdmans, 2007), 46–56; H. S. Versnel,

wrong posture, wrong gesture or indelicate speech would derail the hope for an answered request. The ultimate goal of supplication is for the powerful to hear and answer the suppliant's request. In this way, the suppliant either hopes to draw on or establish a relationship of reciprocity, which was a key feature of the patron-client relationship in the Greco-Roman world.[26] Within Greco-Roman culture, this process resembles a favorable verdict in a legal hearing, and a new bond is formed by the supplicant and supplicandus if the latter grants the petitioner's request.[27] Humans in the Israelite literature also exhibit concern about properly approaching God. The most notable and memorable examples are Moses (Exod. 3) and Isaiah (Isa. 6). Priests also devoted themselves to determining the holiness of people, animals and things as they came close to the sanctuary where one comes into contact with God's holiness.[28] In 1 Enoch 9.4, the angels who petition God on behalf of humans must prepare to come into God's presence.[29] Betz also provides several examples of concern and discussion about proper worship from the Greco-Roman world, especially from philosophers.[30]

With this constellation of examples of the ritualized caution that humans observe when approaching a deity—or caution projected onto angelic beings in 1 Enoch—Betz's suggestion has merit. However, Betz quickly moves from *action* to talk about *theological thinking or ideas*:

> The section of [Matt] 6:1–18, therefore, contains more than rules for proper behavior. These rules, as it were, are only the practical application of underlying theological ideas. These ideas, on which the reflection is based that results in the rules, remain for the most part unstated, but at some points they are stated explicitly. The SM is based primarily on Jewish religious thought.[31]

Here lies a difference between an approach that draws from cognitive science or cultural anthropology and a historical-critical and theological methodology that in the end is interested in thought.

"Religious Mentality in Ancient Prayer," in *Faith, Hope, and Worship: Aspects of Religious Mentality in the Ancient World*, ed. H. S. Versnel (Leiden: Brill, 1981), 1–64.

26. For the place of reciprocity in prayer, see Naiden, *Ancient Supplication*, 79–84; Jerome H. Neyrey, *Give God the Glory: Ancient Prayer and Worship in Cultural Perspective* (Grand Rapids: Eerdmans, 2007), 46–56; Simon Pulleyn, *Prayer in Greek Religion* (Oxford: Clarendon, 1997), 16–38.

27. Naiden, *Ancient Supplication*, 105–6.

28. Rodney A. Werline, "Ritual, Order and the Construction of an Audience in 1 Enoch 1–36," *Dead Sea Discoveries* 22 (2015): 339.

29. For a summary, see Werline, "Ritual, Order," 339. As the article explains, there is a textual problem in 1 En. 9.4.

30. Betz, *The Sermon on the Mount*, 333–5.

31. Betz, *The Sermon on the Mount*, 335.

Ritual Frequency, Memory, and Scripts

Often overlooked in the Sermon on the Mount is that the instructions about piety actually assume a complex knowledge of the pious practices. Such information has been remembered and transmitted "behind" the text. How does this process of memory and transmission function according to some cognitive science theorists?

Whitehouse's theory establishes two modes of religiosity: imagistic and doctrinal. Ritual works differently within these two modes. Religions in the imagistic mode feature religious practices that "are very intense emotionally: they may be rarely performed and highly stimulating ... they tend to trigger a lasting sense of revelation and to produce powerful bonds between small groups of ritual participants."[32] "By contrast," the doctrinal mode features religious activities that "tend to be much less stimulating: they may be highly repetitive or 'routinized,' conducted in a relatively calm and sober atmosphere; such practices are often accompanied by complex theology and doctrine and also tend to mark out large religious communities composed of people who cannot possibly know each other."[33] As Whitehouse clarifies, these two modes are actually "attractor positions," that is, they chart tendencies rather than serve as the only two possible options in talking about religion. One might find features or rituals of imagistic religion in doctrinal religion and vice versa. As he carefully explains, "We cannot say that a particular ritual is doctrinal or imagistic. We can only say that its long-term reproduction through the innumerable thoughts and actions of many people results in the coalescence of features specified by the modal features."[34]

Because Whitehouse designates all "major" world religions, including Judaism and Christianity, as doctrinal, I will focus only on the role of ritual in this mode. Ritual operating in the doctrinal mode tends to be highly "routinized." It assists in storing a "complex of religious teachings in semantic memory."[35] Rituals in this mode also activate "implicit memory," those ritual procedures humans seem to know without being that aware that they know them (e.g., riding a bike).[36] Such knowledge might, at first, come through a series of verbal instructions, directions or repetition of rules. Over time, this combination will develop into intuitive knowledge, a condition in which the practitioner does not need to think in order to be able to perform the required actions. Interestingly, ritual performances in the

---

32. Whitehouse, *Modes of Religiosity*, 63.
33. Whitehouse, *Modes of Religiosity*, 63.
34. Whitehouse, *Modes of Religiosity*, 75–6.
35. Whitehouse, *Modes of Religiosity*, 65.
36. Whitehouse, *Modes of Religiosity*, 65.

doctrinal mode, with their high frequency, especially focus on procedural knowledge.[37] To illustrate this, Whitehouse points out the amount of procedural knowledge required in the performance of a weekly Christian church service.[38]

McCauley and Lawson also explore this phenomenon and refer to the series of remembered actions required in performing a ritual as *scripts*, which, again, people can execute in some instances without much concentrated thought:

> When participants perform rituals routinely, their actions become part of a script. That means, among other things, that they become habitual and automatic. Their memory for carrying out these action sequences is largely procedural (rather than declarative). Participants may have a much richer sense of *how* to proceed than they have for *what* they are doing.[39]

This repetition lends stability to the retention of religious rituals. However, as McCauley and Lawson explain,

> What makes for good recollection, though, may not make for good communication. Frequent repetition may produce reliable memory, on the one hand, but, on the other, the frequent repetition of a cultural representation may diminish the attention people give that material.[40]

As they note, Whitehouse famously refers to this phenomenon as the "tedium effect."[41]

Granted, Whitehouse and McCauley and Lawson are primarily thinking about much longer and more elaborate rituals than a person fasting, giving a gift, or saying a brief prayer. However, even these actions must require some culturally formalized scripts. Concentration on this one particular aspect of fasting when read through cognitive science raises fascinating observations for consideration. First, fasting can require much more procedural information than what the Matthew passage offers. The text does not indicate on which day one should fast. Further, how does a fast begin? Does the fast allow water or other liquid to be consumed? Does the fast include prayer, and, if so, what kind of prayer and when? How does the fast come to a proper end? The *Didache*, for example, answers one of these questions by offering the procedural knowledge that fasting should take place on Wednesday and Friday (*Did.* 8.1), but it does not offer much beyond

---

37. Whitehouse, *Modes of Religiosity*, 93–4.
38. Whitehouse, *Modes of Religiosity*, 92.
39. McCauley and Lawson, *Bringing Ritual to Mind*, 49.
40. McCauley and Lawson, *Bringing Ritual to Mind*, 50.
41. McCauley and Lawson, *Bringing Ritual to Mind*, 50; Whitehouse, *Modes of Religiosity*, 97–9, 130–5.

those directions. Thus, the Matthean text adds only one additional procedural regulation about fasting. This procedural knowledge specifically centers on actions that will bring the performance of the ritual in line with the attitude required for the proper execution for the desired effectiveness of the ritual. Thus, when Jesus' followers fast, they are to give care that they present themselves in such a manner that no one can recognize their fast. The fast should remain a private matter between the practitioner and God. This means that the author assumes the procedural knowledge, implicit knowledge, of the disciples on fasting. Fasting seems to have been a high frequency ritual. One can assume that the Sermon on the Mount assumes all the procedural knowledge from that particular Jewish context in which the tradition developed.

Strangely missing from this instruction about fasting is any explanation of the meaning of the act—the *why* of ritual. Other New Testament passages give some insight into the possibilities of *why* one might fast, but we cannot determine what bearing those passages might have on the Sermon on the Mount. For example, in a Marcan tradition, Jesus explains that his disciples do not fast like the disciples of John the Baptist because the bridegroom is still with them (Matt. 9.14-17; Mark 2.18-22; Luke 5.33-39). When the bridegroom departs, then Jesus' followers will fast. The Sermon on the Mount assumes that the ritual action is already memorable, apparently generated by frequency.

As mentioned, a problematic aspect of high frequency ritual within the doctrinal mode of religion resides in the tendency for the ritual to become routinized so that it can be performed without much thought.[42] This would seem to go against the tone of intentionality in Jesus' instructions about how to perform the rituals, for the *how* focuses especially on the proper attitude needed in the ritual's performance.

Cultural Anthropological Insights

Ritual, Community, and Embodiment

Emile Durkheim recognized the way that religion generated social cohesion and that ritual played a vital role in this process. Durkheim divided religious phenomenon into two basic categories: beliefs and rites.[43] He defined these in the following manner: "The first are states of opinion and consist

---

42. E.g., Whitehouse, *Modes of Religiosity*, 103.
43. Emile Durkheim, *The Elementary Forms of Religious Life*, trans. Karen E. Fields (New York: The Free Press, 1995), 34.

of representations; the second are particular modes of action."[44] While Durkheim understood rites as a means of social integration and as symbolic mechanisms for social control, critics complain that his theory of ritual needed more development and nuance.[45] Influenced by Durkheim, perhaps in part because he was Durkheim's nephew, Marcel Mauss worked on a dissertation on prayer, which he never finished.[46] The uncompleted work has been published, but its usefulness is somewhat limited because of errors, vague generalities and an unpolished argument. However, Mauss's developing notion that prayer is a social act even when performed in private certainly had promise and rings true:

> What we are saying is that prayer is beyond doubt a social phenomenon because the social character of religion is now sufficiently well established … Even when prayer is individual and free, even when the worshippers choose freely the time and mode of expression, what they say always uses hallowed language and deals with hollowed things, that is, one endorsed by social tradition.[47]

His proposition offers an important perspective for a proper reading of all three rituals mentioned in the Sermon on the Mount, not simply the material related to prayer. Jesus' emphasis on practicing the rituals in private does not make them an individualistic and private matter, taking "place in the inmost heart."[48] Rather, the place and function of these rituals is mediated by the culture and participates in a long social history.[49] Mauss also recognized the power wielded by a social action like prayer. Mauss assesses this aspect of prayer, which could be extended to other rituals, as follows: "[O]ne always observes the general principles of ritual simply by not violating those principles. Consciously or not, one conforms to certain norms and adopts an approved attitude."[50] Here Mauss certainly exhibits the influence that Durkheim had on his thinking. While the real effect of ritual action on the participants should not be reduced to an event of "misrecognition," participants sometimes do fail to recognize the power that culture is exerting on them during the moment of the ritual performance.[51]

---

44. Durkheim, *Elementary Forms of Religious Life*, 34.
45. See Bell, *Ritual Theory*, 23–5, 171–3.
46. Marcell Mauss, *On Prayer*, ed. W. S. F. Pickering, trans. Susan Leslie (New York: Durkheim Press; Oxford: Berghahn Books, 2003).
47. Mauss, *On Prayer*, 33.
48. The phrase is borrowed from Mauss, *On Prayer*, 32.
49. Mauss, *On Prayer*, 33. Again, Mauss focuses on prayer, but his observations apply to the other rituals addressed in the Sermon on the Mount.
50. Mauss, *On Prayer*, 34.
51. For a summary of this complex problem, see Bell, *Ritual Theory*, 114–7, 210–1.

Even though a person performs a ritual in private, the action still engages the individual's body. Pierre Bourdieu explored how, through regulating bodily actions and language, cultures shape the dispositions of their members, and in Bourdieu's opinion, produce not a "state of mind," but a "state of the body."[52] As Bourdieu states: "What is 'learned by body' is not something that one has, like knowledge that one can brandish, but something that one is."[53] So, for Bourdieu, rituals such as these in the Sermon on the Mount serve a vital function in shaping an individual as a member of a group. Groups do this not simply through teaching and promulgating ideas, but through the engagement of the members' bodies. The members do not simply think about ideals; they embody values from culture through practice. The construction of space in the practice of these rituals is rather fascinating.

Fasting and the almsgiving perhaps affect the body more than prayer. A fast brings bodily deprivation. Giving flows from possessions most likely acquired through work, which required an engaged, disciplined body over an extended period of time. These actions also call for a special level of commitment from individuals and they both involve a cost for the practitioner. This level of commitment even increases because the actions are to be conducted in secret so that no one else has knowledge of what one is doing. Such actions might separate those who are minimally dedicated to the group from those who are genuinely serious about their commitment.

Jesus' instructions about the rituals move the bodily actions into private space, away from view. This is the realm which God inhabits: "Practice your piety in secret because your *Father in heaven will then see in secret* and will reward you." The author of Matthew seems to assume that the community has complied with the status quo of the culture in which it lived and perhaps engaged in, or admired, public actions of piety. However, Matthew reconstructs that public socially constructed space as off limits to certain ritual actions. Ironically, then, even this movement of the ritual actions out of public view has social implications. Certainly, however, the private has also been socially constructed; the community invades the personal.

The use of the first person plural in the Lord's Prayer brings the community into each recitation. While only Matthew opens with "*Our* Father," for Luke's version begins simply with "Father," both versions of the prayer use first person plural throughout the petitions. These plurals suggest that the prayer might have been constructed for public worship, but the prayer

---

52. Pierre Bourdieu, *The Logic of Practice*, trans. Richard Nice (Stanford, CA: Stanford University Press, 1990), 68.

53. Bourdieu, *Logic of Practice*, 73.

would not necessarily be confined to that setting. In this instance, the plural pronouns possess the power to generate community spatiality without the community being physically present; that is, the suppliant's speech encourages the individual to imagine the community is present even if the prayer is offered in isolation. Strangely, however, the editor of the Sermon on the Mount in Matthew has placed the Lord's Prayer within the context of directives that restrict prayer to "the closet." It is difficult to imagine that the Matthean community never prayed aloud in a communal setting.

Ritual and Politics

As Catherine Bell and Talal Asad have shown, ritual is a way in which people negotiate power relationships within a culture.[54] As Bell writes: "[R]ituals do not refer to politics ... they *are* politics. Ritual is the thing itself. It *is* power; it acts and it actuates."[55] Ritual does not simply communicate power, for it is the area in which this power is acted out. In regard to the acts of piety in the Sermon on the Mount, this applies to all three pious acts addressed in the text—giving alms, fasting, and praying. In the giving of alms, the individual acts within the social layers of society and the distinction between the poor and the more prosperous. Further, the disciples carry out the acts with "hypocrites" in mind who engage in ostentatious displays of their righteousness:

> So whenever you give alms, do not sound a trumpet before you, as the hypocrites do in the synagogues and in the streets, so that they may be praised by others. (Matt. 6.2)

> And whenever you pray, do not be like the hypocrites; for they love to stand and pray in the synagogues and at the street corners, so that they may be seen by others. (v. 5)

> When you are praying, do not heap up empty phrases as the Gentiles do; for they think that they will be heard because of their many words. (v. 7)

> And whenever you fast, do not look dismal, like the hypocrites, for they disfigure their faces so as to show others that they are fasting. Truly I tell you, they have received their reward. (v. 16)

---

54. Bell, *Ritual Theory*; Catherine Bell, *Ritual: Perspectives and Dimensions* (New York: Oxford University Press, 1997). Talal Asad, *Genealogies of Religion*. See also Rodney A. Werline, "Prayer, Politics, and Power in the Hebrew Bible," *Interpretation* 68 (2014): 5–16.

55. Bell, *Ritual Theory*, 195. At the beginning of her next chapter, Bell begins with her thesis: "The argument of this chapter is essentially a simple one: ritualization is first and foremost a strategy for the construction of certain types of power relationships effective within particular social organizations" (p. 197).

The language in these verses matches stock, polemical rhetoric that appears in many texts in the Greco-Roman period.[56] The enemies become caricatures and to what degree any of the condemnation matches anything in reality is difficult to say. In fact, the opponent here might be an imaginary, generic, straw-man hypocrite. For that matter, even the way in which the disciples are to practice giving—"[W]hen you give alms, do not let your left hand know what your right hand is doing" (Matt. 6.3)—is an exaggerated figure of speech. If we combine these features with the analysis above (viz. that the directions about practicing rituals take over some assumed Jewish cultural script) we can only cautiously observe that the execution of these rituals also acts out the politics of the setting. Such generic condemnation as "hypocrite," however, retains the power to be applied over and over again, sometimes for the bad, to future rivals, and, thus, contribute in defining future politics.

Ritual and Moral Obligation

As a social phenomenon, participation in ritual activity can serve to obligate the participants to conform to society as a whole, an aspect which Mauss also seemed to notice. Roy Rappaport noticed this, and even identified it as ritual's "fundamental office: To *perform* a liturgical order, which is by definition a more or less *invariant* sequence of formal acts and utterances *encoded by someone other than the performer* himself, is *necessarily to conform to it*."[57]

This language of encoding leads Rappaport to explore how ritual transmits messages and how those messages are received. Some theorists basically understood ritual as a symbolic action. That means, as a symbol, ritual primarily functioned to communicate a message, but simply one carried out in action. An obvious example of such an approach to ritual lies in Clifford Geertz's understandings of religion and ritual. Since Geertz understood religion as part of culture's webs of meaning, ritual had the job of carrying and conveying message.[58] Certainly, Clifford Geertz is correct on one level. Many rituals communicate a message to both the individual and the group, and that message may be directly related to the beliefs or the worldview of the culture. In fact, Whitehouse and McCauley and Lawson often speak in this way. If ritual provides a method for memory, then the memory likely includes some thought or idea, though, as we have seen, what is received or transmitted may

---

56. Cf. Luke T. Johnson, "The New Testament's Anti-Jewish Slander and the Conventions of Ancient Polemic," *Journal of Biblical Literature* 108 (1989): 419–44.

57. Roy A. Rappaport, *Ritual and Religion in the Making of Humanity* (CSSCA, 110; Cambridge: Cambridge University Press, 1999), 118, (emphasis Rappaport).

58. Clifford Geertz, *The Interpretation of Cultures* (New York: Basic, 1973), 87–125.

not be the intended message of the ritual. However, theorists who limit ritual to this role have missed out on the complexity of the phenomenon. Further, as several have complained, confining ritual to this role perpetuates the Cartesian distinctions between mind and body. If ritual is carrying a message, that message is enacted or arrives in an embodied form.

Unlike anthropological theories that focus on thought, Rappaport acknowledges that ritual communication occurs through embodied message—communication sent through bodies, and in some instances, received in embodied action: "He [the ritual performer] is not merely transmitting messages he finds encoded in the liturgy. He is participating in—that is, *becoming part of*—the order to which his own body and breath give life."[59]

> To say that performers participate in or become parts of the order they are realizing is to say that transmitters-receivers become fused with the messages they are transmitting and receiving. In conforming to the orders that their performances bring into being ... Therefore, by performing a liturgical order the participants accept, and indicate to themselves and to others that they accept whatever is encoded in the canon of that order.[60]

In his explanation of this facet of ritual, he especially had in mind ritualized events like weddings and baptisms. The wedding ceremony conducted before a congregation compels the couple to commit to one another. All those watching hear and see the exchange of vows and the pronouncement that the two are husband and wife. For Rappaport, the ritual action creates moral obligation. The person making the vows has at least said to the community that he or she is willing to submit to the communal ideal. Rappaport explicitly distinguishes between this kind of obligation and real belief. One does not necessarily need to believe the ritual in order to obligate one's self to the community. Rappaport knows that while ritual might misfire or fail, that is, not work, groups rarely think that this is the fault of the ritual.

The language of the Lord's Prayer, when placed on the lips of the petitioner also has a way of committing a person to the implied realities in the prayer. First, the petitions about the arrival of the kingdom ask the suppliant to agree with the community's teaching and vision of the kingdom. If the prayer expects the kingdom's arrival to be near at hand, which I think is the case, then the person praying the prayer in a sense becomes obligated to this view by enunciation of the words.[61] The use of the first person plural in the petitions certainly involves the petitioner in the prayer. Likewise, the

---

59. Rappaport, *Ritual and Religion*, 118.
60. Rappaport, *Ritual and Religion*, 119. All emphases removed from original text.
61. A challenge to the interpretation that the Lord's Prayer is primarily eschatologically oriented can be found in Jeffrey B. Gibson, *The Disciples' Prayer: The Prayer Jesus Taught in its Historical Setting* (Minneapolis, MN: Fortress, 2015).

request for pardoning of sins is grounded in the petitioner's own commitment to forgive the sins of others. With this the supplicant heeds the warning following the prayer that one can only receive forgiveness if one has forgiven the others' sins: "If you do not forgive the sins of others, then your heavenly Father will not forgive you" (Matt. 6.15; cf. Mark 11.26). In this way, the petitioner also expresses a commitment to the ideal of community held in common among the members, which involves dedication to a particular way of living with one another.

Conclusions

Cognitive science of religion and cultural anthropology provide the tools to accomplish what is not possible when only using the historical-critical method; they ground the investigation in the lived experiences of the people within community. This broader frame frees the text from isolation in a domain of thought and places it within a dynamic world of people's actions. The text is not solely about assent to ideas; it is also about the mind-body. Even when the text includes ideas, thoughts, or theology, cognitive science and cultural anthropology emphasize how these attain their staying power or persuasiveness. As a result, the many ways in which humans know and experience become much more apparent.

Biographical Note

Rodney A. Werline is Professor of Religious Studies and the Marie and Leman Barnhill Endowed Chair in Religious Studies at Barton College, Wilson, North Carolina. His research focuses on prayer and ritual in Second Temple Judaism, the Hebrew Bible, and the New Testament.

Bibliography

Asad, Talal. *Genealogies of Religion: Discipline and Reasons of Power in Christianity and Islam*. Baltimore, MD: The Johns Hopkins University Press, 1993.

Barret, Justin L. *Why Would Anyone Believe in God?* Lanham, MD: Alta Mira, 2004.

Bell, Catherine. *Ritual Theory, Ritual Practice*. New York: Oxford University Press, 1992.

—*Ritual: Perspectives and Dimensions*. New York: Oxford University Press, 1997.

Betz, Hans Dieter. *The Sermon on the Mount: A Commentary on the Sermon on the Mount, including the Sermon on the Plain (Matthew 5:3–7:27 and Luke 6:20–49)*. Edited by Adela Y. Collins. Hermeneia. Minneapolis, MN: Fortress, 1995.

Bourdieu, Pierre. *The Logic of Practice*. Translated by Richard Nice. Stanford, CA: Stanford University Press, 1990.

Boyer, Pascal. "Explaining Religious Ideas: Elements of a Cognitive Approach," *Numen* 39 (1992): 27–57. https://doi.org/10.1163/156852792X00159

Durkheim, Emile. *The Elementary Forms of Religious Life*. Translated by Karen E. Fields. New York: The Free Press, 1995.

Geertz, Clifford. *The Interpretation of Cultures*. New York: Basic, 1973.

Gibson, Jeffrey B. *The Disciples' Prayer: The Prayer Jesus Taught in its Historical Setting*. Minneapolis, MN: Fortress, 2015. https://doi.org/10.2307/j.ctt12878s7

Hacham, Noah. "Fasting," 634–6 in *The Eerdmans Dictionary of Early Judaism*. Edited by John J. Collins and Daniel C. Harlow. Grand Rapids, MI: Eerdmans, 2010.

Heinemann, Joseph. *Prayer in the Talmud: Forms and Patterns*. Studia Judaica, 9. Berlin: De Gruyter, 1977. https://doi.org/10.1515/9783110842449

Johnson, Luke Timothy. "The New Testament's Anti-Jewish Slander and the Conventions of Ancient Polemic," *Journal of Biblical Literature* 108 (1989): 419–44. https://doi.org/10.2307/3267112

Mauss, Marcel. *On Prayer*. Edited by W. S. F. Pickering. Translated by Susan Leslie. New York: Durkheim Press; Oxford: Berghahn Books, 2003.

McCauley, Robert N., and E. Thomas Lawson. *Bringing Ritual to Mind: Psychological Foundations of Cultural Forms*. Cambridge: Cambridge University Press, 2002. https://doi.org/10.1017/CBO9780511606410

Mitchell, Nathan D. *Liturgy and the Social Sciences*. Collegeville, MN: Liturgical, 1999.

Naiden, Fred S. *Ancient Supplication*. New York/Oxford: Oxford University Press, 2006. https://doi.org/10.1093/acprof:oso/9780195183412.001.0001

Neyrey, Jerome H. *Give God the Glory: Ancient Prayer and Worship in Cultural Perspective*. Grand Rapids: Eerdmans, MI, 2007.

Obeyeskere, Gananath. "Medusa's Hair: An Essay on Personal Symbols and Religious Experience," 356–67 in *A Reader in the Anthropology of Religion*. Edited by Michael Lambek. 2nd edn. Malden, MA: Blackwell, 2008.

Penner, Jeremy. *Patterns of Daily Prayer in Second Temple Period Judaism*. Studies of the Texts of the Desert of Judah, 104. Leiden: Brill, 2012. https://doi.org/10.1163/9789004230330

Pulleyn, Simon. *Prayer in Greek Religion*. Oxford: Clarendon, 1997.

Rappaport, Roy A. *Ritual and Religion in the Making of Humanity*. Cambridge Studies in Social and Cultural Anthropology, 110. Cambridge: Cambridge University Press, 1999.

Taves, Ann. *Religious Experience Reconsidered: A Building Block Approach to the Study of Religion and Other Special Things*. Princeton, NJ: Princeton University Press, 2009. https://doi.org/10.1515/9781400830978

Versnel, Henk S. "Religious Mentality in Ancient Prayer," 1–64 in *Faith, Hope, and Worship: Aspects of Religious Mentality in the Ancient World*. Edited by H. S. Versnel. Leiden: Brill, 1981. https://doi.org/10.1163/9789004296695

Werline, Rodney A. "Prayer, Politics, and Power in the Hebrew Bible," *Interpretation* 68 (2014): 5–16. https://doi.org/10.1177/0020964313508738

—"Ritual, Order and the Construction of an Audience in 1 Enoch 1–36," *Dead Sea Discoveries* 22 (2015): 339. https://doi.org/10.1163/15685179-12341365

Whitehouse, Harvey. *Modes of Religiosity: A Cognitive Theory of Religious Transmission*. Oxford: Alta Mira, 2004.

PART II
TEXT AND COGNITION

Chapter Six

Emotional Repression and Physical Mutilation? The Cognitive and Behavioral Impact of Exaggeration in the Sermon on the Mount

Thomas Kazen

Introduction

Jesus' special mode of teaching has always been an important topic in New Testament research and a reason for regarding him as "unique," standing apart from his contemporaries. Such a christologically inspired portrait can be discerned already in the characterizations of the gospel narratives, but attempts to confirm it by appeal to the historical Jesus have been less successful.[1] Although Jesus is portrayed as a popular teacher, even the synoptic programmatic gospel narratives seem to associate Jesus' distinctiveness with authority based on miracles and revelatory deeds rather than on special teaching techniques, at least in Mark (Mark 1.22, 27).[2] His distinctiveness is, in fact, underscored by recurring explicit references and implicit allusions to the prophets, whose style and manners were cherished in collective memory. Much of his claimed "uniqueness" can thus be described as similarity or conformity to a commonly recognized role model, which included a liberal use of startling statements and provocative expressions.[3]

---

1. See for example Robert Banks, *Jesus and the Law in the Synoptic Tradition* (Cambridge: Cambridge University Press, 1975), 262–3. Meier criticizes two centuries of historical Jesus studies for being a "modern form of Christology masquerading as a historical quest." John P. Meier, *A Marginal Jew: Rethinking the Historical Jesus.* Vol. 4: *Law and Love* (Anchor Yale Bible Reference Library; New Haven, CT: Yale University Press, 2009), 6, but see my critique of Meier's own portrayal of Jesus as somehow unique, having "a direct pipeline to God's will." Meier, *Law and Love*, 415; Thomas Kazen, *Issues of Impurity in Early Judaism* (Coniectanea Biblica: New Testament Series, 45; Winona Lake, IN: Eisenbrauns, 2010), 153, 167.

2. Cf. William R. Herzog, *Prophet and Teacher: An Introduction to the Historical Jesus* (Louisville, KY: Westminster John Knox, 2005), 71–98. See also Chris Keith, *Jesus against the Scribal Elite: The Origins of the Conflict* (Grand Rapids, MI: Baker Academic, 2014), who argues that Jesus got into conflict with his adversaries because he acted as if he had "scribal authority" although he was not a recognized teacher.

3. For a discussion about Jesus' authority and (purported) uniqueness as an interpreter of the law versus his prophetic role, see Thomas Kazen, *Scripture, Interpretation,*

Many have pointed to Matthew's emphatic portrayal of Jesus as a superior teacher, or perhaps instructor, as his five commonly acknowledged speech constructions somehow indicate an authoritative interpretation of torah.[4] The Sermon on the Mount has attracted most of the attention in this regard. It is brimful of brash and drastic statements that have disturbed interpreters through centuries and triggered numerous attempts to tone down not only the offence, but also the challenge to a general sense of justice and proportionality, posed by this collection of sayings.[5]

This unease probably explains the more principled discussion about how to classify the ethical stance represented by the Sermon. Does it address particular people in a particular context or does it represent a morality expected of believers in general? Does the Sermon reflect a perfectionist or elitist ideal? Is such an ideal possible or impossible to follow? Does the Sermon, perhaps, reflect an interim ethics in view of the expected imminent end?[6] Many Christian exegetes seem to assume that the most difficult instructions must either be explained away or somehow obeyed. A discussion of the authenticity of specific sayings could perhaps be a resort, but results ironically often favor the difficult sayings.[7] A more common approach is to

---

or Authority: Motives and Arguments in Jesus' Halakic Conflicts (WUNT, 320; Tübingen: Mohr Siebeck, 2013), 293–301. Cf. Thomas Kazen, "The Christology of Early Christian Practice," *Journal of Biblical Literature* 127 (2008): 591–614, on Jesus within the framework of a basic prophet typology.

4. Some connection between the five speeches in Matthew and the Pentateuch has been argued at least since B. W. Bacon, "The 'Five Books' of Moses against the Jews," *Expositor* 15 (1918): 56–66. Cf. William D. Davies, *The Setting of the Sermon on the Mount* (Cambridge: Cambridge University Press, 1964), 14–108. This applies in particular to the Sermon. See Dale C. Allison, *The New Moses: A Matthean Typology* (Edinburgh: T&T Clark, 1993), 72–207. For studies emphasizing Jesus role as a teacher, see for example Samuel Byrskog, *Jesus the Only Teacher: Didactic Authority and Transmission in Ancient Israel, Ancient Judaism and the Matthean Community*, (Coniectanea Biblica: New Testament Series, 24; Stockholm: Almqvist & Wiksell International, 1994); Pheme Perkins, *Jesus as Teacher* (Understanding Jesus Today; Cambridge: Cambridge University Press, 1990).

5. For a brief history of interpretation and a discussion of the Sermon's impossible and provocative character, see Ingo Broer, "Die Weisung der Bergpredigt und die Verantwortung der Christen," in *Er stieg auf den Berg ... und lehrte sie (Mt 5,1f.): Exegetische und rezeptionsgeschichtliche Studien zur Bergpredigt*, ed. Hans-Ulrich Weidemann (Stuttgarter Bibelstudien, 226; Stuttgart: Verlag Katholisches Bibelwerk, 2012), 11–24.

6. These basic alternatives were succinctly summarized by Joachim Jeremias, *The Sermon on the Mount* (Facet Books, Biblical Series; Philadelphia, PA: Fortress, 1963 [German 1959]). Harvey K. McArthur presents 12 possible approaches in *Understanding the Sermon on the Mount* (London: Epworth, 1960), 105–27.

7. A quick glance at The Jesus Seminar's *Five Gospels* confirms this. Robert W.

question the literal character of the language and suggest that Jesus, or Matthew, or Q, was speaking figuratively.[8]

To some degree, most interpreters acknowledge the figurative character of the Sermon's language. Among the earliest, John Chrysostom warned against hyperbolical interpretations of the Sermon: Jesus raised the threat of Gehenna because he foreknew that many people would be lax and view some sayings as mere hyperbole. Some even take the prohibition against calling a brother "fool" hyperbolically. "But," says Chrysostom, "I fear that after having misled ourselves by words here, we might suffer the final punishment in deeds there." He further asserts: "Do not therefore think that these sayings are of some hyperbolic sort (*mē toinyn hyperbolēs tinos einai nomize ta legomena*)."[9] McArthur, who refers to Chrysostom, reflects some of Chrysostom's hesitance although he clearly acknowledges the presence of hyperbole in the Sermon.

> Unfortunately there is no objective standard by which hyperbolic and non-hyperbolic statements may be distinguished ... The rigid denial of any hyperbolic element would make interpretation virtually impossible; yet a widespread use of this explanation could reduce the entire Sermon to a series of commonplaces expressed in dramatic and hyperbolic form.[10]

And a little later he confirms that "[i]f the Sermon is to be appropriated it must be recognized that there is an element of *hyperbole* in its statements. But this must not be so stressed that the demands lose their radical character."[11]

This comment is fairly representative of how New Testament scholars deal with the Sermon. The use of hyperbole and metaphor is often mentioned, but rarely seriously considered.[12] While McArthur is right that there are no "objective standards," there are indeed linguistic theories and

---

Funk, Roy W. Hoover, and the Jesus Seminar, *The Five Gospels: What Did Jesus Really Say? The Search for the Authentic Words of Jesus* (San Francisco, CA: HarperCollins, 1993). Part of the explanation is certainly the emphasis on the so-called criterion of dissimilarity in traditional Jesus research.

8. See for example McArthur (*Understanding the Sermon*, 109–11) on the "hyperbole view."

9. John Chrysostom, *Homilies on St. Matthew* XVI, in J.-P. Migne, ed., *Patrologiae cursus completus: Series graeca*, 57 (Paris: J.-P. Migne, 1860), 248, 250.

10. McArthur, *Understanding the Sermon*, 141.

11. McArthur, *Understanding the Sermon*, 148.

12. "Seriously" would in this case often mean acknowledging the *humor* of the saying. Cf. Maurice Casey, *Jesus of Nazareth: An Independent Historian's Account of His Life and Teaching* (London: T&T Clark, 2010), 289–94, who sees jokes in the Sermon and points out that both Christian tradition and modern scholars would have avoided a lot of problems had they taken some of Jesus' teaching less literally.

research on figurative language, its purpose, use, and effects, which could help us gauge the subjective meanings invested in and appropriated through non-literal expressions.[13]

Unfortunately, this is a route rarely taken by interpreters of the Sermon. When it comes to hyperbole, a simple dichotomy between literal and figurative language does not suffice. As the numerous attempts to wrestle with the literal sense of the Sermon's sayings attest, it is exactly the literal imagery that catches attention, and unless these expressions are examples of failed communication, we must conclude that the shock, offence, or surprise of the literal imagery is exactly what is intended. As we will see, however, this is not tantamount to a literal meaning.

In the present chapter, I will explore the character of hyperbole further and interpret its use and effects in the Sermon, taking into account its relationship to literal use, extreme case formulation, and metaphor, with the help of cognitive linguistics, including blending theory, and relevance theory. I will first discuss hyperbole from a theoretical perspective. The insights gained will then be applied to examples of exaggeration in the Sermon on the Mount.

Understanding Hyperbole

Exaggeration, understood as excessive representation, can reflect various kinds of cognitive apprehensions or even misapprehensions of reality. It can result from cognitive distortion, pathological conditions, conventions, or from a perfectly rational wish to communicate. Exaggeration can be used for persuasive, humorous, manipulating, defensive, or aggrandizing purposes.

Definitions

Hyperbole as a rhetorical figure of speech is a particular kind of exaggeration that is used for rhetorical purposes. Rather than indicating a pathological mind, hyperbole must be understood as a communicative strategy. But it is more than that. It is also a cognitive capacity, a way of thinking and imagining. Although exaggeration at first sight distorts reality, the use of hyperbole should not necessarily be understood that way, even if this is exactly how the imagery evoked by hyperbole could be described.

A simple definition of hyperbole is that it "exceeds the (credible) limits of fact in the given context."[14] However, its purpose is not to deceive, as

---

13. For a recent study, see Claudia Claridge, *Hyperbole in English: A Corpus-Based Study of Exaggeration* (Cambridge: University Press, 2011).
14. Claridge, *Hyperbole in English*, 5.

the intended meaning is not identical to the literal meaning of a hyperbolic expression. Instead it results from the contrast between a literal expression which is usually not verbalized (i.e., what actually happened, or an objective fact) and the literal meaning of the hyperbole. What happens between those two is that the contrast, if sufficient, will trigger what Claridge calls "the transferred interpretation,"[15] which takes up a middle position. This transferred interpretation, or meaning, is inferred from the context or at times has to be chosen from a number of available meanings. In any case, hyperbole carries an evaluative and/or emotional component and transmits a subjective meaning.[16] It evokes emotional reaction and facilitates recipients' appropriation or acceptance of the message, including an appropriate behavioral response.

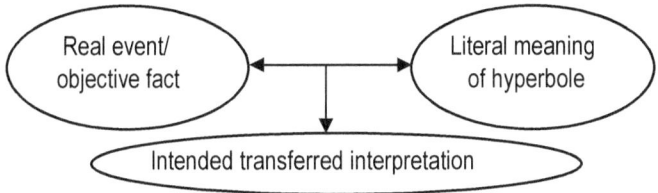

Figure 1. Simplified model of hyperbole (cf. Claridge).

Claridge's model may be compared to the theory of conceptual blending.[17] According to blending theory, our mental representations function within mental spaces or frames, which relate to various cognitive domains and form a network. Such mental spaces can, if they have shared characteristics (called generic space), be combined into a new, blended space, in which certain elements from one input space are mixed with elements from the other. This results in a new conceptual framework and new meaning, which lead to new integrated action.[18] In the case of hyperbole we can think of the

15. Claridge, *Hyperbole in English*, 37.
16. Claridge, *Hyperbole in English*, 37–9.
17. For an introduction, see Gilles Fauconnier and Mark Turner, *The Way We Think: Conceptual Blending and the Mind's Hidden Complexities* (New York: Basic Books, 2002), 17–57; Seanna Coulson and Todd Oakley, "Blending Basics," *Cognitive Linguistics* 11 (2000): 175–96. For an application of blending theory in biblical interpretation, see Thomas Kazen, "The Role of Disgust in Priestly Purity Law: Insights from Conceptual Metaphor and Blending Theories," *Journal of Law, Religion and State* 3 (2014): 62–92.
18. Blends are first and foremost conceptual constructs, being expressed in language. In one of Fauconnier and Turner's introductory examples, a ski instructor compares skiing to a Parisian waiter moving between the tables with a tray, without spilling

(unspoken) literal "expression" or the "real event" and the literal image of the (spoken) hyperbole[19] as two input spaces, creating the blended space of the transferred interpretation,[20] in which the event, fact, or experience is loaded with emotion, intensity, saliency, and subjective evaluation. While only certain aspects of the hyperbole are taken up, these may influence the character of the event or expression to the extent that it is experienced as something rather new or different. As a consequence, the worldview and actions of the recipients will be affected.

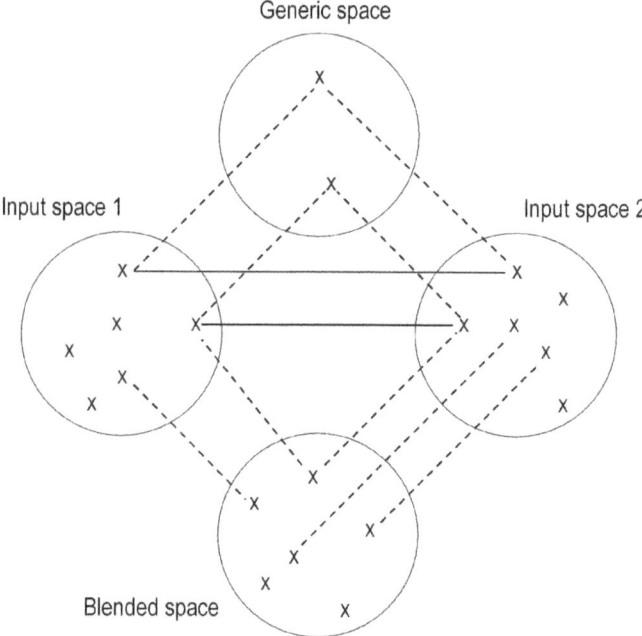

Figure 2. Basic model of blending (cf. Fauconnier and Turner)

Although the resulting blend is thought of as a new space rather than a middle position, both models emphasize the *modified meaning* and *action-oriented*

(*The Way We Think*, 21–2). The integrated action that follows by appropriating this blend is not equal to the sum of its part, but only incorporates certain aspects, while leaving others out. The result nevertheless transcends the parts.

19. That is, the hyperbolic expression in its literal meaning. See Claridge, *Hyperbole*, 27.

20. That is, the hyperbolic expression in its intended transferred interpretation. See Claridge, *Hyperbole*, 27.

effects, resulting from the combination of diverse conceptual frameworks. I use these models heuristically and make no attempt to harmonize them.

Hyperbole as Figurative Language

Literary and rhetorical tropes, including figurative modes of language, have been classified and discussed since the ancient Greeks. Aristotle speaks of four types of metaphor,[21] but uses "metaphor" generically for various forms of figurative language, including simile, hyperbole, and metonymy. Such tropes have in common their non-literal character. Similes and metaphors both employ comparison, in the former case explicitly and in the latter case usually by referring to one thing as another. Instead in metonymy, a thing is referred to by one of its attributes and in irony, the opposite of what is meant is being said. In none of these cases are we supposed to take the trope literally. This is true of hyperbole as well.

Although not *meant* literally, figurative language depends on shared characteristics (generic space) of the figure's literal referent and its figurative referent (input spaces). The literal *imagery* is exactly what evokes the non-literal meaning (blended space) and gives it emphasis. This may be what Aristotle is referring to, when he says that "witticisms are expressed through proportional metaphor and by setting things before the eye" (*ta asteia ek metaphoras te tēs analogon legetai kai tō pro ommatōn poiein*).[22] The point is to signify *energeia*, which Freese in Loeb translates as "actuality," but might be better rendered as "vividness."[23] In the case of hyperbole this is exactly the point, since exaggeration often shocks the recipients, alerts them to the importance of the message and invites them to take it more seriously and act accordingly.

Hyperbole expresses surprise by "*inflat[ing]* the discrepancy between what was expected and what ensues via an overstated description of what happened."[24] Experiments have shown that hyperbole is especially effective in expressing surprise when speaker expectations are not made explicit beforehand.[25] They also show that in the case of an unexpected event, the same degree of surprise can be expressed by a slight hyperbole as by an extreme

---

21. Aristotle, *Poetics* xxi.7-15 (1457b); *Rhetoric* III.ii.7-15; x.7–xi.16 (1405a-b; 1410b-3b). Greek text from J. H. Freese (transl.), *Aristotle: Art of Rhetoric* (LCL, 193; Cambridge, MA: Harvard University Press, 1926).

22. Aristotle, *Rhetoric* III.xi.1 (1411b); cf. Aristotle, *Rhetoric* III.ii.13 (1405b).

23. Aristotle, *Rhetoric* III.xi.2-4 (1411b-2a).

24. Herbert L. Colston and Shauna B. Keller, "You'll Never Believe This: Irony and Hyperbole in Expressing Surprise," *Journal of Psycholinguistic Research* 27 (1998): 499–513, 500.

25. Colston and Keller, "You'll Never Believe This," 502–6.

and impossible one.²⁶ At the same time, the range of inflation helps recipients to interpret the degree of surprise expressed by the speaker correctly, or, in more general terms, the relative strength of emotional involvement and emphasis invested by the speaker in a hyperbolic statement. Extreme hyperboles are thus rhetorically efficient even if not necessary to express the speaker's degree of engagement. The degree of inflation is more significant for the comprehension (effect) of hyperbole than for its production.²⁷

Now and then figurative language turns into conventional idioms and thus becomes "dead."²⁸ When "dead" hyperbolic idioms are used to express what is more or less expected, they neither signal surprise, nor do they have any considerable effect on the recipients.²⁹

True or False?

Aristotle suggests that the use of hyperbole is characteristic for young people (*eisi de hyperbolai meirakiōdes*) and expresses vehemence (*sphodrotēta gar dēlousin*).³⁰ His vocabulary suggests disapproval, and this is confirmed by the subsequent comment that the use of hyperbole is unseemly for older people (*dio presbyterō legein aprepes*).³¹ Although Aristotle's judgment on figurative language in general is not negative, he sometimes calls metaphors obscure speech (*metaphorai gar ainittontai*)³² and regards their use as ornamentation (*kosmein*).³³ He also indicates that this type of language is not truthful: most witticisms come from metaphor and from deception (*esti de kai ta asteia ta pleista dia metaphoras kai ek tou proexapatan*).³⁴ This is not in itself taken as a negative, but rather as a pedagogical method to lead the hearer to understanding by thwarting expectations.

Quintilian similarly characterizes hyperbole as "an elegant straining of the truth" (*decens veri superiectio*). With the use of hyperbole we say more

---

26. Colston and Keller, "You'll Never Believe This," 506–8.
27. Colston and Keller, "You'll Never Believe This," 508–11; cf. Claridge, *Hyperbole*, 7–12.
28. Michael McCarthy and Ronald Carter, "'There's Millions of Them': Hyperbole in Everyday Conversation," *Journal of Pragmatics* 36 (2004): 149–84, 151.
29. Hyperbolic sense can actually be(come) one conventional sense of a word, resulting in a dead metaphor (Claridge, *Hyperbole*, 32). "The more conventional a hyperbolic interpretation is, the weaker will be its emotional impact" (p. 37).
30. Aristotle, *Rhetoric* III.xi.16 (1413a).
31. Aristotle, *Rhetoric* III.xi.16 (1413b).
32. Aristotle, *Rhetoric* III.ii.12 (1405b).
33. Aristotle, *Rhetoric* III.ii.10 (1405a).
34. Aristotle, *Rhetoric* III.xi.6 (1412a).

than actual facts allow (*plus facto dicimus*).³⁵ Quintilian warns against going too far with hyperbole, since "*hyperbole lies, though without any intention to deceive*" (*mentiri hyperbolen nec ita, ut mendacio fallere velit*).³⁶ He explains its use by ordinary and uneducated people:

> ... everybody has an innate passion for exaggeration or attenuation of actual facts, and no one is ever contented with the simple truth. But such disregard of truth is pardonable, for it does not involve the definite assertion of the thing that is not. *Hyperbole* is, moreover, a virtue, when the subject on which we speak is abnormal. For we are allowed to amplify, when the magnitude of the facts passes all words, and in such circumstances our language will be more effective if it goes beyond the truth than if it falls short of it.³⁷

The ambivalence is obvious and it regularly recurs in traditional approaches to metaphor in general and hyperbole in particular, ever since. An understanding of hyperbole as unreliable or untruthful also characterizes some modern linguistic theories, such as David Lewis's convention of truthfulness,³⁸ or the highly influential pragmatics of Paul Grice.³⁹ According to Grice's theory of *conversational implicature*, people expect other participants in a conversation to behave according to certain maxims (quantity, quality, relation, and manner). Although a speaker can occasionally flout a maxim as part of the game, understanding and interpretation generally depend on participants following the rules. Of these, the maxim of quality suggests that speakers are truthful and respect evidence. Irony, metaphor, and hyperbole are examples of flouting the maxim of quality by introducing a categorical falsity.⁴⁰ Applied to hyperbole, Grice's approach suggests that as people encounter a statement, they first assume a literal meaning,

---

35. Quintilian, *Institutio oratoria* VII.vi.67-68. Latin text and translation from Donald A. Russell (ed. and transl.), *Quintilian: The Orator's Education*. Volume III: *Books 6–8* (LCL, 126; Cambridge, MA: Harvard University Press, 2002).
36. Quintilian, *Institutio oratoria* VII.vi.74
37. Quintilian, *Institutio oratoria* VII.vi.75-76 (... *natura est omnibus augendi res vel minuendi cupiditas insita, nec quisquam vero contentus est. Sec ignoscitur, quia non adfirmamus. Tum est hyperbole virtus, com res ipsa, de qua loquendum est, naturalem modum excessit. Conceditur enim amplius dicere, quia dici quantum est, non potest, meliusque ultra quam citra stat oratio*).
38. David K. Lewis, *Convention: A Philosophical Study* (Cambridge, MA: Harvard University Press, 1969); David K. Lewis, "Languages and Language," in *Language, Mind, and Knowledge*, ed. K. Gunderson. (Minnesota Studies in the Philosophy of Science, 7; Minneapolis, MN: University of Minnesota Press, 1975), 3–35.
39. Paul Grice, *Studies in the Way of Words* (Harvard, MA: Harvard University Press, 1989).
40. Grice, *Studies in the Way of Words*, 22–40.

and only if this violates the maxim of quality (truthfulness) do they try out a hyperbolic or metaphorical interpretation.[41]

In recent years, Gricean theory has frequently been criticized. Deirdre Wilson points out that

> traditional approaches to metaphor ... have been increasingly questioned on both theoretical and experimental grounds. Where traditional approaches treat metaphor as departure from a maxim, norm or convention of literal truthfulness, there is a growing consensus that the Romantic critics of classical rhetoric were right to see metaphor as entirely normal, natural and pervasive in language. Where traditional approaches treat metaphor as a purely decorative device with little or no cognitive significance, it is increasingly recognised that most metaphors cannot be paraphrased in literal terms without loss to the meaning.[42]

Deirdre Wilson and Dan Sperber suggest that verbal communication is governed more by expectations of relevance (explained below) than by expectations of truthfulness. Although "hearers expect to be informed and not mislead ... what is communicated is not the same as what is said."[43] Wilson and Sperber point out that although both Lewis and Grice are aware of counterexamples, such as irony and metaphor, where the maxim of truthfulness is flouted, they regard these as departures from literal meaning.[44] Wilson and Sperber demonstrate through numerous examples from "loose talk" that comprehension and communication are often more effectively facilitated by statements that are rough approximations than by strictly true ones. While "I haven't eaten" would by necessity always be untrue if taken strictly literally, it is not misleading as a reply to an invitation for supper. And while "Holland is flat" is strictly untrue, in a certain context it is more relevant and communicates better than a detailed description of the country's topography.[45]

The latter example can either be taken as an approximation ("loose talk" or "loose use") or as a hyperbole. Few people would in fact take "Holland is flat" entirely literally. It is usually understood in a comparative sense, but in a very specific context it could also be understood metaphorically (referring to something else than topography). This illustrates that the meaning of a statement always depends on an implicit contract between speaker and

---

41. Deirdre Wilson, "Parallels and Differences in the Treatment of Metaphor in Relevance Theory and Cognitive Linguistics," *Studia Linguistica Universitatis Iagellonicae Cracoviensis* 128 (2011): 195–213, 206.
42. Wilson, "Parallels," 195–6.
43. Deirdre Wilson and Dan Sperber, "Truthfulness and Relevance," *Mind* 111.443 (2002): 583–632, 583.
44. Wilson and Sperber, "Truthfulness and Relevance," 586–8.
45. Wilson and Sperber, "Truthfulness and Relevance," 592–612.

hearer (or writer and reader), a sharing of mutual expectations, which is informed and shaped by contextual factors.

Rather than assuming a literal interpretation as the default position and moving along a scale of figurative options only if forced to, people usually seem to pick up the relevant level intuitively. In this sense, neither loose talk, nor hyperbole, should be seen as departures from truthful statements. They "involve no violation of any maxim, but are merely alternative routes to achieving optimal relevance."[46] Literal is not equivalent to true.

Relevance

The examples above suggest that hyperbole, like other types of figurative language, is highly context-dependent, both with regard to production and reception. This leads us to consider relevance theory.[47] From a cognitive linguistic perspective, metaphor, including hyperbole, is natural in language because it is pervasive in human thought. According to the commonly known conceptual metaphor theory of George Lakoff and Mark Johnson, our conceptual mappings between different cognitive domains are primary and we use metaphors in language because this is the way we think. Metaphors are not created or do not evolve for the sake of communication, but reflect human experience of being in the world.[48]

Relevance theory, on the other hand, understands metaphor as naturally evolving in intra-human communication in order to express and explain vague and complex thoughts, which in themselves are not necessarily metaphorical. Sperber and Wilson regard metaphor as a continuous range of figures with the literal at one end and hyperbole somewhere along the scale.[49]

Although the two approaches take different perspectives, Wilson suggests that they are complementary. To use one of Wilson's examples, the statement "John is a giant" could, from the perspective of conceptual metaphor theory, be taken metaphorically (e.g., a great scholar [success is size]) or hyperbolically (very tall). The difference would be an increase in quality

---

46. Cf. Deirdre Wilson and Dan Sperber, "Relevance Theory," in *The Handbook of Pragmatics*, ed. L. R. Horn and G. Ward (Oxford: Blackwell, 2004), 607–32. The exact formulation does not appear in the printed version (619), but in the pre-publication version on Sperber's homepage (http://www.dan.sperber.fr/?p=93).

47. For a description of relevance theory, see Wilson and Sperber, "Relevance Theory," and "Truthfulness and Relevance," 600–12.

48. Wilson, "Parallels," 196; cf. George Lakoff and Mark Johnson, *Metaphors We Live By* (Chicago, IL: University of Chicago Press, 1980).

49. Dan Sperber and Deirdre Wilson, "A Deflationary Account of Metaphors," in *The Cambridge Handbook of Metaphor and Thought*, ed. Raymond W. Gibbs Jr. (Cambridge: Cambridge University Press, 2008), 84–105, 84.

as compared to quantity, but metaphors and hyperboles are analyzed in the same way. However, while the metaphor reflects a cross-domain mapping, the hyperbole does not.[50] From the perspective of relevance theory, on the other hand, the context normally provides clues that make some interpretations more relevant than others. For example, the statement "I slept fairly well most of the time" would be understood differently after getting up in the morning, disembarking an aeroplane, or leaving a lecture hall. Lexical meaning is adjusted to satisfy expectations of relevance and a single statement can be intended and understood in a multitude of ways along a continuous scale.[51]

One of Wilson's points is that we will go for a loose interpretation that satisfies our expectations of relevance without even considering a literal one first.[52] Perhaps one could say that while cognitive linguistics explains how metaphors are shaped in our minds through mappings across domains and through blending, we need to consider expectations of relevance in order to understand how speakers and hearers intuitively come to mean the same thing, "distinguishing mere conceptual associations or co-activations from valid inferences," as Wilson expresses it.[53] For our understanding of hyperbole, this suggests that factors such as context and relevance are crucial for deciding whether a statement is meant—and/or understood—as literal, approximate, hyperbolic, ironic, or metaphorical. This will be further explored as we interpret the Sermon.

Interaction, Emotion, and Humor

Aristotle's understanding of metaphor as ornamentation has been influential in literary criticism, where the aesthetic qualities of figurative language are emphasized. From this angle, the role of hyperbole would mainly be to embellish and beautify.[54] Today many linguistic theorists claim otherwise. Laura Cano Mora states:

> Rather than embellishments of ordinary literal language with little cognitive value of their own, hyperboles should be viewed as powerful communicative and conceptual tools. This adheres to a prevailing view among figurative language researchers: figures provide part of the figurative foundation for everyday thought.[55]

---

50. Wilson, "Parallels," 201.
51. Sperber and Wilson, "A Deflationary Account," 201–2.
52. Sperber and Wilson, "A Deflationary Account," 206–7.
53. Sperber and Wilson, "A Deflationary Account," 211.
54. Laura Cano Mora, "All or Nothing: A Semantic Analysis of Hyperbole," *Revista de Lingüística y Lenguas Aplicadas* 4 (2009): 25–35, 26.
55. Cano Mora, "All or Nothing," 34.

After examining a large number of examples of hyperbole in the British National Corpus, Cano Mora emphasizes the emotional factor involved in hyperbole and concludes that it is "a powerful tool for subjective evaluation." Although seemingly focusing more on quantity than on value, hyperbole "should be viewed as a general evaluative resource."[56] Referring to a number of other studies, Claridge similarly points to hyperbole as encoding and transporting emotional attitude. When speakers talk of their own emotions, they regularly use a high amount of figurative language and when emotionally involved they often use hyperbole. Hyperbole can sometimes convey emotional nuance better than literal language.[57]

In addition to this subjective function, there are also interactional aspects of hyperbole expressing emotion.[58] Michael McCarthy and Ronald Carter have stressed the importance of interaction between speaker and listener and argue that hyperbole cannot be fully understood apart from the interactive dimension. It is more than a creative act of the speaker; the listener's contributions are crucial. Like Cano Mora, McCarthy and Carter point to the evaluative context of hyperbole. It both expresses and is received as emotional meaning.[59] By describing the world in disproportionate dimension (rather than "lying"!), hyperbole structures reality according to one out of many possible accounts and brings listeners into a particular perspective.[60]

Hyperbole is thus a powerful tool to promote interaction. From their examination of the CANCODE corpus (Cambridge and Nottingham corpus of Discourse in English), McCarthy and Carter conclude that the interactive character of hyperbole can be clearly observed from numerous expressions of listener involvement and markers.[61]

Examination of hyperbole in interactive contexts also underlines the expressive and interpersonal meanings foregrounded in its use: intensification, humor and banter, empathy, solidarity, antipathy, informality and intimacy, along with evaluative and persuasive goals, are all recurrent features.[62]

Like many other rhetorical figures, hyperbole is intimately associated with human affect. It is caused by, expresses, and effects emotions, as part of an interactive communicative act between speaker and listener.[63]

---

56. Cano Mora, "All or Nothing," 32, 33.
57. Claridge, *Hyperbole*, 74–91.
58. Cf. Claridge, *Hyperbole*, 130–69.
59. McCarthy and Carter, "Millions," 153.
60. McCarthy and Carter, "Millions," 152.
61. McCarthy and Carter, "Millions," 175.
62. McCarthy and Carter, "Millions," 176.
63. For considering the relation of rhetorical figures to emotions, see also Brian

An important aspect of the emotional expression in rhetorical figures is humor. This is true of hyperbole in particular. The humorous aspects of hyperbole have partly to do with its scalar character, meaning that it presents something as being much further along a scale (either larger or smaller) than it actually is, in order to emphasize the direction. Rita Brdar-Szabó and Mario Brdar demonstrate how the upper and lower ends of the scale function like metonyms for the whole scale, in hyperbolic communication, so that large (or small) numbers and absolute expressions like "millions," "the whole world," or "no one" are used for emphasis.[64] Scalar humor is well known and often used. Benjamin Bergen and Kim Binsted argue that

> there is nothing structurally special about these utterances. They use an existing phrasal construction that has an inference built into it. They abuse that inference through the use of imagery, metaphor, and other general-purpose cognitive mechanisms. The resulting mismatch between the hearer's expectations about the utterance and its actual realization, as well as the imagery evoked, are the very things that make the utterances funny.[65]

Scalar humor underscores rather than obscures the message. As we now turn to the Jesus tradition and the Sermon on the Mount, we will see that humor plays a larger role than is often acknowledged.

The Sermon on the Mount

Hyperbole in the Jesus Tradition

The Jesus tradition contains a fair number of harsh and exaggerated sayings, and hyperbolic language is more common than is often acknowledged.[66] Examples of exaggeration are perhaps most frequent in Q material, as the double tradition mainly consists of logia. However, hyperbole and other examples of excessive figurative language are equally found in Mark (and

---

Vickers, "Repetition and Emphasis in Rhetoric: Theory and Practice," in *Repetition*, ed. Andreas Fischer (SPELL, 7; Tübingen: Gunter Narr Verlag, 1994), 85–114, 85–90.

64. Rita Brdar-Szabó and Mario Brdar, "Scalar Model in a Cognitive Approach to Hyperbolic Expressions: With a Little Help from Metonymy," in *Pragmatics Today*, ed. Piotr Cap (Łódź Studies in Language, 12; Frankfurt am Main: Peter Lang, 2005), 75–94, 82–93.

65. Benjamin Bergen and Kim Binsted, "The Cognitive Linguistics of Scalar Humor," in *Language, Culture and Mind*, ed. Michel Achard and Suzanne Kemmer (Stanford, CA: CSLI Publications, 2004), 79–92, 81.

66. Allison regards hyperbole as one of eight prominent features of the sayings tradition. Dale C. Allison, *Jesus of Nazareth: Millenarian Prophet* (Minneapolis, MN: Fortress, 1998), 49–50.

thus in the triple tradition) as well as in the special material of Matthew and Luke.

A classic example from Markan tradition is the camel through the needle's eye (Mark 10.23-27 pars), which still keeps cartoonists busy as they visualize the literal aspects of this grotesque hyperbole. From the double tradition we could mention the hatred of family and even of one's own life (Q 14.25-27), which Matthew slightly softens to make it more palatable (Matt. 10.37-39). And as for special material, Luke's parable of the prodigal son could provide an example, when the father talks of his son as dead and alive again (Luke 15.24, 32). The latter also nicely illustrates the relationship between metaphor and hyperbole, as "dead" and "alive" belong to a different domain of discourse (biological life), but are here taken over and employed in another domain (lost objects/missing people).

The Sermon on the Mount contains a large number of hyperboles and hyperbolic expressions. In the following, hyperboles in the Sermon will be analyzed in view of the cognitive linguistic perspectives discussed above. We will proceed section by section, but give little room for those in which hyperbolic language is missing or unlikely, and obvious hyperboles will receive less attention than more complicated examples.

The Beatitudes

The beatitudes or makarisms (Matt. 5.1-12) are built on contrasts, some of which have the character of overstatement, exaggeration, irony, or paradox. This is particularly the case with the first (poor), second (mourning), and fourth (hungry). The eighth (persecuted) is paradoxical, too, although it is in the subsequent elaboration (5.11-12) that the exaggerated character stands out clearly, as the contents of persecution are spelled out in a way that becomes completely incompatible with any reasonable definition of "blessedness." The other beatitudes (the third, fifth, sixth, and seventh) lack this contrast.

Whether we should speak of hyperbole in the beatitudes is open to discussion, since the contrast also involves a temporal aspect: most of the verbs are in the future tense and one might argue that the blessedness referred to does not describe the present state but the expected future.[67] However, the first and eighth beatitudes suggest that the poor and the persecuted[68] are

---

67. Luke has even added *nyn* to his second and third beatitude, which further emphasizes the temporal contrast.

68. Present, not expected persecution; see Robert A. Guelich, *The Sermon on the Mount: A Foundation for Understanding* (Waco, TX: Word Books, 1982), 93; Hans Dieter Betz, *The Sermon on the Mount: A Commentary on the Sermon on the Mount,*

already blessed since the kingdom is theirs (*hoti autōn estin hē basileia tōn ouranōn*). It would be anachronistic to interpret the kingdom in an entirely futuristic sense;[69] in fact, Matthew's Jesus also proclaims that the kingdom has approached or is at hand (Matt. 4.17; cf. 10.7). The "ninth" beatitude, explicating the eighth (Matt. 5.11) depicts blessedness as simultaneous with persecution (*makarioi este hotan* ...). Although future heavenly reward is seen as the *reason* for joy (*hoti* ...), it must be called hyperbolic to describe the situation of being persecuted and abused as a blessed state.

Hence the first, second, fourth, and eighth (including the ninth) beatitudes function hyperbolically. The poor (*hoi ptōchoi*), the mourning (*hoi penthountes*), and the hungry (*hoi peinōntes*) cannot be expected to receive power, comfort, and satisfaction. Their situation is unequivocally understood to be negative. To call these categories blessed (*makarioi*) breaks with expectation and inflates the discrepancy between expectation and outcome. To some degree, this is toned down by Matthew's additions, which are not found in Luke and unlikely to have been in Q (6.20b-21). To Luke's (presumably Q's) "poor," Matthew adds "in spirit" (*tō pneumati*);[70] "the weeping" (*hoi klaiontes*) in Luke are by Matthew called mourning, and they will be comforted, rather than laugh (*gelasete*), as in Luke; and to those who "hunger," Matthew adds "and thirst for righteousness" (*kai dipsōntes tēn dikaiosynēn*). All of these adjustments soften the three hyperbolic statements, and reduce their contrast with the remaining Matthean beatitudes, which are not found in Luke.

Several explanations for Matthew's move are possible. The relative wealth and comfort of the Matthean church has been argued by some interpreters.[71] More frequently, commentators suggest that Matthew's socio-economic or political consciousness was weaker than Luke's, or that Matthew's interpretation is ethicizing or spiritualizing.[72] In any case, the elements of Matthean

---

including the Sermon on the Plain (Matthew 5:3–7:27 and Luke 6:20–49) (Hermeneia; Minneapolis, MN: Fortress, 1995), 146.

69. Cf. William D. Davies and Dale C. Allison, *A Critical and Exegetical Commentary on the Gospel according to Saint Matthew.* Vol. 1: *Introduction and Commentary on Matthew I-VII* (International Critical Commentary; Edinburgh: T&T Clark, 1988), 446.

70. For a discussion of the meaning of this idiom, see Guelich, *Sermon on the Mount*, 67–75.

71. Aaron M. Gale, *Redefining Ancient Borders: The Jewish Scribal Framework of Matthew's Gospel* (New York: T&T Clark, 2005).

72. See Davies and Allison, *Commentary*, 439; Ulrich Luz, *Matthew 1–7: A Commentary* (Minneapolis, MN: Augsburg, 1989 [German 1985]), 231–2. Davies and Allison are, however, hesitant to call Matthew's interpretation spiritualizing (*Commentary*, 442–4; 451–3), as is Guelich (*Sermon on the Mount*, 87). Betz (*Sermon*, 111–9) also denies a "spiritualization," but theologizes the blessing of the poor, partly with the

redaction are conspicuous as they often seem to intervene or meddle with the intuitive agreement, between speaker and audience, about the contextually relevant level of figurative language that we have discussed. The additions can be understood to partly direct recipients away from the most immediate hyperbolic options, and thereby, perhaps, away from the critical evaluation of poverty and depravity which the strong hyperboles in a tentative Q version indicate.

As in the previous examples, persecution in the eighth beatitude cannot be expected to constitute a blessed state, but what follows (*autōn estin hē basileia tōn ouranōn*) is modelled on the first beatitude and must be understood as Matthean redaction to form an inclusio. It also introduces the subsequent Q saying on persecution in a manner analogous to the preceding eight (*makarioi hoi ...*). In this way, the "ninth" beatitude, which is different in form, becomes an explication of the eighth, and labeled under persecution, while in Luke it stands by itself. Here too, Luke's version is more drastic in its contrasts by using strong and unexpected language (*misēsōsin ... ekbalōsin ... skirtēsate*). The imagery evoked of believers leaping around in joy becomes almost absurd and adds to the emotional force of the saying. The near-comical *imagery* that Luke's version conjures up clearly indicates the non-literal *intended meaning* of the hyperbolic expressions. As the literal images of jumping and laughing are blended with the (unspoken) experience of something quite the opposite, an emotion-laden and highly challenging third, blended space of transferred interpretation is created. In this blend recipients can value themselves within a completely different perspective as uniquely chosen by God, and in which the presently experienced reality is structured according to a different narrative. As in the previous examples, this is somewhat obscured in Matthew. The effect is that recipients cannot be as certain about the intent of the Matthean beatitudes.

It is conspicuous that the Matthean sayings missing from Luke are exactly those that are not based on hyperbole: the meek will inherit the earth, the merciful will receive mercy, the pure in heart will see God, and the peacekeepers will be called God's sons. It is only consistent with this pattern that the Matthean redactions of clearly hyperbolic common sayings serve to make them less extreme. The net effect is that the audience might not intuitively hit the right figurative option or most relevant level instantly, but begins to negotiate with a range of possible meanings. This effect is, in fact, exactly what reception history shows. In a sense we could say that

---

help of Greek philosophy, to speak of the human condition, and associates hunger and thirst for righteousness to an insight into, and wish to overcome, this human condition (*Sermon*, 129–32).

the Matthean redactional layer has obscured the "speaker's level," so that there is no one intended level of figurative meaning for intuition to connect to. This is not to say that Luke or Q are necessarily closer to the narrative speaker, Jesus, but the Lukan version, which I take to be closer to Q, is considerably more univocal.

The beatitudes thus become an example of an originally hyperbolic and emotional plea for a radical reversal of the present order, intuitively understood, influencing behavior, and inducing action, which has through Matthew's redaction been turned into paraenetic moral instruction. Since many of the blessed categories in Matthew are clearly meant to be taken literally and others are explicitly modified, the hyperboles can easily be interpreted along a continuum of figurative meanings, as loose talk, approximation, or even as literal statements. While this broadens the beatitudes' possible range of application, there is a certain risk that even mourning and maltreatment can come to be regarded as blessed states when contrasts are obscured.

Salt and Light

The following two sayings, about salt (5.13) and light (5.14-16), both evoke images that go against general expectation. The juxtaposition of these two sayings is the work of Matthean redaction. Both have corresponding sayings in Mark (9.49-50; 4.21). At the same time, both Matthew and Luke expand the Markan *Vorlage*.

In the saying about salt, Matthew and Luke share a few traits in common, which are not in Mark. Both use the verb *mōranthē* to describe the salt's loss of taste, against the Markan *analon genētai*, and both add that such salt is good for nothing, but thrown out (*blēthen exō* / *exō ballousin*).[73] The metaphorical character of "salt" is evident in Mark, who introduces this saying with "for everyone will be salted with fire" (9.49). Matthew's adaptation rather turns the metaphor into a simile: "you are the salt of the earth" (5.13). The Markan version talks of salt becoming "unsalty" (*analon*) (9.50), which is contradictory and thus shocking. Matthew's (and Luke's, hence probably Q's) *mōranthē* ("become foolish, insipid") softens the contrast somewhat and opens up for loose, approximate, or even literal interpretations. Commentators have excelled in explaining various ways in which salt was used in the ancient world and how it could or could not lose its taste, so as to become useless.[74] Some refer to salt from the Dead Sea containing only a

---

73. This could be explained in a number of ways, but most probably as a Markan-Q overlap. Luke clearly conflates the version he shares with Matthew and the Markan version.

74. A short summary with references is found in Timothy D. Howell, *The Matthean*

certain percentage of table salt, meaning that too high a proportion of other chemicals made such salt dull.[75] The implicit supposition of many interpretive endeavors is that the saying ought to meet audience expectations. Everyone would nod and think: yes, we recognize all of this.[76] However, the way in which hyperbole works is more subtle; it inflates the discrepancy between that which is expected or recognized and that which is communicated. The point here is to trigger emotions, to shock, and to challenge, by evoking an exaggerated, paradoxical, impossible, and hence comical image of literally tasteless salt, which is completely useless, having lost its intrinsic qualities. In real life, there was probably dull or contaminated salt (the unspoken literal meaning), with less taste. The range of inflation in this hyperbole (its absurd literal meaning) facilitates listener comprehension and ensures that communication of the intended message (transferred interpretation) is effective: bad salt is really worthless! This is, of course, a figure for something else being useless because it does not display enough of its intrinsic qualities. In Mark (9.50), salt is associated with the disciples' behavior (keep peace), which might lie behind Matthew's introduction ("you are the salt of the earth"). In Luke (14.34-35), no interpretation is indicated (except perhaps from the general context). The saying could work in a number of contexts, to criticize anyone or anything that does not hold what it promises.

In the saying about light, both Matthew (5.14-16) and Luke (8.16; 11.33) expand on and deviate from Mark (4.21).[77] The saying mixes a common-sense observation with an image of ridiculous behavior (lighting a lamp just in order to hide it). This can be read as a conceptual blend. We must assume that certain things were actually hidden or covered under vessels, or beds (Mark;

Beatitudes in Their Jewish Origins: A Literary and Speech Act Analysis (Studies in Biblical Literature, 144; New York: Peter Lang, 2011), 170. Cf. Davies and Allison, *Commentary*, 472–4. Malina and Rohrbaugh think the "earth" means an earthen oven in which salt was used as a catalyst together with dung for fuel. Eventually its taste was lost. Bruce J. Malina and Richard L. Rohrbaugh, *Social-Science Commentary on the Synoptic Gospels* (2nd edn.; Minneapolis, MN: Fortress, 2003), 41.

75. Luz, *Matthew 1–7*, 250–1.

76. Luz finds it difficult to believe that this is only "a picturesque expression for an impossible possibility" since listeners would then not have agreed to the following image of saltless salt being thrown out (*Matthew 1–7*, 250). This is quite mistaken, however, from a hyperbolic perspective, since the image of the impossible would be the point.

77. There is little to indicate another source, even though Luke offers two variants of the saying. Matthew picks the bushel basket and Luke the bed from Mark's mention of both. In his second variant, Luke invents a cellar. The various options suggest different places where people would put away other "valuables." The Markan *Vorlage* belongs to a series of seemingly unconnected sayings (Mark 4.21-25), probably joined together for mnemonic reason (based on thematic associations and *Stichwörte*).

Luke), or in cellars (Luke), and among these valuables, like food and money. Here something valuable (light) in the domain of vision is imagined to be dealt with as something valuable (money, food) in the domain of subsistence. The blended space produces an absurd image of hiding a lamp under a vessel. The effect is again comical. Matthew then continues to expound the metaphorical meaning of this parable, applying it to the moral behavior of the audience. This is neither found in Mark, nor in Q. The saying about light is not hyperbolic, however. By his redaction and juxtaposition of the two sayings Matthew makes them both speak about disciples' behavior.

Law and Righteousness

Next comes the famous and much-discussed sayings about law and righteousness (Matt. 5.17-20), which introduce the so-called antitheses. This is special Matthean material, except for the introduction (vv. 17-18).[78] This section has been subject to much mishandling due to theological biases and conflicts regarding the place of the "law" in Christian life. It is, however, packed with contrasts, opposites, and strong statements that easily lend themselves to hyperbolic interpretation and should be accounted for.

The very choice between abrogation and fulfillment (*katalysai ... plērōsai*) could be understood as an exaggeration (Matt. 5.17) and the second saying (Matt. 5.18) is best taken hyperbolically. The corresponding Lukan saying (Luke 16.16-17), presumably closer to Q, presents a paradox: the law and the prophets were until John and after that the kingdom, but still, it is easier for heaven and earth to pass away than for one stroke of the law to fall. In Luke (Q), these two sayings do not seem to speak of "law" in the same sense. They may be juxtaposed either because of the *Stichwort* (*nomos*), or to prevent misunderstanding of one saying by balancing it with the other. In Matthew's version, 5.17 almost runs like a comment on Luke 16.16a, in order harmonize the two.[79]

---

78. The source and redaction critical aspects of this section have been discussed endlessly. Cf. Davies and Allison, *Commentary*, 481–503; Luz, *Matthew 1–7*, 257–9. But "the law or the prophets" (*ton nomon ē tous prophētas*) in Matt. 5.17 is probably influenced by Q 16.16, and the saying in Matt. 5.18 about the validity of every single dot or stroke is best understood as a conflation of Mark 13.30-31 (which Matthew repeats elsewhere; Matt. 24.34-35) with Q 16.17, creatively redacted by Matthew. This makes some of the discussion about the relationship between the two temporal clauses in v. 18 redundant: the first clause comes from Q and the second from Mark. The link between the two is the image of heaven and earth passing away. Cf. Roland Deines, *Die Gerechtigkeit der Tora im Reich des Messias: Mt 5,13–20 als Schlüsseltext der matthäischen Theologie* (WUNT, 117; Tübingen: Mohr Siebeck, 2004), 289–94, 345–70

79. Most commentaries make sustained efforts to combine the two sayings and

The second saying (Matt. 5.18/Luke 16.17) does not expect the end of the world, but presents this as an impossibility which nevertheless is easier to envisage than the fall of a single stroke of the law. This hyperbole transmits an extremely strong emotional reaction and subjective evaluation to listeners: the idea that the law would be tampered with is as impossible and shocking as the end of the world would be. The fall of a single stroke of law would be a complete catastrophe. The extreme image says that no one should doubt Jesus' adherence to the law and no one should take it lightly.[80]

The basic hyperbole with its excessive language remains in spite of Matthean redaction, but the substitution of *eukopōteron* with *heōs an* opens the way for a variety of readings by introducing a temporal aspect rather than a simple comparison. The Matthean rendering, "until heaven and earth pass away, no dot or stroke will ever pass away from the law" (*heōs an parelthē ho ouranos kai hē gē, iōta hen ē mia keraia ou mē parelthē apo tou nomou*) is best taken in the same hyperbolic sense as Luke 16.17, but the second *heōs an* clause complicates this. The relationship between the two *heōs an* clauses has often been discussed from syntactical, redactional, and theological perspectives,[81] but it is reasonable to consider rhetorical aspects first. The second temporal clause, *heōs an panta genētai* (until all happens), could be understood as just giving the hyperbole a little boost. Alternatively, it could be seen to negotiate the first, by interpreting the hyperbolic passing away of heaven and earth as an enigmatic reference to fulfillment (cf. the preceding sentence). Instead of a plain and unambiguous evaluation and confirmation of the eternal validity of the law, expressed through extreme hyperbole, we become hesitant as to the level of figurative meaning and the contextual relevance. While antinomian readings are ruled out, a broad range of more or less figurative options become available. Various interpretations through the centuries prove this and demonstrate that these depend as much on ambiguities in the text as on interpreters' biases.[82]

---

explain them in light of each other. Cf. Luz, *Matthew 1–7*, 260–7. But do the sayings need that much harmonization?

80. This hyperbole is analogous to the saying about a camel passing through the eye of a needle being easier than for the rich to enter the kingdom, in its presentation of an impossible image.

81. Is the validity of the law limited in time, and if so, is that limit the passing away of heaven and earth or the fulfilment of everything, or both, and what does that mean? The relationship between and interpretation of the two temporal clauses is a bone of contention. See Guelich, *Sermon on the Mount*, 145–9 and Deines, *Gerechtigkeit*, in n. 78 above.

82. Cf. evidence from the Church Fathers in Manlio Simonetti, *Matthew 1–13* (Ancient Christian Commentary on Scripture, New Testament, IA; Downers Grove, IL: InterVarsity, 2001), 96–7; Luz, *Matthew 1–7*, 261–7.

The subsequent statement about the least (*elachistos*) and the great (*megas*) in the kingdom (Matt. 5.19) is a rather plain example of numerical hyperbole which employs the lower part of a scale for the sake of emphasis and is usually understood intuitively.[83] The asymmetry might be explained by inconsistencies in the Greek use of the various forms of adjective comparison or by Semitic lack of comparatives.[84] Similar considerations apply to the next saying: "if your righteousness does not surpass that of the scribes and the Pharisees, you will never enter the kingdom of heaven" (Matt. 5.20). The construction with the Greek *pleion* reinforces an image of the audience surpassing the legal experts in legal adherence and sets this as a *requirement* for entering the kingdom. If anything, such a statement inflates the discrepancy between the general expectations of the audience and the outcome suggested by the Sermon. Taken as a piece of interactive communication, the extreme imagery should create surprise and laughter. Its function is both evaluative (dishonoring the scribes and the Pharisees) and challenging.

According to relevance theory, the context would provide clues that help listener responses hit the intended figurative level immediately. Assuming for the sake of argument this being spoken by Jesus in a Galilean rural setting, it is not difficult to envisage an intuitive hyperbolic understanding. Although no one would dream of competing with the legal expertise of the specialists—hence the absurdity of the hyperbole!—the image allows laughter and scorn at the shortcomings and misbehavior of the elite, while challenging and strengthening the moral ethos of the community or ordinary people. However, we need not for this reason assume that this special Matthean material goes back to the historical Jesus. The same scenario could work just as well in the Matthean communities, struggling with their opponents, at the end of the first century. Problems appear, however, when later readers encounter this text—readers who associate scribes and Pharisees not with respected elite community leaders or professional specialist, but with hypocrites and immoral rascals, living by double standards. Such assumptions change the contextual clues considerably. The saying releases no laughter, since those "others" are already scorned. To surpass them is easy enough, since "we" are much better already to begin with, by default. The hyperbole is lost. The question that remains is how much righteousness is literally needed for salvation. Perhaps one could sense the beginnings of such a development already with the early recipients of Matthew's gospel.

---

83. Cf. Claridge, *Hyperbole*, 58–61.
84. Davies and Allison, *Commentary*, 498.

The Antitheses

The so-called antitheses (Matt. 5.21-48) are perhaps the most obvious candidates for hyperbolic interpretation. The first, second, and fifth antitheses are similar in their use of obvious hyperboles, as some of the statements clearly go against common sense and jar with a popular sense of justice. This is probably the case with the fourth antithesis, too. In some cases (hell for fool, self-harm, and extreme non-resistance rather than mere non-retaliation) the exaggeration should be obvious. Although the sixth saying about enemy love is similarly counter-intuitive, it is less extreme. The third antithesis, as we will see, is a compound case.

With a reference to murder, the first antithesis (5.21-22) assigns judgment for anger, council for *raka*,[85] hell for "fool," and life sentence for dispute. The suggested punishments are simply out of proportion and obvious examples of hyperbole inflating the discrepancy between expectation and outcome. Punishments for harming others, insulting them, or hurting their honor, rest on a general sense of justice, but that same sense of justice also requires reasonable proportions. This is exactly what talion law (eye for an eye …) expresses and when punishments are out of proportion it is often noticed, as in the archaic Genesis narrative of Lamech, who kills for every wound or hurt (Gen. 4.23-24).

In spite of the inclusion of Gehenna's fire (*tēn geennan tou pyros*) at the bottom of the list, the severity of divine judgment is hardly the issue here. The Greek phrase *enochos estai* ("he is liable"), repeated three times in v. 22, corresponds here to the very common rabbinic idiom *ḥayyāb*, frequently found in halakic discussions from the Mishnah and onwards.[86] This indicates a kind of technical, legal interpretation, exploring case by case the judicial possibilities and limitations of responsibility and punishment for various transgressions, which evolved during the first centuries CE. Such rabbinic discussions can at times become very hypothetical, probing the limits of legal theory rather than solving real cases. At the same time, they usually keep within somewhat realistic limits. Matthew 5.22 goes far off the mark by employing the same technique for stark exaggeration. The effect

---

85. One suggestion for this non-Greek word is a transcription of the Aramaic *rêqā'*, perhaps meaning "empty-head" (Luz, *Matthew 1–7*, 282; Davies and Allison, *Commentary*, 513).

86. The rabbinic *ḥayyāb* ("liable") is so common that any references would be arbitrary. For an example of frequent use, see m. B. Qam. 3. The term is not used in the Hebrew Bible. In the LXX, the corresponding Greek phrase *enochos* (*estai / estin*) is used a few times in Pentateuchal legislation, usually (but not always) in the context of bloodguilt (Exod. 22.2; Lev. 20.9; Num. 35.27; Deut. 19.10; cf. Gen. 26.11; Josh. 2.19). In these cases, however, it does not correspond to any special Hebrew idiom.

is humorous, almost mocking. Instead of exploring the limits and consequences of various related transgressions or insults, the saying shocks its audience and triggers an emotional reaction by going far beyond the reasonable. An unspoken understanding of reasonable punishment is blended with the literal image of an exaggerated expression, and the ensuing intended transferred interpretation will be grasped by the audience as a strong value statement against intra-group animosity.[87]

Hearers in a Matthean context, familiar with evolving contemporary rabbinic discussions, would immediately grasp this at the right level, taking the three verdicts not as a literal scale of punishment.[88] In theory we could envisage a similar scenario at the time of Jesus, but it is uncertain, if not improbable, that Jesus' opponents would have been already arguing in those later rabbinic terms that would resonate with the Matthean saying.[89] These verses (21-22), which are special Matthean material, are a hyperbolic play with early rabbinic halakic style. The effect is to stress the importance of the examples of reconciliation that follow (Matt. 5.23-26), which Matthew has adapted from Mark (Mark 11.25) and Q (Q 12.57-59). These examples, too, are to some degree hyperbolic.

In the first case (Matt. 5.23-24), Matthew has inverted the Markan exhortation to consider forgiving others while praying to God (presumably for forgiveness), into an injunction to leave one's sacrifice in front of the altar and first reconcile with anyone who has a case against oneself. To run away from the altar, leaving the sacrifice behind, definitely sounds like an exaggeration. However, the principle is quite in line with the priestly instructions for the *asham* sacrifice in cases of robbery or fraud, which first require restitution and then sacrifice (Lev. 5.20-26 [ET 6.1-7]).[90] Whether we should

---

87. Notice the repeated reference to "brother" in Matt. 5.22-24. Cf. Luz, *Matthew 1–7*, 288; Davies and Allison, *Commentary*, 512–3. For a discussion of similarities with the *Community Rule*, see Davies, *Setting*, 237–9.

88. It is interesting to note that the *Didache* (3.2) associates anger with murder (*hodēgei gar hē orgē pros ton phonon*). Such an association would make it possible to read Matthew less hyperbolically. Similarly, the insertion "without cause" by a scribe in *Codex Sinaiticus*, also represented by *Codex Bezae*, modifies the command and makes it possible to interpret literally.

89. For a general discussion of the development of halakic reasoning in other areas, see Kazen, *Scripture*.

90. See Thomas Kazen, *Emotions in Biblical Law* (Hebrew Bible Monographs, 36; Sheffield: Sheffield Phoenix, 2011), 158–62; Thomas Kazen, "Self-Preserving and Other-Oriented Concerns in the Jesus Tradition," in *Voces Clamantium in Deserto: Essays in Honor of Kari Syreeni*, ed. S.-O. Back & M. Kankaanniemi (Studier i exegetik och judaistik utgivna av Teologiska fakulteten vid Åbo Akademi, 11; Åbo: Åbo Akademi University, Faculty of Theology, 2012), 124–48, 147.

expect another source or tradition behind this in addition to Mark is a moot question, and the level of figurative meaning depends in part on the context we envisage for the saying.

The second example (Matt. 5.25-26) originates with Q and is quite realistic. Imprisonment for debts did occur in the ancient world.[91] The statement that you would never be released unless the last penny was paid must be taken as an ordinary scalar hyperbole, emphasizing the seriousness of the case. In real life one would expect a number of possible negotiations and compromises.

The second antithesis equates adultery with lustful looks and orders the plucking out of eyes and the cutting off of limbs that cause sin, to avoid the whole body ending up in Gehenna. Except for the introductory vv. 27-28, the material is Markan (Mark 9.43-48), but rearranged. Matthew repeats the same Markan material in the Markan order elsewhere (Matt. 18.8-9). Both Matthew's equation of adultery with lustful looks and the Markan sayings about self-mutilation are clearly hyperbolic. True, the emotional repression demanded for avoiding any sense of attraction could be associated with certain ancient philosophical ideals of self-control and restraint.[92] The extreme actions suggested were not impossible to envisage in the ancient world, as they correspond to a type of punishment common in many honor-and-shame-societies through history.[93] But it is difficult to think that anyone would intuitively take these injunctions literally.[94] In Matthew, these examples of

---

91. At least in non-Jewish contexts. Jewish law does not attest to imprisonment from debt, as pointed out by commentators (cf. Davies and Allison, *Commentary*, 520; Luz, *Matthew 1–7*, 290), but debt slavery was well known. Imprisonment for debts turns up in another Matthean tradition, too (18.23-35).

92. Moderation (*sōphrosynē*), and self-control/abstinence (*enkrateia*), were cardinal virtues in Greek philosophy, both in Plato, Aristotle, and the Stoics. This is reflected for example in Josephus, Philo, and Paul, and in the early Christian tendency towards sexual renunciation and asceticism. Cf. Malcolm Schofield, "Cardinal Virtues: A Contested Socratic Inheritance," in *Plato and the Stoics*, ed. A. G. Long (Cambridge: Cambridge University Press, 2013), 11–28; Teresa M. Shaw, "Sex and Sexual Renunciation," in *The Early Christian World*, Vol. 1, ed. Philip F. Esler (London: Routledge, 2000), 401–21; Leif E. Vaage and Vincent L. Wimbush, eds., *Asceticism and the New Testament* (New York: Routledge, 1999).

93. Numerous examples of this are found in the ancient Near Eastern legal collections; see for example Martha T. Roth, *Law Collections from Mesopotamia and Asia Minor* (2nd edn., SBL Writings from the Ancient World, 6; Atlanta, GA: Scholars Press, 2003).

94. The early Church Fathers often recognized the hyperbole (e.g., Apollinaris), but they were more prone to allegorizing, taking the severed members to represent friendships (Hilary), family and relatives (Jerome), or bishops and priests (Chromatius). See Simonetti, *Matthew 1–13*, 110–1.

self-mutilation are supposedly related to adultery and to avoid that, no elimination of any of the suggested limbs or body parts would suffice. In Mark, the imagery is not explicitly associated with adultery, only with another hyperbole, that of the millstone around the neck (Mark 9.42). The rhetorical focus in Mark is the urgency of the kingdom; to enter it one should do anything necessary, and the hyperbolic examples of self-mutilation underscore the importance of this. The extreme imagery ensures that they are clearly understood as part of a humorous but serious and extremely negative evaluation of adultery and lends weight to the importance of controlling one's desires and behavior.

The third antithesis (Matt. 5.31-32) suggests that divorce causes adultery rather than the other way round. It mainly consists of a saying found in both Mark and Q. In Mark it belongs to the conflict narrative on divorce (Mark 10.2-12). Matthew rewrites this narrative elsewhere, too (Matt. 19.3-9). Luke lacks the narrative, but the saying appears independently (Luke 16.18). Matthew's version of the saying in the Sermon has similarities with Luke, and most scholars assume a Q version behind it. In both places, however, Matthew includes the so-called exceptive clause (except for *porneia*) and there are other minor peculiarities. As I have discussed the relationship between the various versions in detail elsewhere, I will not deal with this any further here.[95] The question in this context is whether hyperbolic language is involved or not. The contrast between a general acceptance of divorce, perhaps for "any matter,"[96] and an outright prohibition (including Q's prohibition of remarriage with a divorcee), is sharp. Without the exceptive clause, the saying could be taken hyperbolically, as a strong value statement against commonly accepted divorce practices. Matthew's version, however, softens the contrast by allowing divorce in cases of *porneia*, with the result that the saying corresponds with known practice, albeit of the stricter kind.[97]

The Q version (excluding Matthew's exceptive clause), could possibly originate with criticisms against Herod Antipas's divorce and remarriage (cf. John the Baptizer). To suggest that Jesus took a similarly critical attitude to Antipas is speculative but possible.[98] This would provide an inter-

---

95. Kazen, *Scripture*, 207–21.
96. Cf. the later rabbinic interpretation of Deut. 24.1-4, attributed to the schools of Hillel and Shammai. For further discussion and references, see Kazen, *Scripture*, 242–59.
97. Often associated with the Qumran sectarians and the school of Shammai. For detailed discussion, see Kazen, *Scripture*, 197–204, 269–76.
98. Kazen, *Scripture*, 200, 202, 205, 219–20, 277–80; cf. Francis Crawford Burkitt, *The Gospel History and Its Transmission* (2nd edn.; Edinburgh: T&T Clark, 1907), 98–102; Raymond F. Collins, *Divorce in the New Testament* (GNS, 38; Collegeville, MN: Liturgical, 1992), 221–2.

active context in which this saying would be intuitively understood. The statement could then be taken as loose talk or approximation, not strictly condemning any divorce and remarriage, but particularly focused on the ruler's deficient morality. However, as the Sermon now stands, including the exceptive clause, the third antithesis is neither intended, nor generally received, as hyperbolic, but rather taken literally.

The fourth antithesis prohibits all oathtaking by contrasting false swearing with constantly truthful talk (Matt. 5.33-37). A somewhat similar saying in 23.16-22 (also uniquely Matthean) does not prohibit swearing altogether, but only the misuse of oaths with specific formulas to avoid their binding effect.[99] Both passages suggest an acquaintance with evolving rabbinic discussions,[100] but the details of the passage from Matthew 23 do not speak for an early date. However, the Sermon's general prohibition of four categories of oaths (by heaven, earth, Jerusalem, and one's head) could perhaps go back to Jesus.[101] The point to speak clearly and truthfully is explicitly made, and in view of that, the saying against swearing should probably be understood hyperbolically. Taking into account the commonality of casual oathtaking, a total ban on swearing would be striking.[102]

If the literal meaning is to speak truthfully (in this case it is almost spelled out in 5.37 as the conclusion), then there is a definite discrepancy between this and the strong prohibitive imagery evoked to drive home the point. The intended transferred interpretation, or blend if we prefer that model, would amount to a stern frown on frivolous talk, a negative value judgment on careless speech, evoking indignation against those who use

---

99. This seem to be an outright polemic against a nominalist (legal formalist) strategy to handle rash oaths, of which the subsequent stages and more elaborate examples can be found in the *Mishnah* (e.g., m. Ned. 2.5; 6.9–7.5).

100. Only that rabbinic texts display so many more categories, and that the four categories in Matt. 5.34-35 cannot be found together in one rabbinic passage. See for example m. Ned. 1.3 or m. Sanh. 3.2.

101. Heaven and earth are found in James 5.12 and seem traditional. Meier (*Law and Love*, 198–206) thinks that they go back to the historical Jesus. Matthew 5.35-36 has two more: Jerusalem and the head. Since Matthew loves triads, Davies and Allison argue that the fourth cannot come from his hand (*Commentary*, 537). This could mean that all four are at least earlier than Matthew.

102. It has also been considered very unpractical, which caused the church in general to allow oaths for serious purposes. However, in the early (especially Greek-speaking) church it was usually more or less literally understood (Luz, *Matthew 1–9*, 318–9; Davies and Allison, *Commentary*, 535–6). For a discussion of the difference between oaths and vows and whether this is reflected in the Jesus tradition, see Meier, *Law and Love*, 183–8, 208–9, nn. 2, 4, and in particular Martin Vahrenhorst, *"Ihr sollt überhaupt nicht schwören": Matthäus im halachischen Diskurs* (WMANT, 95; Neukirchen-Vluyn: Neukirchener Verlag, 2002). A distinction is upheld in m. Nedarim but its details are not explained.

strong language with little backing behind them and challenging listeners to change their own behavior. The bottom line is that oathtaking is useless, since the speaker does not have the power he or she invokes. From this perspective, the saying is indubitably hyperbolic. This remains true whether it is contextualized in Matthew's communities or in Jesus' audience.

The fifth antithesis suggests an extreme policy of non-retaliation (Matt. 5.38-42): turn the other cheek, give away more than what is extorted, go a second mile, give to beggars, and lend to anyone. Just as in the first antithesis, the examples clash with a general sense of justice and proportionality. To turn the other cheek to one who strikes, to give away one's cloak when forced to give up one's shirt (Luke has it the other way round), or to give to those who ask and give up one's rightful belongings, sounds like a stark exaggeration of normal prosocial behavior.[103] Matthew adds going an extra mile when forced to go one.

The sixth antithesis runs in the same vein as it commands enemy love, based on divine generosity as opposed to human tit-for-tat strategies (Matt. 5.43-48). It will be discussed together with the fifth for practical reasons, since the Lukan material corresponding to Matthew's sixth antithesis (Luke 6.27-28, 32-36) surrounds the material corresponding to Matthew's fifth. Reconstructions of Q are usually closer to Luke's order and we will thus consider all of this material together. Matthew places the injunction to love enemies and pray for persecutors in opposition to a purported command to love the neighbor but hate the enemy. Such behavior is motivated by God providing equal care (sun and rain) for everybody. Matthew's argument (5.46-47) is that even tax collectors love those who love them, and even the other nations, that is, the Gentiles (*hoi ethnikoi*), greet their next of kin (*tous adelphous*), while Luke talks of even sinners loving, doing good, and lending (6.32-34).

In Q, enemy love and non-retaliation belong together. The passage can be read as a commentary on a section of the Holiness Code (Lev. 19.17-18),[104] which seems to repudiate earlier talion law (Exod. 21.23-25; Lev. 24.19-22;

---

103. This is also Luz's opinion (*Matthew 1–7*, 325–31). The commandments are not meant literally, but as shocking provocation. Betz, however, objects (*Sermon*, 289); the goal is to combat evil. The fifth antithesis is not an impossible or unrealistic command, but "nonretaliation is a positive gesture of generosity that carries with it the expectation that the adversary will respond in kind" (*Sermon*, 283–4).

104. David R. Catchpole, *The Quest for Q* (Edinburgh: T&T Clark, 1993), 125–33; Kari Syreeni, "The Sermon on the Mount and the Two Ways Teaching of the Didache," in *Matthew and the Didache: Two Documents from the Same Jewish-Christian Milieu?*, ed. H. van de Sandt (Assen: Royal Van Gorcum, and Minneapolis: Fortress, 2005), 87–104, 94–6; Kazen, "Self-Preserving," 139–40.

Deut. 19.21) and regards resentment towards kin and neighbor as unacceptable. This development belongs to a stage in Israelite history (early Persian period) when unity within a small and vulnerable temple state was crucial for survival, and neighbor came to include not only kin but also, to some degree, resident aliens.[105] The topic is taken up by Sirach (28.1-4). From the perspective of Q, enemy love and non-retaliation find their place within an inclusive utopia of a restored Jewish people, including disregarded segments of the population. Love of neighbor is extended to enemies within the group, viewed as "extended family," and supposed to override concerns for retributive justice. I have discussed these issues in more detail elsewhere, including the emotional, psychological, and biological underpinnings for such an inclusive kind of pro-social behavior.[106]

Within such a context the Q sayings would probably be understood as loose or approximate, along a figurative scale. A strictly literal interpretation is unreasonable: one cannot give and lend to anyone, or accept continuous abuse, violence, and extortion. But neither is an overly hyperbolic interpretation likely to have been embraced: while the injunctions to turn the other cheek or give away the rest of one's clothes are exaggerations, provoking emotional reaction and shock, on a singular occasion these actions are not impossible to envisage, and giving or lending are definitely conceivable behaviors.[107] A contextually relevant audience response would take on the challenge to be generous with the more unfortunate within the group, to be more inclusive of "outsiders" as if they were kin, and to be more forbearing of perpetrators, all in the interest of a utopia of kingdom or covenant renewal.[108]

In Matthew's Sermon, these sayings are sorted and separated, so that the words about enemy love and prayer for persecutors are included in the sixth antithesis, while acts of non-retaliaton are presented in the fifth. Through this reordering the sixth antithesis becomes restricted to mental attitudes (including formal greetings), while the fifth contains all the difficult and perhaps unrealistic suggestions that Matthew sets up in contrast to talion law. In addition, he introduces this section with the injunction not to resist

---

105. Christophe Nihan, "Resident Aliens and Natives in the Holiness Legislation," in *The Foreigner and the Law: Perspectives from the Hebrew Bible and the Ancient Near East*, ed. R. Achenbach, R. Albertz, and J. Wöhrle (Wiesbaden: Harrassowitz, 2011), 111–34.
106. Kazen, "Self-Preserving," 139–46. See also Chapter 4 in the present volume.
107. Hence both Betz's and Luz's interpretations can be acknowledged as basically correct in what they affirm.
108. Cf. Markus Cromhout, *Jesus and Identity: Reconstructing Judean Ethnicity in Q* (Eugene, OR: Wipf & Stock, 2007), 301–5, 344–56, 369.

evil, the evil one, or the evildoer (*mē antistēnai tō ponērō*; Matt. 5.39). The meaning of *ponērō* is ambiguous, but we should probably read evildoer.[109] The verb *antistēnai* can be interpreted as "retaliate" rather than "resist."[110] But even if the text is read as "do not take revenge on the evildoer" the subsequent examples of how to act clash with general expectation. This is a typical sign of hyperbole. The instruction is difficult to take strictly literally regardless of the context.

The Matthean community is often envisaged as under pressure and persecuted. The examples, however, do not seem to indicate life-threatening situations. They are not of one piece. Forcing someone to go a mile is usually associated with Roman conscription. Suing for a cloak indicates legal dispute rather than robbery or confiscation by the military. A blow on the right cheek indicates quarrel or humiliation from a superior rather than serious abuse by, for example, a soldier. Some have suggested that these sayings reflect intra-family conflicts as the Jesus movement was breaking up households.[111] As they are phrased, the Matthean examples seem to represent a variety of situations, including but not restricted to intra-family conflicts.

The contents of the fifth and sixth antitheses are also represented in the *Didache* (1.3-5), but here these injunctions are part of very concrete instructions, of which virtually all must be understood literally. Some of the sayings are adapted in a way which makes this obvious. The explanation of the command not to ask for the return of seized property is straightforward (*Did.* 1.4): "because you won't be able to get it" (*oude gar dynasai*). The command to give to everyone who asks without asking for anything back (*Did.* 1.5) is modified, first by a discussion about the responsibility of the

---

109. Betz (*Sermon*, 281) suggests a personal meaning (evildoer) because of all the subsequent examples.

110. Betz, *Sermon*, 280.

111. E.g., Aaron Milavec, "The Social Setting of 'Turning the Other Cheek' and 'Loving One's Enemies' in the Light of the *Didache*," *Biblical Theology Bulletin* 25 (1995): 131–43, and Aaron Milavec, *The Didache: Faith, Hope, and Life of the Earliest Christian Communities, 50–70 C.E.* (New York: Newman Press, 2003), 743–68. He points to evidence for conflict between generations regarding adherence to the Jesus movement. Such an interpretation could work for Luke, who does not include the second mile saying, but only talks of turning the other cheek and of not withholding even your cloak from the one taking (*tou airontos*) your shirt (Luke 6.29). It could perhaps work for the *Didache*, too, which just like Luke uses the verb *airein* (Did. 2.4) rather than the Matthean *tō thelonti soi krithēnai* (Matt. 5.40). But the second mile saying, included in the *Didache* and phrased just like in Matthew with the verb *angareuein* (Matt. 5.41; Did. 2.4), suggests conscription by Roman soldiers. It is not fully convincing to interpret even this saying from an intra-family perspective, as Milavec does, based on a metaphorical reading.

receiver not to accept a gift unless there is a real need (suggesting a context of mutual support), and then by adding a saying (*Did.* 1.6) about letting alms "sweat" in the hands until one knows to whom to give it (*hidrōsatō hē eleēmosynē sou eis tas cheiras sou mechris an gnōs, tini dōs*). Such modifications make a fairly literal interpretation possible.

It seems, then, that the loosely hyperbolic Q sayings, which Matthew has collected in his fifth antithesis, came to be understood much more literally when we find them in the *Didache*, but for that to be possible some adjustments were needed. We cannot assume a literal meaning in Matthew's Sermon for at least three reasons. First, we would expect modifiers that diminish the gap between expectation and outcome, or tone down what is experienced as impossible demands, such as the *Didache* supplies in this case and Matthew provides elsewhere, for example, in the saying on divorce. Secondly, since the surrounding Sermon is full of hyperbole and figurative language we would expect this here, too, unless there is reason not to. Thirdly, the talion law introducing the fifth antithesis does not seem to have been practiced literally at this time, but normally replaced by monetary compensation.[112] I thus suggest a loose figurative interpretation within the context of the Sermon, which would challenge Matthew's audience and motivate them emotionally to waive their claims for retributive justice and include more categories of people in an expanded "kin and family sphere," taking a more generous attitude to strangers and adversaries.

Ritual Practice

Turning to the three special Matthean traditions about almsgiving (Matt. 6.1-4), prayer (6.5-6), and fasting (6.16-18), we must beware of their portrayal of the "hypocrites," which serve as models for the Matthean opponents. All three sections have been subject to various historical or historicizing explanations about trumpet-blowing, street-praying, and disfiguring fasting practices.[113] In the context of the Sermon, these purported practices all function

---

112. Bernard S. Jackson, "Models in Legal History: The Case of Biblical Law," *Journal of Law and Religion* 18 (2002): 1–30, 21; Bernard S. Jackson, *Wisdom-Laws: A Study of the Mishpatim of Exodus 21:1–22:16* (Oxford: Oxford University Press, 2006), 133–8, 157–66; cf. William Ian Miller, *Eye for an Eye* (Cambridge: Cambridge University Press, 2006), 24–7.

113. Few scholars today suggest trumpet-blowing as a historical practice, but Craig Keener mentions Gerhard Friedrich, and Luz mentions K. Bornhäuser, who believed that evidence for this would turn up. See Craig Keener, *The Gospel of Matthew: A Socio-Rhetorical Commentary* (Grand Rapids, MI: Eerdmans, 2009 [1999]), 208; Luz, *Matthew 1–7*, 360. Cf. Davies and Allison, *Commentary*, 579–80; Keener, *Matthew*, 208–11, 226–8.

as contrasts to the suggested proper behavior: to give without letting the left hand know what the right hand does; to pray privately in secret; and to fast invisibly, in secret, too. The first example is phrased in figurative language and an obvious hyperbole expressing a lack of awareness of one's benign acts which is strictly speaking impossible. It creates surprise and was probably heard as funny before it became a dead idiom. It is instantly understood at the intended level. The second and third examples were probably also heard and read hyperbolically; it is difficult to think of any religious tradition in antiquity which would treat ritual behavior like prayer and fasting as an entirely private and individual affair. Since the three commended actions are expressed in hyperbole, their hypocritical contrasts must be expected to be exaggerated, too.[114] Whether we think of these figures as historical adversaries of Jesus or as narrative representatives of the opponents of the Matthean communities, the images which Matthew's hyperbolic descriptions conjure up are designed to make people laugh.

The Matthean audience is thus moved in two ways. First, they are emotionally involved and drawn into a construction of reality in which their opponents are devalued as pathetic. The hyperbolic caricatures induce strong negative emotions against the "hypocrites," both as narrative figures and those whom they represent. Secondly, the hearers are challenged to be modest in their ritual practices. The discrepancy between images of secret practices and experiences of communal gatherings speaks loud and the resulting transferred interpretation is a self-critical scrutiny of one's own attitudes to ritual behavior.

With this perspective in mind, the section on the Lord's Prayer (Matt. 6.9-15) is clearly an insertion into the three parallel sayings on ritual practice, with little of the exaggerated characteristics of the larger context. The introduction (6.7-8) accuses Gentiles of heaping empty phrases (*polylogia*), which might be biased and unfair, but probably corresponds to what the audience expected of non-Jewish religion.[115] It balances the accusation against (other) Jewish adversaries ("hypocrites") in verse 5 and motivates the Lord's Prayer, as a third and proper way to pray.

---

114. This is definitely the case with the trumpet-blowing, as Luz (*Matthew 1–7*, 356–7) points out, and there is no evidence for street-praying either. This is hyperbolic caricature, a "grotesque example" (p. 360).

115. Rhetorically, this is caricature (characterizing true prayer as different both from the prayer of hypocrites and pagans) and fits with Hellenistic Judaism's traditional criticism of idol worship (as for example in Wis. 12–14). However, there may be an allusion here to magical incantations, repeating meaningless syllables (*battalogeō* is "babbling" or "stuttering"), or perhaps to the obscure speech of oracles (Betz, *Sermon*, 347, 364–7). Similar criticism is found in Greek literature.

Three Sayings

The three following Q-sayings (Matt. 6.19-24; cf. Luke 12.33-36; 16.13) about treasures, the eye, and serving two masters, play on colorful contrasts, but contain no obvious hyperboles, except for the claim of the third saying that one would either hate or love one of two masters (6.24). This is a typical end-of-the-scale hyperbole, used for emphasis and intuitively understood to stress that a slave's affection and loyalty would not be equal in relation to the two masters. Hence a pious person cannot be concerned for wealth and vice versa.

Worries

The next passage about worries, also from Q (Matt. 6.25-34), is full of exaggerated statements. While it is true that life is more than food and the body more than clothing (6.25), anyone knows that without food one will die and without clothing the body will suffer or even perish. The analogy between birds and flowers on the one hand and human beings on the other (6.26-28) is obviously flawed, as birds gather seeds incessantly and flowers are of quite a different order. The statement about Solomon (6.29) must be hyperbolic and it is difficult not to think that addressees would have understood the assertion that God will provide those who seek righteousness with everything they need (6.30-33) to be an exaggeration. These are claims that go against general expectations and experience in the ancient world, where ordinary people will starve unless they work hard, whether on their own land, or for others. The audience will know this and their expectations of relevance ensure that no one can misunderstand this saying and stop working for food and clothes. In this case the intended transferred interpretation of the hyperbolic expressions is clearly stated as the conclusion of the section: do not worry about tomorrow (6.34).[116]

The exaggerated imagery is nevertheless provocative, particularly in the context of Q, or perhaps Jesus, with destitute day laborers without land and without regular work. The discrepancy that is created challenges listeners to redescribe their world in terms of confidence, as if the images of birds and flowers were true accounts of reality. If we assume the view that the Matthean community was relatively affluent, or at least far from destitute, the hyperbolic force would not be the same as the experienced

---

116. Cf. Betz, who points to "the peculiar phenomenon that presuppositions and conclusions, which are part of the unwritten text, appear sometimes in the written surface structure, while at other times they remain unstated implications" (*Sermon*, 461).

discrepancy would not be as great, but there would still be a strong push towards changed priorities.

Judging Others

In the subsequent saying (also Q) about judging others (Matt. 7.1-5), we find one of the most illustrious examples of hyperbole in the Jesus tradition: speck versus a log in the eye. Like the camel, it is a favorite of cartoonists, and their attempts aptly bring out the point that envisaging the *imagery* literally is what makes the trick. The absurd idea of both having a log in the eye and of not noticing it is so impossible that it ensures maximal emphasis: no one can doubt the strength of the prohibition against judging others, the condemnation of hypocrisy, or the emotional involvement. The very fact that the hyperbolic image goes far beyond what is reasonable creates a particular combination of humor and seriousness. The image of the log is blended with petty everyday dissatisfactions and disappointments with others, resulting in an interiorization of the demand for self-scrutiny, and abandoning an other-condemning attitude.[117]

The figurative language in the next warning (Matt. 7.6), the special Matthean saying against profaning that which is holy (dogs, swine), is extreme, although not especially hyperbolic.

Divine Care

The examples following the general saying about asking, seeking, and knocking (Matt. 7.7-11), all from Q, are again clearly hyperbolic. Who could be so evil as to give their children stones or snakes to eat instead of bread and fish? This is a highly exaggerated image of inadequate behavior. For parents, this imagery is emotionally upsetting, since no sane parent would ever do such a thing. This is exactly what the hyperbolic descriptions aim at and the point of the rhetorical questions. By invoking parental care and responsibility, the text enlists its recipients' emotional involvement for its real message: a picture of God as caring for human welfare, which acts as motivation for prayer.

---

117. The use of the epithet "hypocrite" in 7.5 suggests that Matthew thinks of this warning as directed against the Pharisees. However, the repeated reference to "brother" in this section indicates its origin as intra-group paraenesis. Cf. Davies and Allison, *Commentary*, 673.

The Sermon's Conclusion

In contrast, the "Golden Rule" (Matt. 7.12; also in Luke 6.31; hence Q) is a perfectly literal statement, summarizing the ethos of much of the previous material.

Finally, the concluding sections, the narrow gate (Matt. 7.13-14), false prophets / good and bad fruit (7.15-20), "lord, lord" (7.21-23), and the houses built on rock and sand (7.24-27) all play with sharp contrasts and often with figurative language. Again, this is mostly Q traditions, ordered by Matthew to provide a fitting conclusion to the Sermon: choose the right way, which is shown by good actions, not just words. The slight exaggeration that "every" tree that does not bear good fruit is cut down and thrown into the fire (7.19) is such a conventional idiom that it does little to affect an audience. Besides that, there are no hyperboles in this section.

Concluding Discussion

Although the Sermon on the Mount contains a number of exaggerations and hyperbolic expressions, not every strong contrast is a hyperbole. There is, for example, no or little hyperbole to speak of in several of the beatitudes (3, 4, 6, and 7), conspicuously those that do not find parallels in Luke but might be Matthean creations. The saying about hiding a light is exaggerated and just as comical as the preceding one about salt, but no hyperbole. Neither the Lord's Prayer, nor the Golden Rule, employ exaggeration and there is little hyperbole in the sayings on treasures, the sound eye, two masters, dogs and swine, the narrow gate, good and bad fruit, "lord, lord," or the two houses, except for a stray end-of-the-scale hyperbole or conventionalized idiom. So, is the Sermon full of hyperbole? As we have seen there are enough of them to play a considerable role in the communication and appropriation of the text.

The most conspicuous examples, plucking out one's eye, cutting off one's hand, not letting the left hand know what the right hand does, the log in the eye, and stones and snakes, are relatively easy to identify and to interpret intuitively, without any linguistic tools or metaphor theories. They simply cannot be taken literally, but their purpose is to emphasize how serious the intended message is. Even in some of these cases, however, contemporary interpreters sometimes strangely enough display an uncertainty about the intended message and how to handle these images with regard to their literal meaning.

This also applies to numerical or scalar hyperboles, which are usually easy to grasp: the least and the great in the kingdom, the last penny, and hating or loving of two masters are examples of hyperbole which employ the ends of the scale for the sake of emphasis. In spite of this pretty obvious use, they have sometimes caused uncertainty, too.

Linguistic considerations and theories of metaphor have proved to be helpful as we have identified and discussed hyperbole in some of the other sayings, which are less apparent at first sight. We can divide these into two groups: one in which the use of hyperbole is quite straightforward and the other in which hyperbolic sayings have been softened by Matthew, or depend on the context or interaction of the audience, to a degree that causes uncertainties as to their intended interpretation along a figurative scale.

In the first group we find the salt saying, the first, second, and fourth antitheses, the ritual practices (almsgiving, prayer, and fasting), and the saying about divine care. These examples all display a wide discrepancy between audience expectation (what some theorists would call the often unspoken literal expression) and the highly exaggerated hyperbolic expression, as it is literally imagined. The latter lends emotional involvement, saliency, and subjective evaluation to the intended or transferred interpretation, influencing audience response. Alternatively, the result can be described as a blend out of two discrepant input spaces, which influences worldview, values, and action. The audience will immediately grasp the messages about intra-group conflict, controlling desires, and speaking truthfully, as serious challenges to which they need to respond. They will know that things or persons that have lost their intrinsic qualities are not worth having, such as hypocrites, and they will value modesty in ritual practice. They will get the picture of God as caring, as a motivation for prayer and trust. They will understand the level of hyperbole intuitively based on experience and contextual factors, without mistaking figurative language for literal.

In the second group we find the first, second, and fourth beatitudes, the saying about law and righteousness, the third, fifth, and sixth antitheses, and the section about worries. What complicates our analysis of their intended interpretation is not only their character, but also our uncertainties regarding their contextualization. If understanding hyperbole partly depends on expectations of relevance, context is sometimes crucial for hitting the right level. Hence we cannot always intuitively do what Matthew's or Q's audience would have done in the past.

Originally, we have argued, the Q beatitudes about poverty, mourning, hunger and thirst, constituted a hyperbolic and emotional plea for a radical reversal of the present order, but together with others and in Matthew's redaction they have rather become paraenetic moral instruction. Similarly, the sayings about law and righteousness which contain clear hyperbolic expressions to the effect that tampering with the law would be as shocking as the end of the world, are opened up for some ambiguity by Matthean redaction, and the obvious impossibility of surpassing the religious experts runs the risk of being turned from a funny and critical challenge to self-righteous scorn. The emotionally-laden statement against divorce is disarmed by the exceptive clause. As for the last two non-retributive antitheses, I have suggested a loose or approximate interpretation along a figurative scale, both for Q and for Matthew. The kind of modification we would expect from Matthew, facilitating a more literal interpretation, is, however, found somewhat later, in the *Didache*. Finally, in the section about worries the hyperboles are not softened by Matthew, but the hyperbolic force in the transferred interpretation of Matthean communities might not remain as strong as in Q, depending on how we situate those communities socially and economically.

In many of the cases discussed we have seen that humor plays an important role. It often results from the use of hyperbole, but not always, and other types of contrasts can be funny, too. While the comical would have been apparent and intuitively understood most of the time by the various audiences envisaged for the Sermon, it is often the identification of a saying as hyperbolic that makes the modern reader or interpreter fully aware of the humor involved. This has to do with one of the points that we have stressed repeatedly, that the figurative or transferred (intended) meaning of a hyperbole is dependent on our imagining it literally. It is exactly that which the hyperbole does *not mean* which is necessary to imagine in order to understand it. This is also why a conventional or "dead" hyperbole stops being recognized, as the absurd literal image no longer appears on an inner screen.

Whether all of this happens because we think (conceptualize) in metaphors (conceptual metaphor theory) or because we grasp for that which has not yet been clearly thought before in our urge to communicate (relevance theory) is a moot question which I will not try to answer. Both models are doable and produce interesting results when applied in textual interpretation.

In any case, hyperbole and hyperbolic expressions, along a broad figurative range, are rhetorically powerful and change people's thoughts and behavior, by investing the intended meaning with saliency, emotion, and subjective evaluation, beyond what any literal language is able to do. Perhaps that is one, major, reason for the successful afterlife of Matthew's sermon construction, just as much as pious, theological, or socially radical explanation would suggest. Perhaps this is what Matthew adds to the Markan Jesus' authority, based on miracles and revelatory deeds: the authority of zestful language—the authority of hyperbole.

Biographical Note

Thomas Kazen is Professor of Biblical Studies, Stockholm School of Theology at University College Stockholm. His research interests include biblical law and Jewish halakha, ritual and purity, Jesus traditions and their development, conceptual metaphors, emotions, sociocognitive and psychobiological approaches, power and hierarchy. Recent books include *Impurity in Early Judaism and the Jesus Tradition: Critical Issues and New Directions* (SBL, 2021); *Dirt, Shame, Status: Perspectives on Same-Sex Relationships in the Bible and Antiquity* (in Swedish; Makadam, 2018); *Scripture, Interpretation, or Authority? Motives and Arguments in Jesus' Halakic Conflicts* (Mohr Siebeck, 2013); and *Emotions in Biblical Law: A Cognitive Science Approach* (Sheffield Phoenix, 2011).

*Bibliography**

Allison, Dale C. *The New Moses: A Matthean Typology*. Edinburgh: T&T Clark, 1993.
—*Jesus of Nazareth: Millenarian Prophet*. Minneapolis, MN: Fortress, 1998.
Bacon, Benjamin W. "The 'Five Books' of Moses against the Jews," *Expositor* 15 (1918): 56–66.
Banks, Robert. *Jesus and the Law in the Synoptic Tradition*. Cambridge: Cambridge University Press, 1975.
Bergen, Benjamin, and Kim Binsted. "The Cognitive Linguistics of Scalar Humor," 79–92 in *Language, Culture and Mind*. Edited by Suzanne Kemmer and Michel Achard. Stanford, CA: CSLI Publications, 2004.
Betz, Hans Dieter. *The Sermon on the Mount: A Commentary on the Sermon on the Mount, including the Sermon on the Plain (Matthew 5:3–7:27 and Luke 6:20–49)*. Edited by Adela Y. Collins. Hermeneia. Minneapolis, MN: Fortress, 1995.
Brdar-Szabó, Rita, and Mario Brdar. "Scalar Model in a Cognitive Approach to Hyperbolic Expressions: With a Little Help from Metonymy," 75–94 in *Pragmatics Today*. Edited by Piotr Cap. Łódź Studies in Language, 12. Frankfurt am Main: Peter Lang, 2005.
Broer, Ingo. "Die Weisung der Bergpredigt und die Verantwortung der Christen," 11–24 in *Er stieg auf den Berg ... und lehrte sie (Mt 5,1f.): Exegetische und rezeptionsgeschichtliche Studien zur Bergpredigt*. Edited by Hans-Ulrich Weidemann. Stuttgarter Bibelstudien, 226. Stuttgart: Verlag Katholisches Bibelwerk, 2012.
Burkitt, Francis Crawford. *The Gospel History and Its Transmission*. 2nd edn. Edinburgh: T&T Clark, 1907.
Byrskog, Samuel. *Jesus the Only Teacher: Didactic Authority and Transmission in Ancient Israel, Ancient Judaism and the Matthean Community*. Coniectanea Biblica: New Testament Series, 24. Stockholm: Almqvist & Wiksell International, 1994.
Cano Mora, Laura. "All or Nothing: A Semantic Analysis of Hyperbole," *Revista de Lingüística y Lenguas Aplicadas* 4 (2009): 25–35. https://doi.org/10.4995/rlyla.2009.731
Casey, Maurice. *Jesus of Nazareth: An Independent Historian's Account of His Life and Teaching*. London: T&T Clark, 2010. https://doi.org/10.5040/9780567691224

---

* The bibliography reflects the fact that this chapter was written in 2015. I regret that I could not interact with subsequent publications, including Ernst Baasland's major work on the Sermon: *Parables and Rhetoric in the Sermon on the Mount* (Mohr Siebeck, 2015).

Catchpole, David R. *The Quest for Q*. Edinburgh: T&T Clark, 1993.
Chrysostom, John. *Homilies on St. Matthew XVI*. Edited by J.-P. Migne. Vol. 1860 of *Patrologiae Cursus Completus: Series Graeca*, 57. Paris: J.-P. Migne, 1860.
Claridge, Claudia. *Hyperbole in English: A Corpus-Based Study of Exaggeration*. Cambridge: University Press, 2011.
Collins, Raymond F. *Divorce in the New Testament*. Good News Studies, 38. Collegeville, MN: Liturgical Press, 1992.
Colston, Herbert L., and Shauna B. Keller. "You'll Never Believe This: Irony and Hyperbole in Expressing Surprise," *Journal of Psycholinguistic Research* 27 (1998): 499–513. https://doi.org/10.1023/A:1023229304509
Coulson, Seanna, and Todd Oakley. "Blending Basics," *Cognitive Linguistics* 11 (2000): 175–96. https://doi.org/10.1515/cogl.2001.014
Cromhout, Markus. *Jesus and Identity: Reconstructing Judean Ethnicity in Q*. Eugene, OR: Wipf & Stock, 2007.
Davies, William D. *The Setting of the Sermon on the Mount*. Cambridge: Cambridge University Press, 1964.
Davies, William D., and Dale C. Allison. *A Critical and Exegetical Commentary on the Gospel according to Saint Matthew*. Vol. 1: *Introduction and Commentary on Matthew I-VII*. International Critical Commentary. Edinburgh: T&T Clark, 1988.
Deines, Roland. *Die Gerechtigkeit der Tora im Reich des Messias: Mt 5,13-20 als Schlüsseltext der matthäischen Theologie*. Wissenschaftliche Untersuchungen zum Neuen Testament, 117. Tübingen: Mohr Siebeck, 2004.
Fauconnier, Gilles, and Mark Turner. *The Way We Think: Conceptual Blending and the Mind's Hidden Complexities*. New York: Basic Books, 2002.
Freese, J. H., trans. *Aristotle: Art of Rhetoric*. Loeb Classical Library, 193. Cambridge, MA: Harvard University Press, 1926.
Funk, Robert W., Roy W. Hoover, and The Jesus Seminar. *The Five Gospels: What Did Jesus Really Say? The Search for the Authentic Words of Jesus*. San Francisco, CA: HarperCollins, 1993.
Gale, Aaron M. *Redefining Ancient Borders: The Jewish Scribal Framework of Matthew's Gospel*. New York: T&T Clark, 2005.
Grice, Paul. *Studies in the Way of Words*. Cambridge, MA: Harvard University Press, 1989.
Guelich, Robert A. *The Sermon on the Mount: A Foundation for Understanding*. Waco, TX: Word Books, 1982.
Herzog, William R. *Prophet and Teacher: An Introduction to the Historical Jesus*. Louisville, KY: Westminster John Knox, 2005.
Howell, Timothy D. *The Matthean Beatitudes in Their Jewish Origins: A Literary and Speech Act Analysis*. Studies in Biblical Literature, 144. New York: Peter Lang, 2011. https://doi.org/10.3726/978-1-4539-0788-7
Jackson, Bernard S. "Models in Legal History: The Case of Biblical Law," *Journal of Law and Religion* 18 (2002): 1–30. https://doi.org/10.2307/1051492
—*Wisdom-Laws: A Study of the Mishpatim of Exodus 21:1–22:16*. Oxford: Oxford University Press, 2006.
Jeremias, Joachim. *The Sermon on the Mount*. Facet Books: Biblical Series. Philadelphia, PA: Fortress, 1963.
Kazen, Thomas. "The Christology of Early Christian Practice," *Journal of Biblical Literature* 127 (2008): 591–614. https://doi.org/10.2307/25610141

—*Issues of Impurity in Early Judaism*. Coniectanea Biblica: New Testament Series, 45. Winona Lake, IN: Eisenbrauns, 2010.
—*Emotions in Biblical Law: A Cognitive Science Approach*. Hebrew Bible Monographs, 36. Sheffield: Sheffield Phoenix, 2011.
—"Self-Preserving and Other-Oriented Concerns in the Jesus Tradition," 124–48 in *Voces Clamantium in Deserto: Essays in Honor of Kari Syreeni*. Edited by S.-O. Back and M. Kankaanniemi. Studier i exegetik och judaistik utgivna av Teologiska fakulteten vid Åbo Akademi, 11. Åbo: Åbo Akademi, 2012.
—*Scripture, Interpretation, or Authority: Motives and Arguments in Jesus' Halakic Conflicts*. Wissenschaftliche Untersuchungen zum Neuen Testament, 320. Tübingen: Mohr Siebeck, 2013. https://doi.org/10.1628/978-3-16-152894-1
—"The Role of Disgust in Priestly Purity Law: Insights from Conceptual Metaphor and Blending Theories," *Journal of Law, Religion and State* 3 (2014): 62–92. https://doi.org/10.1163/22124810-00301004
Keith, Chris. *Jesus against the Scribal Elite: The Origins of the Conflict*. Grand Rapids, MI: Baker Academic, 2014.
Keener, Craig S. *The Gospel of Matthew: A Socio-Rhetorical Commentary*. Grand Rapids, MI: Eerdmans, 2009.
Lakoff, George, and Mark Johnson. *Metaphors We Live By*. Chicago, IL: University of Chicago Press, 1980.
Lewis, David K. *Convention: A Philosophical Study*. Cambridge, MA: Harvard University Press, 1969.
—"Languages and Language," 3–35 in *Language, Mind, and Knowledge*. Edited by K. Gunderson. Minnesota Studies in the Philosophy of Science, 7. Minneapolis, MN: University of Minnesota Press, 1975.
Luz, Ulrich. *Matthew 1–7: A Continental Commentary*. Translated by Wilhelm C. Linss. Minneapolis, MN: Fortress, 1989.
Malina, Bruce J., and Richard L. Rohrbaugh. *Social-Science Commentary on the Synoptic Gospels*. 2nd edn. Minneapolis, MN: Fortress, 2003.
McArthur, Harvey K. *Understanding the Sermon on the Mount*. London: Epworth, 1960.
McCarthy, Michael, and Ronald Carter. "'There's Millions of Them': Hyperbole in Everyday Conversation," *Journal of Pragmatics* 36 (2004): 149–84. https://doi.org/10.1016/S0378-2166(03)00116-4
Meier, John P. *A Marginal Jew: Rethinking the Historical Jesus*. Vol. 4: *Law and Love*. New Haven, CT: Yale University Press, 2009.
Milavec, Aaron. "The Social Setting of 'Turning the Other Cheek' and 'Loving One's Enemies' in the Light of the Didache," *Biblical Theology Bulletin* 25 (1995): 131–43. https://doi.org/10.1177/014610799502500305
—*The Didache: Faith, Hope, and Life of the Earliest Christian Communities, 50-70 CE*. New York: Newman Press, 2003.
Miller, William Ian. *Eye for an Eye*. Cambridge: Cambridge University Press, 2006.
Nihan, Christophe. "Resident Aliens and Natives in the Holiness Legislation," 111–34 in *The Foreigner and the Law: Perspectives from the Hebrew Bible and the Ancient Near East*. Edited by R. Achenbach, R. Albertz, and J. Wöhrle. Wiesbaden: Harrassowitz, 2011.
Perkins, Pheme. *Jesus as Teacher*. Understanding Jesus Today. Cambridge: Cambridge University Press, 1990. https://doi.org/10.1017/CBO9780511621413
Roth, Martha T. *Law Collections from Mesopotamia and Asia Minor*. 2nd edn. SBL Writings from the Ancient World, 6. Atlanta, GA: Scholars Press, 2003.

Russell, Donald A., trans. *Quintilian: The Orator's Education.* Volume III: *Books 6-8.* Loeb Classical Library, 126. Cambridge, MA: Harvard University Press, 2002.

Schofield, Malcolm. "Cardinal Virtues: A Contested Socratic Inheritance," 11–28 in *Plato and the Stoics.* Edited by A. G. Long. Cambridge: Cambridge University Press, 2013. https://doi.org/10.1017/CBO9781139629157.002

Shaw, Teresa M. "Sex and Sexual Renunciation," 401–21 in *The Early Christian World.* Edited by Philip F. Esler. London: Routledge, 2000.

Simonetti, Manlio. *Matthew 1–13.* Ancient Christian Commentary on Scripture: New Testament, IA. Downers Grove, IL: InterVarsity, 2001.

Syreeni, Kari. "The Sermon on the Mount and the Two Ways Teaching of the Didache," 87–104 in *Matthew and the Didache: Two Documents from the Same Jewish-Christian Milieu?* Edited by H. van de Sandt. Assen/Minneapolis: Royal Van Gorcum/Fortress, 2005.

Vaage, Leif E., and Vincent L. Wimbush, eds. *Asceticism and the New Testament.* New York: Routledge, 1999.

Vahrenhorst, Martin. *"Ihr sollt überhaupt nicht schwören": Matthäus im halachischen Diskurs.* Wissenschaftliche Monographien zum Alten und Neuen Testament, 95. Neukirchen-Vluyn: Neukirchener Verlag, 2002.

Vickers, Brian. "Repetition and Emphasis in Rhetoric: Theory and Practice," 85–114 in *Repetition.* Edited by Andreas Fischer. Swiss Papers in English Language and Literature, 7. Tübingen: Gunter Narr Verlag, 1994.

Wilson, Deirdre. "Parallels and Differences in the Treatment of Metaphor in Relevance Theory and Cognitive Linguistics," *Studia Linguistica Universitatis Iagellonicae Cracoviensis* 128 (2011): 195–213. https://doi.org/10.2478/v10148-011-0025-1

Wilson, Deirdre, and Dan Sperber. "Truthfulness and Relevance," *Mind* 111.443 (2002): 583–632. https://doi.org/10.1093/mind/111.443.583

—"Relevance Theory," 607–32 in *The Handbook of Pragmatics.* Edited by G. Ward and L. R. Horn. Oxford: Blackwell, 2004.

Chapter Seven

Parables in the Sermon on the Mount—a Cognitive and Rhetorical Perspective

Lauri Thurén

Introduction

Jesus' most famous speech contains a significant number of parables. If a wide definition of the word is applied, at least 16 such *non-historical, metaphoric narratives appealing to an audience* can be distinguished in the Sermon on the Mount. They encompass about one third of Matthew 5–7.[1] Recent developments in parable research have emphasized that this literary genre sets specific challenges for interpretation.[2] Traditionally, the Sermon has been used as bedrock for Christian ethical and doctrinal issues.[3] Its academic interpretation is typically compromised by historical perspectives, while scholars have paid little attention to the existing text and its communicative functions. These external exigencies have overshadowed its parables as well. They are interpreted by adding historical information to them, which may not be necessary for understanding them—or by reconstructing their original versions.

However, the Sermon's parables in their current literary form were originally written for audiences who were unaware of their possible original versions or later historical reconstructions thereof. Even if the storyline in some instances may presuppose historical information not provided by the author, research on such details does not suffice. In order to find out how

---

1. To be exact, the parables cover no less than 31.3%, or 624 Greek words, of the Sermon, which consists of 1,991 words (according to the Nestle-Aland 28th edition).
2. The parables have particular literary and persuasive functions, which must be identified before a proper interpretation is possible. See, e.g., Charles W. Hedrick, *Many Things in Parables: Jesus and his Modern Critics* (Louisville, KY,: Westminster John Knox, 2004); Ruben Zimmermann, "How to Understand the Parables of Jesus: A Paradigm Shift in Parable Exegesis," *Acta Theologica* 2009: 157–82; Lauri Thurén, *Parables Unplugged – Reading the Lukan Parables in Their Rhetorical Context* (Minneapolis, MN: Fortress Press, 2014).
3. For some overviews, see Donald Hagner, *Matthew 1–13* (Word Biblical Commentary, 33A; Dallas, TX: Word, 1993), 82, and Craig S. Keener, *The Gospel of Matthew: A Socio-Rhetorical Commentary* (Grand Rapids, MI: Eerdmans, 2009), 160–2.

the recipients to whom the author was writing, and the audience to whom his protagonist Jesus was speaking,[4] were supposed to understand these parables, we need a cognitive and rhetorical perspective. We must ask what emotions (*pathos*) and thoughts (*logos*) these parables were designed to produce among their recipients, and how their behavior was supposed to be modified as a result. Moreover, it is vital to recognize the role of the parables in Jesus' argumentation. These questions can be answered with modern approaches to persuasion and argumentation.

Since the parables play a key role in the Sermon, their well-founded assessment is essential for understanding the whole unit. The aim of this chapter is to produce a comprehensive analysis of the parables therein, focusing on their persuasive functions. I hope that the results will shed light on the whole Sermon as well, and even contribute to its historical and ideological studies.

Since parable research easily suffers unwarranted generalizations and omission of problematic material, I will begin with empirical studies regarding all the parables in the Sermon. Then, contrary to the customary theological or historical approaches, each case will be studied with a focus on its cognitive and argumentative functions only. To this end, modern argumentation analysis will be utilized. I will ask how Matthew the author and Jesus the speaker aim to affect their audiences with these parables. In order to understand them, no external sources or manipulation of the text is required. Matthew must be held responsible for everything he writes, irrespective of his sources, of which his audience was hardly aware. From their point of view, deviations from Mark or Luke are not important. For understanding Matthew, the explicit and implicit information in his document suffices.[5]

Identifying and Measuring the Parables

In order to recognize all the parables in the Sermon a workable definition is needed. Dictionaries reflect the general, but imprecise, usage of the word, such as "a simple story used to illustrate a moral or spiritual lesson."[6] Earlier

---

4. By the "author" and the "audience" I refer to the partners of communication as they can be recognized by explicit and implicit signals in the existing document. Unlike the "implied reader" (see Wolfgang Iser, *Der implizierte Leser: Kommunikationsformen des Romans von Bunyan bis Beckett* [München: Fink, 1972]), this approach is not ahistorical, as much of that data refers to historical circumstances. Yet far reaching reconstructions of, e.g., the Matthean community are not relied on.

5. Nevertheless, since 88% of the Sermon's parables are found in Luke as well, some references to them will be made for the sake of curiosity.

6. "Parable," English: Oxford Living Dictionaries, http://www.oxforddictionaries.com/definition/english/parable?q=parable.

scholarship often referred to corresponding, inexact formal or theological features.[7] In particular, the distinction between *metaphor* and *parable* appears difficult. Thus, one cannot rely solely on formal criteria; the parable's function must be observed as well. This is actually done by the best and most comprehensive recent presentations by Klyne Snodgrass and Ruben Zimmermann. According to the in-depth definition by the latter, a parable must be narrative (at least some action or change of status takes place), fictional, realistic, metaphoric, appealing, and context-related.[8]

While Zimmerman correctly captures some features, his definition needs modification, because there are non-fictional, unrealistic, and less "context-related" parables as well. The guidelines for people going before a judge (Matt. 5.25-26, included in the *Kompendium*) are neither fictional nor non-fictional; despite the expanded narrative features toward the end, Jesus simply instructs people on what to do in a certain hypothetical judicial situation. The context suggests that it has a parabolic function.[9] Other parables are not realistic—for example, salt does not lose its taste under any circumstances (Matt. 5.13). Moreover, no parable in the Sermon is "context-related," namely, prompted by any precise exigency; Jesus simply sees the people, sits down, and starts to speak.[10] Thus, I must modify Zimmermann's definition: *A parable is a narrative, non-historical, and metaphoric saying appealing to an audience.*

Despite my theoretical remarks, Zimmermann's list of 13 parables in Matthew 5–7 offers a good point of departure.[11] Some of the parables that include two different images can be bifurcated. Moreover, the parable of the *Narrow Gate* in Matthew 7.13-14 must be included, as it fulfills Zimmermann's criteria and, despite its omission from the catalogue, it is *mirabile dictu*—assessed

---

7. See Thomas Walter Manson, *The Teaching of Jesus: Studies of Its Form and Contents* (Cambridge: Cambridge University Press, 1939), 65.

8. Ruben Zimmermann, "Die Gleichnisse Jesu—eine Hinfügung," in *Kompendium der Gleichnisse Jesu*, ed. R. Zimmermann (Gütersloh: Gütersloher Verlagshaus, 2007), 25–8; Zimmermann, *Parables*, 172–3. The definition is based on theoretical thoughts by Rüdiger Zymner, "Parabel," in *Historisches Wörterbuch der Rhetorik*, ed. J. Walter, et al. (Tübingen: Niemeyer, 2006), 6:502. Klyne R. Snodgrass, *Stories with Intent—A Comprehensive Guide to the Parables of Jesus* (Grand Rapids, MI: Eerdmans, 2008), 9, stays on the same path, albeit less precisely, as he argues: "A parable is an expanded analogy used to convince and persuade."

9. For a discussion about the parabolic nature of these verses, see section 3.4.

10. To be sure, the people include sick and poor individuals (Matt. 4.23-24), but not all of them.

11. Ruben Zimmermann, ed., *Kompendium der Gleichnisse Jesu* (Gütersloh: Gütersloher Verlagshaus, 2007), 392.

as a parable in Dirk Jonas's article in the *Kompendium*.[12] Thus, the Sermon includes 16 clearly distinguishable parables, in order of appearance:

Nr	Name	Verses	Words	Synoptic Parallels
1	*Crazy Salt*	5.13	26	Mark 9.50; 14.34-35
2	*City on a Hill*	5.14	7	- - -
3	*Lamp*	5.15	20	Mark 14.21; Luke 8.16; 11.33
4	*Going before a Judge*	5.25-26	43	Luke 12.58-59
5	*Eye as a Lamp*	6.22-23	45	Luke 11.34-35
6	*Two Masters*	6.24	27	Luke 16.13
7	*Birds*	6.26	28	Luke 12.24
8	*Lilies*	6.28-30	53	Luke 12.27
9	*Measure*	7.2	13	Mark 4.24; Luke 6.38
10	*Speck in the Eye*	7.3-5	64	Luke 6.41-42
11	*Dogs and Pigs*	7.6	25	- - -
12	*Asking*	7.7-8	24	(Luke 11.9)
13	*Bad Fathers*	7.9-11	50	Luke 11.11-13
14	*Narrow Gate*	7.13-14	44	Luke 13.24-29
15	*Bad Tree*	7.16-20	61	Luke 6.43-45
16	*Two Builders*	7.24-27	95	Luke 6.48-49

This catalogue, when connected to corresponding information about the rest of Matthew's parables, yields some interesting results. Above, I already mentioned that 31% of the Sermon consists of parables (602/1,991 words). Likewise, 29% of all of the Matthean parables occur therein (16/56). A certain escalation can be observed: the parables grow longer toward the end of the Sermon.

The same tendency continues in Matthew after the Sermon. On average, the parables in the rest of Matthew are 50% longer than in the Sermon (59 vs. 39 words). This is due to a general tendency in both Matthew and Luke (which is less visible in Mark): the documents start with short parables; they then grow longer toward the end.[13] Other formal features include the number of characters, exigency, type, and credibility. They all support the observation of the simplicity of the parables in the Sermon as compared to the rest of the document. On average, they contain 2 *characters* (individuals

---

12. Dirk Jonas, "Tretet ein!," in *Kompendium der Gleichnisse Jesu*, ed. R. Zimmermann (Gütersloh: Gütersloher Verlagshaus, 2007), 193–9.

13. For closer information and statistics, see Thurén, *Parables Unplugged*, 247–8.

or groups), whereas the other Matthean parables average 2.6 characters. In the Sermon, the parables' *exigency* is always general or undefined, whereas in rest of the document this is true in only 20% of the cases. Other Matthean parables are triggered by a defensive situation (30%) or caused by some other particular demand within the broader narrative (48%).[14] All of the parables in the Sermon are addressed to the disciples (Matt. 5.1-2) and overheard by the general audience (Matt. 7.28), whereas other parables in the document have various audiences, such as the Pharisees, the disciples and the people separately, the disciples of John, the "high priests," and some other individuals.

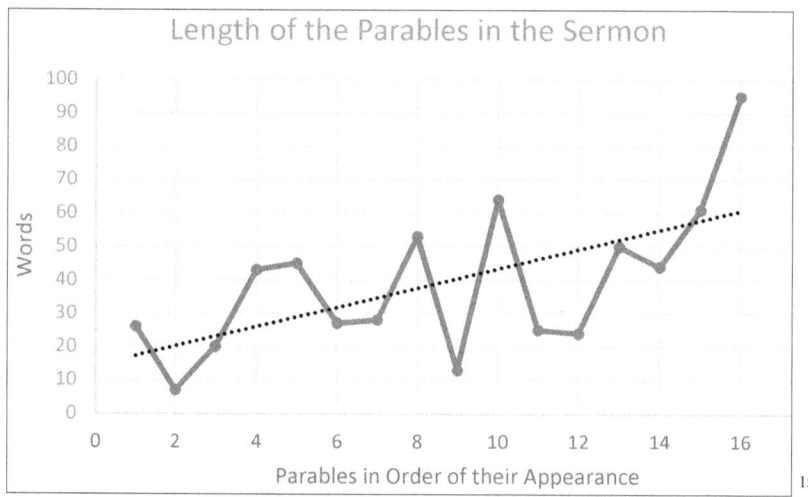
[15]

Based on the definition above, three formal *types* of parables can be found. Some parables are *simple rules*, containing only a minimal amount of "action or change of status." Others present longer *narratives*, where a clear storyline can be identified. Between these types there are parables where at least some narrative element is combined with the basic rule; these cases can be called *extended rules*. Based on these categories, the Sermon contains but one true narrative, 7.24-27 *Two Builders*. Five cases are extended rules: 5.25-26 *Going before a Judge*, 6.28-30 *Lilies*, 7.6 *Dogs and Pigs*, 7.9-11 *Bad Fathers*, and 7.13-14 *Narrow Gate*. The remaining ten parables are simple rules. Other parables in Matthew are longer and more developed.

---

14. Matt. 11.27 remains unclassified, as this parable is a prayer to God.
15. The trend line is calculated with Microsoft Excel. Excel's trend function uses the standard method of least square to calculate the trend.

	Simple rules	Extended rules	Narratives
Sermon on the Mount	63% (10)	31% (5)	6% (1)
Rest of Matthew	40% (16)	20% (8)	40% (16)

An interesting feature of the parables is their *credibility*. Assessing this feature sounds difficult, but they contain some simple indicators by which they can be measured and which I assess according to four levels of certainty. Parables based on pure reason and general knowledge are not expected to be met with any objections: "A city set on a hill cannot be hidden" (Matt. 5.14). They can be introduced with a rhetorical question (Who among you would not do this?), or they can be negative statements (Nobody behaves like this). Their expected credibility is thus high (level 5). Five parables in the Sermon belong to this category: 5.14 *City on a Hill*, 5.15 *Lamp*, 6.22-23 *Eye as a Lamp*, 7.3-5 *Speck in the Eye*, and 7.16-20 *Bad Tree*.

In the opposite case, a parable may include an *oxymoron*, or the storyline is highly suspicious. Such parables have the lowest level of credibility, level 2. In Matthew, for example, *The Great Wedding* (22.1-14) belongs to this category; a king inviting rugged people from the street to the feast sounds most unlikely. In the Sermon, *Dogs and Pigs* (7.6), where the latter tear the hearers to pieces, and *The Narrow Gate* (7.13-14) may sound correspondingly odd.

Between the extremes, there are five rules that appeal to experience more than pure logic (level 4): presumably, no father gives his son a stone for a bag lunch (7.9-11, *Bad Fathers*); yet fathers can do even worse things to their sons. Finally, there are incidents that may or may not happen (level 3): not every house built on sand will collapse (7.24-27, *Two Builders*). Four parables belong to this group.

NR	Title	Verses	Credibility	Type
1	*Crazy Salt*	5.13	4	Simple rule
2	*City on a Hill*	5.14	5	Simple rule
3	*Lamp*	5.15	5	Simple rule
4	*Going before a Judge*	5.25-26	3	Extended rule
5	*Eye as a Lamp*	6.22-23	5	Simple rule
6	*Two Masters*	6.24	4	Simple rule
7	*Birds*	6.26	4	Simple rule
8	*Lilies*	6.28-30	4	Extended rule
9	*Measure*	7.2	3	Simple rule
10	*Speck in the Eye*	7.3-5	5	Simple rule

NR	Title	Verses	Credibility	Type
11	Dogs and Pigs	7.6	2	Extended rule
12	Asking	7.7-8	3	Simple rule
13	Bad Fathers	7.9-11	4	Extended rule
14	Narrow Gate	7.13-14	2	Extended rule
15	Bad Tree	7.16-20	5	Simple rule
16	Two Builders	7.24-27	3	Narrative

The distribution of degrees of credibility across the Sermon's parables corresponds to the range of credibility of parables within the rest of Matthew.

Parables' credibility grade	High (5)	Good (4)	Fair (3)	Poor (2)
Sermon on the Mount	31%	31%	25%	13%
The rest of Matthew	32%	30%	25%	13%

A comparison between the whole of Matthew, Luke, and Mark shows an escalation of the parables' difficulty toward the end of the document.[16] The weak credibility and the greater length roughly correlate with each other.

The following chart displays all of the data about the parables in the Sermon discussed above. Moreover, corresponding analyses of other synoptic parables will enable several comparative studies.

No.	Title	Verses	Synoptic parallels	Words	Credibility	Type	Character
1	Crazy Salt	5.13	M 9.50; L 14.34-35	26	4	Simple rule	2
2	City on a Hill	5.14		7	5	Simple rule	0
3	Lamp	5.15	M 14.21; L 8.16; 11.33	20	5	Simple rule	2
4	Going before a Judge	5.25-26	L 12.58-59	43	3	Extended rule	4
5	Eye as a Lamp	6.22-23	L 11.34-35	45	5	Simple rule	1
6	Two Masters	6.24	L 16.13	27	4	Simple rule	3
7	Birds	6.26	L 12.24	28	4	Simple rule	2

---

16. See Thurén, *Unplugged*, 248.

No.	Title	Verses	Synoptic parallels	Words	Credibility	Type	Character
8	*Lilies*	6.28-30	L 12.27	53	4	Extended rule	2
9	*Measure*	7.2	M 4.24; L 6.38	13	3	Simple rule	2
10	*Speck in the Eye*	7.3-5	L 6.41-42	64	5	Simple rule	2
11	*Dogs and Pigs*	7.6		25	2	Extended rule	3
12	*Asking*	7.7-8	L 11.9	24	3	Simple rule	2
13	*Bad Fathers*	7.9-11	L 11.11-13	50	4	Extended rule	2
14	*Narrow Gate*	7.13-14	L 13.24-29	44	4	Extended rule	2
15	*Bad Tree*	7.16-20	L 6.43-45	61	5	Simple rule	2
16	*Two Builders*	7.24-27	L 6.48-49	95	3	Narrative	2

Focusing on the Cognitive and Persuasive Dimension

After the formal characterization, I will turn to the function of the parables. With all respect to historical and theological enquires regarding the parables, it is high time to ask what the messages of the author and his speaker are, as they appear in the finished form of the gospel. When analyzing the parables in this way, one need not know anything less or more than what was known by the audience to which the author was writing. Jesus' reconstructed utterances, hypothetical situations, even some per se correct pieces of information about first-century Palestine, as well as Trinitarian images, do not belong to the context provided or assumed by the author.[17] When trying to understand what kinds of reactions he wanted to create with his texts, and how he wanted to shape the attitudes, values, and behaviors of his readers, the finished form of the document must be respected. The same applies to the message of his hero, Jesus the speaker, and his audience.

All synoptic gospels present the parables as pieces of argumentation. They are tools with which the author attempts to persuade his readers. Instead of providing any new information about topics such as God, Christ, eschatology, or ethics, the parables appeal to the recipients' emotions and

---

17. Contra Snodgrass, *Stories*, 25, and many others emphasizing knowledge of the historical Jesus' context.

reasoning by telling stories that, typically, are non-religious. Usually, they refer to what is customary, reasonable, or at least acceptable in daily life or in some profession. Sporadically, exceptional but moving emotions are displayed instead.[18] The principle illustrated by the parable is then to be applied to the addressees' lives and relationship with God or other people.

In order to analyze the process of persuasion, appropriate tools are required. I will use Stephen Toulmin's famous model for argumentation analysis.[19] It offers a classical, state-of-the-art system in a form that is simple enough to be understood by a non-specialist. Perhaps its best advantage for studying parables is that it provides a controllable way of explicating the unexpressed parts of the argumentation. In Jesus' parables, such thoughts abound.

In brief, argumentation consists of certain stereotypical parts. First, there must be a *claim*, the opinion put forward. Second, there must be a common point of departure, something supporting the claim and agreed upon by the audience. This part is called the *data*. Third, there must be a general rule, the *warrant*, connecting the data and the claim. Since this rule is seldom completely accepted by the audience, it needs *backing*, namely, generally accepted information or examples supporting the warrant.

---

18. For example, the *Samaritan* (Luke 10.30-37) or the *Prodigal Son* (Luke 15.11-32) depend on the protagonist's emotion instead of their customary behavior: their sudden compassion (*splanchnizomai* in the aorist form). The longer parables typically end with a surprise, but if it is too weird for the audience, the parable has failed and does not serve the persuasion (for example Luke 20.16b; unlike Matt. 21.41). Many of the least acceptable and thus weakest parables deal with a master, who acts against standard customs, for example the *Bad Servant* (Matt. 24.45-51), *Bridesmaids* (25.1-13), *Talents* (25.14-30). Yet they are based on the audience's acceptance of the master's *patria potestas*. This, following the Jewish *qal wahomer*-reasoning, suggests that God too can act accordingly.

19. Stephen Edelston Toulmin, *The Uses of Argument* (Cambridge: Cambridge University Press, 1958), and Stephen Edelston Toulmin, et al, *An Introduction to Reasoning* (2nd edn.; New York: Macmillan, 1984). Toulmin was one of the founding fathers of modern argumentation analysis. Biblical scholars are finally becoming aware of the benefits of this widely used and sophisticated discipline. See closer Frans H. van Eemeren, Rob Grootendorst, and Tjark Kruiger, *Handbook of Argumentation Theory: A Critical Survey of Classical Backgrounds and Modern Studies* (Studies of Argumentation in Pragmatics and Discourse Analysis, 7; Dordrecht and Providence: Foris Publications, 1987); Niilo Lahti, *The Maneuvering Paul – a Pragma-Dialectical Analysis of Paul's Argumentation in First Corinthians 4:18–7:40* (Dissertation; Joensuu: University of Eastern Finland, 2017). For reasons why ancient approaches to argumentation are problematic, see Lauri Thurén, "Is There Biblical Argumentation?," in *Rhetorical Argumentation in Biblical Texts,* ed. A. Eriksson, et al. (Harrisburg, PA: Trinity Press International, 2002), 77–92.

> Backing: The proportion of Roman Catholic Swedes is less than 2%
> ▼
> Warrant: A Swede is not a Roman Catholic
> ▼
> Data: Petersen is a Swede ─► Claim: Petersen is not a Roman Catholic

In real argumentation, such as that connected to the parables, all of the parts are seldom visible. By closely following Toulmin's descriptions, they can, however, be estimated. Despite this seemingly simple structure, applying it to real text requires some expertise. Too often, the general parts (backing and warrant) are confused with the particular data. Fortunately, the results of a Toulminian analysis are easy to understand and scrutinize.

When a parable's persuasive function is expressed according to Toulmin's model, it is usually best labeled as a backing. When the author tells his audience a parable, he distances them from the actual situation. He tries to show how some general principle applies in another setting. Only then does he ask the audience to relate the same principle to the case at hand. This theory is based on reading the parables as coherent narratives instead of applying particular details therein. Such an *allegorical* reading would lack any persuasive force. If Jesus claimed something about God or the audience by just using cover names, this is unlikely to add to the credibility of his proclamation.[20] Instead, he can tell a story where a king gets mad at his fraudulent servants. Then, he refers to typical Jewish *qal wahomer* reasoning: if an earthly master acts in this way, how much more will God do the same?

The Parables in the Sermon as Persuasive Devices

All the parables in the Sermon take place in the same situation. Matthew, the author, refers to "large crowds ... from Galilee and the Decapolis and Jerusalem and Judea and from beyond the Jordan," as well as to the disciples. Jesus presents them with a single speech, and the people are astonished (ἐξεπλήσσοντο). Despite any per se feasible hypotheses about the origins of the different elements of these chapters, Matthew presents the

---

20. The *Sower* (13.3-8) appears to contradict this idea, since Matthew's Jesus gives it an allegorical explanation (13.18-23). Unlike the Lukan version, no narrative climax can be discerned. However, even there the parable as a whole, not only its details, should be applied to the audience's situation. As a backing, it illuminates a general warrant: understanding the message is more important than merely hearing it.

Sermon as given in one session. In order to understand the message and the assumed impact of his text, it ought to be studied accordingly.[21]

The absence of any specific exigency presents a challenge to the analysis. The persuasive function of Matthew's longer narratives is easier to detect, as there he typically provides more information about the situation. Most of the Sermon's parables (88%) occur in Luke as well, but their setting there is not much clearer: only three cases have a particular situation.[22] In the following, I will briefly scrutinize each parable by first assessing its formal features and then estimating its argumentative structure.

1. Crazy Salt, 5.13

You are the salt of the earth; but if the salt goes crazy (μωρανθῇ) how can it be made salty again? It is no longer good for anything, except to be thrown out and trampled underfoot by men (cf. Mark 9.50; Luke 14.34-35).

This brief simple rule contains 26 words and displays one obscure group. The credibility is good (4), but not excellent, as it requires some knowledge about salt.

The surprising word *mōranthē* explicitly reminds of the popular rhetorical technique called *oxymoron*, referring to something irrational, absurd, and impossible:[23] it is chemically impossible for salt to become not salty. Commentators' attempts to find substances in Palestine that were falsely called *salt* and could lose their effect are out of place, as there is no guarantee that Matthew's recipients were aware of them. Likewise, hypotheses about where salt was used, or whether the word has some metaphorical meaning, are superfluous.[24] Without adding any new information to the parable, it must be stated that for Matthew's audience, the image sounds impossible, not customary. This is probably exactly what he wants.[25] A corresponding

---

21. While Hagner, *Matthew*, 83, may well be historically right when referring to the wide scholarly consensus that the Sermon "is 'clearly' a compilation of the sayings of Jesus by the evangelist," this is not what the author and his speaker tell their audiences. In order to understand their messages, Matthew 5–7 must be studied as a coherent entity. To be sure, *tous logous toutous* (7.28) could refer to several speeches as well, but nothing else in the text supports this idea.

22. Luke's versions of *Crazy Salt* (Luke 14.34-35), *Asking* (Luke 11.9), and *Bad Fathers* (Luke 11.11-13) are presented in a particular situation; yet he aims six parables at the disciples instead of a general audience.

23. Heinrich Lausberg, *Handbook of Literary Rhetoric: A Foundation for Literary Study*, trans. M. T. Bliss, et al; ed. D. E. Orton and R. D. Anderson (Leiden: Brill, 1998), §807.

24. Hagner, *Matthew*, 99, refers to such explanations.

25. John Drury, *The Parables in the Gospels—History and Allegory* (Crossroad: New York, 1985), 138, correctly notes the absurdity of the parallel parable in Luke.

rhetorical technique is used in *Camel* (19.24):[26] even if impossible things happen, rich people do not enter the Kingdom. Contrary to Luke, Matthew's Jesus compares his audience with salt. The particular purpose for using salt is not revealed; thus, no implicit qualities are to be applied to the audience. Jesus emphasizes *that* salt must be used, not *how* it is used. What counts is that salt must maintain its quality in order to be used properly. Otherwise, it cannot do anything, *eis ouden ischyei*. The reasoning consists of two parts, of which Luke only has the second. Matthew's Jesus begins with a metaphor: "You are the salt of the earth."

Part I

W: Salt cannot be used improperly
▼
D: (As disciples) you are the salt of the earth ─▶ C: You must perform your task properly

Part II

B: **Salt becoming "crazy" would make it useless**[27] (4)
▼
W: Losing their essential characteristics makes things useless
▼
D: You must perform your task properly ─▶ C: You shall not lose the
characteristics of discipleship
▲
Counter-*rebuttal*:[28] even if impossible things happened, this shall not take place

2. City on a Hill, 5.14

You are the light of the world. A city set on a hill cannot be hidden (Matthew only).

This simple rule consists of seven words—or 13, if the reference to *light* is included. The brief version is Matthew's shortest parable. The credibility is excellent (5), since no objections are assumed.[29] Like the previous parable, this one too refers to the audience, illustrating a principle that ought to be applied. No human characters are involved. The parable stays on a general level; there is no exhortation to do good works.[30]

---

26. See also Isa. 49.15 (a woman forgetting her nursing child) and 54.10 (mountains being removed).
27. The parable will be referred to using **bold text**.
28. The *rebuttal* expresses the circumstances under which the claim is valid (Toulmin, *Uses*, 81–101).
29. Apparently, Jesus did not think of heavy fog. Axiomatic references to Jerusalem (Hagner, *Matthew*, 100) are out of place, since the sermon was given in Galilee.
30. Contra Hagner, *Matthew*, 100.

B: **Example of a city on a hill** (5)
▼
W: Visible things cannot be hidden
▼
D: (As disciples or as "light") You are highly visible —▶ C: You cannot hide yourselves
(without losing your characteristics)

3. Lamp, 5.15

Nor does anyone light a lamp and put it under a basket, but on the lampstand, and it gives light to all who are in the house (cf. Mark 14.21; Luke 8.16; 11.33).

This simple rule consists of 20 words, displaying a domestic issue. The credibility is good (5), indicated by a negative introduction: nobody does this. Two characters are involved. The parable differs from the parallel in Luke, especially by allegorically introducing the audience in the parable. Nevertheless, its primary function is that of a backing: to exemplify and support a general rule (warrant).

B: **No one after lighting a lamp puts it under a basket** (5)
▼
W: All things must be used properly
▼
D: You are the light of the world (5.13) —▶ C: You must shine before men (5.16)

Verse 16 presents an additional reasoning, which glides from the parable to the real world. To put it simply:

W: Good works cause glorification
▼
D: You want God to be praised —▶ C: You must do good works

All three of the opening parables stay on an abstract level. They emphasize the importance of keeping a high profile as disciples, but no specific issues are discussed. In one sense, however, the parable about the lamp differs from its predecessors: while it is virtually impossible for salt to become non-salt, and for a city to be hidden, a light can technically be hidden. Thus, this parable marks the climax of this section, discouraging the audience from acting in an improper way.

4. Going before the Judge, 5.25-26

Make friends quickly with your opponent at law while you are with him on the way, so that your opponent may not hand you over to the judge, and the judge

> *to the constable, and you be thrown into prison. Truly I say to you, you will not come out of there until you have paid up the last cent* (cf. Luke 12.58-59).

These verses appear to be nothing else but practical guidelines in an awkward situation. However, their theological context makes them a parable. The preceding threats in verse 22 do not refer to human sanctions; no court would find somebody guilty for getting angry at his brother and calling him a fool; and nobody can send another to *Gehenna*. Thus, when read in its context within the Sermon, the *prison* here apparently has some theological connotation as well. Like in Matthew 23.3-12 (or Luke 14.8-14), the seemingly practical guidelines for decent behavior function as parables referring to divine vindication.

This extended rule is rather similar to Luke's version. It has 43 words, but no fewer than four characters (you, the opponent, the judge, and the constable). The credibility is not very good (3)—why could not the opponent lose the case and be thrown in jail instead? To be sure, 5.26 suggests that the quarrel is about money, but since an official verdict is needed, the case is far from solved.

Apparently, the reasoning is built upon the idea that a judge's decision cannot be anticipated. As typical for the Sermon, the story is aimed at a general audience without any particular exigency. It refers to the audience's behavior, but simultaneously says something about God. However, as in the previous parable, both the data and the claim are unclear. The latter is expressed in verse 25, which is hardly a practical warning against anger.[31] It stresses that things must be sorted out before it is too late. An allegorical reading would lead to disarray: is God the debtor, the judge, or the constable? Alternatively, who else could they be? Instead, one should look at the principle illustrated by the parable. There are many minor pieces of reasoning within the parable, such as the comparison between the costs of settling the case with the opponent compared to the fines to be paid in order to get out of prison. The time factor is also important: the opportunity to make things right will soon be lost. In any case, the basic structure is clear.

B: **Preparing for an unpredicted court trial** (3)
▼
W: Better safe than sorry
▼
(D: You will face the trial of God in the near future ─▶ C: Be prepared soon, even if it may cost you)

---

31. Contra Hagner, *Matthew*, 118.

The more implicit theological version could read as follows:

B: **Preparing for an unpredicted court trial** (3)
▼ ▼
W: Better safe than sorry W: If an earthly judge is to be avoided, how much more the heavenly judge
▼ ▼
(D: You will face the trial of God →▶ C: Be prepared for it soon, even if it may cost you)

5. Eye as a Lamp, 6.22-23

The eye is the lamp of the body; so then if your eye is "simple" (ἁπλοῦς),[32] *your whole body will be full of light. But if your eye is bad* (πονηρός), *your whole body will be full of darkness. If then the light that is in you is darkness, how great is the darkness!* (cf. Luke 11.34-35).

Despite its length (45 words), this is a simple rule, since no real action is presented. There is but one character. Although both adjectives πονηρός and ἁπλοῦς are difficult to understand in this context, their function is clear: they indicate opposite qualities of an eye: the "bad eye" makes the body dark, the "simple" makes it light. Thus, only the latter functions well. The idea of illuminating the inner parts of the body may seem strange to modern readers, in the ancient world it was hardly exceptional.[33] Thus, this is one of the few parables where some knowledge outside of the text is required when assessing the credibility as good (4). What general rule does the parable refer to, and how is this to be applied? It argues that a dysfunctional eye makes the whole body dark, which is to be avoided. Allegorical allusions for example to an *evil eye*,[34] would dismiss the parable, where the eye plays an integral role, illuminating a general rule. A single word is not to be separated as a metaphor from its meaning in the whole narrative.

The parable is close to its Lukan parallel, but here a clear application is missing. The data apparently refers to something to be observed, and the claim argues that the audience ought to take care of their ability to do so. Unfortunately, the Matthean Jesus is no more explicit about the subject

---

32. Anssi Voitila, "ἁπλοῦς, ἁπλότης," in *Historical and Theological Lexicon of the Septuagint*. Vol. 1: *Alpha – Gamma*, ed. E. Bons (Tübingen: Mohr-Siebeck, 2020), 927–38, offers a fresh, comprehensive study of the different meanings of the word. Here, the sense can be derived from the opposite adjective.

33. Cf. Prov. 20.27, "The spirit of man is the lamp of the Lord, searching the chambers of the body."

34. Hagner, *Matthew*, 158–9.

to be observed.³⁵ The closest reference would be the difference between earthly and heavenly treasures (Matt. 6.19-21, 24). Just as a good vision is important for the body, so is the ability to observe the heavenly treasures important for the disciples. Since parables typically support a general rule, the following argumentation scheme can be detected:

B: **A dysfunctional eye makes the whole body dark** (3)
▼
W: Inability to see is dangerous for a person
▼
D: Earthly assets [are visible but]   ─▶ C: Take care of your ability
cannot be trusted   to see the [invisible] heavenly treasures

6. Two Masters, 6.24

No one can serve two masters; for either he will hate the one and love the other, or he will be devoted to one and despise the other. You cannot serve God and Mammon (cf. Luke 16.13).

This simple rule has 27 words and three characters. It refers to a domestic setting, the servants' experience. The credibility is good (4). Although two master characters are present, their roles remain passive. The strong language has misguided some interpreters to mollify the message, which is clear indeed.³⁶ The reasoning can be depicted in two ways. Since the metaphorical use of *serving* continues in the claim, the parable could exceptionally be a warrant; then the extension in verse 24b, connected to the rule with γάρ, would serve as a backing, supporting the warrant. In this interpretation, the real characters (God, Mammon) are directly—and allegorically—identified with the two masters.

B: General image of servants
▼
W: **Nobody can serve two masters, but hates one and loves the other** (4)
▼
D: God and Mammon require your obedience ─▶ C: You cannot serve them both

However, since verse 24b continues the imagery of the rule in verse 24a, they together serve as a backing; they illustrate a more general rule. In this case, no

---

35. Contrary to Luke 11.29-33, referring to Jesus as an important sign.
36. Hagner, *Matthew*, 159, argues based on Jesus' hard saying in Luke 14.26 about hating one's relatives that *hatred* cannot mean "hatred as we understand the word." However, Jesus does not tell his audience to love Mammon less than God, but to choose between two options.

allegory is required. Although not available to the implied audience, Gospel of Thomas 47.1-2 offers an interesting parallel, which does not invite direct allegory: "It is impossible for a man to mount two horses or to stretch two bows."

B: **Nobody can serve two masters, but hates one and loves the other** (4)
▼
W: Two authorities cannot be held simultaneously
▼

D: God and Mammon require your obedience —▶ C: You cannot serve both God and Mammon

7. Birds, 6.26

Look at the birds of the air, that they do not sow, nor reap nor gather into barns, and yet your heavenly father feeds them. Are you not worth much more than they? And who of you by being worried can add a single hour to his life? (cf. Luke 12.24).

This simple rule has but 28 words and two characters. Unlike in Luke, the species of bird is not stated. The parable refers to a natural phenomenon, even when God is mentioned. The credibility is good (4), as the parable relies on the recipients' own observation, not only on traditional Jewish thinking.[37] The message of the parable deals explicitly with God. Instead of simply promoting a careless attitude, it carries a specific message in the context, which speaks of discipleship: it must not be compromised by economic problems.[38]

Although the parable is brief, the reasoning is based on several stages. Actually, it serves as a rebuttal to the addressees' assumed thinking:

W: Maintaining life requires concern about several issues
▼

D: You want to maintain your life —▶ C: You must be anxious about what to eat, etc.
▲
R: Unless 6.26

First, Jesus urges his audience to observe the birds in order to prove that they are not anxious:

I.

W: Who does not sow is not anxious about eating
▼

D: Observing the birds ▶ Birds do not sow, etcetera —▶ C: Birds are not anxious

---

37. Pace Hagner, *Matthew*, 163–4.
38. Cf. Hagner, *Matthew*, 164.

Second, the birds' example is used to illustrate a general rule:

II.

           B: **Birds are not anxious about life, yet God feeds them** (4)
                      ▼
        W: Anxiety is not required for maintaining life
                      ▼
D: You want to maintain your life (eat, etc.) ⎯▶ C: You must not be anxious
                    [⎯▶ Do not let economic problems compromise your
                           discipleship]

Third, a *qal wahomer* structure boosts the effect of the reasoning:

III.

                B: General concept of *qal wahomer*
                           ▼
            W: One takes better care of more valuable things
                           ▼
D: God takes care of the birds
D: You are more valuable than birds   ⎯▶ C: God takes better care of you

8. Lilies, 6.28-30

> *And why are you worried about clothing? Observe how the lilies of the field grow; they do not toil nor do they spin, yet I say to you that not even Solomon in all his glory clothed himself like one of these. But if God so clothes the grass of the field, which is alive today and tomorrow is thrown into the furnace, will He not much more [clothe] you? You of little faith!* (cf. Luke 12.27).

This sister parable is an extended rule; the rule is enriched by telling in verse 30 how the grass is processed. It has 51 words and two characters: Solomon and the field-workers. It too refers to an observation of nature, despite having a theological dimension. The credibility is likewise good (4), and the audience, exigency, and reference remain the same. A combined and simplified structure, including the *qal wahomer* reasoning, can be displayed:

B: **God clothes lilies better than Solomon** (4) (B2: General concept of *qal wahomer*)
          ▼   ▼
  W1: God takes care of nature   W2: Will he not [take care] much
                                               more of you?
         ▼
D: You are more valuable than nature ⎯▶ C: God certainly takes care of you
                                                   ▶ Do not worry about your clothing,
                                                      etcetera

9. Measure, 7.2

For in the way you judge, you will be judged; and by your standard of measure, it will be measured to you (cf. Mark 4.24; Luke 6.38b).

This brief parable (12 words, two characters) is unlike the Lukan parallel, which is not supported by an example from the marketplace. Thus, its credibility is weaker (3): who guarantees that the maxim will work in practice? The saying is a rule that is repeated later as the Golden Rule, or actually *Ius talionis*: "In everything, therefore, treat people the same way you want them to treat you" (Matt. 7.12). This first version is a parable, referring to general social and business conventions, hardly to judicial issues. The data can be retrieved from 7.1b, "in order not to be judged": you want to avoid being judged. The *passivum divinum* may refer to God's judgment as well.

B: General social and business conventions (7.2)
▼
W: *Ius talionis* (3)
▼
D: You want to avoid being judged (by God) ⎯▶ C: Do not judge other people

10. Speck in the Eye, 7.3-5

Why do you look at the speck that is in your brother's eye, but do not notice the log that is in your own eye? Or how can you say to your brother, 'Let me take the speck out of your eye,' and behold, the log is in your own eye? You hypocrite, first take the log out of your own eye, and then you will see clearly to take the speck out of your brother's eye (cf. Luke 6.41-42).

Despite its length (64 words, two characters), this parable is a simple rule—actually a rhetorical question "Why?" It presupposes that the audience replies: "I have no reason to do so." According to an everyday experience, one feels a speck in the own eye even when nobody else observes it. Finding a speck in the brother's eye before he does is not probable, especially with a log in one's own eye. Thus, it has excellent (5) credibility.[39] Surprisingly, unlike the context (7.1-2), the parable does not actually speak of judging others, but of helping them (v. 4: "Let me take the speck out of your eye"). Healing another's eye is not automatically identical to criticizing him. The final exhortation in 7.5, to take the log out of one's own eye, is part of the parable and not the actual claim. Yet, together with the context it provides two options for formulating the data and the claim. Instead of supporting the

---

39. However, despite the sensible reasoning, the whole setting as such is far from credible. In this sense, the parable resembles *Crazy Salt* (5.13).

prohibition (not to judge), the parable aims at doing something: becoming a better person.⁴⁰

B: **You cannot find the speck that is in your brother's eye with a log in your own eye** (5)
▼
        W: Only a healthy/faultless individual can help others
        ▼

a) D: You want to help other people   —▶ C: Make sure you are healthy
b) D: You want to criticize other people   —▶ C: Make sure you are beyond criticism

11. Dogs and Pigs, 7.6

Do not give what is holy to dogs, and do not throw your pearls before swine, or they will trample them under their feet, and turn and tear you to pieces (στραφέντες ῥήξωσιν) (Matthew only).

Although this parable is brief (25 words), it is an extended rule, as the simple guideline is augmented by a detailed description of the animals' attack. Three characters are involved, but only one human group. The credibility of the storyline cannot be very high: hardly anyone has witnessed the peculiar course of action described. To be sure, wild swine could be dangerous, but their great interest in pearls and fierce attacks against their owners sounds exceptional (2). No synoptic parallels exist. The basic reasoning within the parable is clear:

   B: **Dogs and pigs may destroy holy things, pearls, and their owner** (2)
        ▼
      W: Lack of appreciation is destructive to holy things
        ▼

D: You own holy things   —▶ C: Do not present holy things to ill-advised people

The reference of the parable is not evident, since the context gives no precise clues. Little is gained through allegorical comparison of the dogs and swine to Gentiles, Gentile Christians, or any other ethnic or religious groups.⁴¹ Peculiar enough, the problem with the pigs here is not that Jews considered them unclean, but that they can be physically dangerous. Thus, the interpretation must stay on a general level.

"What is holy" may refer to Jesus' message, but not to issues pertaining to the Church:⁴² Jesus' audience consists of haphazard people simply interested

---

40. Against the common interpretation, e.g. by Hagner, *Matthew*, 169.
41. For such an attempt, see Hagner, *Matthew*, 171–2.
42. Thus, rightly Hagner, *Matthew*, 171.

in his healing and teaching (Matt. 4.23-25). If 7.1-5 warns against too critical of an attitude toward other people, here the message is the opposite.

B: **Example of dogs and pigs** (2)
▼
W: Credulity can be dangerous
▼
D: You have got something valuable ─▶ C: Do not entrust it to ill-advised people

12. Asking, 7.7-8

Ask, and it will be given to you; seek, and you will find; knock, and it will be opened to you. For everyone who asks receives, and he who seeks finds, and to him who knocks it will be opened (cf. Luke 11.9).

It is unclear whether these sayings can be labeled as a parable. *Asking* and *seeking* can apply directly to non-material issues as well. Only the third command, to knock on the door so that it will be opened, presents a tiny simple rule including some action. There are 24 words; two characters are involved. The credibility is only fair (3), since in real life, a door may or may not be opened. The exhortations emphasize that the hearers must do something: ask, seek, and knock. Thereby, they are not just comforted by God's help.[43] This parable presents a basic scheme, preparing the audience for the essential message in the following parable.

B: **Experience about knocking on the door** (3)
▼
W: Ask and it will be given to you
▼
D: God is able to help ─▶ C: Actively request God's help

13. Bad Fathers, 7.9-11

Or what man is there among you who, when his son asks for a loaf, will give him a stone? Or if he asks for a fish, he will not give him a snake, will he? If you then, being evil, know how to give good gifts to your children, how much more will your father who is in heaven give what is good to those who ask him! (cf. Luke 11.11-13).

This parable is an extended rule, consisting of 50 words. It is credible (4), as the rhetorical question does not expect a negative answer. The parable refers to the audience's own imaginable behavior. Whereas the previous parable supported the simple correlation between asking and receiving, this parable

---

43. Contra Hagner, *Matthew*, 174.

is more theological: Jesus assures that God's help is not just a possibility. Instead, he will help the audience—who in the text are implied to be God's *children*, namely Jews by default. He cannot be worse than bad people, who do so to their children.

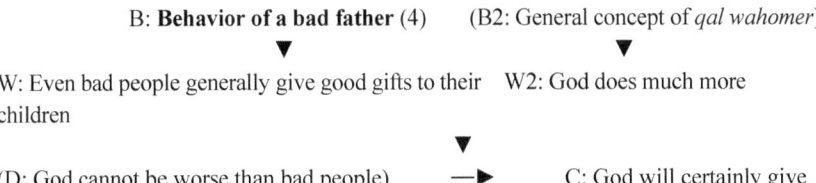

14. Narrow Gate, 7.13-14

Enter through the narrow gate; for the gate is wide and the way is broad that leads to destruction, and there are many who enter through it. For the gate is small and the way is narrow that leads to life, and there are few who find it (cf. Luke 13.24-29).

This parable is an extended rule, consisting of 44 words and two characters. The parable refers to the audience's behavior. The credibility is poor (2): why would a wider and more crowded passage be more dangerous than a discreet one? Since no explicit grounds are provided, the support must be found in the traditional metaphor of *two ways*. Perhaps the author and the speaker trust that their recipients are aware of it.[44] However, in this version, the spatial imagery does not emphasize the difficulty of proceeding (unlike in, for example, Luke 13.24).[45] The reason for the unpopularity of the way leading to life is merely that it is difficult to detect. Since the parable is not self-supporting, but a general rule requiring a backing (B), it can exceptionally be characterized a warrant (W) according to Toulmin's system:

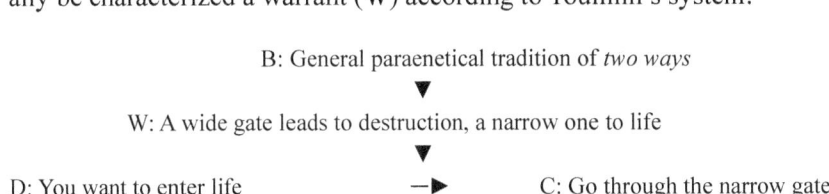

---

44. For early Jewish references, see Hagner, *Matthew*, 178–9.
45. Contra Hagner, *Matthew*, 178–9, according to whom the broadness of the other way implies "an easiness and comfort," whereas the narrow road emphasizes "the genuine e [sic] difficulty of this way."

However, "going through a gate" is a parabolic saying. Thereby, the whole parable functions as a backing to a general rule, which resembles the message of *Two Builders* (7.24-27):

> B: **A wide gate leads to destruction, a narrow one to life** (2)
> ▼
> W: Popular and easy solutions are dangerous
> ▼
> D: You want to protect your life ─▶ C: Choose an unpopular solution

15. Bad Tree, 7.16-20

> *You will know them by their fruits. Grapes are not gathered from thorn bushes nor figs from thistles, are they? So every good tree bears good fruit, but the bad tree bears bad fruit. A good tree cannot produce bad fruit, nor can a bad tree produce good fruit. Every tree that does not bear good fruit is cut down and thrown into the fire. So then, you will know them by their fruits* (cf. Luke 6.43-45).

This simple rule consists of 61 words and two characters. It refers to an experience of agriculture with excellent (5) credibility.[46] It does not refer to the quality of a tree (although the peculiar statement in v. 19 can be interpreted in this way), but to different types of trees (v. 16). It is not a general warning against hypocrisy, but tells the audience how to judge other people.[47] Matthew 12.33 uses the parable for another purpose, to urge the audience to do good.

> B2: **Example of different types of trees** [v. 16] (5)
> ▼
> B1: **Each tree is known by its fruits** [v. 17]
> ▼
> W: Appearances are unreliable, only deeds count
> ▼
> D: Bad prophets look nice ─▶ C: You will know bad prophets by their outcomes (vv. 16, 20)

Actually, the parable provides a rebuttal to a naïve trust in people's appearance, implied in verse 15:

---

46. In Luke, the credibility is weaker, since Jesus needs to support his opening statement with several examples. One could argue that occasionally even a good tree produces some bad fruit.

47. Against Hagner, *Matthew*, 184, who has to admit that this word is not even used here.

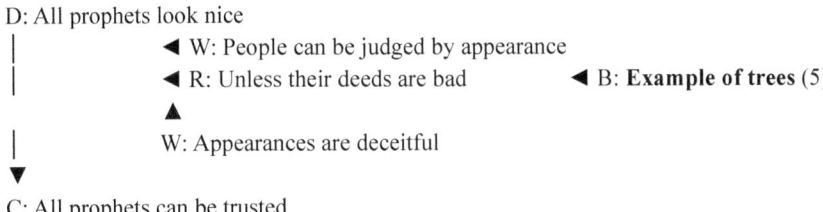

16. Two Builders, 7.24-27

Therefore everyone who hears these words of mine and acts on them, may be compared to a wise man who built his house on the rock. And the rain fell, and the floods came, and the winds blew and slammed against that house; and yet it did not fall, for it had been founded on the rock. Everyone who hears these words of mine and does not act on them, will be like a foolish man who built his house on the sand. The rain fell, and the floods came, and the winds blew and slammed against that house; and it fell—and great was its fall (cf. Luke 6.48-49).

The first narrative in Matthew (and in Luke) is longer (95 words, two characters) than the previous ones and less credible (3) than most of them. It refers to a construction worker's occupation. It too is aimed at a general audience and contains general teaching, illuminating something about them.

This proper story ends with a mighty climax, which nevertheless is not too surprising. Unlike in Luke 6.48-49, the audience is told at the outset that the second builder was a fool. The colorful story is entertaining, but where is the *point*? A wise man built a good house, a stupid man a poor one! There must be more than meets the eye. Why on earth did the second builder do such a lousy job?

Sandy soil, where rivers (οἱ ποταμοί) can surprisingly flow, refers to a *wadi* or any knowledge of floodplains. This parable does not require specific information of first-century Palestine.[48] Despite the risk, building a house on such a foundation had its benefits: it was faster and cheaper.[49] Unfortunately, the risk the man took came back to haunt him in the end. Although he is called "stupid," the story could have ended differently. What if the man lived well in his house when the rainy season began, while the other was still digging and laying the foundation? Since the ending of Jesus' story is but one of the possible outcomes, the message of the parable is possible, but not self-evident.

---

48. Thus, rightly Hagner, *Matthew*, 191.

49. However, unlike Luke 6.48, Matthew does not emphasize the man's heavy work, which makes the parable more difficult for the audience to understand. Yet nothing more than common knowledge of the relative difficulty of building on rock is required. In any case, besides revealing the man's wisdom at the outset, this is another point where Matthew appears to be a less talented storyteller than Luke.

The parable has inspired several allegorical interpretations, such as identifying a crisis with the eschatological judgment of God, allusions to the Temple, Israel, and so on.[50] Hagner sees here an attack against Paulinism "that (unlike Paul himself) champions a gospel of cheap grace."[51] All of these additions are superfluous. The parable is best seen as illustrating a general rule, which is applied to the addressees' situation.

Indeed, despite its length and lower credibility, a general rule can be identified behind this story, too. It could be formulated "Sweat saves blood" or "Making great effort to do things the right way ensures great rewards in the end." This principle is not self-evident; one could argue that in every project, some risks must be taken, and unnecessary work is to be avoided. The parable with its vivid and dramatic story aims at covering those objections or other problems inherent in the principle, which it exemplifies. Nobody is expected to identify with the man who lost his house.

B: **Narrative of two men building houses** (3)
▼
W: Great effort to do something right will reward you in the end
▼
D: You hear the teaching ─▶ C: Obey Jesus despite the costs

Conclusions

Toulmin's model combined with the principle of reading the parables *unplugged*, with neither reconstructed historical additions or exclusions nor with religious eyeglasses, yielded simple ways of understanding several tricky parables. Their messages can now be summarized. Instead of making general statements based on occasional parables or by intuition, I will put together all of the warrants supported by the parables, and all of the claims supported by these warrants. By classifying these expressions, it is possible to see more clearly the goal of the parables in this text.

These themes can be classified into the following types:

1) Miscellaneous *paraenesis* (3)
2) Keep a high profile as disciples (3)
3) Do not worry (4)
4) Do not worry, despite the costs (4)
5) Beware the antagonists (2)

---

50. Snodgrass, *Stories*, 334–7, discusses several options, including an eschatological interpretation. See also Hagner, *Matthew*, 189–90. Most of them require massive additions to the text.
51. Hagner, *Matthew*, 191–2.

C Nr	Title	Verses	Warrants	Claims	Type	Credi-bility
1	*Crazy Salt*	5.13	Losing their essential characteristics makes things useless	You shall not lose the characteristics of the discipleship	2	4
2	*City on a Hill*	5.14	Visible things cannot be hidden	You cannot hide yourselves	2	5
3	*Lamp*	5.15	All things must be used properly	You must shine before men	2	5
4	*Going before a Judge*	5.25-26	Better safe than sorry	Be prepared soon, even if it may cost you	4	3
5	*Eye as a Lamp*	6.22-23	Inability to see is dangerous for a person	Take care of your ability to see invisible treasures	1	5
6	*Two Masters*	6.24	Two authorities cannot be held simultaneously	You cannot serve both God and Mammon	4	4
7	*Birds*	6.26	Anxiety is not required for maintaining life	Do not be anxious for your life	3	4
8	*Lilies*	6.28-30	God takes care of the nature	Do not worry about you clothing etc.	3	4
9	*Measure*	7.2	Ius talionis	Do not judge other people	1	3
10	*Speck in the Eye*	7.3-5	Only a healthy / faultless individual can help others	Make sure you are healthy	1	5
11	*Dogs and Pigs*	7.6	Lack of appreciation is destructive to holy things	Do not present holy things to ill-advised people	5	2
12	*Asking*	7.7-8	Ask and it will be given to you	Actively request God's help	3	3
13	*Bad Fathers*	7.9-11	Even bad people can give good gifts to their children	God will certainly give you good things	3	4
14	*Narrow Gate*	7.13-14	A wide gate leads to destruction, a narrow one to life	Do not choose an easy solution	4	2
15	*Bad Tree*	7.26-20	Each tree is known by its fruits	You will know bad prophets by their outcome	5	5
16	*Two Builders*	7.24-27	Great effort to do something right will reward you in the end	Obey Jesus despite the costs	4	3

The parables in the Sermon do not support any particular theological or practical theme. Instead, they mostly stay on a *meta-level*, speaking of the conditions of discipleship in general. For example, by referring to birds and lilies, Matthew's Jesus emphasizes that no economic worries should prevent a full-hearted life as a disciple. Thereby, the parables prepare the hearers for the difficulties connected with discipleship. The speaker ensures that it pays to maintain a high profile, despite the difficulties. In this regard, the last parable, *Two Builders* (7.24-27), serves as a proper *peroratio* to the Sermon.[52] God will take care of Jesus' disciples, so there is no need to put trust in earthly assets such as money or people—especially not religious teachers and miracle-worker, who are discussed immediately before the *Two Builders* (7.15-23). Simultaneously, they are advised not to lose their identity. Yet, they are not motivated by any harsh threats.

The type of claim supported by the parables and the credibility grades correlate in an interesting way:

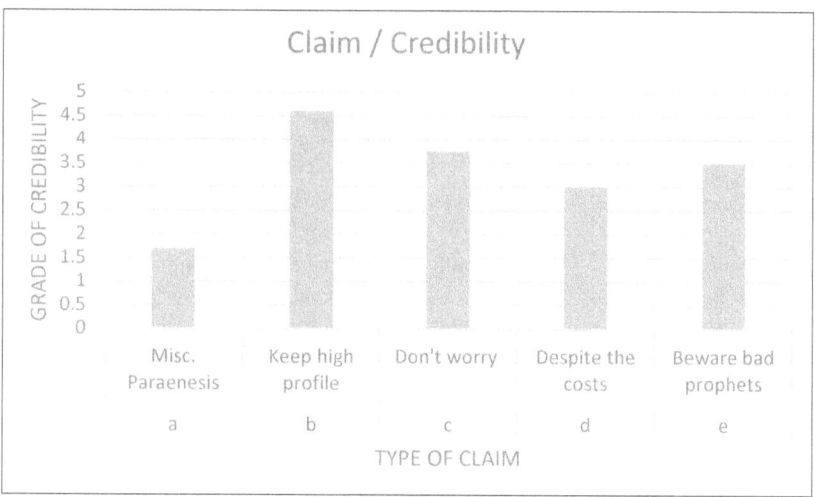

Parables supporting exhortation to keep a high profile (b) and miscellaneous commands (a) are the most credible, whereas warnings against bad prophets (e) and especially encouragement not to worry despite the costs (d) are less convincingly supported.

Compared to the rest of the document, these parables are preparatory and general. Theological narratives focusing on God's extreme goodness and extreme austerity, for example, *Workers in the Vineyard* (20.1-16), *Wicked Tenants* (21.33-46), *Wedding Banquet* (22.1-14), or *Servants* (24.45-51),

---

52. The aim of the *peroratio* is to repeat and emphasize the essential message of the presentation and exhort the audience toward action (see Lausberg, *Handbook*, §431–42).

and explicit eschatology such as in *Dragnet* (13.47-50) and *Weather Forecast* (16.2-3), are yet to come. The long narratives starting from Matthew 13.3 are more vivid, emotional, and carry deeper ideological messages than the simple rules of the Sermon.

Interestingly enough, the Sermon around the parables is different. Its fame is based on its specific commands and threats, which are often strict *ad absurdum* (for example, the social guidelines in 5.21-22 and sexual advice in 5.27-29). Their actual aims and messages have always been a riddle, and explanations abound.[53] Perhaps the nature of the parables provides an additional clue to understanding these exhortations. Based on the parables, one can suggest that the main aim of the whole Sermon is to prepare the audience for the forthcoming teaching of Jesus and Matthew's narrative about Jesus' fate. Thereby, the Sermon's function is not so much to give some virtually inapplicable pieces of advice,[54] but to add to Jesus' ethos and in other ways prepare the audience for Matthew's forthcoming presentation. A more comprehensive study could substantiate this hypothesis.

Since my goal is to read Matthew as his audience would, synoptic comparisons have been kept to a minimum. However, it is interesting to note that Matthew uses several almost identical parables in a different way or for different purposes than Luke. Unlike Luke, Matthew does not even hint at Jesus in the parables *Crazy Salt* (5.13), *Lamp* (5.15), or *Eye as a Lamp* (6.22-23). *Bad Tree* (7.16-20) refers to other people, not to the audience. Moreover, Luke has a better idea of how to tell a story—he does not reveal the stupidity of the second builder (7.24-27) at the outset, and he emphasizes the wise man's hard work. Yet, based on these stories, no essential narratological or theological differences between the two evangelists can be demonstrated. The one parable Luke would really envy, epitomizing his emphasis on God's sovereign love toward people who do not deserve it, is found in Matthew's *Workers in the Vineyard* (20.1-16).

Finally, the cognitive and rhetorical role of the parables in the Sermon may be discussed. This analysis has given support to the hypothesis that through his parables, Matthew's Jesus does not actually tell the audience anything new. Little is said about theology, Christology, eschatology, or even ethics. Instead, the parables present commonly acceptable images and stories illustrating some general, mostly non-theological principles. These ideas are then supposed to be applied to the audience's own situation. By moving their thoughts for a moment from their real lives and

---

53. For a brief overview, see Hagner, *Matthew*, 82–3.
54. For example, the lifetime expectancy of people practicing the guidelines in 5.29-30 must be short.

actual circumstances to an imaginary story-world, Jesus gives them some leeway: they are invited to contemplate the issue not in a theoretical context, but in a narrative one. When following any story, the audience "makes an agreement" with the speaker to follow him into that story-world in order to experience something.[55] This experience is often emphasized with emotional components and a good storyline.[56] Afterwards, the audience is then encouraged to apply the experience or lesson they have learnt to their real lives. Contrary to a dozen other parables in Matthew, the Sermon's audience does not include any explicit antagonists, so this shift of worlds serves for overcoming the conventional paths of thinking and behavior only.

The narratological and rhetorical strategy, which is based on the parables' ability to distance the audience from the actual situation or daily life, can be compromised, especially by one effective tool: allegorical interpretation. If the characters and events in the story are closely identified with some real-life individuals or phenomena, the narrative loses its persuasive power as a parable. Describing some situation with cover names does not add to the credibility of any argumentation. In some cases, which seem to encourage such a reading, the Jewish *qal wahomer* reasoning offers a more persuasive alternative. Thus, despite its alluring nature, allegory does not explain the power of the parables of Matthew in early phases of the tradition.

Yet, as the patristic allegorical interpretation of the parables indicate, they may have other ways of serving religious proclamation at a later stage, when the readers are already committed to the worldview promoted by these stories. Moreover, these parables provide an important source for studying the historical Jesus and his environment. However, these valuable goals should not prevent us from seeing their argumentative role in their actual context.

Biographical Note

Lauri Thurén gained his PhD in theology in 1990, from Åbo Akademi University. He undertook further studies at University of Turku (Finland), Uppsala University (Sweden), and Graduate Theological Union (CA, USA). Since 2001, he has been Professor of Biblical Studies at University of Eastern Finland. Major monographs include *Parables Unplugged: Reading the*

---

55. See Erwin M. Segal, "A Cognitive-Phenomenological Theory of Fictional Narrative," in *Deixis in Narrative: A Cognitive Science Perspective*, ed. J. F. Duchan, G. A. Bruder, and L. E. Hewitt (Hillsdale, NJ: Lawrence Erlbaum, 1995), 70–1.

56. Perhaps the most sophisticated model for analyzing storytelling as a cognitive process is developed by Monika Fludernik, *Towards a 'Natural' Narratology* (London/New York: Routledge, 1996) and *An Introduction to Narratology*, trans. P. Häusler-Greenfield and M. Fludernik (London: Routledge, 2010).

Lukan Parables in Their Rhetorical Context (Fortress, 2014), *Derhetorizing Paul: A Dynamic Perspective on Pauline Theology and the Law* (Mohr Siebeck, 2000), and *Argument and Theology in 1 Peter: The Origins of Christian Paraenesis* (Sheffield Academic Press, 1996). His current research interests cover the parables of Jesus, the antagonists in the New Testament, rhetorical criticism, and argumentation analysis.

Bibliography

Drury, John. *The Parables in the Gospels—History and Allegory*. New York: Crossroad, 1985.
van Eemeren, Frans H., Rob Grootendorst, and Tjark Kruiger. *Handbook of Argumentation Theory: A Critical Survey of Classical Backgrounds and Modern Studies*. Studies of Argumentation in Pragmatics and Discourse Analysis, 7. Dordrecht, Holland: Foris Publications, 1987. https://doi.org/10.1515/9783110846096
Fludernik, Monika. *Towards a "Natural" Narratology*. London: Routledge, 1996. https://doi.org/10.1515/jlse.1996.25.2.97
—*An Introduction to Narratology*. Translated by M. Fludernik and P. Häusler-Greenfield. London: Routledge, 2010. https://doi.org/10.4324/9780203882887
Hagner, Donald. *Matthew 1–13*. Word Biblical Commentary, 33A. Dallas, TX: Word, 1993.
Hedrick, Charles W. *Many Things in Parables: Jesus and his Modern Critics*. Louisville, KY: Westminster John Knox, 2004.
Iser, Wolfgang. *Der implizierte Leser: Kommunikationsformen des Romans von Bunyan bis Beckett*. München: Fink, 1972.
Jonas, Dirk. "Tretet ein!," 193–9 in *Kompendium der Gleichnisse Jesu*. Edited by R. Zimmermann. Gütersloh: Gütersloher Verlagshaus, 2007.
Keener, Craig S. *The Gospel of Matthew: A Socio-Rhetorical Commentary*. Grand Rapids, MI: Eerdmans, 2009.
Lahti, Niilo. *The Maneuvering Paul – a Pragma-Dialectical Analysis of Paul's Argumentation in First Corinthians 4:18–7:40*. Dissertation; University of Eastern Finland, Joensuu, 2017.
Lausberg, Heinrich. *Handbook of Literary Rhetoric: A Foundation for Literary Study*. Edited by D. E. Orton and R. D. Anderson. Translated by M. T. Bliss. Leiden: Brill, 1998.
Manson, Thomas Walter. *The Teaching of Jesus: Studies of Its Form and Contents*. Cambridge: Cambridge University Press, 1939.
Segal, Erwin M. "A Cognitive-Phenomenological Theory of Fictional Narrative," 70–1 in *Deixis in Narrative: A Cognitive Science Perspective*. Edited by J. F. Duchan, G. A. Bruder, and L. E. Hewitt. Hillsdale, NJ: Lawrence Erlbaum, 1995.
Snodgrass, Klyne R. *Stories with Intent—a Comprehensive Guide to the Parables of Jesus*. Grand Rapids, MI: Eerdmans, 2008.
Thurén, Lauri. "Is There Biblical Argumentation?," 77–92 in *Rhetorical Argumentation in Biblical Texts*. Edited by A. Eriksson. Harrisburg, PA: Trinity Press International, 2002.
—*Parables Unplugged – Reading the Lukan Parables in Their Rhetorical Context*. Minneapolis, MN: Fortress, 2014. https://doi.org/10.2307/j.ctt9m0vdv

Toulmin, Stephen Edelston. *The Uses of Argument.* Cambridge: Cambridge University Press, 1958.
Toulmin, Stephen Edelston, Richard Rieke, and Allan S. Janik. *An Introduction to Reasoning.* 2nd edn. New York: Macmillan, 1984.
Voitila, Anssi. "ἁπλοῦς, ἁπλότης," 927–38 in *Historical and Theological Lexicon of the Septuagint.* Vol. 1: Alpha – Gamma. Edited by E. Bons. Tübingen: Mohr-Siebeck, 2020.
Zimmermann, Ruben. "Die Gleichnisse Jesu—eine Hinfügung," 25–8 in *Kompendium der Gleichnisse Jesu.* Edited by R. Zimmermann. Gütersloh: Gütersloher Verlagshaus, 2007.
—"How to Understand the Parables of Jesus: A Paradigm Shift in Parable Exegesis," *Acta Theologica1* (2009): 157–82. https://doi.org/10.4314/actat.v29i1.44175
Zimmermann, Ruben, ed. *Kompendium der Gleichnisse Jesu.* Gütersloh: Gütersloher Verlagshaus, 2007.
Zymner, Rüdiger. "Parabel," *Historisches Wörterbuch der Rhetorik* 6:502.

Chapter Eight

Is There a Reason to Worry?
A Pragma-Dialectical Analysis of Matthew 6.25-34

Niilo Lahti

Introduction

The complexity and fascination of the Sermon on the Mount derive partially from Jesus' extreme exhortations and commands, which often seem poorly justified. To be sure, I hope that it will be paid attention to, whether my claim about the Introduction holds in the final version of the book,[1] even those who do not consider Jesus as an authoritative figure have referred to them and considered them important. What is this effect based on? What are the cognitive and argumentative features that enable it?[2] Part of the answer to these questions lies in the analysis of the argumentative and rhetorical aspects of a discourse, using the pragma-dialectical approach to argumentation. Pragma-dialectics is considered by some to be "the most important argumentation theory in the world today."[3] The method examines argumentation

---

1. Chapter 1, this volume.
2. Charles E. Carlston, "Matthew 6:24–34," *Interpretation* 41 (1987): 179–83, 179 rightly asks: "How then shall these transparent statements be understood, since they evidently cannot mean exactly what they say?"
3. Frans H. van Eemeren and Rob Grootendorst, *A Systematic Theory of Argumentation: The Pragma-Dialectical Approach* (Amsterdam/Philadelphia: John Benjamins, 2004), back cover. Pragma-dialectics and its extension, strategic maneuvering, has been applied full-scale only once to a biblical text. Such a study was conducted by Mika Hietanen when he analyzed Paul's argumentation in Galatians (*Paul's Argumentation in Galatians: A Pragma-Dialectical Analysis* [New York: T&T Clark, 2007], based on Hietanen's doctoral thesis, which was published in 2005). However, Hietanen did not apply strategic maneuvering to its full potential, partially because the notion was not developed to the degree it is in the monograph *Strategic Maneuvering* (Frans H. van Eemeren, *Strategic Maneuvering in Argumentative Discourse: Extending the Pragma-Dialectical Theory of Argumentation* [Amsterdam: John Benjamins, 2010]). See also Niilo Lahti, "Shameful Corinthians: A Pragma-Dialectical Analysis of 1 Corinthians 6:12–v20," in *Proceedings of the 8th International Society for the Study of Argumentation*, ed. B. J. Garssen, et al. (Amsterdam: Sic Sat, 2015), 825–35, which deals with the pragma-dialectical analysis of 1 Cor. 6.12-20 in the latest ISSA conference article collection. My dissertation is a full-scale pragma-dialectical analysis of 1 Cor. 4.18–7.40: Niilo Lahti, *The Maneuvering Paul*

through a model for critical discussion, which promotes the resolution of a dispute on the merits. In addition, pragma-dialectics considers the speaker's efforts to win the dispute by employing rhetorical devices and tactics. This aspect is accounted for in the notion of strategic maneuvering.

The attempt to be reasonable and effective and the interplay of these two goals is prominent in Matthew 6.25-34, in which Jesus argues for not needing to worry. The section of the Sermon holds several arguments that support this claim, but some of them appear problematic at least at first sight. Is there a reason to worry about the reasons whether one should worry or not? In this chapter, I shall conduct a pragma-dialectical analysis of Matthew 6.25-34 in order to scrutinize the curious argumentative and rhetorical features of the section.

Pragma-Dialectics

From a pragma-dialectical viewpoint, the goal of argumentation is to resolve a difference of opinion in a *critical discussion*. In order to clarify what is involved in viewing argumentative discourse as aimed at resolving a dispute,[4] the notion of critical discussion is given shape in an *ideal model*. The model describes what argumentative discourse would be like if it were optimally aimed at resolving a dispute regarding the tenability of a standpoint. Features that do not contribute to the critical resolution process, such as repetitions, digressions, and expressions of emotions, are ignored. The model specifies the various *argumentative stages* in the resolution process, which are as follows:[5]

– *a Pragma-Dialectical Analysis of Paul's Argumentation in First Corinthians 4:18–7:40* (Dissertation; Joensuu: University of Eastern Finland, 2017).

4. In a monologue, the speaker or author discusses with an implied audience. In this case, the arguer molds his or her approach according to the assumed changes that happen in the thoughts and attitudes of the audience during the argumentation process. Consequently, even a monologue is interaction, not one-way communication.

5. Frans H. van Eemeren, Rob Grootendorst, and Francisca Snoeck Henkemans, *Fundamentals of Argumentation Theory: A Handbook of Historical Backgrounds and Contemporary Developments* (Mahwah, NJ: Erlbaum, 1996), 280; Frans H. van Eemeren and Peter Houtlosser, "Strategic Maneuvering: Maintaining a Delicate Balance," in *Dialectic and Rhetoric: The Warp and Woof of Argumentation Analysis*, ed. Frans H. van Eemeren and Peter Houtlosser (Dordrecht: Kluwer Academic, 2002), 132. See also Frans H. van Eemeren, Rob Grootendorst, Sally Jackson, and Scott Jacobs, *Reconstructing Argumentative Discourse* (Tuscaloosa, AL: The University of Alabama Press, 1993), 25–34; Frans H. van Eemeren, Rob Grootendorst, and Tjark Kruiger, *Handbook of Argumentation Theory: A Critical Survey of Classical Backgrounds and Modern Studies* (Studies of Argumentation in Pragmatics and Discourse Analysis, 7: Dordrecht, Holland: Foris Publications, 1987), 527–9.

1. *The confrontation.* In the confrontation stage a difference of opinion (*mixed* or *nonmixed*)[6] arises: a party presents a standpoint that another party does not accept. It becomes clear that there is a need for an argumentation.
2. *The opening.* In the opening stage the parties choose to attempt to resolve the difference of opinion. The roles of *protagonist* and *antagonist* are assigned.[7] Also the possibilities for an agreement are evaluated. This is done by discovering if there is enough common ground that the parties share—things such as the discussion format, background knowledge, values, and so on.
3. *The argumentation.* In the argumentation stage the protagonist(s) defends the standpoint at issue and the antagonist(s) challenges this standpoint. The argumentation is carried out by exchanging standpoints, defenses, and critical responses to these standpoints.
4. *The conclusion.* In the concluding stage the outcome of the argumentation is assessed. If the standpoint is withdrawn, the difference of opinion has been resolved in the favor of the antagonist. If the doubt is withdrawn, the dispute has been resolved in the favor of the protagonist. If the parties cannot agree on the outcome of their argument, then it has not ended in a resolution of a difference of opinion.[8]

---

6. See Frans H. van Eemeren, Rob Grootendorst, and Francisca Snoeck Henkemans, *Argumentation: Analysis, Evaluation, Presentation* (Mahwah, NJ: Lawrence Erlbaum, 2002), 8–9. In a nonmixed difference of opinion only one party is committed to defending a standpoint. In a mixed dispute, one party adopts a positive and the other party a negative standpoint pertaining the same proposition.

7. In our case, Jesus is the protagonist, since he is committed to defending the standpoint that he puts forward in the text. The group of disciples (5.1) is considered the antagonist. Jesus has to take into account their implicit criticism. Explicit criticism is not displayed in the text. The crowds should not be considered an active party in the argumentation. They may still affect the argumentation process with their presence.

8. The description of the four argumentation stages is based on: Van Eemeren, Grootendorst, and Snoeck Henkemans, *Fundamentals*, 281–2; Van Eemeren, Grootendorst, and Kruiger, *Handbook*, 529–30; Van Eemeren, Grootendorst, and Snoeck Henkemans, *Argumentation*, 25; Frans H. van Eemeren, Rob Grootendorst, Sally Jackson, and Scott Jacobs, *Speech Acts in Argumentative Discussions: A Theoretical Model for the Analysis of Discussions towards Solving Conflicts of Opinion* (Doldrecht: Foris Publications, 1984), 85–7; Frans H. van Eemeren and Rob Grootendorst, *Argumentation, Communication, and Fallacies: A Pragma-Dialectical Perspective* (Hillsdale, NJ: Lawrence Erlbaum, 1992), 35; Van Eemeren and Grootendorst, *Systematic*, 60–2; Hietanen, *Paul's Argumentation*, 56–7, n. 162. The concluding stage does not appear in Matt. 6.25-34. Thus, it is left unconsidered in the analysis.

With these basic features in mind, it is possible to begin the analysis. First, I will establish an *analytic overview* based on the text. Second, I will assess its *strategic maneuvering*. I shall explain these two concepts below. After the analysis proper, I will scrutinize the possible problematic features of Jesus' argumentation based on the *code of conduct* presented in the pragma-dialectical theory. Jesus puts forward shocking and provocative argumentation. How does such communication stand against a set of rules designed to promote reasonableness and critical attitude? I shall return to the evaluation later in the chapter.

In the analytic overview, the goal is to reconstruct the argumentation of a discourse in a way that reflects the process of resolving a dispute in accordance with the ideal model. The reconstruction occurs through a number of phases, which differ depending on the aim of the analysis. In this article, the reconstruction consists of the following steps: (i) Standpoint; (ii) Common starting points; (iii) Arguments; (iv) Argumentation structure.[9] The first three steps correspond with the first three argumentation stages. In the confrontation stage the standpoint is put forward, in the opening stage the common starting points are brought up, and in the argumentation stage arguments and criticisms are exchanged. After the identification of the standpoint(s), common starting points and arguments, the argumentation structure is reconstructed based on the first three steps.

The relationships between arguments can conveniently be displayed by applying schematic presentation for complex argumentation structures. When this is done, one can easily examine which arguments support which other arguments. Besides a *single* argumentation, which consists of two and only two premises, pragma-dialectics suggest three *complex* argumentation structures, which consist of more than two premises: *multiple*, *coordinative*, and *subordinative* argumentation.[10] (See Figure 1.) Complex argumentation can be broken into single argumentations. Furthermore, when applicable, arguments can be presented in chains.

---

9. On analytic overview, Van Eemeren and Grootendorst, *Argumentation*, 93–4; Van Eemeren and Grootendorst, *Systematic*, 118–22; Van Eemeren, Grootendorst, and Snoeck Henkemans, *Fundamentals*, 288–9; Van Eemeren, Grootendorst, and Kruiger, *Handbook*, 536–7. Often the *argument schemes* are also analyzed. However, I will not scrutinize them, since it is not specifically useful for my purposes. In addition, assessing the schemes would render this article too long. Consequently, in the section Possible Problematic Features in Jesus' Argumentation (p. 229). I will refrain from assessing whether the argument scheme rule (rule 7) has been violated or not.

10. Van Eemeren and Grootendorst, *Argumentation, Communication*, 73–89; Van Eemeren, Grootendorst, and Snoeck Henkemans, *Argumentation*, 64–72.

Single argumentation

Multiple argumentation

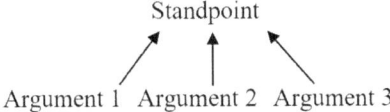

Coordinative argumentation

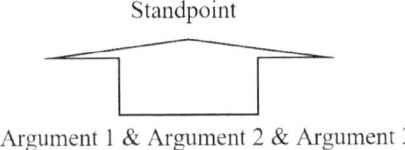

Subordinative argumentation

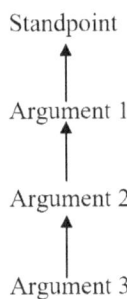

Figure 1. Single argumentation and complex argumentation structures.[11]

In multiple argumentation, each argument functions as a separate sufficient defense for the same standpoint. This is the strongest structure from the viewpoint of the arguer, since even if one of the arguments would turn out to be inconclusive, the argumentation does not fall apart. In coordinative argumentation, a combination of arguments must be taken together to constitute an adequate support for a standpoint. If one of the arguments is regarded

---

11. Van Eemeren, Grootendorst, and Snoeck Henkemans, *Argumentation*, 64: Usually, one of the premises is implicit. Then, the single argument appears to consist of only one premise. Implicitness of the argument is indicated by the brackets.

as inconclusive the argumentation does not hold. Multiple and coordinative argumentation are not always easy to distinguish from each other. When in doubt, the analyst is recommended to assume that it is multiple rather than coordinative argumentation.[12] That is, the analyst should be charitable to the arguer. In subordinative argumentation, a standpoint is defended with an argument, which in turn is in need of an argument, which in turn may be in need of an argument, and so on.

The second phase of the analysis consists of assessing the strategic maneuvering which is dealt with theoretically in the extended pragma-dialectical model.[13] The analytic overview functions as a basis for its analysis and for a critical evaluation. Strategic maneuvering deals with the integration of rhetorical insights into the dialectical viewpoint of the argument. In so doing, it attends to the continual efforts of the speaker, made in all moves in argumentative discourse, to keep the balance between *reasonableness* and *effectiveness*.[14] "This moving about is aimed at ending up in the best possible position" depending on the stage of the discussion.[15] Regarding these stages, every dialectical aim that they have has its rhetorical analogue.[16] Thus, discussion party

---

12. Van Eemeren and Grootendorst, *Argumentation, Communication*, 81–2; Van Eemeren, Grootendorst, and Snoeck Henkemans, *Argumentation*, 75–6.

13. Van Eemeren, *Strategic Maneuvering*, 22–23.

14. Frans H. van Eemeren and Peter Houtlosser, "Strategic Maneuvering: Examining Argumentation in Context," in *Examining Argumentation in Context: Fifteen Studies on Strategic Maneuvering* (ed. Frans H. van Eemeren; Amsterdam: John Benjamins, 2009), 4–5; Van Eemeren, *Strategic Maneuvering*, 40. A speech-act, which plays a role in resolving a difference of opinion, is considered a single "move." From the pragma-dialectical point of view, speech-act theory is discussed elaborately in Van Eemeren, Grootendorst, Jackson and Jacobs, *Speech Acts*. On reasonableness, Van Eemeren, *Strategic Maneuvering*, 29: "My stipulative (but lexically based) definition delineating the meaning of the term *reasonable* is: *using reason in a way that is appropriate in view of the situation concerned*." See further pp. 29–36. On effectiveness, p. 39: "It should be noted that 'effectiveness' is not completely synonymous with 'persuasiveness,' because aiming for effectiveness is not limited (as in the case of persuasiveness) to those parts of argumentative discourse (arguments) that can be reconstructed as belonging to the argumentation stage but applies also to the parts of the discourse that belong to the confrontation stage, the opening stage or the concluding stage, to which the term *persuasiveness* does not naturally pertain."

15. Van Eemeren, *Strategic Maneuvering*, 40.

16. Van Eemeren and Houtlosser, "Strategic Maneuvering," 5. Pertaining the dialectical aims, Van Eemeren, *Strategic Maneuvering*, 45: Confrontation stage: "To achieve clarity concerning the specific issues at stake and the positions held by the parties in the difference of opinion"; Opening stage: "To achieve clarity concerning the point of departure for the discussion with regard to ... starting points"; Argumentation stage: "To achieve clarity concerning the protagonist's argumentation in defense of the standpoints at issue and the antagonist's doubts concerning these standpoints and the argumentation

maneuvers strategically by making use of the combination of dialectic and rhetoric to create an effective discourse.

The strategic choices available at each of the four argumentation stages depend on the *topical potential, audience demand*, and *presentational devices* available to the speaker.[17] Even though these aspects can be distinguished analytically, in practice, they work together. They run parallel with the three prominent areas of interest of classical rhetoricians: topics, audience orientation, and stylistics.[18] Topical potential concentrates on the choice that the arguer makes, when selecting specific topics from the available pool. Second, to analyze audience demand is to study how the arguer takes the audience and its presuppositions and attitudes into account when formulating the arguments. Third, presentational devices refer to a choice as to how an argumentative move is to be presented in the strategically best way.[19]

Analysis

In my translation of Matthew 6.25-34, below, I have marked the confrontation stage (the standpoint) with underlining and the opening stage (common starting points) with **bold**. The argumentation stage appears as normal text.

Matthew 6.25-34
> 25 <u>Because of this I say to you: do not be concerned for your life, what you eat [or what you drink], and not about your body, what to put on.</u> Is not life more than food and the body more than clothing? 26 **Look at the birds of the sky** that they do not sow, nor do they harvest into barns, yet heavenly father feeds them. Are you not worth more than them? 27 But who of you, by being concerned, is able to add one cubit to his age? 28 So why are you concerned for clothing? **Consider carefully the lilies of the field, how they grow**: they do not labor nor do they spin. 29 But I say to you that not even **Solomon in all his glory** was clothed like one of them. 30 But if God in this way clothes the grass of the field which is today and tomorrow is cast into the oven, will he not much more do so to you, you of little faith? 31 <u>Therefore do not be concerned, saying: "what shall we eat," "or what shall we drink," or "what shall we wear."</u> 32 For all these the Gentiles seek after. For your heavenly

---

in their defense"; Concluding stage: "To achieve clarity concerning the results of the critical procedure as to whether the protagonist may maintain his standpoints or the antagonist his doubts." See Van Eemeren, *Strategic Maneuvering*, 45 also for the rhetorical aims.

17. The three aspects are introduced in Van Eemeren, *Strategic Maneuvering*, 93–127.

18. Van Eemeren *Strategic Maneuvering*, 94–5.

19. Van Eemeren and Houtlosser, "Strategic Maneuvering," 5; Van Eemeren, *Strategic Maneuvering*, 93–4, 165. See Van Eemeren, Grootendorst, and Kruiger, *Handbook*, 552–7.

father knows that you need all these things. 33 But seek first the kingdom [of God] and his righteousness, and all these things will be added to you. 34 Therefore do not be concerned for tomorrow, for tomorrow will be concerned for itself. Sufficient for the day is its own trouble.

Standpoint

The standpoint of the section is fairly simple to detect. Jesus repeats three times the same commandment in different words in verses 25a, 31, and 34a: "Do not be concerned for your life, what you eat [or what you drink], and not about your body, what to put on"; "Do not be concerned when saying: 'what shall we eat,' 'or what shall we drink,' or 'what shall we wear'"; "Do not be concerned for tomorrow."

Each of the three directives forbid worrying about everyday concerns. In verse 25a, I interpret "life"[20] as including what follows in the phrase, namely, food and clothing.[21] Food and clothing are thus examples of what a person can worry about in life.[22] The same goes with what to drink in verse 31 and, according to some manuscripts, also in verse 25a. Verses 25a and 31 resemble each other significantly. The formulation in 34a is different to some degree. It also forbids concern but this time for "tomorrow." However, I regard "tomorrow" as entailing all concerns that a person can worry about in the future.[23] In other words, regarding what may happen "tomorrow," one can be concerned about the things that Jesus has already mentioned in verses 25a and 31. Consequently, the point in all three formulations is that one should not be concerned about everyday concerns.

Why everyday concerns? In verse 33, Jesus contrasts the things that a person can be worried about with God's kingdom and his righteousness.[24]

---

20. Ulrich Luz, *Matthew 1–7: A Commentary* (ed. Helmut Koester, trans. James E. Crouch, rev. edn., Hermeneia; Minneapolis, MN: Fortress, 2007), 342: "ψυχή is not 'soul,' since it eats and drinks, but (Semitically) 'life.'" Cf. also Donald A. Hagner, *Matthew 1–13* (Dallas: Texas, 1993), 163. However, Hans Dieter Betz: "The juxtaposition of ψυχή and σῶμα ('body') in v. 25 speaks in favor of 'soul' rather than life." In Betz, *The Sermon on the Mount: A Commentary on the Sermon on the Mount, including the Sermon on the Plain (Matthew 5:3–7:27 and Luke 6:20–49)* (Minneapolis, MN: Fortress, 1995), 470. I agree with Luz and Hagner. However, certain ambiguousness may be intended in the text. St. Augustine, *The Lord's Sermon on the Mount* (Westminster, MD: The Newman Press, 1948), 136 claims "the word 'soul' stands for 'life' whose support is that material nourishment."

21. Betz, *Sermon*, 471.

22. Hagner, *Matthew*, 163.

23. Augustine, *Lord's Sermon*, 143: "… the word 'tomorrow' is not used except in speaking of time where the future follows upon the past."

24. Hagner, *Matthew*, 165: "V 33 concisely states the climatic point of the entire

The disciples (5.1) should focus on seeking the kingdom and righteousness and the mundane things will be provided to them, too.[25] What the kingdom and righteousness have in common and how they differ from food, drink, and clothing is that they are especially theological concepts in their context.[26] The kingdom and righteousness relate intimately to God and his will in comparison to the mundane things, which are vital to both the disciples and Gentiles. Consequently, verse 33 can be paraphrased as follows: "First do God's will and all the everyday concerns will be given to you." In addition, Jesus claims that the Gentiles seek what I call everyday concerns. Consequently, Jesus dissociates the Gentiles, who do not trust in God, from the disciples, who do trust.[27]

I reformulate Jesus' standpoint in a positive manner when he addresses his disciples: "*You do not need to worry about everyday concerns (what to eat, [drink,] wear) (25a, 31, 34a).*" The imperative that Jesus employs in verses 25a, 31, and 34a could be colored in one of two ways: either in the direction of a moral necessity or as an invitation to freedom from anxiety. In the arguments, Jesus promises that God will take care of the disciples and their mundane needs. The matter at hand is positive in itself. Consequently, I interpret Jesus extending a positive invitation. The disciples are called to assume a carefree attitude.

---

pericope." In addition, Betz, *Sermon*, 481: "This most important statement [verse 33] is the culmination of the argument." Indeed, this may be Jesus' overall point, but in terms of the argumentation structure, verse 33 functions as an argument for the standpoint.

25. Hagner, *Matthew*, 165 rightly observes that "The passive voice of προστεθήσεται, 'will be added,' is, with v 32 in mind, a divine passive (it is God who will add these things)."

26. Luz, *Matthew 1–7*, 344: "As is usually the case in Matthew, in v.33 'kingdom' means God's coming rule into which the community hopes to enter by passing through judgment. 'Righteousness' probably means, as in 3:15; 5:6, 10, 20; 6:1, the righteousness required of people, that is, the activity that God desires and that corresponds to his kingdom." According to Luz, "the relationship between 'kingdom' and 'righteousness' here is the same as the relationship between the second and third petitions of the Lord's Prayer," p. 344, Overall, Luz holds that the Sermon "is built symmetrically around a core, namely, the Lord's Prayer in 6:9–13. The sections before and after the Lord's Prayer parallel one another…" p. 172. To me, this kind of structuring appears too complex for an ordinary listener of the Gospel to able to comprehend. Thus, I do not regard it plausible. If such a structuring was the case, then it would not be persuasive. Section 6:19–34, renders dealing with "questions about possessions…" p. 328. For a discussion regarding the structure of the Sermon, see Hagner, *Matthew*, 83–4. According to him (p. 84), "the Lord's Prayer does indeed stand at the approximate center of the sermon, and its content is related generally to some of the themes in the material that follows, though it seems doubtful that deliberate structural correspondence is intended."

27. Jesus also dissociates the disciples from the Gentiles in the Sermon in 6.8 and 7.11.

In addition to the repetition, the standpoint is indicated with the phrases "because of this" (*dia touto*) in verse 25a and "therefore" (*oun*) in verses 31 and 34. The phrases suggest that what follows is a conclusion of what has been stated previously. In verses 32 and 34b, Jesus employs the words "for" (*gar*) to put forward further arguments in support of the standpoint.

Common Starting Points

There is no material in the text that one can mark or distinguish as common starting points without controversy. Nevertheless, Jesus does point to sources and phenomena that he believes and that the recipients agree with and share with him. For example, in verse 26a, Jesus states that birds do not "sow" or "harvest into barns." At face value, this is pretty obvious. However, for the phrase to have a sensible meaning the sowing and harvesting must point beyond the immediate observation. When people perform these tasks, they reserve food for the future and, thus, they take "tomorrow" into consideration and, in a sense, worry about it. The birds, according to Jesus, do not perform such a task, and consequently do not worry about tomorrow.[28] However, the disciples could, in theory, criticize the argument by stating that even though the birds do not reserve food for tomorrow (which may not be true in all cases), they still have to worry about getting food or otherwise they would perish. Thus, the heavenly father may feed them, but the birds still have to do their part.[29] All in all, the common starting point includes the view regarding birds and especially the literal phrasing. It is a separate matter, however, whether the disciples would agree with the application of such a view.[30]

In verse 28b, Jesus treats another case similar to that of the birds. This time he brings up lilies of the field as an example of a carefree attitude. As the birds did not sow or harvest into barns, the lilies do not labor or spin. This is, again, obvious. Consequently, to labor and spin must refer to something else besides the literal meaning. Since in the case of the birds the sowing and harvesting alluded to concern about the future, the tasks that the lilies do not perform should be interpreted in the same way. Again, the

---

28. Hagner, *Matthew*, 164.
29. Betz, *Sermon*, 475 also witnesses another kind of problem in the argument: "One is to draw the conclusion *a minori ad maius*: if anxiety over food is unnecessary for animals, how much more so for human beings? The vexing question why, granted this presupposition, human beings must still work for their upkeep is not raised at this point" [his italics]. On *a minori ad maius* and *a maiori ad minus* –argumentation in Matthew 6 (and Luke 12), see Richard J. Dillon, "Ravens, Lilies, and the Kingdom of God (Matthew 6:25–33 / Luke 12:22–31)," *CBQ 53* (1991): 605–27, 616–7.
30. See Luz, *Matthew 1–7*, 343 for a discussion on verse 26 and its problems.

disciples would agree with the literal phrasing of verse 28. The lilies may be an easier example for Jesus, since they do not seem to perform any tasks as actively as the birds do. They clearly do not worry about the future, since they just stand still. However, in this sense they do not resemble the life of a human as much the birds either. From this point of view, Jesus' argument can be criticized: "Although the lilies are not concerned about the future, their situation does not resemble ours, since they really do not have the option to be worried in the first place."

In verse 29, Jesus refers to a tradition of which he and the recipients are both aware. He mentions Solomon and his glory and thus alludes to King Solomon's reign and to his rich kingdom. During Solomon's era, Israel was at the height of its grandeur, at least according to the tradition (see 1 Kgs. 3.13; 10.14-27; 2 Chr. 9.13-28).[31] When Jesus combines the tradition with the phrase "not even" in verse 29, he suggests that the lilies of the field are significantly better clothed than the mighty Solomon himself. In a sense, this is an absurd statement. Realistically speaking, Solomon was better clothed, since he had clothes in the first place, whereas the lilies do not wear them at all. This metaphor suggests that Jesus has another point in mind. Nevertheless, he appeals to a common tradition, but employs it in a surprising and, in a sense, absurd manner.

List of common starting points:

- Birds do not sow or harvest into barns (26a)
- Lilies grow without laboring or spinning (28b)
- Tradition regarding King Solomon and his glory (29)

Arguments

The majority of the text material consists of arguments. Based on the three appearances of the standpoint (25a, 31, 34a), I have divided the text into three subsections: verses 25-30,[32] 31-33, and 34. I shall argue that the parts consist of argumentative wholes that formulate three separate lines of defense for the standpoint.[33]

---

31. Betz, *Sermon*, 477–88.

32. Hagner, *Matthew*, 165: "This verse [31] is a summarizing recapitulation of the passage (vv. 25-30) …"

33. According to Luz, *Matthew 1–7*, 339 the arrangement is as follows: "an introductory prohibition (v. 25); a first argument from experience (v. 26); a second, parallel argument from experience (vv. 28b–30) with a short introduction (v. 28a); the summarizing admonition that repeats the prohibition (vv. 31–33)." Betz, *Sermon*, 55–6 has roughly the same structure as I do. He labels verses 25c-34 as "argumentation" and consequently verses 25c-30 as "first argument," verses 31-33 as "second argument," and

The first everyday concern that Jesus mentions in verses 25a and 31 is food. In verse 26a, he addresses this example and implicitly argues that there is no reason to be concerned about food (arg. 1.1a). Jesus brings up the birds of the sky as a role model for the disciples. He claims that the birds do not sow or harvest into barns meaning that they do not worry (extensively) about food in the same way that people generally do. Nevertheless, God feeds the birds (arg. 1.1a.1a). In verse 26b, Jesus asks rhetorically whether the disciples are not more worthy than the birds. The disciples are expected to answer "yes." They want to regard themselves higher than mere birds (arg. 1.1a.1b.1).[34] However, the argument in verse 26b does not connect immediately to verse 26a. An implicit argument needs to be supplied in order to make sense of the connection between them.

The idea is that since, according to Jesus, God feeds the birds and at the same time the disciples are worth more than birds, they will surely be fed as well (arg. 1.1a.1b).[35] Two arguments are combined coordinatively: God feeds the birds *and* if God feeds the birds, then he will surely feed the disciples. Consequently, the disciples do not need worry about food, because God will feed them, since he feeds the birds, which are of lesser worth than the disciples.

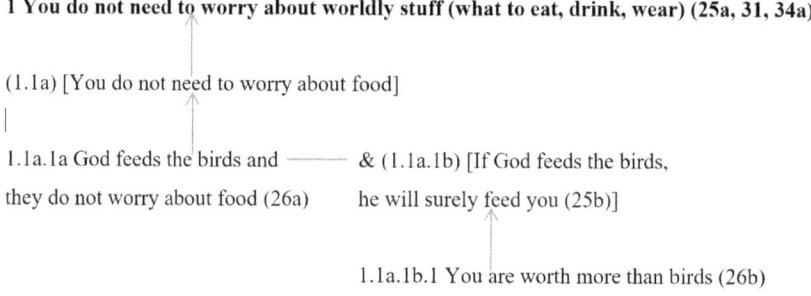

Figure 2. No need to worry about food[36]

verse 34 as "third argument." See also p. 461. Betz (p. 62) states that the body of the Sermon (5.17–7.12) "is constructed as a ring composition," as indicated by the expression law and the prophets in 5.17 and 7.12." He renders verses 6.19–7.12 as the third section of the main body "devoted to the affairs of daily life."

34. See Augustine, *Lord's Sermon*, 136. The argument represents typical Jewish *qal wahomer* argumentation.

35. Betz, *Sermon*, 479 rightly observes the rule behind the argumentation: "what it true of the less important is true also of the more important."

36. If the numbering of an argument is in parenthesis and the text of the argument is in brackets, it should be regarded as an implicit argument. In terms of representing

Jesus already puts forward a similar argument in verse 25b. He suggests that "life is more than food and the body is more than clothing." God's influence is implied. Since God has provided the disciples life and body, he will surely provide them sustenance, too.[37] Consequently, verse 25b introduces the premise that is employed in the implicit argument (arg. 1.1a.1b) regarding the birds and also later regarding the lilies (arg. 1.1c.1b, see Figures 3 and 6).

In verse 27, Jesus asks rhetorically whether the disciples can "add one cubit" to their age by being concerned. The formulation "but who of you" and the nature of the standpoint both indicate that the question is expected to receive the answer "no."[38] The disciples cannot (and in the end nobody can) extend their life by worrying (arg. 1.1b).[39] This argument is separate from the group of arguments dealing with food (arg. 1.1a ...). However, the word "but" (δέ) indicates some kind of connection between the arguments. Furthermore, even though one can extend one's life with food, one cannot extend it by worrying. Due to these issues, I render a coordinative connection between the food-arguments (arg. 1.1a ...) and the argument regarding extending one's life (arg. 1.1b). The judgment that the argument is coordinative is further supported by that in verses 28-30 Jesus deals with arguments concerning clothing in a similar fashion to the arguments concerning

---

the argumentation structure schematically, I follow the examples given in Van Eemeren, Grootendorst, and Snoeck Henkemans, *Argumentation*, 69–72.

37. Augustine, *Lord's Sermon*, 136. Carlston, "Matthew," 180 makes the same conclusion, although hesitantly.

38. Hagner, *Matthew*, 164.

39. Luz, *Matthew 1–7*, 344: "One has understood it [verse 27] to mean either that people cannot add even a little bit to the length of their lifetime or that people cannot add a cubit to his height. The usual interpretation today is the former interpretation, since prolonging one's life is a desirable goal and an object of concern, while increasing one's height is not." Luz himself opts for the second view. Hagner, *Matthew*, 164 maintains that "in the context, it makes the best sense to take ἡλικία as length of life and then to take πῆχυς as a fraction of time." W. F. Albright and C. S. Mann, *Matthew: Introduction, Translation, and Notes* (Grden City, NY: Doubleday, 1971), 82: "*Pēchus* (cubit) is a measure of space, which we have translated simply by 'anything,' while *hēlikia* can mean either stature or span of life" [their italics]. Willoughby C. Allen, *A Critical and Exegetical Commentary on the Gospel according to S. Matthew* (Edinburgh: T&T Clark, 1922), 64 states that πῆχυς is a measure of space, not of time. ἡλικία can mean either age, duration of life, or stature. In Mt the latter seems more appropriate." Be as it may, the idea behind the phrase is that one cannot extend one's life by worrying. Carlston, "Matthew," 180 points out rightly: "Whether the Greek word is to be translated as 'span of life' ... or 'physical stature' ... is unclear but irrelevant. In either case the emphasis has moved completely away from God's providential care to a thoroughly secular reminder that some things are beyond our control."

food in verse 26.⁴⁰ Thus, the argument in verse 27 is located between two argumentative wholes that are coordinative, since they refer to food and clothing which are both brought up in the standpoint. The argument in verse 27 is, then, loosely connected thematically to the groups of argument in verses 26 and 28-30.

In verses 28-30, Jesus puts forward a group of arguments that functions quite similarly to that appearing in verse 26.⁴¹ Instead of not being concerned about food, Jesus argues that the disciples do not need to be worried about clothing (arg. 1.1c). This is indicated by the rhetorical question in verse 28a. The question is expected to receive an answer such as: "We cannot come up with any reason." Instead of birds, Jesus brings up lilies of the field. They do not labor or spin and still they grow. Yet the lilies do not worry about clothing (arg.1.1c.1a). The case of the birds was similar: they did not sow or harvest into barns and still they managed. In verse 29, Jesus claims that the lilies are not just clothed but clothed better than the mighty Solomon. This adds a *hyperbolical* flavor to the argument.

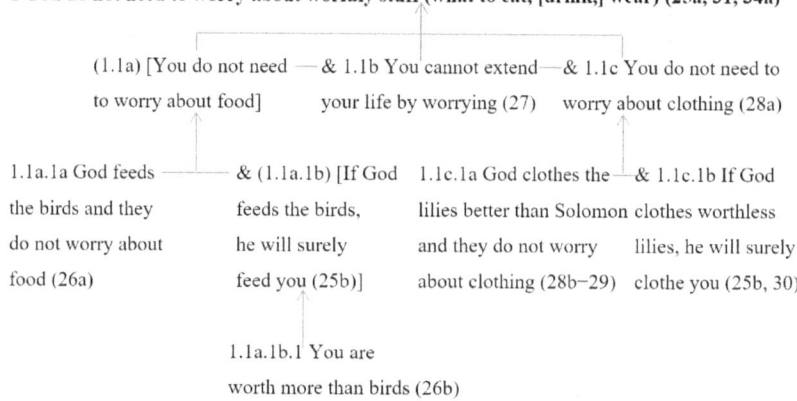

Figure 3. No need to worry about food or clothing and worrying does extend one's life.

In verse 30, Jesus asks again rhetorically that if God clothes the lilies, which are not much of worth, does he not then clothe the disciples. The expected answer is "yes," of course God clothes the disciples, which are much worthier to him than lilies (arg. 1.1c.1b). Consequently, whereas the logical link between 1.1a.1b was left implicit, this time Jesus puts a similar argument

---

40. Hagner, *Matthew*, 164: "The parallelism [of verses 28-39] in form with v 26 is striking, if nevertheless incomplete."

41. In terms of rhetoric, Luz, *Matthew 1–7*, 343 states that "The second image [verses 28-30] is somewhat more detailed and thus increases the effect of the first one."

forward explicitly; however, this time he does not provide a support as to why it is so that if God clothes worthless lilies, he will surely clothe the disciples.[42] Based on the argument 1.1a.1b.1, it can be presumed that a similar argument might be imagined as a support in this case, too, but since it is not put forward explicitly, it is not added to the argumentation structure (the argument would be numbered as 1.1c.1b.1).

The second argumentative whole in section 6.25-34 consists of verses 31-33. In this case, Jesus does not deal with such examples as food or clothing but contrasts the behavior of the disciples to that of the Gentiles.[43] In addition, he contrasts the seeking of the kingdom of God and his righteousness to the seeking of everyday concerns.

In verse 32, Jesus states that the Gentiles seek such everyday concerns as indicated in the previous verse. This is portrayed somewhat implicitly as an undesirable behavior (arg. 1.2a). The Gentiles are unaware of the blessings of the heavenly father. They are oblivious to the pursuit of the kingdom of God, whereas Jesus portrays it as of prime importance to the disciples. Moreover, if the disciples follow his advice and seek the kingdom and righteousness, they are promised the everyday concerns that they need and are allegedly concerned about (arg. 1.2b).[44] In the structure, I have interpreted the kingdom and righteousness referring more broadly to the will of God. That the disciples will receive what they need is supported by Jesus' emphatic notion that their heavenly father knows their needs (arg. 1.2b.1) and consequently will supply them accordingly. The example of the Gentiles (arg. 1.2a) and the objective of the disciples (arg. 1.2b) should be regarded as a coordinative argument in which the former is regarded as an undesirable example and the latter as a proper alternative to such an example.

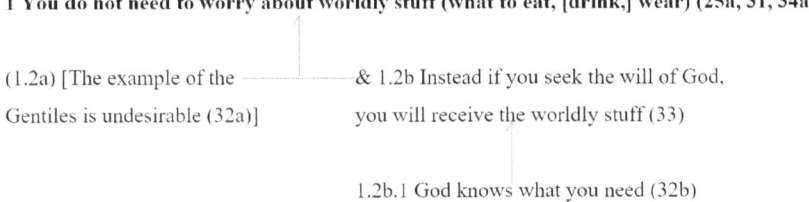

Figure 4. The way of the Gentiles and the way of the disciples.

---

42. Hagner, *Matthew*, 165.
43. Betz, *Sermon*, 466.
44. See Betz, *Sermon*, 483.

The third and final line of defense is portrayed in verse 34.[45] The first part of the first sentence repeats the standpoint. Thus, the phrases "for tomorrow will be concerned for itself" and "sufficient for the day is its own trouble" are arguments. Both phrases sound like known sayings.[46] Consequently, they have a certain appeal that stems from their poetic formulation and familiarity. Both phrases, however, require interpretation for them to make sense argumentatively. Literally speaking, tomorrow concerning for itself is not a sensible sentence argumentatively.[47]

The latter phrase is easier to interpret. After reinterpreting it, the sentence states that there are enough problems every day even without worrying.[48] Consequently, worrying is in a sense useless, since the same (amount of) problems will occur anyway. From this point of view, the former phrase appears understandable as well. The disciples would be well off letting tomorrow worry for itself meaning that they should not worry about the future, since problems are bound to happen regardless of their concern. Consequently, I render the two phrases referring to the same idea, namely, that trouble will exist even without worrying (arg. 1.3).[49]

1 You do not need to worry about worldly stuff (what to eat, [drink,] wear) (25a, 31, 34a)

1.3 Trouble will exist even without worrying (34bc)

Figure 5. Trouble will exist even without worrying.

---

45. Betz, *Sermon*, 484: "The third argument is extremely brief, but it is supposed to be at the same level as the two preceding arguments (vss 25c–30 and 31–33)."

46. Carlston, "Matthew," 180. Luz, *Matthew 1–7*, 346: "Verse 34 is one of the secondary interpretations of our text in wisdom style." Betz, *Sermon*, 486 characterizes verses 34bc as "half-philosophical statements in which observations on the affairs of daily life combine with practical conclusions to be drawn from them."

47. Luz, *Matthew 1–7*, 346 states that "The content [of verse 34] is equally difficult [as it is linguistically]. One can choose between a more optimistic and a more pessimistic interpretation: (a) Understood optimistically this verse can speak of the possibility of living fully in the present. (b) The pessimistic interpretation is more probable, however, because with v. 34c the verse ends on a pessimistic note: all planning is futile; it is enough for a person to bear the burden of each day." I concur with option (b); Betz, *Sermon*, 485.

48. Betz, *Sermon*, 486 has the correct idea: "People are foolish to be concerned with tomorrow since, as vs 27 has shown, it is not under human control."

49. Hagner, *Matthew*, 166.

Argumentation Structure

From the argumentation structure we should note that arguments 1.1a, 1.1b, and 1.1c and also 1.2a and 1.2b are *cumulative* coordinative arguments.[50] In other words, they do not necessarily need each other to provide sufficient support but they clearly reinforce each other and thus should not be considered as multiple argumentation. For instance, the bad example of the Gentiles would by itself warn the disciples not to follow such a behavior. However, Jesus provides them a positive alternative to follow which would also function as a sufficient defense by itself. Now, they reinforce each other and make the support that much stronger.

All the second level arguments (arg. 1.1a.1a, 1.1a.1b, 1.1c.1a, 1.1c.1b, 1.2b.1) are theologically colored in the sense that God appears in each of them. Jesus' overall point is to argue that God will take care of the disciples' needs. Jesus has a positive approach to the issue. However, the arguments 1.1b and 1.3 also provide negatively flavored examples. Besides God's willingness to take care of the disciples, their concern is argued to be useless, since they cannot extend their life by worrying and they have to face the future trouble anyway. The first line of defense consists mostly of arguments which, by example, attempt to show God's care. The second line of defense presents the worry for everyday concerns as the way of the Gentiles.[51] The disciples are provided with an alternative goal, seeking the kingdom and God's righteousness, which also guarantees them the worldly needs they may have. The third line of defense consists of short sayings which emphasize the uselessness of worrying: the trouble will occur despite the disciples' concern.[52]

---

50. Van Eemeren, Grootendorst, and Snoeck Henkemans, *Fundamentals*, 308: "If the coordinative argumentation is used in a direct defense, it is 'cumulative'; if used in an indirect defense, it is 'complementary.' Due to their function with regard to the sufficiency of the argumentation, the arguments are in both cases interdependent." See Van Eemeren, Grootendorst, and Kruiger, *Handbook*, 569.

51. See Betz, *Sermon*, 480.

52. Betz, *Sermon*, 485 claims that "the third argument [in verse 34] is worded sparsely, but it presupposes the same train of thought as the previous two arguments. It is characterized of all three arguments that they complement one another ..." This should not be misunderstood that the three lines of defense (1.1a, 1.1b, 1.1c and 1.2a, 1.2b and 1.3) should be taken together as cumulative coordinative arguments. Instead, they indeed provide independent support for the standpoint. Naturally, there is, however, some topical reinforcement between the arguments, but this does not affect the argumentation structure.

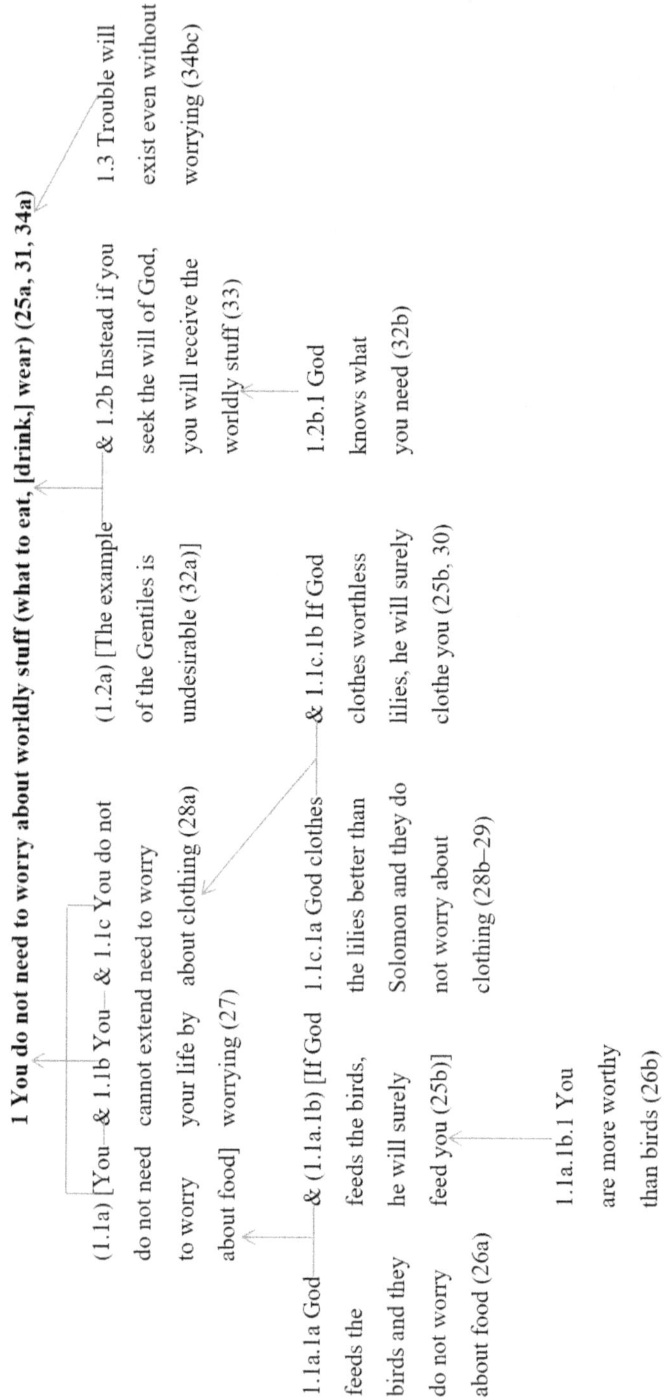

1 You do not need to worry about worldly stuff (what to eat, [drink,] wear) (25a, 31, 34a)

(1.1a) [You do not need to worry about food] & 1.1b You cannot extend your life by worrying (27) & 1.1c You do not need to worry about clothing (28a) (1.2a) [The example of the Gentiles is undesirable (32a)] & 1.2b Instead if you seek the will of God, you will receive the worldly stuff (33) 1.3 Trouble will exist even without worrying (34bc)

1.1a.1a God feeds the birds and they do not worry about food (26a) & (1.1a.1b) [If God feeds the birds, he will surely feed you (25b)] 1.1c.1a God clothes the lilies better than Solomon and they do not worry about clothing (28b–29) & 1.1c.1b If God clothes worthless lilies, he will surely clothe you (25b, 30) 1.2b.1 God knows what you need (32b)

1.1a.1b.1 You are more worthy than birds (26b)

Figure 6. The complete argumentation structure of Matthew 6.25-34.

Strategic Maneuvering

In assessing the strategic maneuvering, we analyze the rhetorical aspects of the arguments and the interplay of rhetoric and argumentation. The three inseparable aspects of strategic maneuvering, topical potential, audience demand, and presentational devices, are scrutinized in the argumentation stages in order starting from the confrontation stage. However, since the concluding stage is not represented in the text, it is excluded from the analysis.

Confrontation stage

- Because of this I say to you: do not be concerned for your life, what you eat [or what you drink], and not about your body, what to put on. (25a)
- Therefore, do not be concerned when saying: "what shall we eat," "or what shall we drink," or "what shall we wear." (31)
- Therefore, do not be concerned for tomorrow. (34a)

Topical potential. The topic that Jesus brings up in all formulations of the standpoint has to do with letting go of concern. This is a positive topic; a carefree attitude is implied.[53] However, Jesus does not command the disciples to have a carefree attitude but instead not to be concerned. Thus, although the topic is positive, the formulation is negative: not to do something rather than to do something. The negative formulation opens up different possibilities in terms of which arguments to employ. In addition, Jesus lists various issues that one can be concerned about when worried about one's life or body: food, drink, and clothing. These issues, in turn, allow Jesus to address them as examples (1.1a and 1.1c and the arguments in their support). If he is able to argue successfully for their relevance, their success can be generalized to all such worldly issues: God the creator takes care of its lesser created beings, so all the more he will take care of people and Jesus' disciples who are created as God's image. These images of the creation are not mentioned explicitly in the text, but topically speaking they lurk in the background. After all, the arguments that Jesus employs include birds of the heaven and the lilies of the field, two aspects of the creation.

---

53. Betz, *Sermon*, 464 claims that "this defense appears to have been caused by a profound crisis of faith in God's providence." This view that represents mirror-reading does not necessarily hold. The disciples or the supposed Matthean community did not have to doubt God's providence. The text and Jesus' argumentation may have other purposes. I claim that the section's (6.25-34) main aim is to promote Jesus' authority through the topic at hand.

Moreover, the negative formulation of the standpoint allows Jesus to forbid the issue at hand, namely worrying. This, in turn, enables an approach that emphasizes Jesus' authority more than a positive formulation. By denying any reasons for being concerned, he allows the disciples to adopt a carefree attitude. In verse 25, the authoritative approach is emphasized by the famous phrase "I say to you," which appears at least nine times in the Sermon alone and in verse 29 in the argumentation stage.[54]

The standpoint and its topic are brought up in the first place as a response for Jesus' point in 6.24.[55] He has argued prior to the argumentative section at hand that the disciples cannot serve two masters, namely mammon and God.[56] The response in verses 25-34 is indeed a positive one. They do not have to serve mammon, since God will provide everything that they need and possibly even more, the kingdom of God and his righteousness, according to verse 33. God is a better master than mammon.[57]

Audience demand. The positive aspect of the topic of the standpoint will likely appeal to the audience. The issues listed in the first two formulations cover the most basic needs: hunger, thirst, and warmth. The disciples are promised sufficiency. Some of them were fishermen (4.18, 21) and perhaps they had to struggle for their living from time to time. Now, they are told not worry about those things. Implicitly already in the standpoint it is suggested that they will receive food, drink, and clothing from somewhere, not having to struggle for it. The positive promise may be appealing but on the other hand it may sound extraordinary and thus not too convincing.

---

54. Luz, *Matthew 1–7*, 342 "The authority of the Lord Jesus stands behind the following words ['I say to you']." See Hagner, *Matthew*, 163.

55. An indication of this is that verse 24 brings God into the picture, since section 6.25-34 mentions him several times. Luz, *Matthew 1–7*, 340: "In v. 25a therefore (διὰ τοῦτο) makes the connection to what has preceded." See also pp. 342, 345. Hagner, *Matthew*, 163 states that *dia touto* "refers at least to v 24, but probably to the whole preceding section, vv 19–24." According to Betz (*Sermon*, 469) "If they [the words 'because of this'] refer to vs 24, the relationship remains unclear." In my mind, section 6.25-34 is a clear response to verse 24 and perhaps to verses 19-24 overall. On p. 469, however, Betz continues: "... vs 24 raises the question of the necessities of life: If one is to serve God alone, how is one to take care of daily needs? Verses 25–34 provide an answer, in the sense that serving God alone takes care of daily needs (vs 33)."

56. Betz, *Sermon*, 454 holds that "the saying [in verse 24d] is peculiar in that it sees this undivided loyalty as threatened by the service to another deity, Mammon, that is directly opposed to God." P. 458: "Naming this pseudo-deity by a foreign name indicates its demonic and even magical character." Hagner, *Matthew*, 159: "[mammon] is here [in verse 24] personified and regarded as a potential master."

57. Betz, *Sermon*, 457: "God is not a slave master; serving him is a voluntary acknowledgement of his beneficence and rulership."

Presentational devices. Jesus phrases the standpoint differently in verse 25a than in verse 31. The contents are, however, fairly close to one another. In light of verse 25a, the disciples would not address the everyday concerns, whereas according to a version of verse 31 they do ponder out loud "what shall we eat" and so on. In a sense, the second formulation portrays a more realistic situation in which the disciples wonder about their needs, but they are still instructed not to be concerned.

It appears that with the third repetition of the standpoint, it gains further realistic features. The disciples are not to abandon their worry for everyday concerns completely but only regarding "tomorrow" and, hence, the conceivable future. The argument regarding the birds supports this idea. Jesus relates that the birds do not sow nor harvest into barns, meaning that they do not store food for the future. Consequently, the consecutive formulations of the standpoint emphasize the thought that the disciples should not play it safe by taking the future too much into consideration, but to trust in God, who will provide them everything as they seek the kingdom.[58]

Opening stage
– Look at the birds of the heaven (26a)
– Consider carefully the lilies of the field, how they grow (28b)
– Solomon in all his glory (29)

Topical potential. Only fragments of the opening stage occur in the text material. The phrases are used as parts of the argumentation stage so that the two stages are seamlessly integrated.

Jesus employs two images from nature which may fit to the surroundings in which he gave his speech: birds and lilies.[59] Since the issue at hand deals with the basic needs of people, the two topics relate to them well, because they all stem from nature in a straightforward manner.[60] Furthermore, birds and lilies are distinctly dependent on what nutrition and sustenance they are able to get daily, since they cannot store in the same sense that people can.

---

58. According to Hagner, *Matthew*, 160, "the issue in view in these passages is not wealth primarily, but an absolute and unqualified discipleship ... Most important is where one's heart lies, i.e., what controls one's interests, energy, and commitment ... Jesus asks for uncompromising commitment to God's will and purposes."

59. Betz, *Sermon*, 465: "Surprisingly positive is the way in which the natural order is treated in our passage."

60. Carlston, "Matthew," 180: "Birds and lilies ... are not so much mere examples as natural witnesses to the providence of God ..."

Thus, they function for Jesus' purpose. Birds and lilies represent remarkably the attitude that he wants the disciples to adopt.[61]

The reference to Solomon and to his glory is brief. Consequently, the recipients do not have to be aware of any details regarding Solomon but only his general reputation as a glorious king of Israel. When he is compared to the lilies of the field in terms of clothing, one would presume that Solomon would be the clear winner. The contrast is meant to be huge. Thus, when Jesus states the opposite—that the lilies are better clothed than the king—the disciples are certainly surprised.

Audience demand. The birds and the lilies may have special appeal to the audience, since they are readily available as visible examples for the disciples. Both can be seen in the wild fairly easily. Thus, the disciples are bound to have had experience of the birds and lilies.[62]

Presentational devices. The phrase "Solomon in all his glory" is a brief reference to the wealth and reputation of the king. Jesus refers to the archetype, not any particular detail regarding Solomon. The allusion to the "glory" further indicates that Jesus wants the disciples to pay attention to the king's possessions as part of his reputation. The glory of Solomon is immediately connected to his clothing.

Argumentation stage
- Is not life more than food and the body more than clothing? (25b)
- (Look at the birds of the heaven)[63] that they do not sow, nor do they harvest into barns, yet heavenly father feeds them. (26a)
- Are you not worth more than them? (26b)
- But who of you (by) being concerned is able to add one cubit to his age? (27)
- So why are you concerned for clothing? (28a)

---

61. Betz, *Sermon*, 475 provides two reasons why the birds do not worry: "they rely on nature's abundance, and they have no presumptions about controlling the future." While this could be imagined to be so, such points are not provided in the text.

62. Betz, *Sermon*, 465: "… calling attention to things as they stand before one's eyes, things that one can verify immediately. The goodness of life is thus grounded in daily experience. At first sight, calls to observation seem stunningly naïve but undeniable …"

63. The parentheses indicate the phrases that are part of the opening stage. They are, however, included here in the text in order to maintain the train of thought of the arguments.

- (Consider carefully the lilies of the field, how they grow:) they do not labor nor do they spin. (28b)
- But I say to you that not even (Solomon in all his glory) was clothed like one of them. (29)
- But if God in this way clothes the grass of the field which is today and tomorrow is cast into the oven, not much more you, you of little faith? (30)
- For all these the Gentiles seek after. (32a)
- For your heavenly father knows that you need all these things. (32b)
- But seek first the kingdom [of God] and his righteousness, and all these things will be added to you. (33)
- for tomorrow will be concerned for itself. (34b)
- Sufficient for the day its own trouble. (34c)

Topical potential. The argumentation that Jesus employs to argue for lack of worry about everyday concerns can be divided roughly into two categories: (a) God provides mundane matters and; (b) Worrying is useless in itself. Arguments beginning with 1.1a, 1.1c, and 1.2b belong to the group (a) and arguments 1.1b and 1.3 belong to the group (b). The argument 1.2a can be also regarded belonging to group (a), since it portrays the Gentiles as unaware of God's blessings and thus indirectly emphasizes the disciples' close relation to their "heavenly father."

The arguments of category (a) promote the disciples' trust in God. In a sense, this appears to be Jesus' top priority. The directive in verse 33 supports this interpretation. Jesus does not want the disciples only to refrain from being worried but to go one step further and seek the kingdom of God and his righteousness. Seeking the kingdom is made possible by relinquishing one's worry about mammon and everyday concerns. By contrast, the arguments of category (b) are not necessarily theological in nature since God is not mentioned in them; instead, they appeal to common sense. The argument in verse 27 (arg. 1.1b) suggests that nobody can extend their life by worrying. If being concerned is regarded as a mere thought process, then the argument appears to be valid. Indeed, nobody can gain food or something to drink or clothing merely by thinking about it. However, if worrying entails the action of storing mundane issues for the rainy day as the birds or lilies did not do, then the argument 1.1b becomes debatable.

Audience demand. Several of the arguments appeal to the disciples' esteem. In 1.1a.1b.1, Jesus suggests that they are worth more than birds. In addition, in verse 30 he implies that, of course, God holds the disciples in high regard, since he even takes care of the "grass of the field." Furthermore, Jesus places the lilies higher than Solomon himself suggesting that the disciples are even higher than the king when it comes to clothing them. In verse 30, however, Jesus calls the disciples those of "little faith." With this maneuver he assumes an authoritative position over them. Still, in verse 32, Jesus distinguishes the Gentiles from the disciples (see arguments 1.2a and 1.2b). The former do not have such a relationship with God as the latter do. Consequently, the disciples' heavenly father will take care of them, his children. It is left unexpressed whether God's generosity extends also to the Gentiles as well. The dissociative phrasing implies that it does not, but this is not guaranteed. According to 5.45 God provides the same blessings to both the Gentiles and the disciples which creates tension between that verse and 6.32, if it is assumed that the dissociation in the latter verse implies that the Gentiles are to receive less than the disciples.[64]

Jesus assumes that the disciples already have a relationship with God.[65] He builds on that foundation by attempting to deepen the existing connection. Jesus argues that God is willing to provide them their needs more than willingly, since even birds and lilies get their share. Moreover, Jesus calls God as the "heavenly father" in verse 26 and "your heavenly father" in verse 32b. These labels are meant to make the disciples trust God even more than they did prior to the section at hand.

Presentational devices. Jesus employs the imperative throughout the section and the argumentation stage.[66] He directs the disciples to "look at the birds of the heaven," "consider carefully the lilies of the field," and to "seek first the kingdom [of God] and his righteousness." These formulations promote Jesus' authority and his position over the disciples.

Another prominent feature is the use of rhetorical questions. Jesus employs them to activate the audience and to address the disciples closely. More specifically, Jesus uses the questions to emphasize how clear—allegedly—his points are. For instance, the answer that the phrase "is not life more than food and the body more than clothing" is expected to elicit is not only "yes" but "yes, of course." This applies also to the rhetorical question in verse 26b.[67]

---

64. Carlston, "Matthew," 181 claims that "the promise of God's providential care, in other words, is not for everyone (cf. 'Gentiles,' in v. 32) but for those who have heeded the demand of 5:17–20 by putting the will of the Creator first."

65. Luz, *Matthew 1–7*, 345: "They [Jesus' audience] are men and women who know about the kingdom of God and are touched by it."

66. Luz, *Matthew 1–7*, 339. For the relation of the imperative expressions and the argumentative reasoning of the Q text, see Dillon, "Ravens, Lilies," 617.

67. Betz, *Sermon*, 475.

Of course the disciples are worthier than the birds. These questions are likely to add to the persuasiveness of Jesus in the sense that, if he is able to receive the answers he expects, the disciples may see the other argumentation more acceptable as well. Moreover, the questions have an accusatory tone, since they portray the information as self-evident. This is especially evident in verse 30 in which Jesus calls the disciples those of "little faith." That the disciples worry and do not realize or believe how important they are to God suggests that their faith is not strong. Through the accusatory tone, Jesus again attempts to claim authority. He puts himself in a position in which he confronts his disciples for modest faith. This is contrasted in verse 32b. Naturally, their heavenly father knows the disciples' needs. Jesus portrays himself as having complete trust in God and the disciples as lacking in that regard.

As in the confrontation stage in verse 25a, Jesus employs the phrase "I say to you" in verse 29. The purpose is the same in both cases: to promote authority.[68] The tension of verse 29 has already been discussed. Jesus claims that the lilies are better clothed than Solomon. This is meant to shock the audience. It is interesting that Jesus combines this notion with the authoritative phrase. It appears that the argument should be accepted primarily on the basis of Jesus' authority. Even if he says something shocking and odd, his authority guarantees the statement's truth value.

Possible Problematic Features in Jesus' Argumentation

In this section, I will assess Jesus' argumentation in Matthew 6.25-34 based on the pragma-dialectical *code of conduct* (see Table 1).[69] Throughout the analysis, I have already discussed several of the problems occurring in the text. Here, I will bring up those not mentioned previously. The rules and their violations reveal technically the features in the argumentation that hinder the dispute resolution process. In practice, however, some hesitation must be maintained in the evaluation. Since there is relatively little information regarding either the context or the acceptable and unacceptable argumentative conventions by the discussion parties, and since the disciples do not speak with Jesus in the text, I will only point out possible problematic features in Jesus' argumentation instead of putting forward a decisive

---

68. Betz, *Sermon*, 477 claims that "the introductory formula 'but I tell you' (λέγω δὲ ὑμῖν) is intended to call attention to something [verse 29] easily overlooked or taken for granted …" I render the attempt to gain authority a simpler aim than what Betz proposes. Moreover, the shocking statement in verse 29 is hardly something that would be overlooked or taken for granted. Betz notices the startling nature of the argument himself, too (p. 478).

69. Van Eemeren, Grootendorst, and Snoeck Henkemans, *Fundamentals*, 283.

claim about its shortcomings. To be sure, the author of the gospel indicates the reaction of the crowds in 7.28. This may suggest what Jesus' rhetorical purpose in 6.25-34 is, but it is not enough for a holistic evaluation. Consequently, I will not apply the rules mechanically but as a backdrop.

Table 1. Pragma-dialectical code of conduct.

   1.   Freedom rule
Parties must not prevent each other from putting forward standpoints or casting doubt on standpoints.

   2.   Burden-of-proof rule
A party who puts forward a standpoint is obliged to defend it if asked to do so.

   3.   Standpoint rule
A party's attack on a standpoint must relate to the standpoint that has indeed been advanced by the other party.

   4.   Relevance rule
A party may defend his or her standpoint only by advancing argumentation related to that standpoint.

   5.   Unexpressed premise rule
A party may not falsely present something as a premise that has been left unexpressed by the other party or deny a premise that he or she has left implicit.

   6.   Starting point rule
No party may falsely present a premise as an accepted starting point, or deny a premise representing an accepted starting point.

   7.   Argument scheme rule
A standpoint may not be regarded as conclusively defended if the defense does not take place by means of an appropriate argument scheme that is correctly applied.

   8.   Validity rule
The reasoning in the argumentation must be logically valid or must be capable of being made valid by making explicit one or more unexpressed premises.

   9.   Closure rule
A failed defense of a standpoint must result in the protagonist retracting the standpoint, and a successful defense or a standpoint must result in the antagonist retracting his or her doubts.

   10.   Usage rule
Parties must not use any formulations that are insufficiently clear or confusingly ambiguous, and they must interpret the formulations of the other party as carefully and accurately as possible.[70]

The first potential problem in Jesus' argumentation concerns the ambiguity of the standpoint.[71] The three formulations in verses 25a, 31, and 34a are

---

70. This is the non-technical variation of the rules, from Van Eemeren, Grootendorst, and Snoeck Henkemans, *Argumentation*, 182–3. For the technical version, see Van Eemeren and Grootendorst, *Systematic*, 136–57.

71. Betz, *Sermon*, 461 rightly sees a positive aspect to the ambiguousness in

different from one another, especially the third from the other two. All of them project a view regarding worry. Furthermore, the arguments regarding the birds and the lilies (1.1a.1a and 1.1c.1a) offer another phrasing about worry even though they do not mention the notion explicitly. Based on these arguments, I have rendered the concern referring to the future in terms of survival. Based on verse 31, the disciples are allowed to worry about their immediate daily needs; otherwise their prime concern should be following God's will and consequently most likely Jesus. However, the reconstruction of the specific nature of the standpoint has required significant amount of effort and this indicates that ambiguity exists.[72]

The rhetorical question in verse 27 (1.1b) is problematic. Again, the issue has to do with the notion of "being concerned." If it means merely the thought process, then the argument obviously stands. By thinking about worrisome thoughts, one does not extend one's life. However, since worrying refers (also) to storing mundane items for the future, the argument becomes problematic. If one cannot get food on a particular day, but has previously stored it, one survives that much longer. It appears that the formulation of the rhetorical question is intended to make the argument such that it is expected to receive a negative answer.

Jesus' statement in verse 29 is designed to shock the disciples. In contrast to common belief, he suggests that Solomon was less well clothed than lilies of the field. This may be problematic in itself and the argument appears to rely on Jesus' authority based on the phrase "I say to you." The hierarchy that Jesus puts forward in verses 29-30 is that Solomon is at the bottom, because the lilies are better clothed than him and the disciples are on top, since they are better clothed than the lilies. This may be persuasive, since it privileges the disciples to a great degree. However, the hierarchy and the logic may seem suspicious. Would the disciples regard themselves higher than a great

---

general: "... the SM is fond of engaging the reader in semantic word games. Apparent ambiguities, such as the meaning of the terms ψυχή or σῶμα ... appear to be intended to stimulate the reader's or hearer's thinking. It would therefore be wrong for translators and interpreters to remove such ambiguities and straighten out what they could view as 'problems,' because by doing so they would edit out much of the force of the argument." On p. 470, he continues that "the term [ψυχή] may be intentionally ambiguous." I disagree with Betz that the analyst should not attempt to assess the problematic features of ambiguities by attempting straightening them out. Both the persuasive and unpersuasive aspects and the dialectical violations should be scrutinized neutrally.

72. Luz, *Matthew 1–7*, 341: "One main question for the interpretation is: What does the warning against anxiety actually mean? Is it a warning against anxiousness, against inner lack of freedom, against being a prisoner of worry? Is it a warning against greed and covetousness? Or is the issue not only an inner attitude but also a specific behavior, such as the challenge to renounce possessions or refusing to work?"

king of their nation from the past? Besides being a king, Solomon is a person like the disciples. If God clothes lilies better than a person with high regard, what guarantees are there that the heavenly father will clothe them? One way to solve the problem is to interpret being clothed in some other metaphorical way. However, even if one is able to put forward a sensible interpretation, the verse still contributes to the confusion regarding the meaning of being clothed.

In sum, these three problematic features in the Jesus' argumentation consist mainly of ambiguous (Rule 10) and unrealistic features regarding the standpoint and arguments. Several of these features are so obvious that it seems likely that they are put in the text knowingly and despite of the potential criticism.[73]

Conclusion

Jesus' aim in 6.25-34 is to convince the disciples that they do not need to worry about everyday concerns. More specifically this means that they do not have to worry about their future in terms of food, drink, and clothing. The disciples are better off serving God instead of mammon (6.24), since the former will take care of them. In addition, since trouble will surface despite of their concern, there is no point to it. Not having to worry about their future, the disciples are free to follow Jesus and seek the kingdom of God.

Jesus builds up his authority through a variety of means. Among these tactics are the accusatory rhetorical questions, the shocking statement regarding Solomon, and the authoritative phrase "I say to you." In addition,

---

73. Luz, *Matthew 1–7,* 341 refers to extensive criticism on Jesus' argumentation: "Few Gospel texts have evoked such harsh criticism. It is said that every 'starving sparrow' contradicts Jesus, not to mention every famine and every war; that the text gives the appearance of being extremely simpleminded; that it acts as if there were no economic problems, only ethical ones, and that it is a good symbol of the economic naïveté that characterized Christianity in the course of its history ... it speaks of work 'in the most disdainful terms' and appears to encourage laziness. The admonition not to be anxious about tomorrow appears to be naïve not only in the age of global nuclear threats ... Correspondingly, for long stretches of its history the interpretation of this text reads like an attempt to defend it against attacks." Carlston, "Matthew," 179 holds that "these verses [6.24-34], carefully thought through, are so full of difficulties that they raise in a striking way the fundamental problem of the nature of theological language." See p. 179 for further examples of difficulties. Betz, *Sermon,* 460, on the other hand, has a more positive perspective: "The argument laid out in SM/Matt 6:25–34 is well constructed. The great care displayed by the composition must be accredited to the author of the SM." In addition, he praises the rhetorical skill used in the passage (p. 466).

he appeals to the disciples' esteem and at the same time lets them know that their faith is not strong. In this way, Jesus assumes an authoritative position over them. It appears that some of the arguments are deliberately unrealistic and even easy to criticize. Therefore, the emphasis is on Jesus' authority and on his way of presenting the case, not in the reasonableness of the arguments. Jesus presents himself as the embodiment of the carefree attitude.

A person who criticizes Jesus is likely to argue that his reasoning is unrealistic and causes danger to one's physical well-being. Consequently, the antagonist expresses a worried attitude—the opposite of what Jesus promotes. However, Jesus' argumentation is intimately connected to his person and authority representing his innate view of the world. The question becomes whether one can and is willing to trust Jesus and share his view of the world. An antagonist, who cannot or is not willing to, is simply left with his/her worrisome attitude, which is in principle assumed to be inferior to the carefree attitude. Rhetorically speaking, who would not want be free of everyday concerns in comparison to being concerned? Even a successful criticism of Jesus' arguments still cannot discount his personal view to which the argumentation is tied with presentational devices. The rhetorical style that simplifies matters a great deal may prove persuasive to those, who seek to unburden themselves of everyday concerns.[74]

Intuitively speaking, this kind of argumentation that is designed to promote Jesus' authority may be characteristic of the Sermon. This possibility is supported by the verses in 7.28-29, which indicate the effect of the Sermon and Jesus' presentational style. The purpose of the argumentation is not to be logically sound but to portray Jesus as a holistic representative of the kingdom of God. The arguments are meant to portray this image and impact the audience with an uncompromising force. It can be tentatively argued that the passage I have analyzed exemplifies how the Sermon functions as part of the *exordium* of the Gospel.

In the introduction, I suggested that besides the followers of Jesus, other readers have found the argumentation of Matthew 6.25-34 appealing. Even though the argumentation has elements that promote Jesus' authority, it also holds other, more universally persuasive qualities as well. The appealing factors include the topic of the standpoint and arguments and the style of argumentation. Jesus presents a positive, almost ideal case with clearly naïve arguments. They may be persuasive if not convincing logically, since they appeal to emotion. People characteristically wish to obtain a carefree attitude. What Jesus proposes is a lens through which this attitude

---

74. Populistic approaches, in which complex matters are simplified by rhetorical means, are still persuasive in today's politics.

can be achieved. In addition, some of the arguments do not refer to God (explicitly), which may help to convince those who do not trust in him. For instance, trouble will ensue despite being concerned. In addition, some of the arguments that do mention God can, in a sense, function without bringing God up. The arguments hold such universal ideas that do not necessarily require God. For instance, the arguments concerning birds and lilies could be seen as follows: "The animals and plants do fine without stress, why would not you?"

In the end, Matthew 6.25-34 functions in two ways. First, it encourages the disciples who already believe in God and in Jesus to deepen their relationship. It invites the audience to stop being worried about everyday concerns and to follow Jesus by seeking the kingdom of God. Second, it attempts to persuade those outside of the group to get to know Jesus by portraying him as an uncompromising preacher, who applies universal ideas and promises a lot to those who are willing to answer his call.

Biographical Note

Niilo Lahti is a post-doctoral researcher in the Philosophical Faculty, School of Theology, at University of Eastern Finland, Joensuu. He is expert in biblical argumentation, especially through the lens of pragma-dialectics and the Toulmin model. Lahti was awarded the Young Researcher award in 2018 and granted the honor of *primus doctor* in 2019 by the University of Eastern Finland. During his PhD period, Lahti studied Paul's argumentation in First Corinthians. Currently, as a member of the project "Parables as Persuasive Narratives," funded by the Finnish Academy, Lahti aims to contribute to uncovering a novel model for analyzing and understanding all of Jesus' parables.

Bibliography

Albright, William F., and Christopher S. Mann. *Matthew: Introduction, Translation, and Notes*. Garden City, NY: Doubleday, 1971.

Allen, Willoughby C. *A Critical and Exegetical Commentary on the Gospel according to S. Matthew*. The International Critical Commentary. Edinburgh: T&T Clark, 1922.

Augustine, St. *The Lord's Sermon on the Mount*. Westminster, MD: The Newman Press, 1948.

Betz, Hans Dieter. *The Sermon on the Mount: A Commentary on the Sermon on the Mount, including the Sermon on the Plain (Matthew 5:3–7:27 and Luke 6:20–49)*. Edited by Adela Y. Collins. Hermeneia. Minneapolis, MN: Fortress, 1995.

Carlston, Charles E. "Matthew 6:24–34," *Interpretation* 41 (1987): 179–83. https://doi.org/10.1177/002096438704100208

Dillon, Richard J. "Ravens, Lilies, and the Kingdom of God (Matthew 6:25–33 / Luke 12:22–31)," *Catholic Biblical Quarterly* 53 (1991): 605–27.

van Eemeren, Frans H. *Strategic Maneuvering in Argumentative Discourse: Extending the Pragma-Dialectical Theory of Argumentation*. Amsterdam: John Benjamins, 2010. https://doi.org/10.1075/aic.2

van Eemeren, Frans H., and Rob Grootendorst. *Argumentation, Communication, and Fallacies: A Pragma-Dialectical Perspective*. Hillsdale, NJ: Lawrence Erlbaum, 1992.

—*A Systematic Theory of Argumentation: The Pragma-Dialectical Approach*. Amsterdam: John Benjamins, 2004. https://doi.org/10.1017/CBO9780511616389

van Eemeren, Frans H., Rob Grootendorst, Sally Jackson, and Scott Jacobs. *Speech Acts in Argumentative Discussions: A Theoretical Model for the Analysis of Discussions towards Solving Conflicts of Opinion*. Doldrecht, Holland: Foris Publications, 1984. https://doi.org/10.1515/9783110846089

—*Reconstructing Argumentative Discourse*. Tuscaloosa, AL: The University of Alabama Press, 1993.

van Eemeren, Frans H., Rob Grootendorst, and Tjark Kruiger. *Handbook of Argumentation Theory: A Critical Survey of Classical Backgrounds and Modern Studies*. Studies of Argumentation in Pragmatics and Discourse Analysis, 7. Dordrecht, Holland: Foris Publications, 1987. https://doi.org/10.1515/9783110846096

van Eemeren, Frans H., Rob Grootendorst, and Francisca Snoeck Henkemans. *Fundamentals of Argumentation Theory: A Handbook of Historical Backgrounds and Contemporary Developments*. Mahwah, NJ: Erlbaum, 1996.

—*Argumentation: Analysis, Evaluation, Presentation*. Mahwah, NJ: Lawrence Erlbaum, 2002. https://doi.org/10.4324/9781410602442

van Eemeren, Frans H., and Peter Houtlosser. "Strategic Maneuvering: Maintaining a Delicate Balance," 132 in *Dialectic and Rhetoric: The Warp and Woof of Argumentation Analysis*. Edited by Frans H. van Eemeren and Peter Houtlosser. Dordrecht: Kluwer Academic, 2002. https://doi.org/10.1007/978-94-015-9948-1

—"Strategic Maneuvering: Examining Argumentation in Context," 4–5 in *Examining Argumentation in Context: Fifteen Studies on Strategic Maneuvering*. Edited by Frans H. van Eemeren. Amsterdam: John Benjamins, 2009. https://doi.org/10.1075/aic.1

Hagner, Donald. *Matthew 1–13*. Word Biblical Commentary, 33A. Dallas: Word, 1993.

Hietanen, Mika. *Paul's Argumentation in Galatians: A Pragma-Dialectical Analysis*. New York: T&T Clark, 2007.

Lahti, Niilo. "Shameful Corinthians: A Pragma-Dialectical Analysis of 1 Corinthians 6:12–20," 825–35 in *Proceedings of the 8th International Society for the Study of Argumentation*. Edited by B. J. Garssen, D. Godden, G. Mitchell, and A. F. Snoeck Henkemans. Amsterdam: Sic Sat, 2015.

—*The Maneuvering Paul – a Pragma-Dialectical Analysis of Paul's Argumentation in First Corinthians 4:18–7:40*. Dissertation. Joensuu: University of Eastern Finland, 2017.

Luz, Ulrich. *Matthew 1–7: A Commentary*. Edited by Helmut Koester. Translated by James E. Crouch. Rev. edn. Hermeneia. Minneapolis, MN: Fortress, 2007.

PART III
SOCIAL DYNAMICS

Chapter Nine

Hypocrites and the Pure in Heart:
Religion as an Evolved Strategy for In-Group Formation

John Teehan

Introduction

What we are about to engage in is a new sort of hermeneutics, a cognitive-critical approach to Scripture. Just as the historical-critical approach seeks to uncover the influences of the historical context of scripture—placing its construction in a particular historical context, reading it against the assumptions and concerns of that historical period, problematizing its subsequent theological readings through treating the document as a product of historical processes—the cognitive-critical method seeks to read through the semantics of the text to uncover the influence of various cognitive processes. These cognitive processes, or mental tools, are the means through which humans apprehend their experiences and environment. We do not think *with* these processes but rather think *through* these processes. That is, these processes construct the basic categories that constitute human cognition. As such, their influence goes unnoticed; they work outside of conscious awareness, indeed they structure conscious awareness, unless we are led to reflect on the structures of these mental categories, seeking insight into their genesis and the nature of their influence. This is, essentially, the work of cognitive science: an umbrella term for numerous disciplines that are seeking to understand how the mind processes input from the environment and generates thoughts, beliefs, behavior, feelings—and this includes religious beliefs, behaviors and feelings.

While this is a complex and still developing paradigm, we can set out a working model that will suffice for the purposes at hand. In *Thinking, Fast and Slow*, Daniel Kahneman[1] presents, in extensive detail but also in quite accessible form, the myriad cognitive biases that shape our perception of and reaction to our world. This important work also gives us a simple, though not simplistic, framework for approaching human cognition. There

---

1. Daniel Kahneman. *Thinking, Fast and Slow*. New York: Farrar, Straus & Giroux, 2011.

are two basic methods of cognitive processing, System 1 and System 2. System 1 processes are quick, non-reflective, automatic processes working outside of conscious awareness that generate intuitively, and even emotionally compelling beliefs. System 2 processes are slower, reflective, deliberative processes that are readily available to conscious awareness and generate "reasoned" beliefs. I put "reasoned" into scare quotes because often System 2 functions to provide rationalization of the intuitions generated by a System 1 process, rather than a neutral rational judgment. It is, of course, possible for System 2 to overcome the compelling, intuitive outputs of System 1—possible, but not easy. Evidence clearly demonstrates the relative weakness of System 2 processes compared to System 1 processes.[2]

These System 1 processes bear more than a passing similarity to the Freudian conception of unconscious forces. We need not delve into this topic in detail here, but they are different in (at least) two important ways. For Freud, these processes were not directly available to conscious inspection and only made themselves manifest indirectly, significantly through dreams. Cognitive science holds that we can uncover these processes through empirical, experimental procedures; that we can discern consistent patterns of judgments and biases through, for example, a review of anthropological and ethnographic studies, historical records and psychological experimentation—and these findings can be further tested through experimental manipulation. A second key distinction is that for Freud these unconscious forces were largely the result of conflicts in psycho-sexual development, while for cognitive science these processes are the result of our species' evolutionary history; they were shaped by natural selection to address concrete, transcultural challenges of humans in the pursuit of inclusive fitness. While this evolutionary context is not always brought to the forefront of cognitive science, and for some researchers it may not be deemed relevant to their particular focus and so not explicitly endorsed, the evolutionary aspect of our cognitive functions is the context for understanding the ultimate cause for why we have the mental tools we do—and in regards to understanding issues of morality and human sociality, I believe it is a central concern.

The relevance of all of this should be evident: the cognitive processes that structure our experiences and judgments are all System 1 processes. The cognitive-critical method postulates that since these cognitive processes constitute the means through which we apprehend the world, they will

---

2. Jonathan Haidt, "The Emotional Dog and its Rational Tail: A Social Intuitionist Approach to Moral Judgment," *Psychological Review* 108 (2001), 814–34; Jonathan Haidt, *The Righteous Mind: Why Good People Are Divided by Religion and Politics* (New York: Pantheon, 2012); Kahneman, *Thinking*.

shape how we think about the world, and how we express those thoughts. The relevant implication for our topic is that these tools have given contour and structure to how we think about religion, and that evidence of this influence is discernable in the pages of Scripture. Our case study here is the Sermon on the Mount (Matt. 5–7), and the thesis to be developed is that we can see the Sermon as an example of how religion is, in part, an evolved cultural adaptation to promote the formation of cohesive, morally-bounded groups that extend beyond the relatively small, homogeneous groups characteristic of our hunter-gatherer ancestors. So, the first task is to understand the evolutionary dynamics involved with group formation.

The Evolution of Society

How are human societies possible? A defining characteristic of the human species is that we live in the largest, most complex groups in the animal kingdom—a fact not always appreciated. What may be even less appreciated is just how complicated and difficult this was to achieve. Living as a member of a group poses a serious problem from an evolutionary perspective: natural selection favors those behaviors that maximize the inclusive fitness of an individual, namel, behavior that provides an individual and its genetic kin with a competitive advantage against other individuals. However, successful group living requires that individuals act in ways that, at times, go against their direct interests and instead benefits others in the group. Group living, on the other hand, provides benefits in terms of shared risks, increased security, group productivity, that have clear evolutionary value, and accordingly, social species are found throughout the animal kingdom. Each species has developed, throughout its evolutionary history, a way to resolve the conflict between individual and group interests. One of the most efficient resolutions was hit upon by the so-called *eusocial* insects, for example, ant, bees, wasps. In these species there are high levels of genetic relatedness between all members of the group, such that there is no ultimate distinction between the good of an individual and the good of the group. For as William Hamilton demonstrated, the successful propagation of genes occurs not only through direct reproduction but also though the reproductive success of kin.[3] High levels of social coordination is achieved in such species through a tightly structured, genetically based, social hierarchy.[4]

---

3. William D. Hamilton, "Genetic Evolution of Social Behavior, I and II," *Journal of Theoretical Biology* 7 (1964): 1–52.
4. Bert Holldobler and Edward O. Wilson, *The Superorganism: The Beauty, Elegance, and Strangeness of Insect Societies* (New York: W. W. Norton, 2008).

But humans are not ants; we did not achieve the levels of social development we have through extended genetic connections. Contemporary human societies are composed of networks of unrelated strangers, who not only are not kin, but often will not even know or directly interact with one another—and yet all societies are able (to greater and lesser degrees of success) to coordinate social cooperation sufficient to allow the continued survival of the group. Of course, humans did not always live in groups of this nature. Although we have always been a social species, descended from an ancient lineage of social species, earliest human communities were relatively small and largely genetically based. The greater the genetic relatedness between members of a group, the less problematic is social cooperation. But at some point, clearly before the advent of agriculture some 10,000 years ago, humans burst through the limits of kin-based groups and began to grow. How we developed from small, kin-based groups of perhaps 150 individuals[5] to groups of thousands at the dawn of recorded history, to groups of millions found in numerous ancient civilizations, is an accomplishment in need of an explanation—and one important element of that explanation is the development of religion. Let's try to trace this out.

In evolutionary terms, committing resources that could be used to promote your own good to instead promote the good of another, often referred to as altruism, is a bad strategy, as this may put you, and your family, at a competitive disadvantage (sacrificing for your children, on the other hand, is an investment in the future success of your genes). Evolution should not look favorably on altruists. However, committing resources to someone else can also function as an investment in your own good, if that investment is repaid. This is a strategy know as reciprocal altruism.[6] In this case, sharing resources that can be spared today provides security when it is paid back at a future time when you may have insufficient resources; but reciprocation need not be made directly. If my investment of resources results in, for example, the strengthening of my group—the locus of my efforts to promote my inclusive fitness—then this too is a benefit to me. Indirect reciprocity, or indirect altruism[7] is recognized to be a major method for establishing systems of social cooperation.

While these theoretical insights constitute a major step toward understanding the evolution of human sociality, they also raise challenges that

---

5. Robert Dunbar, "Neocortex Size as a Constraint on Group Size in Primates," *Journal of Human Evolution* 6 (1992): 469–93.
6. Robert L. Trivers, "The Evolution of Reciprocal Altruism," *Quarterly Review of Biology* 46 (1971): 35–57.
7. Richard Alexander, *The Biology of Moral Systems: Foundations of Human Behavior* (New York: Aldine de Gruyter, 1987).

need to be addressed. Such systems can only work if reciprocity occurs. If I commit my resources to you and you do not pay me back, or if you enjoy a social benefit without contributing to the social good, or if you fail to follow through on a cooperative venture—strategies referred to as "cheating" or "defecting"—that commitment of resources constitutes a failed investment, and whether in financial terms or evolutionary terms, this poses serious risks as repeated failed investments can be disastrous. For a group to survive and thrive it must develop a system that encourages cooperation and discourages cheating and defection—and from an evolutionary perspective, this is just what a moral system does. It sets out the conditions of social living, what is expected and what is prohibited, and crucially, the consequences for violating the moral code—conditions which, as varied as they may be in specifics, are grounded in evolved cognitive and emotional predispositions.[8] The picture being painted by this account is that of humans predisposed to cooperate with others, but also keenly aware of who reciprocates and who cheats; who is a reliable partner in social cooperation and who is looking for a free ride.

We do not need to delve into all the specifics of our evolved moral psychology. For our present purposes we can focus on one particular, and particularly important, fact: from an evolutionary perspective, morality is an in-group adaptation. Morality is a system for social cooperation based on networks of reciprocation, both direct and indirect, and it is the individual members of my group who are potential partners in social cooperation; it is they who contribute to the well-being and success of the group in which I pursue my inclusive fitness; it is they who are in a position to reciprocate my acts of altruism—they are the targets of my moral concern. Members of out-groups are not situated in such morally significant positions; they are not invested in the success of my group, in fact they may, and throughout human history often did, pose a threat to the welfare of my group. The psychological mechanisms that predispose us to pro-sociality, to sacrifice, to compassion and concern, are biased toward those recognized as members of the in-group. They do not function in the same way toward out-group members.

Significant support for this deeply ingrained, in-group evolved moral bias is being provided by neuroscience. Experimental evidence is revealing

---

8. Robert Axelrod and William D. Hamilton, "The Evolution of Cooperation," *Science* 211 (1981): 1390–6; Alexander, *Biology*; Robert Boyd and Peter J. Richerson, "The Evolution of Reciprocity in Sizable Groups," *Journal of Theoretical Biology* 132 (1988): 337–56; Herbert Gintis, "Strong Reciprocity and Human Sociality," *Journal of Theoretical Biology* 206 (2000): 169–79; Ernst Fehr and Urs Fischbacher, "Social Norms and Human Cooperation," *Trends in Cognitive Sciences* 8 (2004): 185–90; Michael A. Nowak, "Five Rules for the Evolution of Cooperation," *Science* 314 (2006): 1560–3.

that our brains are less sensitive to the perception of pain in out-group members, and in fact, witnessing the suffering of out-group members can trigger reward centers in the brain. We are primed to respond to the faces of out-group members as a threat-cue; and in some situations, out-group members are not even processed on a neurological level as persons but instead trigger a disgust response similar to that triggered by pathogens.[9] Scientific studies of morality are zeroing in on empathy as a key proximate cause for altruistic behavior, and neuroscience is revealing the empathy systems of the brain to be sensitively tuned to in-group/out-group distinctions. As Frans de Waal put it: "The empathy mechanism is biased the way evolutionary theory would predict."[10]

The evolution of these moral mechanisms made possible the extension of altruism and moral concern beyond the limits of genetic relatedness and so paved the way for the development of larger societies, but even these mental tools face a limit—they are triggered by cues of in-group membership. This method of policing social exchange works well in the type of group characteristic of the extended hunter-gatherer phase of our history. In these relatively small groups, keeping track of the reputations of all the members was not such a challenge. You knew who was in your group because these were the people you met and interacted with every day. You could evaluate their commitment to the group and its code because you witnessed it on a regular basis. However, as a group grows larger and more anonymous, this task becomes more difficult. Our moral psychology did not evolve to function in the sorts of large-scale societies characteristic of developed civilization. To see how this shift may have occurred we need to look at two further issues: signaling theory and punishment. This will also allow us to see how religion plays into this process.

We are not born with an innate knowledge of who is in our group, but it seems that we are innately predisposed to respond to various environmental

---

9. Hillary A. Elfenbein and Nalini Ambady, "Is there an In-Group Advantage in Emotion Recognition?" *Psychological Bulletin* 128 (2002): 243–9; Susan T. Fiske, "What We Know about Bias and Intergroup Conflict: The Problem of the Century," *Current Directions in Psychological Science* 11 (2002): 123–8; Tania Singer, et al., "Empathic Neural Responses Are Modulated by the Perceived Fairness of Others," *Nature* 439 (2006): 466–9; Joan Y. Chiao, et. al., "Cultural Specificity in Amygdala Response to Fear Faces," *Journal of Cognitive Neuroscience* 20 (2008): 2167–74; Xiaojing Xu, et al., "Do You Feel My Pain? Racial Group Membership Modulates Empathic Neural Responses," *The Journal of Neuroscience* 29 (2009): 8525–9; Alessio Avenanti, Angela Sirigu, and Salvatore Aglioti, "Racial Bias Reduces Empathic Sensorimotor Resonance with Other-Race Pain," *Current Biology* 20 (2010): 1018–22.

10. Frans B. M. de Waal, "Putting Altruism Back into Altruism: The Evolution of Empathy," *Annual Review of Psychology* 59 (2008): 279–300.

cues as signals of in-group status. This is the basis of signaling theory.[11] Two very simple heuristics employed are based on phenotypic similarity and on social familiarity. Someone who looks like you has a reasonable probability of being genetically related to you, and so this triggers mechanisms of kin selection.[12] It is also a good bet, in evolutionary terms, that individuals you regularly interact with from an early age are also closely related to you. This may not hold true in more complex societies but was standard in smaller hunter-gatherer groups—and we must always keep in mind that that was the period, and those the conditions, that laid down the basics of our moral psychology.

Another important signal of in-group membership is language—people who speak your language, or your particular dialect of a language, are likely to be connected to your larger group. They have been raised by people who speak and sound like you, and indeed studies by developmental psychologists show that even infants show a preference for individuals speaking their native language, even before the child has acquired that language.[13]

Shared behavior can also prime the empathetic systems, and this helps to explain the ubiquity of rituals. The communal synchronization of bodily movements contributes to a shared emotional experience that bonds participants together.[14] Chanting, singing, dancing, or other rhythmic movements not only promote social coordination, such ritualistic behaviors can also function as costly-signals-of-commitment.

Costly signaling is found throughout the animal kingdom. The excessive plumage of the peacock, the super-sized antlers of elk, or the stotting behavior of antelope, are costly in evolutionary terms. They serve as a handicap in the struggle to survive and so should have been eliminated by natural selection pressures.[15] These costly traits have evolved however because their

---

11. Randolph M. Nesse, ed., *Evolution and the Capacity for Commitment* (The Russell Sage Foundation Series on Trust, 3; New York: Russell Sage Foundation, 2001); William Irons, "Religion as a Hard-To-Fake Sign of Commitment," in Nesse, *Evolution*, 292–309.

12. Lisa M. DeBruine, "Facial Resemblance Enhances Trust," *Proceedings of the Royal Society of London B: Biological Sciences* 269 (2002): 1307–12.

13. Paul Bloom, *Just Babies: The Origins of Good and Evil* (New York: Crown, 2013).

14. Paul Reddish, Ronald Fischer, and Joseph Bulbulia, "Let's Dance Together: Synchrony, Shared Intentionality and Cooperation," *PLoS ONE* 8 (2013): e71182; Paul Reddish, Joseph Bulbulia, and Ronald Fischer, "Does Synchrony Promote Generalized Prosociality?" *Religion, Brain and Behavior* 4 (2014): 3–19.

15. In examples such as these, the phenomenon is referred to as the handicap principle: "The investment that animals make in signals is similar to the 'handicaps' imposed on the stronger contestants in a game or a sporting event: for example, the removal of

very costliness serves as a signal, whether to predators or potential mates, of the vitality of the individual who can bear such costs and yet survive. Only a truly healthy and quick antelope could afford to signal its presence to a predator and hope to survive, and so it also signals that it will be costly to the predator to expend energy trying to take it down.

There are human behaviors and rituals that also signal important fitness information to others. For example, conspicuous displays of wealth serve to signal the individual's fitness as a procurer of resources, much like the elaborate nests built as mating strategies by males in various species of birds. But costly rituals can also signal another vital piece of social information: that the person performing the ritual, which may be costly in any number of ways—in terms of physical pain, investment of resources, devotion of time to learn the intricacies of the ritual, and so on—is sincerely committed to the group. If she or he were not committed to the group, how or why would they be willing to invest such efforts in such a display? Costly signals of commitment indicate who has invested in the group and so who is likely to be a reliable partner in social exchange; and by signaling in-group status it primes our empathy systems. It is here that religion comes into the picture.

William Irons points out that religions function as very effective costly-signals of commitment. He writes:

> Most religions are expressed in elaborate rituals that are costly in time and sometimes in other ways. These rituals also provide extensive opportunities for members of a community to monitor one another's commitments to the community and its moral code thereby facilitating the formation of larger and better-united groups.[16]

They are also often hard to learn and impenetrable to those not reared in the religious traditions which renders them hard-to-fake, and in regard to the effectiveness of signals "to be successful they must be hard to fake. Other things being equal, the costlier the signal the less likely it is to be false."[17]

---

the superior player's queen in a chess match, the extra weight the swifter race horse must carry, or the score of several strokes that the more accomplished golfer starts with. A handicap proves beyond a doubt that the victor's win is due to mastery, not chance. The peacock's tail and the stag's antlers are not mere disabilities; rather, they are handicaps in this very special sense: they allow an individual animal to demonstrate its quality." Amotz Zahavi and Avishag Zahavi, *The Handicap Principle: A Missing Piece of Darwin's Puzzle* (Oxford: Oxford University Press, 1997), xiv.

16. Irons, "Religion."

17. Irons, "Religion"; see also Richard Sosis and Candace Alcorta, "Signaling, Solidarity, and the Sacred: The Evolution of Religious Behavior," *Evolutionary Anthropology* 12 (2003): 264–74; Richard Sosis, "Religious Behaviors, Badges, and Bans: Signaling Theory and the Evolution of Religion," in *Where God and Science Meet: How Brain and Evolutionary Studies Alter our Understanding of Religion*. Vol. 1 of *Evolution, Genes*

This then, is one aspect of religion that facilitated the expansion of human groups. By providing a set of signals of commitment, religious behavior, symbols, and beliefs signal membership in a moral community and help to clarify the boundaries of the in-group.[18] You do not need to be related to someone or know them personally to recognize them as one of your own. Their participation in the rites of a shared set of beliefs and behaviors signals in an effective way that they are part of the in-group, which primes the mental tools that underlie social cooperation. We will look at this function in detail when we turn to a consideration of the Sermon on the Mount, but we can now set out our thesis: *the Sermon on the Mount functions to help define the boundaries of the new Christian in-group and does so by establishing a set of signals of membership in, and commitment to, that in-group.*

Before turning to that discussion, there is one further aspect of religion that allows it to contribute to the formation of cohesive and functioning social units and this stems from what is known as the Supernatural Punishment Hypothesis. As we discussed, a basic goal of any social code is the promotion of cooperation. Cooperation is risky as there is always the chance that the investment of resources will not be reciprocated (whether directly or indirectly) and this is a serious threat to the psychology of altruism. So dangerous is this that evolution has equipped us with a keen sensitivity to cheaters[19] and a readiness to punish those who do cheat—even when the punishment is itself costly. Indeed, the evidence suggests that the threat of punishment is a more effective means of promoting cooperation than is the promise of reward.[20] The threat of punishment raises the potential cost of cheating, thereby reducing its value as a strategy; this in turns lowers the

---

and the Religious Brain, ed. P. McNamara (Westport, CT: Praeger Publishers, 2006), 61–86.

18. Sosis, "Religious Behaviors."

19. E.g., Robert Dunbar, *Grooming, Gossip and the Evolution of Language* (Cambridge, MA: Harvard University Press, 1997); Nesse, *Evolution*; Sven Vanneste, et al., "Attention Bias toward Noncooperative People: A Dot Probe Classification Study in Cheating Detection," *Evolution and Human Behavior* 28 (2007): 272–6; Jan Verplaetse, Sven Vanneste, and Johan Braeckman, "You Can Judge a Book by Its Cover: The Sequel. A Kernel of Truth in Predictive Cheating Detection," *Evolution and Human Behavior* 28 (2007): 260–71.

20. E.g. Joseph Henrich and Robert Boyd, "Why People Punish Defectors: Weak Conformist Transmission Can Stabilize Costly Enforcement of Norms in Cooperative Dilemmas," *Journal of Theoretical Biology* 208 (2001): 78–89; Michael E. Price, Leda Cosmides, and John Tooby, "Punitive Sentiment as an Anti-Free Rider Psychological Device," *Evolution and Human Behavior* 23 (2002): 203–31; Robert Boyd, et al., "The Evolution of Altruistic Punishment," *Proceedings of the National Academy of Sciences* 100 (2003): 3531–5; Joseph Henrich, et al., "Costly Punishment across Human Societies." *Science* 312 (2006): 1767–70; Tobe Ellingsen and Magnus Johannesson,

potential costs of cooperating (i.e., by reducing the chance of being cheated, it lowers the chance that one will not recoup on one's altruistic act). Therefore, a credible threat of punishment plays a crucial social role.

Punishment raises its own problems, however. For one, the act of imposing punishment has risks and costs. The cost of imposing punishment, added to the cost of what was lost as a result of being cheated, may make punishing a losing proposition, so much so that it may just not seem worth it. This mitigates the contribution punishment makes to the calculus of cooperation—if, that is, you are making a rational calculation about punishing someone. Here signaling theory comes into play again. If you have a reputation for being a cool-headed, rational person then I might be inclined to cheat you whenever it seems punishing me does not make sense. However, if you have a reputation for being short-tempered and prone to irrational outbursts of anger, then the rational assessment of cost/benefit is not in the picture, and I need to think twice about testing you. Just as having a reputation for being a reliable cooperator is to your advantage, so too is a reputation for being irrationally driven to revenge. Theorists have argued that emotions and their outward displays evolved as hard-to-fake signals of commitment to act; and in the case of anger and moral outrage, to act in a retributive manner, despite the costs.[21]

Of course, your irrational resolve to punish me for cheating you works as a disincentive to my cheating only to the degree that I fear being caught—something much more likely in small groups of familiars, less so in large anonymous groups. Here is another role for religion to play: the communal belief in morally-interested gods shifts some of the work of detecting and punishing cheaters away from temporal powers.

There is ample experimental evidence that shows that levels of cooperation rise, and cheating decreases, when actors are not guaranteed anonymity. Cooperation games staged face to face yield higher rates of generosity and trust than when the players are in separate rooms; yet even in those situations, if there is the possibility of players meeting after the game, cooperativeness is higher than when that possibility does not exist. Studies show that even a stylized image of eyes in the room raises levels of cooperation, lending support to the maxim, "watched people are nice people."[22] More

---

"Anticipated Verbal Feedback Induces Altruistic Behavior," *Evolution and Human Behavior* 29 (2008): 100–5.

21. Robert H. Frank, *Passions within Reason: The Strategic Role of Emotions* (New York: W. W. Norton, 1988); Nesse, *Evolution*.

22. Ernst Fehr and Urs Fischbacher, "The Nature of Human Altruism," *Nature* 425 (2003): 785–91; Kevin J. Haley and Daniel M. T. Kessler, "Nobody Is Watching? Subtle Cues Affect Generosity in an Anonymous Economic Game," *Evolution and Human*

pertinent to our topic, it has been shown that even priming subjects with cues about disembodied beings (e.g., an invisible Princess Alice with children, the ghost of a recently departed researcher with adults) significantly impacts rates of cheating.[23] All of this makes sense given what we know about our evolved moral psychology. If someone is watching me, then my reputation is at stake, and having a reputation of being a cheater is harmful to my long-term interests. Also, being watched means crimes do not go undetected, and this raises the specter of suffering costly punishment.

Gods are perfectly suited to provide the watchful eye that societies need to guard against violations of the social code in large, complex societies, and it may be that the bigger the society, the bigger the god that will be needed.[24] Work in the cognitive science of religion is setting out the parameters of a default schema for gods.[25] We need not address this in detail here, but one aspect of our evolved god-beliefs is particularly pertinent: while humans are recognized to be "limited-access strategic agents" who, because of their limited access to all the relevant facts of any social exchange, including what is in the minds of other agents, can readily be deceived, gods are often conceived as "full-access strategic agents" not subject to such constraints.[26] It is not enough that gods have access to all relevant social information, they must in some way be interested in this information. The literature points to three ways gods may be morally involved: they may act as moral role models, they may be moral legislators, or they may be moral enforcers.[27] Of the three, the most essential is that they be interested in enforcing the code of the group, for this involves them directly, and in a uniquely effective way, with the calculus of punishment. A morally interested god, who is committed to enforcing the rules of the group strengthens the cohesiveness of that group by raising the likelihood of being caught cheating, and therefore the likelihood of being punished. This can act as a deterrent to cheating, but it also promotes cooperation by lowering the risks associated with altruistic

---

Behavior 26 (2005): 245–56; Martin A. Nowak and Karl Sigmund, "Evolution of Indirect Reciprocity," *Nature* 437 (2005): 1291–8; Ellingsen and Johannesson, "Anticipated."

23. Jesse Bering, "On Reading Symbolic Random Events: Children's Causal Reasoning about Unexpected Occurrences" (Paper Presented at Psychological and Cognitive Foundations of Religiosity Conference. Atlanta, GA, 2003); Jesse Bering, "The Folk Psychology of Souls," *Behavioral and Brain Sciences* 29 (2006): 453–62.

24. Ara Norenzayan, *Big Gods: How Religion Transformed Cooperation and Conflict* (Princeton, NJ: Princeton University Press, 2013).

25. Pascal Boyer, *Religion Explained: The Evolutionary Origins of Religious Thought* (New York: Basic Books, 2001); Scott Atran, *In Gods We Trust: The Evolutionary Landscape of Religion* (Oxford: Oxford University Press, 2002).

26. Atran, *In Gods We Trust*.

27. Boyer, *Religion Explained*.

acts. This is the Supernatural Punishment Hypothesis, which is supported by experimental research, as well as ethnographic studies.[28]

Let's pull this together: humans are social creatures, descended from a long evolutionary lineage of social species. Group living is a major adaptation for our species. Coordinated group action provided advantages in accessing resources and defending against threats, compensating for our relatively vulnerable physical nature. Group activity requires the commitment of resources away from strictly individual fitness, toward the group. The conditions for cohesive group living are easier to achieve in relatively small, kin-based units. However, as groups compete, numbers begin to matter and larger groups gain an advantage, but for larger, more anonymous groups to develop, there must be conditions that allow for the extension of our evolved moral psychology. A credible system of punishment supports social cohesion, but this too is strained by the increasing size of groups. However, by outsourcing the enforcement of social rules to a morally interested, full-access strategic agent, that is, a god, the group's moral bonds may be upheld. But for all of this to work, there must be widespread commitment to the god that oversees the moral code of the group, and so signals of commitment to a group's god indicates that one is subject to the watchful influence of that god. Religion, then, becomes an important element in the formation and maintenance of group identity, and by identifying an individual as a member of that in-group it primes the empathetic responses of the brain that constitute moral concern and sensitivity. Religion is not the only way to accomplish these goals, but it is one of the oldest, and arguably most effective means to establishing morally bonded and significant groups. From the perspective of an evolutionary cognitive science, religions have been shaped by the interplay of cognitive mechanisms and shifting social

---

28. Domonic Johnson and Oliver Krüger, "The Good of Wrath: Supernatural Punishment and the Evolution of Cooperation," *Political Theology* 5 (2004): 159–76; Dominic Johnson, "God's Punishment and Public Goods: A Test of the Supernatural Punishment Hypothesis in 186 World Cultures," *Human Nature* 16 (2005): 410–46; Jesse Bering and Dominic Johnson, "'O Lord … You Perceive My Thoughts from Afar': Recursiveness and the Evolution of Supernatural Agency," *Journal of Cognition and Culture* 5 (2005): 118–42; Dominic Johnson and Jesse Bering, "Hand of God, Mind of Man: Punishment and Cognition in the Evolution of Cooperation," *Evolutionary Psychology* 4 (2006): 219–33; Azim Shariff and Ara Norenzayan, "Mean Gods Make Good People: Different Views of God Predicting Cheating Behavior," *International Journal of the Psychology of Religion* 21 (2011): 85–96; Quentin Atkinson and Pierrick Bouratt, "Beliefs about God, the Afterlife and Morality Support the Role of Supernatural Policing in Human Cooperation," *Evolution and Human Behavior* 32 (2011): 41–9; Azim Shariff and Mijke Rhemtulla, "Divergent Effects of Beliefs in Heaven and Hell on National Crime Rates," *PloS ONE* 7 (2012): e39048.

environments to play just this role, and religious texts offer testimony to this evolutionary function of religion.[29] In order to exemplify this claim, let us turn now to the *Gospel of Matthew*, and in particular, the Sermon on the Mount, to see how it fits this evolved cognitive schema, and how it is designed to trigger the moral-cognitive tools that promote group formation.

Defining the New (Christian) In-group

As we turn to this task it is crucial to keep in mind just what we are doing, and what we are not doing. We are going to read the Sermon on the Mount through the lens of the cognitive-critical method. In doing so, we seek to discern the influence of various moral-cognitive tools essential to group formation in shaping the content of the Sermon. It is just because the text has been shaped by these System 1 tools that the text can function to promote the formation of a new moral community—by virtue of having been shaped by these tools it can serve to trigger these same cognitive tools, the tools that generate the appropriate moral/social instincts that make group living possible.

What I am not doing is ascribing such motives to the historical Jesus or to "Matthew," at least not as intentional motives. These moral-cognitive tools, as System 1 processes, work outside of conscious awareness; they are not being strategically employed by the author of this gospel (at least this need not be the case), rather, they find expression through the writing of the text, as they structure the way we apprehend social exchanges. What we are aiming for is a cognitive-critical analysis, not a theological or confessional analysis. Therefore, it would be entirely beside the point to argue that there are other ways to read the text or a certain passage—of course there are, but here the focus is strictly on how the text functions to promote group formation through the triggering of evolved moral intuitions; this is not about what Jesus meant, or what subsequent theologians or traditions understand Jesus to have meant, but rather about how these texts are cognitively processed and how that processing promotes group formation.

It is also important not to ascribe an overly reductionistic intent to this analysis. That this text functions to trigger evolved mechanisms does not mean that is all it can do, nor that it can only be employed to generate group

---

29. For a more detailed discussion, see John Teehan, *In the Name of God: The Evolutionary Origins of Religious Ethics and Violence* (Malden, MA: Wiley-Blackwell, 2010); John Teehan, "Religion and Morality: The Evolved Cognitive Nexus," in *The Oxford Handbook of Evolutionary Psychology and Religion*, ed. T. Shackelford and J. Liddle (Oxford. Oxford University Press, 2016). (Publication forthcoming 2021; currently available online, DOI: 10.1093/oxfordhb/9780199397747.0.13.11.)

dynamics constrained by our evolutionary past. Indeed, religion is an evolved cultural innovation whose very function is to enable humans to develop modes of sociality that extend beyond those natural to our environment of evolutionary adaptation. While our focus will be on System 1 processes, we must respect the role System 2 processes, relatively weak as they may be, can play in modifying, reframing, and resisting the intuitive outputs of System 1. This adds an element of plasticity, and even creativity, into the story—and this is a very important element of the story. Nothing here should be taken to deny or diminish that element, it is simply not the primary concern of this essay. With that said, let us consider hypocrites and the pure in heart.

What we come to know as Christianity emerged out of its Jewish background during a period that has been described as the "heyday of Jewish sectarianism."[30] The destruction of the Second Temple by the Romans in 70 CE left established Jewish groups and signals of group identity in shambles. In this situation, how does one know who to trust to reciprocate cooperation and who to avoid as a possible cheater? If I cannot answer these questions with some degree of certainty then my cooperation becomes foolish, a potential waste of resources on those who will not contribute to my own inclusive fitness. As we have seen, evolution makes us very wary of this danger. The breakdown of established group boundaries can be no more than a transitional phase if society itself is not to collapse.

Such a situation is a fertile breeding ground for the rise of competing sects,[31] and the appearance of numerous sects during this period is well attested. It is just in this period that a group of Jews from Jerusalem and the region of Galilee began to develop a sect centered on the teachings of Jesus of Nazareth. The origins of Christianity are part of the development of first-century Jewish sectarianism, with early Christians as one of several groups of Jews struggling to redefine their understanding of Judaism and forge an identity for themselves as the true children of the covenant.

For a sect to be successful it must both connect itself and distinguish itself from a more established tradition. To claim validity for its perspective it must criticize the original tradition as corrupted, while affirming some selected aspects of that tradition that it claims to preserve. In the terms of our evolutionary analysis, the sect becomes the in-group, drawing a boundary around itself that distinguishes it from an older tradition, now denigrated to the status of out-group. The sectarians, in turn, are seen from the

---

30. Shaye J. D. Cohen, *From the Maccabees to the Mishnah* (Louisville, KY: Westminster John Knox, 1987).

31. John E. Stambaugh and David L. Balch, *The New Testament in its Social Environment* (Philadelphia, PA: Westminster Press, 1986).

perspective of the more established group as defectors who threaten the stability of the in-group. For the Jesus movement to succeed in this environment it needed to distinguish itself from other Judaisms, while claiming the mantle of heirs to the covenant. We can recognize numerous practices and moral innovations introduced in the gospel as means of signaling this distinction and as markers of identity in a new in-group. The function of the moral tradition found in the New Testament is more complicated than this, however. In signaling its distinctiveness from Judaism, Christianity, as it developed, needed to avoid the opposite danger of identifying itself with paganism. Thus, Christianity came to represent itself as a third race, "neither Jew nor Greek."[32]

Early in the Sermon, Jesus makes clear that he is not a defector from the moral in-group that all his listeners would be identifying with:

> Do not think that I have come to abolish the law or the prophets; I have come not to abolish but to fulfill. For truly I tell you, until heaven and earth pass away, not one letter, not one stroke of a letter, will pass from the law until all is accomplished. Therefore, whoever breaks one of the least of these commandments, and teaches others to do the same, will be called least in the kingdom of heaven; but whoever does them and teaches them will be called great in the kingdom of heaven. (Matt. 5.17-19)

This signals that Jesus is committed to the moral code that binds the group together and that he recognizes and endorses the Supernatural Punishment that is to come to those who violate that code. He is no out-group member come to disrupt the moral order, in fact he presents himself as one seeking to strengthen the group by setting out a higher moral standard: "For I tell you, unless your righteousness exceeds that of the scribes and Pharisees, you will never enter the kingdom of heaven" (Matt. 5.20).

This is a brilliant rhetorical move as it establishes the moral commitment of Jesus while denigrating that of the ostensible moral leaders of the community. This subtly shifts from an endorsement of the group's moral code to a critique of that code, at least as it is practiced by the leaders of the group. This continues in greater specificity in the teachings known as the Antitheses. In this group of teachings, Jesus reminds the crowd of basic moral teachings of the group, but then gives a new reading of them, for example:

> You have heard that it was said to those of ancient times, "You shall not murder"; and "whoever murders shall be liable to judgment." But I say to you that if you are angry with a brother or sister, you will be liable to judgment. (Matt. 5.21-22)

---

32. Judith Lieu, *Neither Jew nor Greek? Constructing Early Christianity* (Edinburgh: T&T Clark, 2002).

> You have heard that it was said, "You shall not commit adultery." But I say to you that everyone who looks at a woman with lust has already committed adultery with her in his heart. (Matt. 5.27-28)

> Again, you have heard that it was said to those of ancient times, "You shall not swear falsely, but carry out the vows you have made to the Lord." But I say to you, Do not swear at all, either by heaven, for it is the throne of God, or by the earth, for it is his footstool ... Let your word be "Yes, Yes" or "'No, No"; anything more than this comes from the evil one. (Matt. 5.33-37)

These three Mosaic commandments express concerns central to successful group living, and the successful pursuit of inclusive fitness: survival, reproduction, cooperation. Whatever the new group teaches about morality, such concerns must be addressed, and here Jesus tacitly endorses them while significantly altering their expression: it is not enough to refrain from killing, one must seek harmonious relationships; sexual faithfulness is not sufficient, as covetousness is sufficient to upset the social order; your word must be your bond, only then can your neighbors truly trust you. Jesus is redefining the moral code of the group. He is setting a higher standard, a costlier standard. Those who seek membership in this redefined in-group must set themselves apart from the older manifestation of the group and its understanding of the moral code by engaging in costlier forms of signaling.

Here again we can also see Jesus separating his followers from other Jews, not by an outright rejection of Jewish tradition, but by presenting his vision as a truer, deeper understanding of the tradition, and by denigrating the contemporary standard bearers of that tradition:

> So whenever you give alms, do not sound a trumpet before you, as the hypocrites do in the synagogues and in the streets, so that they may be praised by others. Truly I tell you, they have received their reward. (Matt. 6.2)

> And whenever you pray, do not be like the hypocrites; for they love to stand and pray in the synagogues and at the street corners, so that they may be seen by others. Truly I tell you, they have received their reward. (Matt. 6.5)

> And whenever you fast, do not look dismal, like the hypocrites, for they disfigure their faces so as to show others that they are fasting. Truly I tell you, they have received their reward. (Matt. 6.16)

These religious rituals—charity, prayer, fasting—are traditional Jewish signals of commitment that bind together the moral in-group, and Jesus does not do away with them, as practices, but rather critiques the way the ostensible leaders of the community engage in these rituals, thus undermining their value as reliable signals of commitment. Those who perform these rituals in this manner are "hypocrites," that is, those who say one thing, but mean another. They are cheaters who signal commitment to the group but are actually only committed to their own good reputation. This is why they make such public displays of how much the ritual is costing them—to be seen as valuable in-group members, that is their reward. This is set in stark contrast to how Jesus' followers should engage in these rituals, "in secret" (Matt. 6.4) so that they "may be seen not by others" (Matt. 6.18).

This admonition to perform these rituals in secret is clearly designed to avoid the possibility of hypocrisy. If you are fasting in such a way that no one knows you are making this sacrifice then you cannot be accused of doing it for dishonest motives, as the hypocrites do. This is in keeping with the general thrust of Jesus's teachings in the Antitheses toward a more inward understanding of the moral code—that is, not simply refraining from an act of killing or infidelity, but refraining from the inner states that may give rise to those acts—and as such it is unproblematic in terms of establishing a moral code for the new in-group to set it apart from the established in-group. Still, these religious rituals also function as costly signals of commitment. While doing them in private does not reduce their costliness, it does seem to negate their value as signals; what good is a signal that no one sees? But of course, someone does see them, God sees you, "and your Father who sees in secret will reward you" (Matt. 6.4, 6, 18). Here Supernatural monitoring comes into play, with God distributing reward and, it is clearly implied, punishment to those who do or do not adhere to the moral practices of the group. We do not need to go to the synagogue or temple to monitor signals of group commitment, God is watching and knows who has already received their reward and who truly deserves to be rewarded.

This still leaves a problem, for as we have seen a group does require reliable signals of commitment in order to stabilize cooperation across an expanding social horizon. If Jesus is going to undermine established Jewish costly signaling, then he needs to replace them with signals particular to the new in-group. As Christianity developed it acquired a varied set of ways to signal commitment, all of which could come with significant costs during its formative period, given its political status in the larger Roman world. In the Sermon on the Mount we can see two defining strategies. One, that we have been discussing, was to refrain from public displays signaling commitment to the Jewish tradition; not praying or fasting as the hypocrites do, exceeding the behavior of the scribes and Pharisees. This strategy receives further elaboration in the Gospels as we hear Jesus rework the meaning of the Sabbath (e.g., Matt.12.1-12) and Jewish dietary laws (Matt. 15.10-11), both of which served to distinguish Jews from Gentiles. In effect, what Jesus is doing, and not only the Sermon, is rejecting Jewish ethnicity as a signal of group identity.[33]

---

33. See David C. Lahti, "'You Have Heard … but I Tell You …': A Test of the Adaptive Significance of Moral Evolution," in *Evolution and Ethics: Human Morality in Biological*

Still, all of this could be read to identify one as a Gentile. It was not enough for the followers of Jesus to identify as non-Pharisaic, they had to also distinguish themselves from the larger polytheistic community. We see this in the Sermon, as Jesus often adds Gentiles to the hypocrites as models of how not to do things: "Do not even the Gentiles do the same?" (Matt. 5.47), "do not heap up empty phrases as the Gentiles do" (Matt. 6.7). The key move, however, in keeping this new in-group distinct from pagans was continued commitment to the one, true God worshiped by the Jews, and the concomitant rejection of the pantheon of the gods worshiped by everyone else. This is one reason why it was so important for Jesus to walk the line between re-interpreting Jewish beliefs and practices and rejecting them outright. Yet, it is not enough to signal "we are not them," the Jesus movement needed a positive identification of who they were, and positive means of signaling that identity—and this second strategy in group formation consists in signaling commitment to Jesus, himself.

Jesus begins the Sermon by identifying those who are "blessed." This can be read as an invitation to join the new in-group by identifying those who are prime candidates for inclusion as they have already been effectively rejected or ill-served by the established in-group: the "pure in heart" and "poor in spirit," not those rich in possessions; the suffering, not the comfortable; the "meek" not the proud leaders; the merciful, not those with the power to wreak vengeance; the peacemakers, not the warriors; those who are persecuted, not the politically privileged persecutors (Matt. 5.3-10). These, and not the powerful ones—those hypocrites and Gentiles—will reap the benefits of the community, "the kingdom of heaven." What makes this benediction something more than a compassionate rally for social justice is the last blessing Jesus announced: "Blessed are you when people revile you and persecute you and utter all kinds of evil against you falsely on my account" (Matt. 5.11). On one level, this does not necessarily seem the best recruitment strategy—things will get worse when you follow me—but on another level, it works quite effectively. This is already a group that is suffering and disempowered, with little hope of things getting better. What hope they might have been holding on to, particularly if they embraced a reading of Judaism that held out the possibility of a resurrection, was that of living a righteous life and being justified in the eyes of God, and this is just what Jesus is promising them. "Rejoice and be glad, for your reward is great in heaven, for in the same way they persecuted the prophets who were before you" (Matt. 5.12). Note again how Jesus reaffirms the familiar

and Religious Perspective, ed. P. Clayton and J. Schloss (Grand Rapids, MI: Eerdmans, 2004), 132–50.

tradition—the persecution of the prophets (thus aligning the disempowered listener with the moral heroes of old)—while shifting authority to himself.

We can also recognize that the danger inherent in following Jesus, rather than being a disincentive to joining the group, functions as a costly signal of commitment. Those willing to join a group that comes with this cost (a cost that was already being realized by the time Matthew was written) must truly be committed to the group and so can be trusted to be cooperative and caring community members, and belonging to such a group is a deep, evolutionarily-based, human need. It is a well-established aspect of group dynamics that costly membership is correlated with group cohesiveness and longevity.[34]

At the end of the Sermon Jesus also implicitly signals that he is the path to the Kingdom. He tells the crowd:

> Not everyone who says to me, "Lord, Lord," will enter the kingdom of heaven, but only the one who does the will of my Father in heaven. On that day many will say to me, "Lord, Lord, did we not prophesy in your name, and cast out demons in your name, and do many deeds of power in your name?" Then I will declare to them, "I never knew you; go away from me, you evildoers." (Matt. 7.21-23)

This does two things, it implicitly signifies that it is through commitment to Jesus that one enters the Kingdom and it reconfirms that it is not through dramatic public displays that one signals they are reliable members of the new in-group (even hypocrites do that) but through moral behavior, here sanctified as the will of God.

This is quite a proposal Jesus presents to the crowds on the mountain: a promise of a new community that—on the explicit level—provides rewards that compensate for the sufferings of this world, rewards that neither other Jewish nor Gentile groups can offer, and which on the implicit level—that is, the evolved cognitive level of System 1—holds out the chance for membership in a caring, morally-bounded group that provides the necessary conditions for the individual pursuit of inclusive fitness and human flourishing, something that those marginalized within the larger Jewish community were clearly lacking.

As appealing as such a proposal must have been, and still is, we must always be wary of "false prophets, who come to you in sheep's clothing but inwardly are ravenous wolves" (Matt. 7.15). Even prophets need to signal their reliability, and Matthew is sensitive to this, as we can recognize in

---

34. Richard Sosis and Eric R. Bressler, "Cooperation and Commune Longevity: A Test of the Costly Signaling Theory of Religion," *Cross-Cultural Research* 37 (2003): 211–39.

the final verse of the Sermon: "Now when Jesus had finished saying these things, the crowds were astounded at his teaching, for he taught them as one having authority, and not as their scribes" (Matt. 7.28-29). Jesus has authority, and Matthew's readers would have understood that to have authority was to have been given that authority from a higher authority—and Jesus had already indicated that it is the will of God that is speaking through his teachings; and once more this is set in contrast to those who presume to speak with authority for the established in-group, the "scribes."

While the Sermon ends there, Matthew makes clear that the lesson has not. For in the very next chapter we are informed that as Jesus descended the mountain, the crowds followed him. The lesson continues now not through words but through actions—and what do we find?

> And there was a leper who came to him and knelt before him, saying, "Lord, if you choose, you can make me clean." He stretched out his hand and touched him, saying, "I do choose. Be made clean!" Immediately his leprosy was cleansed. (Matt. 8.1-3)

Jesus not only teaches with authority, he acts with authority, healing one suffering from a gruesome and feared disease simply be pronouncing the words, just as God created simply by pronouncing the words. This is a powerful testimony to the role Jesus can play for the community—not simply as God's prophet, but as someone with the power to dispense rewards and punishments himself, that is, Jesus can fulfill the role required by the Supernatural Punishment Hypothesis.

Chapter 8 is filled with stories of Jesus' healing powers, but in terms of our topic here it will be worthwhile to consider just one more story, the healing of the centurion's servant. A centurion, one with a position of authority within the Roman military, comes to Jesus and asks him to heal his servant, who is at the centurion's home suffering terribly from paralysis, and Jesus agrees to go. But the soldier demurs,

> "Lord, I am not worthy to have you come under my roof; but only speak the word, and my servant will be healed. For I also am a man under authority, with soldiers under me; and I say to one, 'Go', and he goes, and to another, 'Come', and he comes, and to my slave, 'Do this', and the slave does it." (Matt. 8.8-9)

Jesus is amazed. Here a representative of a powerful and feared out-group recognizes the authority of Jesus, even if the scribes and Pharisees will not. And this Roman not only recognizes Jesus' authority, he has faith in his power and in his word—he does not need proof—and his faith is rewarded: "And to the centurion Jesus said, 'Go; let it be done for you according to your faith.' And the servant was healed in that hour" (Matt. 8.13). The centurion may not have needed a demonstration of the rewards of faith, but

Matthew understood that the crowds did. These acts of power make Jesus a more credible moral monitor for the nascent in-group.

This story does even more than attest to the credibility of Jesus, it allows him to drive home his message about the nature of membership in his new in-group:

> Truly I tell you, in no one in Israel have I found such faith. I tell you, many will come from east and west and will eat with Abraham and Isaac and Jacob in the kingdom of heaven, while the heirs of the kingdom will be thrown into the outer darkness, where there will be weeping and gnashing of teeth. (Matt. 8.10-12)

This is not the in-group as Jews understood it; it is not a Jewish in-group, even though Jesus is here speaking to a Jewish audience. This is an in-group that will not be defined by ethnicity, nor by religious commitment to the Jewish faith, as it was traditionally understood—it will be defined by faith in the Lord Jesus, that is, it will form through costly signaling to a supernatural agent who functions as moral monitor for the group that can then grow to encompass members not bound by kinship or ethnicity—this is the evolved-cognitive formula that makes possible the development of larger and yet still cohesive, functioning groups. The success of this small, first-century Jewish sect's development into a worldwide religion that would continue into the twenty-first century is in no small part a result of its effective triggering of the evolved-cognitive tools that constitute that formula.

Biographical Note

John Teehan is Professor, Department of Religion, at Hofstra University in New York, where he also teaches in the Department of Philosophy, and the Cognitive Science program. He is the author of *In the Name of God: The Evolutionary Origins of Religious Ethics and Violence* (Wiley-Blackwell, 2010). His research is in the Cognitive Science of Religion, with a focus on the connections between religion and morality. His publications have focused on theoretical research into these topics, as well as the implications of this research for theology and the philosophy of religion.

Bibliography

Alexander, Richard. *The Biology of Moral Systems: Foundations of Human Behavior*. New York: Aldine de Gruyter, 1987.

Atkinson, Quentin, and Pierrick Bouratt. "Beliefs about God, the Afterlife and Morality Support the Role of Supernatural Policing in Human Cooperation," *Evolution and Human Behavior* 32 (2011): 41–9. https://doi.org/10.1016/j.evolhumbehav.2010.07.008

Atran, Scott. *In Gods We Trust: The Evolutionary Landscape of Religion*. Oxford: Oxford University Press, 2002.

Avenanti, Alessio, Angela Sirigu, and Salvatore Aglioti. "Racial Bias Reduces Empathic Sensorimotor Resonance with Other-Race Pain," *Current Biology* 20.11 (2010): 1018–22. https://doi.org/10.1016/j.cub.2010.03.071

Axelrod, Robert, and William D. Hamilton. "The Evolution of Cooperation," *Science* 211 (1981): 1390–6. https://doi.org/10.1126/science.7466396

Bering, Jesse. "On Reading Symbolic Random Events: Children's Causal Reasoning about Unexpected Occurrences." Paper Presented at the Psychological and Cognitive Foundations of Religiosity Conference, Atlanta, GA, August 2003.

—"The Folk Psychology of Souls." *Behavioral and Brain Sciences* 29 (2006): 453–62. https://doi.org/10.1017/S0140525X06009101

Bering, Jesse, and Dominic Johnson. "'O Lord … You Perceive My Thoughts from Afar': Recursiveness and the Evolution of Supernatural Agency," *Journal of Cognition and Culture* 5.1–2 (2005): 118–42. https://doi.org/10.1163/1568537054068679

Bloom, Paul. *Just Babies: The Origins of Good and Evil*. New York: Crown, 2013.

Boyd, Robert, Herbert Gintis, Samuel Bowles, and Peter J. Richerson. "The Evolution of Altruistic Punishment," *Proceedings of the National Academy of Sciences* 100 (2003): 3531–5. https://doi.org/10.1073/pnas.0630443100

Boyd, Robert, and Peter J. Richerson. "The Evolution of Reciprocity in Sizable Groups," *Journal of Theoretical Biology* 132 (1988): 337–56. https://doi.org/10.1016/S0022-5193(88)80219-4

Boyer, Pascal. *Religion Explained: The Evolutionary Origins of Religious Thought*. New York: Basic Books, 2001.

Chiao, Joan Y., Tetsuya Iidaka, Heather L. Gordon, Junpei Nogawa, Moshe Bar, Elissa Aminoff, Norihiro Sadato, and Nalini Ambady. "Cultural Specificity in Amygdala Response to Fear Faces," *Journal of Cognitive Neuroscience* 20 (2008): 2167–74. https://doi.org/10.1162/jocn.2008.20151

Cohen, Shaye J. D. *From the Maccabees to the Mishnah*. Louisville, KY: Westminster John Knox, 1987.

DeBruine, Lisa M. "Facial Resemblance Enhances Trust," 1307–12 in *Proceedings of the Royal Society of London B: Biological Sciences* 269.1498, 2002. https://doi.org/10.1098/rspb.2002.2034

Dunbar, Robert. "Neocortex Size as a Constraint on Group Size in Primates," *Journal of Human Evolution* 6 (1992): 469–93. https://doi.org/10.1016/0047-2484(92)90081-J

—*Grooming, Gossip and the Evolution of Language*. Cambridge, MA: Harvard University Press, 1997.

Elfenbein, Hillary A., and Nalini Ambady. "Is There an In-Group Advantage in Emotion Recognition?" *Psychological Bulletin* 128 (2002): 243–9. https://doi.org/10.1037/0033-2909.128.2.243

Ellingsen, Tobe, and Magnus Johannesson. "Anticipated Verbal Feedback Induces Altruistic Behavior," *Evolution and Human Behavior* 29 (2008): 100–5. https://doi.org/10.1016/j.evolhumbehav.2007.11.001

Fehr, Ernst, and Urs Fischbacher. "The Nature of Human Altruism," *Nature* 425 (2003): 785–91. https://doi.org/10.1038/nature02043

—"Social Norms and Human Cooperation," *Trends in Cognitive Sciences* 8 (2004): 185–90. https://doi.org/10.1016/j.tics.2004.02.007

Fiske, Susan T. "What We Know about Bias and Intergroup Conflict: The Problem of the

Century," *Current Directions in Psychological Science* 11 (2002): 123–8. https://doi.org/10.1111/1467-8721.00183

Frank, Robert H. *Passions within Reason: The Strategic Role of Emotions.* New York: W. W. Norton, 1988.

Gintis, Herbert. "Strong Reciprocity and Human Sociality," *Journal of Theoretical Biology* 206 (2000): 169–79. https://doi.org/10.1006/jtbi.2000.2111

Haidt, Jonathan. "The Emotional Dog and its Rational Tail: A Social Intuitionist Approach to Moral Judgment," *Psychological Review* 108 (2001): 814–34. https://doi.org/10.1037/0033-295X.108.4.814

——*The Righteous Mind: Why Good People Are Divided by Religion and Politics.* New York: Pantheon, 2012.

Haley, Kevin J., and Daniel M. T. Fessler. "Nobody Is Watching? Subtle Cues Affect Generosity in an Anonymous Economic Game," *Evolution and Human Behavior* 26 (2005): 245–56. https://doi.org/10.1016/j.evolhumbehav.2005.01.002

Hamilton, William D. "Genetic Evolution of Social Behavior, I and II," *Journal of Theoretical Biology* 7 (1964): 1–52. https://doi.org/10.1016/0022-5193(64)90039-6

Henrich, Joseph, and Robert Boyd. "Why People Punish Defectors: Weak Conformist Transmission Can Stabilize Costly Enforcement of Norms in Cooperative Dilemmas," *Journal of Theoretical Biology* 208 (2001): 79–89. https://doi.org/10.1006/jtbi.2000.2202

Henrich, Joseph, Richard McElreath, Abigail Barr, Jean Ensminger, Clark Barrett, Alexander Bolyanatz, Juan Camilo Cardenas, Michael Gurven, Edwins Gwako, Natalie Henrich, Carolyn Lesorogol, Frank W. Marlowe, David P. Tracer, and John Ziker. "Costly Punishment across Human Societies," *Science* 312.5781 (2006): 1767–70.

Holldobler, Bert, and Edward O. Wilson. *The Superorganism: The Beauty, Elegance, and Strangeness of Insect Societies.* New York: W. W. Norton, 2008.

Irons, William. "Religion as a Hard-to-Fake Sign of Commitment," 292–309 in *Evolution and the Capacity for Commitment.* Edited by R. M. Nesse. New York: Russell Sage Foundation, 2001.

Johnson, Dominic. "God's Punishment and Public Goods: A Test of the Supernatural Punishment Hypothesis in 186 World Cultures," *Human Nature* 16 (2005): 410–46. https://doi.org/10.1007/s12110-005-1017-0

Johnson, Dominic, and Jesse Bering. "Hand of God, Mind of Man: Punishment and Cognition in the Evolution of Cooperation," *Evolutionary Psychology* 4 (2006): 219–33. https://doi.org/10.1177/147470490600400119

Johnson, Dominic, and Oliver Krüger. "The Good of Wrath: Supernatural Punishment and the Evolution of Cooperation," *Political Theology* 5 (2004): 159–76. https://doi.org/10.1558/poth.2004.5.2.159

Kahneman, Daniel. *Thinking, Fast and Slow.* New York: Farrar, Straus & Giroux, 2011.

Lahti, David C. "'You Have Heard … but I Tell You …': A Test of the Adaptive Significance of Moral Evolution," 132–52 in *Evolution and Ethics: Human Morality in Biological and Religious Perspective.* Edited by J. Schloss and P. Clayton. Grand Rapids, MI: Eerdmans, 2004.

Lieu, Judith. *Neither Jew nor Greek? Constructing Early Christianity.* Edinburgh: T&T Clark, 2002.

Nesse, Randolph M., ed. *Evolution and the Capacity for Commitment.* The Russell Sage Foundation Series on Trust, 3. New York: Russell Sage Foundation, 2001.

Norenzayan, Ara. *Big Gods: How Religion Transformed Cooperation and Con-*

flict. Princeton, NJ: Princeton University Press, 2013. https://doi.org/10.2307/j.ctt32bbp0

Nowak, Martin A., and Karl Sigmund. "Evolution of Indirect Reciprocity," *Nature* 437 (2005): 1291. https://doi.org/10.1038/nature04131

Nowak, Michael A. "Five Rules for the Evolution of Cooperation," *Science* 314.8 (2006): 1560–3. https://doi.org/10.1126/science.1133755

Price, Michael E., Leda Cosmides, and John Tooby. "Punitive Sentiment as an Anti-Free Rider Psychological Device," *Evolution and Human Behavior* 23 (2002): 203–31. https://doi.org/10.1016/S1090-5138(01)00093-9

Reddish, Paul, Joseph Bulbulia, and Ronald Fischer. "Does Synchrony Promote Generalized Prosociality?," *Religion, Brain and Behavior* 4 (2014): 3–19. https://doi.org/10.1080/2153599X.2013.764545

Reddish, Paul, Ronald Fischer, and Joseph Bulbulia. "Let's Dance Together: Synchrony, Shared Intentionality and Cooperation," *PLoS ONE* 8.8 (2013): 71182. https://doi.org/10.1371/journal.pone.0071182

Shariff, Azim, and Ara Norenzayan. "Mean Gods Make Good People: Different Views of God Predicting Cheating Behavior," *International Journal of the Psychology of Religion* 21 (2011): 85–96. https://doi.org/10.1080/10508619.2011.556990

Shariff, Azim, and Mijke Rhemtulla. "Divergent Effects of Beliefs in Heaven and Hell on National Crime Rates," *PloS ONE* 7.6 (2012): 39048. https://doi.org/10.1371/journal.pone.0039048

Singer, Tania, Ben Seymour, John P. O'Doherty, Klaas E. Stephan, Raymond J. Dolan, and Chris D. Frith. "Empathic Neural Responses Are Modulated by the Perceived Fairness of Others," *Nature* 439.7075 (2006): 466–9. https://doi.org/10.1038/nature04271

Sosis, Richard. "Religious Behaviors, Badges, and Bans: Signaling Theory and the Evolution of Religion," 61–86 in *Where God and Science Meet: How Brain and Evolutionary Studies Alter our Understanding of Religion*. Edited by P. McNamara. Vol. 1 of *Evolution, Genes and the Religious Brain*. Westport, CT: Praeger Publishers, 2006.

Sosis, Richard, and Candace Alcorta. "Signaling, Solidarity, and the Sacred: The Evolution of Religious Behavior," *Evolutionary Anthropology* 12 (2003): 264–74. https://doi.org/10.1002/evan.10120

Sosis, Richard, and Eric R. Bressler. "Cooperation and Commune Longevity: A Test of the Costly Signaling Theory of Religion," *Cross-Cultural Research* 37 (2003): 211–39. https://doi.org/10.1177/1069397103037002003

Stambaugh, John E., and David L. Balch, *The New Testament in its Social Environment*. Philadelphia, PA: Westminster, 1986.

Teehan, John. *In the Name of God: The Evolutionary Origins of Religious Ethics and Violence*. Malden, MA: Wiley-Blackwell, 2010. https://doi.org/10.1002/9781444320695

—"Religion and Morality: The Evolved Cognitive Nexus," in *The Oxford Handbook of Evolutionary Psychology and Religion*. Edited by J. Liddle and T. K. Shackelford. Oxford: Oxford University Press, 2016. Currently available online, publication forthcoming 2021. https://doi.org/10.1093/oxfordhb/9780199397747.013.11

Trivers, Robert L. "The Evolution of Reciprocal Altruism," *The Quarterly Review of Biology* 46 (1971): 35–57. https://doi.org/10.1086/406755

Vanneste, Sven, Jan Verplaetse, Alain van Hiel, and Johan Braeckman. "Attention Bias toward Noncooperative People: A Dot Probe Classification Study in Cheating Detection," *Evolution and Human Behavior* 28 (2007): 272–6. https://doi.org/10.1016/j.evolhumbehav.2007.02.005

Verplaetse, Jan, Sven Vanneste, and Johan Braeckman. "You Can Judge a Book by Its Cover: The Sequel. A Kernel of Truth in Predictive Cheating Detection." *Evolution and Human Behavior* 28 (2007): 260–71. https://doi.org/10.1016/j.evolhumbehav.2007.04.006

de Waal, Frans B. M. "Putting Altruism Back into Altruism: The Evolution of Empathy," *Annual Review of Psychology* 59 (2008): 279–300. https://doi.org/10.1146/annurev.psych.59.103006.093625

Xu, Xiaojing, Xiangyu Zuo, Xiaoying Wang, and Shihui Han. "Do You Feel My Pain? Racial Group Membership Modulates Empathic Neural Responses," *The Journal of Neuroscience* 29 (2009): 8525–9. https://doi.org/10.1523/JNEUROSCI.2418-09.2009

Zahavi, Amotz, and Avishag Zahavi. *The Handicap Principle: A Missing Piece of Darwin's Puzzle*. Oxford: Oxford University Press, 1997.

Chapter Ten

"Whoever is kind to the poor lends to Yahweh, and will be repaid in full" (Proverbs 19.17): Patterns of Indirect Reciprocity in the Book of Proverbs and in the Sermon on the Mount

Anne Katrine de Hemmer Gudme

Introduction

In the Book of Proverbs 19.17 in the Hebrew Bible, cited in the title above, we encounter the idea that benefiting the poor will result in being owed a favor by God.[1] In the present study, I suggest that this idea is a forerunner of the concept of a reward in heaven in exchange for alms, which is expressed in the Sermon on the Mount in the Gospel of Matthew 6.1-4.

In terms of gift-giving, which has been explored intensively within the field of social anthropology, Proverbs 19.17 and Matthew 6.1-4 are both examples of "indirect" or "generalized" reciprocity. Whereas direct reciprocity is a simple question of "tit for tat"—A gives to B and B gives to A, indirect reciprocity creates a chain of giving, where A gives to B, who gives to C, and so on until someone eventually gives to A.

In the first half of the chapter, I give a brief introduction to gift-giving theory and to the opposing concepts of free gifts and friend-making gifts.[2] Then I trace the above-mentioned pattern of indirect reciprocity from Proverbs in the Hebrew Bible, through the Books of Daniel and Tobit, and in selected Mesopotamian wisdom texts, until I end up in the New Testament with the Sermon in Matthew. What makes our examples special of course is that A, a human, gives to B, another human, and then eventually a deity gives to A.

In the remainder of the chapter, I use insights from evolutionary studies, such as evolutionary biology, evolutionary psychology, and evolutionary

---

1. Here, and in the following, I am using the New Revised Standard Version of the Bible.
2. This introduction to gift-giving is based on pp. 21–36 in Anne Katrine de Hemmer Gudme, *Before the God in This Place for Good Remembrance: A Comparative Analysis of the Aramaic Votive Inscriptions from Mount Gerizim* (Berlin: De Gruyter, 2013).

theory of religion, to discuss the relationship between altruism, such as charity and alms-giving (indirect reciprocity), and the evolution of religious systems featuring "Big Gods," that is gods that are perceived to be morally interested in their worshipers' behavior. These insights help us to see that the demand for charity and altruistic behavior may not simply be a value in religious systems such as Christianity and Judaism, but that it most likely is a time-tested and superior evolutionary strategy that helps cooperating groups to get ahead.

At the very end, I bring in a discussion of "true" altruism, inspired by the Swedish economist Jan Tullberg.

First, however, we shall turn to gift-giving theory and reciprocity in general and in the Book of Proverbs in particular.

Reciprocity and Gift-giving

In recent years, there has been a renewed interest in gift-giving and reciprocity in ancient societies. This interest has led to a near-consensus on how to define reciprocity, namely as "the principle and practice of voluntary requital, of benefit for benefit (positive reciprocity) or harm for harm (negative reciprocity)."[3] Reciprocity is most commonly conceptualized as involving two parties and is known as direct reciprocity. But indirect reciprocity, involving a third party, is also well known.

Direct reciprocity is straightforward: A offers something, a gift, a challenge, respect, threats and so on to B who requites it at a later time. Indirect reciprocity is the kindness (or insult) directed at a stranger who is unlikely to make a direct return, but who may extend the courtesy to a third party, C, who does a favor for D and so on until the chain eventually reaches A, who regards this as an indirect form of repayment for the favor done to B.[4]

As indicated in the title indirect reciprocity is the main focus of this chapter and I shall return to this below. First, however, I shall give a brief introduction to the nature of gift-giving in general.

---

3. This definition was put forward by Richard Seaford, "Introduction," in *Reciprocity in Ancient Greece,* ed. C. Gill, N. Postlethwaite, and R. Seaford (Oxford: Oxford University, 1998), 1–12, and has since been adopted by several scholars. See also Daniel C. Ullucci, *The Christian Rejection of Animal Sacrifice* (Oxford: Oxford University, 2012), 24–30, Göran Eidevall, *Sacrificial Rhetoric in the Prophetic Literature of the Hebrew Bible* (Lewiston, NY: Edwin Mellen, 2012), 38–41, and Gudme, *Before the God,* 22–23. Hans van Wees offers a very similar definition: "exchange conceptualized as the performance and requital of gratuitous actions." Hans van Wees, "The Law of Gratitude: Reciprocity in Anthropological Theory," in Gill, Postlethwaite, and Seaford, *Reciprocity in Ancient Greece,* 1998, 13–50, 20.

4. Van Wees, "The Law of Gratitude," 21–4; Peter P. Ekeh, *Social Exchange Theory: The Two Traditions* (Harvard, MA: Harvard University, 1974), 52–6 and 58–60.

Modern scholarship's interest in the gift began in earnest with the French anthropologist and sociologist Marcel Mauss and his famous work, *Essai sur le don/The Gift*, which was first published in 1925.[5] Mauss was fascinated and intrigued by the mechanism of reciprocity and he expressed his puzzlement in the following manner:

> What rule of legality and self-interest, in societies of a backward or archaic type, compels the gift that has been received to be obligatorily reciprocated? What power resides in the object given that causes its recipient to pay it back?[6]

In *The Gift*, Mauss reacted against the Polish anthropologist Bronislaw Malinowski's concept of "pure gifts," which Malinowski defined as a non-reciprocal action: "An act, in which an individual gives an object or renders a service without expecting or getting any return."[7] In response to Malinowski, Mauss stressed that gifts are neither freely given nor disinterested, and that they come with a threefold obligation, to give, to receive, and to reciprocate.[8] Mauss also stressed that because gifts are inalienable objects and never completely detached from their givers and receivers, gifts are able to create strong and lasting social bonds and relationships. Perhaps the most notable feature of the gift according to Mauss is that it is a friend-making gift.[9]

The "Maussian gift" is often described in contrast to commodity exchange or trade.[10] This comparison helps to clarify the nature of reciprocity in

---

5. For an introduction to studies on the gift before Mauss, see Beate Wagner-Hasel, "Egoistic Exchange and Altruistic Gift: On the Roots of Marcel Mauss's Theory of the Gift," in *Negotiating the Gift: Pre-Modern Figurations of Exchange*, ed. G. Algazi, V. Groebner, and B. Jussen (Göttingen: Vandenhoeck & Ruprecht, 2003), 141–71.

6. Marcel Mauss, *The Gift*, trans. W. D. Halls, with foreword by M. Douglas (London: Routledge, 1990), 4, italics in original. Mauss found his answer in the Maori concept of hau. The hau is the spirit of the thing given, which compels the receiver to reciprocate (Mauss, *The Gift*, 14–6; italics in original). Mauss's use and understanding of hau has subsequently been much criticized by, among others, Claude Lévi-Strauss, Raymond Firth, and Marshall Sahlins, see Marshall Sahlins, *Stone Age Economics* (London: Routledge, 2004 [1972]), 149–83 and Jacques T. Godbout in collaboration with Alain Caillé, *The World of the Gift* (Montreal: McGill-Queen's University, 1998), 118–28.

7. Bronislaw Malinowski, *Argonauts of the Western Pacific: An Account of Native Enterprise and Adventure in the Archipelagoes of Melanesian New Guinea* (London: Routledge, 1922), 177–80, 177.

8. Mauss, *The Gift*, 94, see also p. 4: "… apparently free and disinterested but nevertheless constrained and self-interested." Malinowski subsequently modified his category of "Pure Gifts," see Bronislaw Malinowski, *Crime and Custom in Savage Society* (London: Kegan Paul, 1926), 40–1.

9. Mauss, *The Gift*, 16–7, 42. To quote the now famous pun made by Marshall Sahlins: "If friends make gifts, gifts make friends" (Sahlins, *Stone Age Economics*, 186).

10. Perhaps the best-known advocate of this distinction is C. A. Gregory, who

gift-giving as a particular kind of exchange. As opposed to commodity exchange reciprocity is voluntary. Although there are moral and social expectations of requital, there is no actual law to enforce this.[11] Therefore, reciprocity presupposes and is dependent on goodwill and an understanding of the social norm that lies behind the exchange.[12]

The price is another important difference between commodity and gift: commodities carry a fixed price and commodity exchange involves an exact equivalence between the objects exchanged. Reciprocity, on the other hand, only involves a rough equivalence between the exchanged objects, and an equivalence that is heavily dependent on the social status and financial means of the giver and receiver.[13] In fact, it is generally considered to be very bad form to return a gift with an identical object. If one does so the exchange echoes commercial exchange, where objects have a price, to too great an extent, and thus the spirit of gift-giving is endangered. This has to do with a fact that was pointed out by the French sociologist Pierre Bourdieu, namely that gift-giving entails a certain amount of social deceit or concealment. For gift-giving to be successful the aspect of exchange in the commercial sense must be toned down. Therefore, according to Bourdieu, a gift given in return must be both "deferred and different."[14] "Different," because to return a gift with the same gift is to cancel the transaction and thereby the gift; and "deferred," because the time which passes between gift and countergift is necessary to veil the fact that a form of exchange is actually taking place.[15] This concealment achieves both individual and collective "misrecognition" of what goes on in the exchange.[16]

---

defines gift-exchange as "the exchange of inalienable objects between people in a state of reciprocal dependence" as opposed to commodity-exchange, which is "the exchange of alienable objects between transactors who are in a state of reciprocal independence." C. A. Gregory, "Gifts to Men and Gifts to God: Gift Exchange and Capital Accumulation," *Man* 15 (1980): 626–52, 640. For a more detailed definition see C. A. Gregory, *Gifts and Commodities* (London: Academic Press, 1982), 100–1. Cf. J. van Baal, *Reciprocity and the Position of Women* (Assen, NL: Koninklijke Van Gorcum, 1975), 39–51.

11. Seaford, "Introduction," 2; Alvin Gouldner, "The Norm of Reciprocity: A Preliminary Statement," *American Sociological Review* 25 (1960): 161–78, 171.

12. Ullucci, *The Christian Rejection*, 25–6.

13. J. van Baal, "Offering, Sacrifice and Gift," *Numen* 23 (1976): 161–78, 164; cf. Ullucci, *The Christian Rejection*, 24–7.

14. Pierre Bourdieu, *The Logic of Practice*, trans. R. Nice (Cambridge: Polity Press, 1990), 105.

15 Bourdieu, *The Logic of Practice*, 107. This point was stressed already by Mauss: "Time is needed in order to perform any counterservice" (Mauss, *The Gift*, 47–8).

16. Pierre Bourdieu, *Outline of a Theory of Practice*, trans. R. Nice (Cambridge: Cambridge University, 1977), 5–6; Bourdieu, *The Logic of Practice*, 105.

The Free Gift

There are at least two kinds of gift in gift-giving theory: the "Maussian" friend-making gift, which is characterized by reciprocity and the so-called "free gift," Malinowski's "pure gift," which is given without expecting or receiving anything in return.

It was the difference between these two concepts of gift that made the French-Algerian philosopher Jacques Derrida write that *The Gift* was in fact a book that dealt with anything but the gift, that is the free gift.[17] According to Derrida, the free gift is a paradox and in truth an impossibility.[18] For the free gift to exist there can be no exchange and no expectation of exchange on either part. Gift and exchange are incompatible. Therefore the recipient must not conceive of the gift as a gift, because the mere indication of gift would suggest an indebtedness or obligation, which leads to circulation and exchange.[19] At the same time the giver must not think of the gift as gift, because by doing so he would inevitably reward himself for giving a gift—simply by feeling good about himself. So with Derrida we reach this tantalizing paradox that for the free gift to exist it must not exist, because as soon as something is recognized as a gift it destroys the very concept of a gift.[20] According to Derrida, this does not mean that there is no such thing as exchanged gifts. They do exist as a phenomenon, but they contradict and annul the idea of the free gift.[21]

The free gift is impossible, it seems, in anything but theory, but the ideal of the free gift is of crucial importance for our understanding of the gift in general and indeed there are examples of gifts that struggle to resemble the free gift: The gift called *Supatra dan*, which has been studied by among others the social anthropologist James Laidlaw, is an example of a gift that comes close to the ideal of the free gift. The *dan* is a gift of food given to renouncers by practitioners of Shvetamber Jainism. The renouncers are a group of itinerant celibate ascetics who rely on lay people for food and clothing. Renouncers spend their lives performing ritualized confessions, prayer, preaching, and study to reach an ultimate goal of spiritual purification and salvation. When lay Jains give alms to renouncers, a huge effort is made to make the gift, the *dan*, as anonymous, impersonal, and free as

---

17. Jacques Derrida, *Given Time*. 1: *Counterfeit Money*, trans. P. Kamuf (Chicago, IL: University of Chicago, 1992), 24 (italics in original).
18. Derrida, *Given Time*, 16.
19. Derrida, *Given Time*, 13–4, 37; James Laidlaw, "A Free Gift Makes No Friends," *The Journal of the Royal Anthropological Institute* 6 (2000): 617–34, 621.
20. Derrida, *Given Time*, 14.
21. Derrida, *Given Time*, 37.

possible; the renouncers never visit the same house on two successive days, they only receive a little food from each house and they never say thank you or praise the food, but make sure to act reluctant to receive. When the food is eaten it is all mixed in one large dish, so that no one knows where the individual dishes came from. In short, every effort is made to alienate the *dan* and make it into a free gift, an impersonal gift.[22] This is an important point, which I shall return to below; the free gift, which attempts to be completely selfless and disinterested, is also deeply impersonal. A free gift does not create bonds between people. A free gift makes no friends.

Interestingly, the Maussian gift strives for the ideal of the free gift while in fact being an "embryonic" form of commodity exchange. As expressed by Laidlaw, the Maussian gift "is located on the logical and phenomenological trajectory between pure gift and commodity."[23] This is the "polite fiction" and "social deceit," which Mauss claimed to be connected with gift exchange. The gift takes the form of the free gift, "the present generously given," but in fact it involves obligation and economic self-interest.[24] This is the gist of Bourdieu's notion of misrecognition mentioned earlier. Bourdieu stresses that there is a difference between the phenomenological or subjective view of gift-giving and the objective view.[25] The observer, who sees the act of gift-giving from "above," sees the gift as reversible, as an almost mechanical model of exchange, but to the agents involved in gift-giving the act is irreversible.[26]

Bourdieu's dual perspective helps us to see the gift as an open-ended social relation and not as a closed system. There is always an element of insecurity or gambling in gift-giving, because although there may be an expectation or norm of reciprocity, the nature of the exchange, like all social transactions, is continuously negotiated. When one gives a gift, one never knows if there will be one in return, what it will be or when it will come.[27]

---

22. Laidlaw, "A Free Gift," 617–9; Jonathan Parry, "The Gift, the Indian Gift and the 'Indian Gift'," *Man* 21 (1986): 453–73.

23. Laidlaw, "A Free Gift," 628.

24. Mauss, *The Gift*, 4.

25. Bourdieu, *Outline of a Theory*, 4–5. Bourdieu directs his critique to Lévi-Strauss's idea of a "cycle of reciprocity." Cf. Bourdieu, *Logic of Practice*, 98: "the analyst reduces the agents to the status of automata or inert bodies moved by obscure mechanisms towards ends of which they are unaware. 'Cycles of reciprocity', mechanical interlocking of obligatory practices, exist only for the absolute gaze of the omniscient, omnipresent spectator, who, thanks to his knowledge of the social mechanics, is able to be present at the different stages of the 'cycle'."

26. Bourdieu, *Outline of a Theory*, 5.

27. Gadi Algazi, "Introduction: Doing Things with Gifts," in *Negotiating the Gift: Pre-Modern Figurations of Exchange*, ed. G. Algazi, V. Groebner, and B. Jussen

If the gift did not imply the risk of refusal, it would simply lose its capacity as a friend-making gift.[28]

Gifts to the Gods

A nuanced understanding of reciprocity and gift-giving is of great importance to the study of sacrifice and offerings in ancient societies. Ancient sacrificial systems have often been denigrated and dismissed as "primitive" attempts to barter with the divine realm. However, it is more accurate to think of gifts to the gods not as bribes but as proper Maussian gifts, intended to create a lasting and mutually beneficial relationship between the giver and the receiver.[29] As with all kinds of gift-giving, gifts to the gods entail the risk of refusal but when one wishes to exchange gifts with the gods the outcome of the exchange is always a matter of interpretation. As the archaeologist Robin Osborne points out, gifts to gods are doubly affected by uncertainty:

> To give a gift to the gods is to enter into a relationship from which the return is uncertain. Both when and how a supernatural power will react to a gift are not only unknown at the time that the object is dedicated, but remain unknown. What might count as blessing is defined, and may be debated, by those who experience or observe the blessing; that blessings relate to past, or future, gifts is an "item of faith."[30]

Another interesting aspect of gift-giving between human beings and deities is that the exchange is always asymmetrical. Humans give sacrificial animals, votive figurines, prayers and praise whereas the gods give life, health, prosperity, crops, and offspring.[31] The asymmetry between the exchanged objects and the exchanging partners is quite similar to asymmetrical exchange among humans, even if the difference is intensified in the case of gifts to the gods. Historian of religion Daniel Ullucci mentions the stereotypical example of students who give apples to their teachers:

> We do not conclude from this either that teachers are too poor to purchase their own apples, or that teachers subsist solely on student-brought apples and will die without them. We immediately parse the social act for what it is: an attempt to create a reciprocal relationship.[32]

(Göttingen: Vandenhoeck & Ruprecht, 2003), 9–27 ,10, 17, 21–2; Bourdieu, *Outline of a Theory*, 105.

28. Bourdieu, *Outline of a Theory*, 99.
29. Gudme, *Before the God*, 30–36.
30. Robin Osborne, "Hoardes, Votives, Offerings: The Archaeology of the Dedicated Object," *World Archaeology* 36 (2004): 1–10, 2.
31. Osborne, "Hoardes, Votives, Offerings," 3.
32. Ullucci, *The Christian Rejection*, 29.

Thus, gods are not assumed to need or to depend upon gifts given to them by humans. They are, however, expected to appreciate the gifts as "perks" and marks of honor.[33]

In sum, gift exchange between people and gods mirrors gift exchange between people as an invested social transaction, where both parties are assumed to benefit from the exchange.

The most common form of exchange between people and gods in the ancient Mediterranean world and in the Hebrew Bible is direct reciprocity; a person (A) offers something, a sacrifice, a votive offering and so on to a deity (B), who requites it at a later time.[34] However, there are also examples of indirect reciprocity between people and gods. I shall return to these examples below.

Reciprocity in the Book of Proverbs

If we turn now to the Book of Proverbs, it is clear that the friend-making capacity of the gift was not lost to the author(s) of the text. The social potential of reciprocal exchange is expressed very clearly in Proverbs 18.16: "A man's gift (*mattan*) makes room for him, and brings him before the great." And along the same lines, although perhaps with a hint of sarcasm it says in chapter 19: "Many seek the favour of a generous man, and every one is a friend to the man who gives gifts (*mattan*)."[35]

In Proverbs 3.9-10, there is a precise description of direct reciprocity between human beings and Yahweh: "Honour Yahweh with your wealth and with the first fruits of all your produce; then your barns will be filled

---

33. Robert Parker, "Pleasing Thighs: Reciprocity in Greek Religion," in Gill, Postlethwaite, and Seaford, *Reciprocity in Ancient Greece*, 1998, 105–26.

34. In this system of exchange the gods are usually seen as the initiators of the cycle, cf. Stanley Stowers, "The Religion of Plant and Animal Offerings versus the Religion of Meanings, Essences, and Textual Mysteries," in *Ancient Mediterranean Sacrifice*, ed. J. Knust and Z. Varhelyi (Oxford: Oxford University, 2011), 1–29, 29: "The gods regularly give the fruit of the land – the grain, the oil, the offspring of animals, and the children of humans. These new products mysteriously come from somewhere. Why not from someone? This assumption, together with the default intuition that the gods are persons, forms the context for practices of social reciprocity with the gods."

35. In chapter 19, the context may be that of borderline bribery. Verse 4 contrasts the rich man who has many friends with the poor man, who loses his one friend. Verse 5 is about false witnesses and then verse 6 returns to the topic of gifts that make friends. The fact that the verse about lying and testifying falsely is sandwiched between two verses about gift giving may justify that the gift is interpreted as a bribe here. Cf. Peter T. H. Hatton, *Contradiction in the Book of Proverbs: The Deep Waters of Counsel* (Burlington, VT: Ashgate, 2008), 137–48, especially 146–7.

with plenty, and your vats will be bursting with wine." This verse is concerned with the world of agri- and viticulture and the point is basically that if you give a gift to Yahweh, Yahweh will give gifts to you in return.

Of prime interest to the topic of indirect reciprocity is the claim in Proverbs 19.17: "Whoever is kind (*khonen*) to the poor (*dal*) lends (*malveh*) to Yahweh and will be repaid in full (*ugmulo yeshallem lo*)". Gary A. Anderson has argued convincingly that the verb *khanan* in this verse most likely carries the meaning "to give generously," that is to give alms, rather than the more general meaning of being kind or gracious.[36] The statement in Proverbs 19.17 corresponds very well with the general attitude to the poor in the Book of Proverbs. The poor and the helpless are generally seen to be under Yahweh's special protection and therefore one should treat them kindly.[37] This is expressed in, for instance, Proverbs 14.31: "He who oppresses (*osheq*) the poor (*dal*) insults his maker, but he who is kind (*khonen*) to the needy (*ebyon*) honor him." The sentiment in Proverbs 19.17 also corresponds well with the general attitude to almsgiving in the Book of Proverbs. For instance, in Proverbs 28.27: "He who gives (*noten*) to the poor (*larosh*) will lack nothing, but he who shuts his eyes will have many curses."

There is nothing surprising as such in the general view of Proverbs 19.17 on the poor and giving alms. What is new and different here is the very explicit statement that Yahweh is indebted to the person who gives to the poor and that Yahweh will be sure to pay (*shillem*) his debt. In this way, Proverbs 19.17 creates a chain of indirect reciprocity, where A gives to the poor and Yahweh gives to A.

Marduk's Basket

In Mesopotamian wisdom literature, there are a couple of interesting parallels to Proverbs 19.17. In the *Counsels of Wisdom*, the reader is given instructions on a range of subjects, such as proper company, proper speech, proper marriage, benefits of religion, and how to behave towards those in need. First, in lines 57–60 there is a prohibition, which in a way is an example of negative indirect reciprocity: "Do not insult the downtrodden and ... Do not sneer at them autocratically. With this a man's god is angry, it is not pleasing to Shamash, who will repay him with evil." In the following lines (61–5) the prohibition is succeeded by a command to do good: "Give food

---

36. Gary A. Anderson, "Redeem your Sins by the Giving of Alms: Sin, Debt, and the 'Treasury of Merit' in Early Jewish and Christian Tradition," *Letter & Spirit* 3 (2007): 39–69, especially 48–9.

37. Cf. Prov. 22.22-23: "Do not rob the poor because they are poor, or crush the afflicted at the gate; for Yahweh pleads their case and take the life of those who rob them."

to eat, beer to drink, grant what is asked, provide for and honour. In this a man's god takes pleasure, it is pleasing to Shamash, who will repay him with favour. Do charitable deeds, render service all your days."[38]

What we have here are descriptions of firstly negative indirect reciprocity, insulting the weak will be repaid with evil by a third party, and positive indirect reciprocity, charity will be repaid with favor by a third party. In both examples, the third party is a deity, namely the Mesopotamian sun-god Shamash.

A similar idea is expressed in *The Dialogue of Pessimism*, where the master says to his servant: "Servant, listen to me." "Yes, master, yes." "I will do a good deed for my country." "So do it, master, do it. The man who does a good deed for his country, his good deed rests in Marduk's basket."[39] In a footnote to the just cited passage from *The Dialogue of Pessimism*, the assyriologist Benjamin R. Foster writes that the meaning of the expression "Marduk's Basket" is unclear: "the idea may be that if one distributes largesse, the recipient is god himself, so good will thereby accrue to the giver."[40] I believe that *The Dialogue of Pessimism* is actually describing a case of indirect reciprocity, where altruism, a good deed for the country, is stored in Marduk's basket and later "repaid" to the donor somehow.[41] This means that to have good deeds resting in Marduk's basket is similar to being owed a favor by Yahweh (cf. Prov. 19.17) or Shamash (cf. *Counsels of Wisdom* ll. 64–5). Thus, in Proverbs 19.17, *Counsels of Wisdom* and *The Dialogue of Pessimism* we have examples of indirect reciprocity, where charity or altruism leads to a reward from the deity.

In his recent works on the history of sin and the history of charity in biblical thought, Gary A. Anderson has traced the development of this idea in biblical literature.[42] In Proverbs 19.17, the gift or favor that the generous person is to receive from Yahweh is unspecified, but in a passage in the Book

---

38. Wilfred G. Lambert, *Babylonian Wisdom Literature* (Oxford: Clarendon Press, 1960; repr. Oxford University Press, 1996), 102–3.

39. Benjamin R. Foster, *Before the Muses: An Anthology of Akkadian Literature*. Vol. II: *Mature, Late* (Bethesda: ML: CDL Press, 1996), 801. Lambert reads kippat, "ring," instead of qappat, "basket," see Lambert, *Babylonian Wisdom Literature*, 149 and W. H. Ph. Römer, and W. von Soden, eds., *Texte aus der Umwelt des Alten Testaments*, III/1 (Gütersloh: Mohn, 1990), 162 n. 73.

40. *Foster, Before the Muses*, 801, n. 1.

41. Cf. Victor Avigdor Hurowitz, who compares these lines in *The Dialogue of Pessimism* with two passages in the *Shamash Hymn* (lines 118–21 and 122–7), "An Allusion to the Šamaš Hymn in the Dialogue of Pessimism," in *Wisdom Literature in Mesopotamia and Israel*, ed. R. J. Clifford (Atlanta, GA: Society of Biblical Literature, 2007), 33–6.

42. Gary A. Anderson, *Sin: A History* (New Haven, CT: Yale University Press,

of Daniel giving to the poor is explicitly linked with redeeming one's sins. In Daniel chapter 4, Daniel is summoned to king Nebuchadnezzar to interpret the king's dream about a magnificent tree that is cut down. Daniel explains to Nebuchadnezzar that the tree is the king himself and that the dream predicts that the king will spend a number of years as a wild animal until he understands that God has dominion over everything and then his kingdom will be returned to him. In the following verse, Daniel gives this advice: "Therefore, O King, may my advice be acceptable to you: redeem your sins by almsgiving (*betsidqah*) and your iniquities by generosity (*bemikhan*) to the poor; then your prosperity may be prolonged."[43] Here it seems that almsgiving no longer results in an unspecified countergift from Yahweh, but that it quite specifically is understood as a way to redeem sins.[44]

In the roughly contemporary Book of Tobit, the saving power of almsgiving is elaborated upon in a farewell speech given by Tobit to his son, Tobias. The passage is rather long, but it deserves to be quoted in full:

> To all those who practice righteousness give alms (*eleēmosynēn*) from your possessions, and do not let your eye begrudge the gift when you make it. Do not turn your face away from anyone who is poor, and the face of God will not be turned away from you. If you have many possessions, make your gift from them in proportion; if few, do not be afraid to give according to the little you have. So you will be laying up a good treasure (*thēsaurizeis*) for yourself against the day of necessity. For almsgiving delivers from death and keeps you from going into the Darkness. Indeed, almsgiving, for all who practice it, is an excellent offering (*dōron agathon*) in the presence of the Most High. (4.7-11)[45]

Besides giving an excellent description of asymmetrical gift-giving, where the equivalence of the exchange is dependent on the social status and financial means of the giver and receiver, this text repeats the idea that kindness to the poor will result in kindness from Yahweh. And the idea is expanded

---

2009); Gary A. Anderson, *Charity: The Place of the Poor in the Biblical Tradition* (New Haven, CT: Yale University Press, 2013).

43. Anderson, "Redeem your Sins," 43–4.

44. "This verse is something of a watershed in the history of biblical thought because here, for the first time, we have a clear and unambiguous reference to almsgiving as a penitential act" (Anderson, "Redeem your Sins," 44). This development should probably be seen in relation to the development of the conceptualization of sin as debt that can be paid off, see Gary A. Anderson, "From Israel's Burden to Israel's Debt: Towards a Theology of Sin in Biblical and Early Second Temple Sources," in *Reworking the Bible: Apocryphal and Related Texts at Qumran*, ed. E. G. Chazon, D. Dimant, and R. A. Clements (Leiden: Brill, 2005), 1–30.

45. Translation from *The New Oxford Annotated Apocrypha. New Revised Standard Version* (Oxford: Oxford University Press, 2010).

with reference to a treasure, which a person can accumulate by giving alms. Furthermore, it is stated that almsgiving can save a person from death and, finally, almsgiving is likened with an offering or gift to God.[46]

This means that according to the Book of Tobit giving alms to the deserving poor is just as beneficial as giving a gift or offering to God.[47] Or to phrase it in gift-giving terms, indirect reciprocity where A gives to the poor and God gives to A is just as rewarding as direct reciprocity where A gives to God and God gives to A.

Treasures in Heaven

This leads us to the Sermon on the Mount in Matthew 6. In the passage on alms in verses 1-4, we recognize the chain of indirect reciprocity, where a person's charity to someone in need is rewarded by God:

> Beware of practising your piety before others in order to be seen by them; for then you have no reward (*misthon*) from your Father in heaven. So whenever you give alms, do not sound a trumpet before you, as the hypocrites do in the synagogues and in the streets, so that they may be praised by others. Truly I tell you, they have received their reward. But when you give alms, do not let your left hand know what your right hand is doing, so that your alms may be done in secret; and your Father who sees in secret will reward (*apodōsei*) you.

The novelty in Matthew, of course, is the condition that almsgiving in itself is not sufficient, but that it has to be charity given if not in secret then at least discreetly. In truth, "The others," the hypocrites who give alms in order to receive praise, will be given a reward as well (v. 2), but it seems that this reward is something that one should try to avoid. In this way, the author(s) of Matthew pushes almsgiving further in the direction of the ideal of the free gift. The donor knows that he has given a gift, and God, who "sees in secret," knows of the gift and will give a reward, but the donor is not allowed to reward himself with the praise and recognition of others as well.

Another difference worth noting is the understanding of the treasure in heaven in Matthew 6.19-21, which is most likely the same as the reward for charity mentioned in 6.1 and 6.4. Whereas the treasure in Heaven in

---

46. Cf. Prov. 10.2 and 11.4, where righteousness is said to save from death. See also Anderson, "Redeem your Sins," 50–1 and Gary A. Anderson, "A Treasure in Heaven: The Exegesis of Proverbs 10:2 in the Second Temple Period," *Hebrew Bible and Ancient Israel 1* (2012): 351–67. See also *Ben Sira* 29.12-13; *PsSol.* 9.5; *SyrBar.* 24.1; *4 Ezra* 7.77; 1 Tim. 6.18-19 and Matt. 19.21.

47. "Tobit is suggesting that placing coins in the hand of a beggar is like putting a sacrifice on the altar – for both the hand and the altar provide direct access to God" (Anderson, "Redeem your Sins," 54).

Matthew refers to an "other-worldly" reward, the gift that one is owed by Yahweh in Proverbs 19 and the treasure accumulated by almsgiving which is said to "deliver from death" in Tobit 4 are certainly restricted to this world.[48] This is most likely also the case in regard to the favor owed by Shamash in *The Counsels of Wisdom* and the benefits from having good deeds stored in Marduk's basket in *The Dialogue of Pessimism*.[49]

In spite of their difference in eschatology though, all these texts operate with the idea that almsgiving is meritorious through a chain of indirect reciprocity, where good deeds directed at other human beings are rewarded by the deity.

A similar idea seems to be present in another New Testament text, namely in Acts 10.4, where the officer Cornelius is addressed by an angel, who tells him that he should invite the apostle Peter to his house. The angel explains why Cornelius has been singled out for this task by referring to his meritorious behavior: "Your prayers (*proseukhai*) and your alms (*eleēmosynai*) have ascended as a memorial before God." Cornelius is being rewarded for his faithfulness and his charity with the gift of baptism (cf. 10.47-48).[50] In the case of the latter it is another example of indirect reciprocity.

To sum up, in the Mesopotamian, Hebrew Bible, and New Testament text examples mentioned above it is possible to trace a pattern of indirect reciprocity, where a person shows charity by doing good deeds and/or giving alms to the poor. This gift is repaid not by the receiver of the gift, which would make it direct reciprocity, but by a third party, a deity, either Yahweh, Marduk, Shamash, or the Christian God. What separates these texts is their eschatology; it is very likely that the favor being owed by the deity in Proverbs, Tobit and the two Mesopotamian wisdom texts are "worldly" rewards, granted to the receiver in this life, since these texts seem to have no conception of an afterlife based on merit.[51] In Matthew and Acts, however, the reward from the Father and the gift of baptism may very well be thought to entail salvation after death.

---

48. Anderson, "A Treasure in Heaven," 367; Anderson, *Charity*, 123-6. Cf. Matt. 19.16-29.

49. For a very interesting comparative survey of "Treasures in Heaven" in biblical and Zoroastrian sources, see Almut Hintze, "Treasures in Heaven: A Theme in Comparative Religion," *Irano-Judaica VI* (2008): 9–36.

50. This view of prayer as meritorious corresponds well with the passage in Matt. 6.5-6, where prayer is described in similar terms as almsgiving in vv. 1-4 as something that should be done discretely and which will trigger a reward from the Father in heaven.

51. Heikki Räisänen, *The Rise of Christian Beliefs: The Thought World of Early Christians* (Minneapolis, MN: Fortress, 2010), 79–86.

However, what unites these texts is the view that charity—acts of altruism—are gifts that will be rewarded by a deity through a chain of indirect reciprocity.

In the following, we shall look closer at the problem of altruism by consulting insights from evolutionary psychology and the cognitive science of religion. If human behavior is developed through evolution and based on the principle of the survival of the fittest, how then do we explain the fact that human beings *do* behave altruistically and why do religions promote altruism such as charity and almsgiving?

The Problem of Altruism

Within the fields of evolutionary studies, indirect reciprocity is often referred to as "prosocial behavior" and it is defined as "an act that increases the fitness of some other individual at the expense of one's own fitness."[52]

Whereas direct reciprocity or "tit for tat" is fairly easy to make sense of when it comes to improving the condition of the individual—I help you and you help me—it is more difficult to explain the existence of indirect reciprocity, that is, you help me and I'll help someone else, or I help you and someone else will help me.[53] It is particularly the risk of cheaters and free-riders—that is individuals who will receive but not reciprocate—that pose a challenge to an explanation of indirect reciprocity as a sound evolutionary strategy.[54] There is always the risk of being exploited when one offers a gift or a kindness. This is true both when it comes to direct reciprocity and indirect reciprocity. However, indirect reciprocity is much riskier because it is significantly harder to monitor and control. In a relationship of direct reciprocity, if a gift or service is not reciprocated within a reasonable amount of time one can simply interrupt any future exchange with the non-reciprocating party. Direct reciprocity is not immune to free-riders, but it is fairly easy to limit one's losses.

In a relationship of indirect reciprocity, where A helps B, B helps C, C helps D and so on, it is much more difficult to limit the loss in case the

---

52. Matthijs van Veelen, "Does it Pay to be Good? Competing Evolutionary Explanations of Pro-Social Behaviour," in *The Moral Brain*, ed. J. Verplaetse, et.al. (New York: Springer, 2009), 186.

53. Martin A. Nowak and Karl Sigmund, "Evolution of Indirect Reciprocity," *Nature* 437 (2005): 1291. Indirect reciprocity can be described as "upstream" when it is based on a positive experience: B has received help from A and therefore B helps C, or as "downstream" when it is based on (positive) reputation: A has helped B and therefore A receives help from C (see p. 1292, figure 1).

54. Daniel Nettle and Robin I. M. Dunbar, "Social Markers and the Evolution of Reciprocal Exchange," *Current Anthropology* 38 (1997): 93–9, 93–4.

reciprocal chain is broken because the roles of giver and recipient are distributed among a larger group of people. In other words, indirect reciprocity is more vulnerable to free-riders and cheaters, because the risk of detection if one does not reciprocate is much smaller.

If direct reciprocity is almost always a low-risk investment when it comes to increasing the fitness of the individual and indirect reciprocity seems to be such a high-risk investment, why then do we see examples of indirect reciprocity or so-called prosocial behavior all the time?

The principle of kin selection may to some extent help to explain prosocial behavior. An individual may give away food or offer help to a family member if this action furthers the long-term survival of the gene that both individuals are carrying. Acting in favor of the reproduction of a gene may sometimes lead to a loss of fitness for one individual but this loss is made up for by the increase in fitness for the other related individual and the gene that they have in common.[55] The problem with kin selection as an explanatory model is that prosocial behavior can frequently be observed among non-kin, both in the animal world and in human societies.[56] So even if kin selection explains some cases of indirect reciprocity it does not sufficiently explain all.

The Israeli evolutionary biologist Amotz Zahavi, who has based most of his research on thorough observations of the group-breeding songbird called the Arabian Babbler, proposes an explanation based on individual selection, that is, behavior that improves the fitness of a single individual. According to Zahavi, prosocial behavior can be interpreted as a signal that is intended to advertise the individual's qualities and thereby to increase the social prestige of the individual. As such, prosocial behavior can be described as a handicap that signals fitness just as the tail of a peacock and it works as an investment that generates social prestige, which enhances coalition and mating opportunities for the signaling individual.[57] According to this model, the benefits to the group that follow the prosocial behavior

---

55. Van Veelen, "Does it Pay": 191–2; Ara Norenzayan, *Big Gods: How Religion Transformed Cooperation and Conflict* (Princeton, NJ: Princeton University Press, 2013), 5.

56. Amotz Zahavi, "Altruism as a Handicap: The Limitations of Kin Selection and Reciprocity," *Journal of Avian Biology* 26 (1995): 1–3.

57. Amotz Zahavi and Avishag Zahavi, *The Handicap Principle: A Missing Piece of Darwin's Puzzle* (Oxford: Oxford University, 1997), 133–47. For further studies on human employment of competitive altruism in order to enhance cooperation and mating opportunities, see Zahavi and Zahavi, *Handicap Principle*, 209–27; Pat Barclay, "The Evolution of Charitable Behaviour and the Power of Reputation" in *Applied Evolutionary Psychology*, ed. S. C. Roberts (Oxford: Oxford University Press, 2012), 149–72; Wendy Iredale and Mark van Vugt, "Altruism as Show Off: A Signalling Perspective

is merely a consequence of the handicap and not a factor in the selection of the behavior itself.[58]

A third option is group selection, that is, behavior that improves the fitness of a group as a whole. Group selection is promoted by, for instance, the evolutionary biologist David Sloan Wilson as an explanatory model for prosocial behavior.[59] Wilson and his associates have observed how prosociality seems to be selectively advantageous at a larger scale. In the long run, groups of prosocial individuals appear to outcompete less social groups and this long-term success in fitness justifies the risk of exploitation by cheaters and free-riders.[60] This means that, even though indirect reciprocity is a risky investment, it is an investment that pays off over time.

It is perfectly possible, of course, that the evolution of prosocial behavior should not be explained by only one of these models, but rather by a combination of individual selection, kin selection, and group selection.[61] An interesting aspect which has been treated recently by the psychologist Ara Norenzayan in his book *Big Gods* is the interplay between the evolution of religion and the evolution of morality.[62] According to Norenzayan, Big Gods, that is morally interested gods, facilitate the success of large-scale cooperating communities, because Big Gods are thought to observe human behavior and to intervene and demand loyalty displays that are difficult to fake. A good example of a morally interested Big God is the Father in heaven, who "sees in secret" in Matthew 6, but Shamash, and Marduk, and Yahweh, who all keep a record of favors owed to deserving worshipers, also belong in this category. The presence of Big Gods increases prosociality, which in turn increases the fitness of the group in accordance with Wilson's group selection argument, mentioned above, and this leads to what Norenzayan calls a "runaway process of cultural evolution," where expanding

---

on Bystander Helping, Charity Giving, Environmental Sustainability and Other Acts of Kindness," in Roberts, *Applied Evolutionary Psychology*, 173–85.

58. Zahavi, "Altruism as a Handicap".

59. David Sloan Wilson, Daniel Tumminelli O'Brien, and Artura Sesma, "Human Prosociality from an Evolutionary Perspective: Variation and Correlations at a City-Wide Scale," *Evolution and Human Behavior* 30 (2009): 190–200; Elliott Sober and David Sloan Wilson, *Unto Others: The Evolution and Psychology of Unselfish Behavior* (Cambridge, MA: Harvard University Press, 1998), 132–58. For a critical discussion of the notion of group selection see Steven Pinker, "The False Allure of Group Selection: An Edge Original Essay" (6.18.2012), https://www.edge.org/conversation/the-false-allure-of-group-selection.

60. Wilson, O'Brien, and Sesma, "Human Prosociality."

61. Cf. van Veelen, "Does it Pay to be Good?" 196–7.

62. Norenzayan, *Big Gods*.

groups of cooperating individuals take their prosocial religious beliefs with them and thereby instigate ever-growing systems of social cooperation.[63]

This means that there appears to be a fruitful interrelation between prosocial behavior and religions with Big Gods—they mutually promote each other. To some extent this helps to explain why religious systems featuring Big Gods so often encourage altruistic behavior and acts of indirect reciprocity. And when one takes into account the high-risk character of indirect reciprocity on the individual level it also helps to explain why it is necessary to have a deity to offer security on the loan that is a gift or a service. If A gives a gift or a service to B, A may not be rewarded by C, D or E, but by God, Yahweh, Shamash, or Marduk himself.

The Free Gift and True Altruism

Here I would like to make a brief detour and bring in a discussion instigated by the Swedish economist Jan Tullberg. Tullberg has studied the practice of indirect reciprocity and he has questioned whether it is in fact correct to label it as prosocial behaviour and altruistic. Tullberg has argued that indirect reciprocity is in fact a selfish act and as such is should not be labelled as altruism.[64]

One could argue that this terminological disagreement simply stems from different academic practices. In evolutionary studies, altruism is an action that increases the fitness of some other individual at the expense of one's own fitness, but altruism also seems to be a sound evolutionary strategy in the long run. This definition collides with Tullberg's understanding of altruism as a self-less act. Interestingly, Tullberg's discussion of altruism shares many features with the discussion of the free gift which I mentioned at the beginning of this study. According to Tullberg, if prosocial behaviour turns out to pay off in the long run, then we cannot call it altruism.[65] And indeed, according to the evolutionary models discussed above, prosocial behaviour does seem to pay off both on the individual level, where an individual improves

---

63. Norenzayan, *Big Gods,* 8–9; Ara Norenzayan and Azim F. Shariff, "The Origin and Evolution of Religious Prosociality," *Science* 322 (2008): 58–62.

64. Jan Tullberg, "On Indirect Reciprocity: The Distinction between Reciprocity and Altruism, and a Comment on Suicide Terrorism," *The American Journal of Economics and Sociology* 63 (2004): 1193–212.

65. Tullberg stresses that he categorizes actions according to their effects, that is according to their statistically expected results: "... in contrast to the two variants of intention – what the actor intended and what we as observers think he intended. Such an expected effect is also in contrast to actual outcome – credit loss of a bank should not be regarded as ex post facto altruism" (Tullberg, "On Indirect Reciprocity," 1196).

its fitness through social prestige, and on a group level, where the overall fitness of the group is enhanced by prosocial behavior. This, says Tullberg, can be categorized as indirect reciprocity because it serves the self-interest of the individual or the group, but it is wrong to call it altruism, because altruism should only be used to describe actions that entail a net cost, a loss of fitness, and no benefits.[66] One hears an echo of Derrida's paradox that for the free gift to exist it must not exist, because as soon as something is recognized as a gift it destroys the very concept of a gift.[67]

Tullberg remarks that religious systems often include patterns of indirect reciprocity, where A gives to B and God then rewards A.[68] This pattern is similar, of course, to the kinds of indirect reciprocity that are represented in Proverbs 19, and in the Sermon in Matthew 6, and in the other text examples that we have reviewed above.

If we stick with Tullberg's distinction between indirect reciprocity and altruism, it is clear that the idea of a metaphysical reward is no guarantee against egoism. Tullberg mentions the example of Mother Teresa: "If Mother Teresa got to Heaven, her deeds were not altruistic but self-serving in the long run: doing extremely well by doing good."[69] If, on the other hand, there is no God and no heaven then Mother Theresa turns out to have been a true altruist in deeds, whereas her motivation does not oppose her own long-term self-interest.[70] It follows from the nature of this discussion that the solution to the problem must remain a matter of faith.[71]

Tullberg's discussion of true altruism is, of course, intended as a provocation and it does not in any way topple the insights on prosocial behaviour reached by evolutionary scientists. It does encourage an interesting reflexion, however, on the nature of gifts and charity.

---

66. Tullberg, "On Indirect Reciprocity," 1195.

67. Derrida, *Given Time,* 14.

68. Tullberg, "On Indirect Reciprocity," 1202. Tullberg mentions "reincarnation and Paradise" as examples of metaphysical rewards and these of course are per definition otherworldly benefits that will only prove themselves true or false after death. There are however also divine rewards that may occur in this life and the identification of these as exactly divine gifts or blessings and not just as a stroke of luck is an "item of faith," cf. Osborne, "Hoardes, Votives, Offerings," 2, and the discussion of giving gifts to the gods above.

69. Jan Tullberg, "The Golden Rule of Benevolence versus the Silver Rule of Reciprocity," *Journal of Religion and Business Ethics* 3 (2011): Art. 2, 6.

70. Tullberg continues, "These judgments do not in any way disclaim that she has manifested an extreme strength of will in forsaking her short-term interests and wants. But her example also illustrates the internal inconsistency in the arguments for altruism" (Tullberg, "The Golden Rule," 6).

71. Cf. Osborne, "Hoardes, Votives, Offerings."

In broad terms, we have an opposition between a friend-making, personal, and reciprocal gift and a "free," impersonal, and non-reciprocal gift. The latter may be truly altruistic in Tullberg's understanding of the term, but it does not bind people together, nor does it further cooperation. A free gift makes no friends. The reciprocal, friend-making gift, on the other hand, may be entirely governed by self-interest, but it also works as a kind of social glue. What direct and indirect reciprocity have in common is exactly their ability to establish and maintain sociality and cooperation. Direct reciprocity works best at the local level, whereas indirect reciprocity has the potential to form the basis of large cooperative networks.[72] For indirect reciprocity to work on a group level, self-interest oddly enough is more important than generosity. This is because indirect reciprocity roughly works in two ways; it is called "upstream," when a person gives a gift or a service because one has personally experienced being given a gift or a service, and "downstream," when a person gives a gift or a service to another individual, who has been known to do the same to others. Interestingly, in these patterns of exchange a reciprocal reputation appears to be better than a reputation for being generous. Individuals who participate in indirect reciprocity seek out other individuals, who have been seen to, or who are rumored to, be good at reciprocal exchange. This is most likely a way to steer clear of cheaters. Very generous givers are generally avoided, probably because they are considered to be foolhardy or undependable.[73]

When viewed from the perspective of the exchanging parties, both kinds of reciprocity entail a real risk of failure, a risk of being snubbed or cheated or exploited. This is what ensures their ability to create social cohesion, even if the long-term benefit of the transaction seems guaranteed when viewed "from above."

For the reciprocal gift to work it does not require complete selflessness, but it does require a certain amount of faith (or risk-taking) in other people or—in the case of metaphysical rewards—in God.[74]

---

72. Cf. Nowak and Sigmund, "Evolution of Indirect Reciprocity"; Norenzayan, *Big Gods*, 4–7.

73. Tullberg, "The Golden Rule," 1199; Nowak and Sigmund, "Evolution of Indirect Reciprocity," 1291–2.

74. Tullberg claims that the Sermon on the Mount is in fact a "hostile attack on reciprocity," because it expands the demand for an eye for an eye (tit for tat) by requiring that one turns the other cheek and thus behaves truly altruistic in Tullberg's sense and acts "according to the egoistic demands of the other" ("The Golden Rule of Benevolence," 2). But see Teehan's claim (indirectly contra Tullberg) that the Sermon is in fact still governed by reprocity because one turns the other cheek in order to receive a metaphysical reward from God (John Teehan, *In the Name of God* [Oxford: Wiley-Blackwell, 2010], 138–40).

Biographical Note

Anne Katrine de Hemmer Gudme is Professor of Hebrew Bible at the University of Oslo, Norway. Her research focuses on religious ritual and semi-ritualized social practices in the Hebrew Bible, and she has published several studies on sacrifices, votive practice, gift-giving and hospitality.

Bibliography

Algazi, Gadi. "Introduction: Doing Things with Gifts," 9–27 in *Negotiating the Gift: Pre-Modern Figurations of Exchange*. Edited by G. Algazi, V. Groebner, and B. Jussen. Göttingen: Vandenhoeck & Ruprecht, 2003.

Anderson, Gary A. "From Israel's Burden to Israel's Debt: Towards a Theology of Sin in Biblical and Early Second Temple Sources," 1–30 in *Reworking the Bible: Apocryphal and Related Texts at Qumran*. Edited by E. G. Chazon, R. A. Clements, and D. Dimant. Leiden: Brill, 2005. https://doi.org/10.1163/9789047416142_002

—"Redeem Your Sins by the Giving of Alms: Sin, Debt, and the 'Treasury of Merit' in Early Jewish and Christian Tradition," *Letter & Spirit* 3 (2007): 39–69.

—*Sin: A History*. New Haven, CT: Yale University Press, 2009.

—"A Treasure in Heaven: The Exegesis of Proverbs 10:2 in the Second Temple Period," *Hebrew Bible and Ancient Israel* 1 (2012): 351–67. https://doi.org/10.1628/219222712804556608

—*Charity: The Place of the Poor in the Biblical Tradition*. New Haven, CT: Yale University Press, 2013.

van Baal, J. *Reciprocity and the Position of Women*. Assen, NL: Koninklijke Van Gorcum, 1975.

—"Offering, Sacrifice and Gift," *Numen* 23 (1976): 161–78. https://doi.org/10.1163/156852776X00094

Barclay, Pat. "The Evolution of Charitable Behaviour and the Power of Reputation," 149–72 in Roberts, *Applied Evolutionary Psychology*, 2012. https://doi.org/10.1093/acprof:oso/9780199586073.003.0010

Bourdieu, Pierre. *Outline of a Theory of Practice*. Translated by R. Nice. Cambridge: Cambridge University, 1977. https://doi.org/10.1017/CBO9780511812507

—*The Logic of Practice*. Translated by Richard Nice. Cambridge: Cambridge Polity Press, 1990.

Derrida, Jacques. *Given Time. 1: Counterfeit Money*. Translated by P. Kamuf. Chicago, IL: University of Chicago, 1992.

Eidevall, Göran. *Sacrificial Rhetoric in the Prophetic Literature of the Hebrew Bible*. Lewiston, NY: Edwin Mellen, 2012.

Ekeh, Peter P. *Social Exchange Theory: The Two Traditions*. Cambridge, MA: Harvard University Press, 1974.

Foster, Benjamin R. *Before the Muses: An Anthology of Akkadian Literature*. Volume II: *Mature, Late*. Bethesda, ML: CDL Press, 1996.

Gill, Christopher, Norman Postlethwaite, and Richard Seaford, eds. *Reciprocity in Ancient Greece*. Oxford: Oxford University, 1998.

Godbout, Jacques T., and Alain Caillé. *The World of the Gift*. Montreal: McGill-Queen's University, 1998.

Gouldner, Alvin. "The Norm of Reciprocity: A Preliminary Statement," *American Sociological Review* 25 (1960): 161–78. https://doi.org/10.2307/2092623

Gregory, Chris A. "Gifts to Men and Gifts to God: Gift Exchange and Capital Accumulation," *Man* 15 (1980): 626–52. https://doi.org/10.2307/2801537

—*Gifts and Commodities*. London: Academic Press, 1982.

Gudme, Anne Katrine de Hemmer. *Before the God in This Place for Good Remembrance: A Comparative Analysis of the Aramaic Votive Inscriptions from Mount Gerizim*. Berlin: De Gruyter, 2013. https://doi.org/10.1515/9783110301878

Hatton, Peter T. H. *Contradiction in the Book of Proverbs: The Deep Waters of Counsel*. Burlington, VT: Ashgate, 2008.

Hintze, Almut. "Treasures in Heaven: A Theme in Comparative Religion," *Irano-Judaica* VI (2008): 9–36.

Hurowitz, Victor Avigdor. "An Allusion to the Šamaš Hymn in the Dialogue of Pessimism," 33–6 in *Wisdom Literature in Mesopotamia and Israel*. Edited by R. J. Clifford. Atlanta, GA: Society of Biblical Literature, 2007.

Iredale, Wendy, and Mark van Vugt. "Altruism as Show Off: A Signalling Perspective on Bystander Helping, Charity Giving, Environmental Sustainability and Other Acts of Kindness," 173–85 in Roberts, *Applied Evolutionary Psychology*, 2012. https://doi.org/10.1093/acprof:oso/9780199586073.003.0011

Laidlaw, James. "A Free Gift Makes No Friends," *The Journal of the Royal Anthropological Institute* 6 (2000): 617–34. https://doi.org/10.1111/1467-9655.00036

Lambert, Wilfred G. *Babylonian Wisdom Literature*. Oxford: Clarendon Press, 1960. Repr. Oxford University Press, 1996.

Malinowski, Bronislaw. *Argonauts of the Western Pacific: An Account of Native Enterprise and Adventure in the Archipelagoes of Melanesian New Guinea*. London: Routledge, 1922.

—*Crime and Custom in Savage Society*. London: Kegan Paul, 1926.

Mauss, Marcel. *The Gift*. Translated by W. D. Halls. London: Routledge, 1990.

Nettle, Daniel, and Robin I. M. Dunbar. "Social Markers and the Evolution of Reciprocal Exchange," *Current Anthropology* 38 (1997): 93–9. https://doi.org/10.1086/204588

Norenzayan, Ara. *Big Gods: How Religion Transformed Cooperation and Conflict*. Princeton, NJ: Princeton University Press, 2013. https://doi.org/10.2307/j.ctt32bbp0

Norenzayan, Ara, and Azim Shariff. "The Origin and Evolution of Religious Prosociality," *Science* 322 (2008): 58–62. https://doi.org/10.1126/science.1158757

Nowak, Martin A., and Karl Sigmund. "Evolution of Indirect Reciprocity," *Nature* 437 (2005): 1291. https://doi.org/10.1038/nature04131

Osborne, Robin. "Hoardes, Votives, Offerings: The Archaeology of the Dedicated Object," *World Archaeology* 36 (2004): 1–10. https://doi.org/10.1080/0043824042000192696

Parker, Robert. "Pleasing Thighs: Reciprocity in Greek Religion," 105–26 in Gill, Postlethwaite, and Seaford, *Reciprocity in Ancient Greece*, 1998.

Pinker, Steven. "The False Allure of Group Selection: An Edge Original Essay," (6.18.2012), https://www.edge.org/conversation/the-false-allure-of-group-selection.

Räisänen, Heikki. *The Rise of Christian Beliefs: The Thought World of Early Christians*. Minneapolis, MN: Fortress, 2010.

Roberts, S. Craig ed. *Applied Evolutionary Psychology*. Oxford: Oxford University Press, 2012.

Römer, W. H. Ph., and W. von Soden, eds. *Texte aus der Umwelt des Alten Testaments*, III/1. Gütersloh: Mohn, 1990.

Sahlins, Marshall. *Stone Age Economics*. London: Routledge, 2004.
Seaford, Richard. "Introduction," 1–12 in Gill, Postlethwaite, and Seaford, *Reciprocity in Ancient Greece*, 1998. https://doi.org/10.1093/acprof:oso/9780198777250.003.0001
Sober, Elliott, and David Sloan Wilson. *Unto Others: The Evolution and Psychology of Unselfish Behavior*. Cambridge, MA: Harvard University Press, 1998.
Stowers, Stanley. "The Religion of Plant and Animal Offerings versus the Religion of Meanings, Essences, and Textual Mysteries," 1–29 in *Ancient Mediterranean Sacrifice*. Edited by J. Knust and Z. Varhelyi. Oxford: Oxford University, 2011. https://doi.org/10.1093/acprof:oso/9780199738960.003.0001
Teehan, John. *In the Name of God: The Evolutionary Origins of Religious Ethics and Violence*. Oxford: Wiley-Blackwell, 2010. https://doi.org/10.1002/9781444320695
Tullberg, Jan. "On Indirect Reciprocity: The Distinction between Reciprocity and Altruism, and a Comment on Suicide Terrorism," *The American Journal of Economics and Sociology* 63 (2004): 1193–212. https://doi.org/10.1111/j.1536-7150.2004.00341.x
—"The Golden Rule of Benevolence versus the Silver Rule of Reciprocity," *Journal of Religion and Business Ethics* 3 (2011).
Ullucci, Daniel C. *The Christian Rejection of Animal Sacrifice*. Oxford: Oxford University, 2012. https://doi.org/10.1093/acprof:oso/9780199791705.001.0001
van Veelen, Matthijs. "Does it Pay to Be Good? Competing Evolutionary Explanations of Pro-Social Behaviour," 185–200 in *The Moral Brain: Essays on the Evolutionary and Neuroscientific Aspects of Morality*. Edited by J. Verplaetse. New York: Springer, 2009. https://doi.org/10.1007/978-1-4020-6287-2_8
Wagner-Hasel, Beate. "Egoistic Exchange and Altruistic Gift: On the Roots of Marcel Mauss's Theory of the Gift," 141–71 in *Negotiating the Gift: Pre-Modern Figurations of Exchange*. Edited by G. Algazi, V. Groebner, and B. Jussen. Göttingen: Vandenhoeck & Ruprecht, 2003.
van Wees, Hans. "The Law of Gratitude: Reciprocity in Anthropological Theory," 13–50 in Gill, Postlethwaite, and Seaford, *Reciprocity in Ancient Greece*, 1998.
Wilson, David Sloan, Artura Sesma, and Daniel Tumminelli O'Brien. "Human Prosociality from an Evolutionary Perspective: Variation and Correlations at a City-Wide Scale," *Evolution and Human Behavior* 30 (2009): 190–200. https://doi.org/10.1016/j.evolhumbehav.2008.12.002
Zahavi, Amotz. "Altruism as a Handicap: The Limitations of Kin Selection and Reciprocity," *Journal of Avian Biology* 26 (1995): 1–3. https://doi.org/10.2307/3677205
Zahavi, Amotz, and Avishag Zahavi. *The Handicap Principle: A Missing Piece of Darwin's Puzzle*. Oxford: Oxford University Press, 1997.

Chapter Eleven

Macarisms and Identity Formation: Insights from the Comparison of 4Q525 and the Sermon on the Mount

Elisa Uusimäki

Introduction

The collection of nine macarisms or beatitudes, which begins with the Sermon on the Mount (Matt. 5.3-11), is not one of a kind in its ancient context, as similar lists are known in early Jewish and Christian literature.[1] This article examines how two series of macarisms, those found in 4QBeatitudes (4Q525) and in the Gospel of Matthew, shape and construct the identity of their audiences.[2] Philip Esler has previously analyzed the Matthaean macarisms in light of social identity theory and pointed out how they embody group norms.[3] In terms of 4Q525, I have written on the social function of macarisms (frag. 2 ii) in relation to the description of curses (frag. 15).[4] The aim of this article, on the other hand, is to highlight specific points of

---

1. Hermann Lichtenberger, "Makarisms in Matthew 5:3ff. in Their Jewish Context," in *The Sermon on the Mount and Its Jewish Setting*, ed. H.-J. Becker and S. Ruzer (Cahiers de la Revue Biblique, 60; Paris: Gabalda, 2005), 40–56.
2. For the Hebrew text and its French translation, see Émile Puech, "4QBéatitudes," in *Qumrân Grotte 4 – XVIII: Textes Hébreux (4Q521–4Q528, 4Q576–4Q579)*, ed. Émile Puech (Discoveries in the Judean Desert, 25; Oxford: Clarendon, 1998), 115–78.
3. Philip F. Esler, "Group Norms and Prototypes in Matthew 5.3–12: A Social Identity Interpretation of the Matthaean Beatitudes," in *T&T Clark Handbook to Social Identity in the New Testament*, ed. J. Brian Tucker and Coleman A. Baker (London: Bloomsbury, 2014), 147–71, 164–70. Esler's study, based on a seminal presentation delivered in 1994, moves forward the discussion on whether the macarisms of Matthew should be characterized as eschatological blessings or (ethical) entrance-liturgies by focusing on their social role instead. For an overview of past scholarship on Matthaean macarisms, see Esler, "Group Norms," 149–55.
4. Elisa Uusimäki, "Wisdom, Scripture, and Identity Formation in 4QBeatitudes," in *Social Memory and Social Identity in the Study of Early Judaism and Early Christianity*, ed. Samuel Byrskog, Raimo Hakola, and Jutta Jokiranta (Novum Testamentum et Orbis Antiquus/Studien zur Umwelt des Neuen Testaments, 116; Göttingen: Vandenhoeck & Ruprecht, 2016), 175–86.

contact between the macarisms in 4Q525 and Matthew that can illuminate the question of identity formation in these texts in a fresh way.⁵

There are significant differences between these texts, which were composed in different settings and for different audiences, but there are parallels as well; the aim of my comparison is not to deny the differences, but to highlight the resemblances. I do not claim that all lists of macarisms functioned in exactly the same way, but instead I consider certain similarities that can be observed between 4Q525 and Matthew. The macarisms documented in both texts describe prototypical figures and, accordingly, shape their target audiences by providing them with models to follow. Also being performative utterances, macarisms contribute to an establishment of in-group identity; it will be argued that this effect relates to the placements of the series. Finally, the theme of kingship shared by both texts further illuminates the self-images promoted and constructed by them. Before proceeding to these questions, the examination will begin with a brief look at 4Q525, an overview of the macarism tradition, a description of the theoretical framework employed in this article, and structural comments on the series to be treated.

While the Sermon on the Mount does not require further introduction,⁶ a brief overview may be given for 4Q525, a Jewish wisdom instruction from the late Second Temple era. The extant copy was found at Qumran, although the likely origin of the text is non-sectarian.⁷ The manuscript consists of 50

---

5. An earlier version of this paper was presented at the "Social and Cognitive Sciences in the Analysis of Texts and History. Special Theme: Sermon on the Mount" meeting, organized by the NordForsk network "Socio-Cognitive Perspectives on Early Judaism and Early Christianity" in Helsinki in January 2014. I thank all of the participants for the lively discussion that contributed to this article. In particular, many thanks are due to Petri Luomanen, Nina Nikki, Rikard Roitto, and Hanna Tervanotko, who read and commented on a later version of the article.

6. The amount of scholarly literature on the Sermon is enormous. This was already the case in the 1970s, as is indicated by the introductory remarks of Robert A. Guelich, "Matthean Beatitudes: 'Entrance-Requirements' or Eschatological Blessings?" *Journal of Biblical Literature* 95 (1976): 415–34, 415. The Sermon also has a rich and somewhat chequered reception history in Christian theology from ancient authors until modernity; see the Introduction to this volume, Chapter 1.

7. The remaining copy originates from the turn of the era, but the date of composition is perhaps in the mid-second century BCE. For the origin of 4Q525, see, e.g., Puech, "4QBéatitudes," 116–9; John I. Kampen, *Wisdom Literature* (Eerdmans Commentaries on the Dead Sea Scrolls; Grand Rapids, MI: Eerdmans, 2011), 308. Jacqueline C. R. de Roo, "Is 4Q525 a Qumran Sectarian Document?" in *The Scrolls and the Scriptures: Qumran Fifty Years After*, ed. Stanley E. Porter and Craig A. Evans (Journal for the Study of Pseudepigrapha Supplement Series, 26; Sheffield: Sheffield Academic Press, 1997), 338–67, argues for the sectarian provenance of 4Q525, but her thesis has not received support by other scholars.

fragments with six lengthier passages (frags. 2 ii-iii; 5; 14 ii; 15; 24 ii). In terms of its pedagogical purpose, form, and content, 4Q525 shares a myriad of elements with Proverbs 1–9. It exhorts the reader to pursue a virtuous life, but in addition to stressing the importance of human efforts, it underlines the role of torah as a divine source of wisdom.[8] Moreover, the worldview reflected in 4Q525 includes eschatological beliefs that are foreign to Proverbs.[9]

In line with 4Q525's modern title, previous research on the text has primarily dealt with the series of macarisms (frag. 2 ii).[10] Scholars have analyzed its content and structure, often in connection with the similar lists in Matthew (5.3-12) and Luke (6.20-23), while its social and spiritual functions have

---

8. The author even rewrites parts of Proverbs 1–9 in order to show that wisdom is embodied in torah; Elisa Uusimäki, "Use of Scripture in 4QBeatitudes: A Torah-Adjustment to Proverbs 1–9," *Dead Sea Discoveries* 20 (2013): 71–97. Note that the term "torah" is not capitalized in this article, in order to highlight its multiple meanings that range from "instruction" to "Pentateuch" and "law." For the non-fixed content of the term in late Second Temple Judaism, see, e.g., Eva Mroczek, "Thinking Digitally about the Dead Sea Scrolls: Book History before and beyond the Book," *Book History* 14 (2011): 241–69, 251.

9. These concern future judgment and punishment, as well as demonic beings (esp. frags. 15–23). For comments on the eschatological nuances of 4Q525, see, e.g., Matthew J. Goff, *Discerning Wisdom: The Sapiential Literature of the Dead Sea Scrolls* (Supplements to Vetus Testamentum, 116; Leiden: Brill, 2007), 221–2; Kampen, *Wisdom Literature*, 312–3.

10. Émile Puech, "Un hymne essénien en partie retrouvé et les Béatitudes," *Revue de Qumran* 13 (1988): 59–88; George J. Brooke, "The Wisdom of Matthew's Beatitudes," *Scripture Bulletin* 19 (1989): 35–41; reprinted in George J. Brooke, *The Dead Sea Scrolls and the New Testament* (Minneapolis, MN: Fortress Press, 2005), 217–34; Émile Puech, "4Q525 et les péricopes des Béatitudes en Ben Sira et Matthieu," *Revue Biblique* 98 (1991): 80–106; Heinz-Josef Fabry, "Der Makarismus – mehr als nur eine weisheitliche Lehrform: Gedanken zu dem neu-edierten Text 4Q525," in *Alttestamentlicher Glaube und Biblische Theologie: Festschrift für Horst Dietrich Preuß zum 65. Geburtstag*, ed. Jutta Hausmann and Hans-Jürgen Zobel (Stuttgart: Kohlhammer, 1992), 362–71; Joseph A. Fitzmyer, "A Palestinian Collection of Beatitudes," in *The Four Gospels 1992: Festschrift Frans Neirynck*, ed. F. van Segbroeck, et al., 3 vols. (Bibliotheca Ephemeirdum Theologicarum Lovaniensium, 100; Leuven: Leuven University Press, 1992), 1:509–15; Émile Puech, "The Collections of Beatitudes in Hebrew and in Greek (4Q525, 1–4 and Matt 5, 3–12)," in *Early Christianity in Context: Monuments and Documents: Essays in Honour of Emmanuel Testa*, ed. Frédéric Manns and Eugenio Alliata (Studim Biblicum Franciscanum Collectio Maior, 38; Jerusalem: Franciscan, 1993), 353–68; Benedict T. Viviano, "Eight Beatitudes at Qumran and in Matthew?" *Svensk exegetisk årsbok* 58 (1993): 71–84; James H. Charlesworth, "The Qumran Beatitudes (4Q525) and the New Testament (Mt 5:3–11; Lk 6:20–26)," *Revue de l'histoire et de philosophie religieuses* 80 (2000): 13–35.

received less attention.[11] It is only appropriate, therefore, that this article specifically addresses the role of macarisms in the process of identity formation.

Macarisms: Intentional Speech Acts

The term "macarism" designates a formula that begins with the Hebrew word *ashre* or the Greek *makarios*. The formula is generally translated into English as "happy" or "fortunate." The term "blessed" is used as well, but a macarism is actually a proclamation of happiness and a form of congratulations; an illuminative example of this role of a macarism is Psalm 1.1-2, which states: "Happy is the man who has not followed the counsel of the wicked, or taken the path of sinners, or joined the company of the insolent; rather, the teaching of the Lord is his delight, and he studies that teaching day and night."[12] Nevertheless, a macarism is a fundamentally religious statement because the prosperous condition is considered to follow divine blessing and favour.[13]

A blessing, on the other hand, has been described as an act of granting and receiving favor, which is meant to form a bond between the divine being(s) and human beings.[14] In the Hebrew Bible, blessedness means fullness of life, including family, prosperity, honor, and well-being. Since these features largely correspond with the promises given in macarisms, Waldemar Janzen has argued that the content of blessing forms the basis for the macarism. Macarisms acknowledge that all blessings come from God and they point to the state of blessedness, but they do not *cause* that state.[15] Unlike a blessing, which seeks to effect a change, the proclamation of happiness reinforces a blessed state that already is (in part) reality for the recipient. Despite not being identical, the formulae of macarisms and blessings have, therefore, a relationship of some kind.

In spite of being declarative, macarisms are typically conditional and serve as implicit exhortations, admonitions, and even warnings.[16] This

---

11. The major exception is my article "Wisdom, Scripture, and Identity Formation in 4QBeatitudes."
12. The English translation is from *JPS Hebrew-English Tanakh* (2nd edn.; Philadelphia, PA: Jewish Publication Society, 2003).
13. Walter Käser, "Beobachtungen zum alttestamentlichen Makarismus," *Zeitschrift für die alttestamentliche Wissenschaft* 82 (1970): 235–50.
14. Prapod Assavavirulhakarn, "Blessing," in *Encyclopedia of Religion*, ed. Lindsay Jones, 15 vols. (2nd edn.; Detroit, MI: Macmillan, 2005), 2:979–85, 2:979–80.
15. Waldemar Janzen, "'AŠRÊ in the Old Testament," *Harvard Theological Review* 58 (1965): 215–26, 222–3.
16. See, e.g., Georg Bertram, "μακάριος in the LXX and Judaism," in *Theological Dictionary of the New Testament*, ed. Gerhard Kittel, 10 vols. (Grand Rapids, MI:

makes them naturally fitting for pedagogical contexts; the biblical forms predominantly occur in psalms and wisdom literature. As macarisms require the performance of certain things, they can be located somewhere between blessings and instructions in terms of function as well.

Macarisms (like blessings) have social functions, although this aspect has not received much attention in biblical scholarship.[17] As I hope to show in this article, they can operate to forge a sense of identity. This is natural in that the proclivity for group formation is intrinsic to all human beings;[18] the human tendency toward categorization on both cognitive and social levels is also a basic assumption related to the concept of social identity. The aspect of group formation is specifically pertinent to religious texts that often strengthen the in-group identity of the target audience.

The comparison of 4Q525 and Matthew will draw on the insights of two "twin" theories of social sciences: self-categorization theory (SCT) and social identity theory (SIT).[19] As put forward by Penelope J. Oakes, S. Alexander Haslam and John C. Turner, the concept of *self-categorization* designates "the cognitive grouping of the self"; in other words, a person identifies himself/herself with "some class of stimuli" and respectively contrasts it with another "class of stimuli." Self-categories operate on interpersonal, intergroup, and interspecies levels.[20] As for the second theory, the theory and concept of *social identity* is related to intergroup interaction.

Eerdmans, 1967), 4:364–7, 4:365; Samuel Terrien, "Wisdom in the Psalter," in *In Search of Wisdom: Essays in Memory of John G. Gammie*, ed. Leo G. Perdue, Bernard Brandon Scott, and William Johnston Wiseman (Louisville, KY: Westminster John Knox, 1993), 51–72, 55.

17. The major exception is K. C. Hanson, "How Honourable! How Shameful! A Cultural Analysis of Matthew's Makarisms and Reproaches," *Semeia* 68 (1994): 81–111, who highlights the formula's link to the cultural values of honor and shame in the Mediterranean region and suggests that *ashre* should be translated as "honorable" instead of "blessed" or "happy." While the formula was used in a culture concerned with the honor of a person, and it might reflect some of those concerns, I have chosen to employ the translation "fortunate," since the rich connotations of *ashre* cannot be confined to "honorable" alone, nor does that translation seem to embody the primary nuances of the term.

18. James A. Boon, *Other Tribes, Other Scribes: Symbolic Anthropology in the Comparative Study of Cultures, Histories, Religions, and Texts* (Cambridge: Cambridge University Press, 1982), 230.

19. For a helpful introduction to SIT and SCT, see Philip F. Esler, "An Outline of Social Identity Theory," in Tucker and Baker, eds., *T&T Clark Handbook to Social Identity*, 13–39.

20. Penelope J. Oakes, S. Alexander Haslam, and John C. Turner, "The Role of Prototypicality in Group Influence and Cohesion: Contextual Variation in the Graded Structure of Social Categories," in *Social Identity: International Perspectives*, ed. Stephen Worchel, et al. (London: Sage, 1998), 75–92, 76–7, 80.

It was introduced by Henri Tajfel, who defined it as the self-concept of an individual related to group membership. Social identity results from a person's knowledge of his/her participation in a social group (or several groups) "together with the value and emotional significance attached to that membership."[21] The formation of social identity typically causes depersonalization, which results in self-stereotyping or the perception of oneself increasingly as an example of a category or a member of an in-group, and decreasingly as a distinctive person.[22]

The role of norms (ethics) is essential in the formation and maintenance of social identity because they tell the members of a group how to behave in order to belong to it. Michael Hogg and Scott Reid have defined group norms as the "regularities in attitudes and behavior that characterize a social group and differentiate it from other social groups."[23] Prototypical figures, for their part, embody these norms as the ideal "cognitive representations of group norms."[24] These remarks, which form the theoretical frame for the present discussion, direct attention to the social functions of macarisms in the expression of group norms and the self-categorization process of the audience.

Macarisms in 4Q525 and Matthew: A Remark on Structure

A few structural observations on the lists of macarisms are necessary before their thematic comparison. The series in 4Q525 (frag. 2 ii) is well-preserved apart from the first macarism, while the poem that succeeds the series is preserved only in part. The passage reads as follows:

> ... 1 with a pure heart and does not slander with his tongue. *vacat* Fortunate are those who hold fast to her statutes and do not hold fast to 2 the ways of injustice. *vacat* Fortu[nate] are those who rejoice in her and do not pour out into the ways of folly. *vacat* Fortunate are those who seek her 3 with pure hands and do not search her with a deceitful heart. *vacat* Fortunate is the one who attains wisdom. *vacat* He walks 4 in torah of the Most High: he establishes his heart in her ways. *vacat* He restrains himself with her teachings and favors her chastisements const[an]tly. 5 He does not leave her in the face of [his] affliction[s], during the time of distress does not abandon her, does not forget her [in the day] of terror, 6 and in the humility of his soul does not

---

21. Henri Tajfel, *Human Groups and Social Categories: Studies in Social Psychology* (Cambridge: Cambridge University Press, 1981), 255.
22. Oakes, Haslam, and Turner, "The Role of Prototypicality in Group Influence and Cohesion," 77.
23. Michael A. Hogg and Scott A. Reid, "Social Identity, Self-Categorization, and the Communication of Group Norms," *Communication Theory* 16 (2006): 7–30, 7.
24. Hogg and Reid, "Social Identity," 11.

despise [her]. But he reflects on her constantly, in his distress muses [on her and in al]l 7 his being [comprehends] her. [He sets her] in front of her eyes, lest he walk in the ways of ... [25]

The first four macarisms are antithetical: they begin with a positive half-line (... *ashre*) and continue with a negative one (... *we-lo*). These formulae concerned with the pursuit of wisdom are followed by the fifth macarism with only one half-line. The following lines comment on it and expand into another poem, which portrays the ideal actions of a wise person. The unit begins with four positive half-lines, followed by four negative ones, a tricola consisting of three half-lines, and other fragmentary remnants of the poem.

The initial series probably contained six to nine macarisms. The first extant macarism hardly initiates the series, as the feminine suffix *he* must go back to an aforementioned feminine noun. Thus, the series would have contained at least six macarisms, five shorter ones and one longer one. Émile Puech argues that the scribes rarely used the number six, and he suggests that there were originally a total of seven to nine macarisms.[26] The number nine might be supported by the structure of the Matthaean series. Yet it should be noted that there is conclusive evidence for five macarisms alone, although George Brooke convincingly prefers to speak of 8+1 or 4+1 macarisms, owing to the different last macarism.[27]

Brooke's observation points to a major structural similarity between the series: Matthew's list of 8+1 is aligned with the closest parallel to the 4+1 macarisms in 4Q525. In 4Q525, the final macarism opens into another related section, a poem on the completed search for wisdom, the wise ones and torah-dedicated life. This literary technique brings to mind Matthew's last macarism, which is commented on by Charles H. Dodd as follows: "Instead of the extreme brevity which characterizes the others, there is a striking fullness of detail in the clause ... Formally, therefore, this ninth beatitude offers at every point a contrast to the others. We may best regard verses 11–12 as a transition to the next following section of the Sermon."[28] It can also be noted that both texts repeat the same elements at the beginning

---

25. The English translations of 4Q525 are my own, but they have been strongly influenced by the previous English translations of the text, to which I am indebted. Particularly influential has been the translation of Michael Wise, et al., published in Donald W. Parry and Emanuel Tov, eds., *The Dead Sea Scrolls Reader: Calendrical and Sapiential Texts* (6 vols.; Leiden: Brill, 2004), 4:246–65.

26. Puech, "Collections of Beatitudes," 356–62.

27. Brooke, "Wisdom of Matthew's Beatitudes," 221.

28. Charles H. Dodd, "The Beatitudes," in *Mélanges bibliques rédigés en l'honneur de André Robert* (Travaux de l'Institut catholique de Paris, 4; Paris: Bloud & Gay, 1956), 404–5.

and end of the *extant* lists; 4Q525 mentions "heart" and Matthew "heaven" in those places.[29]

The resemblance—that a series of compact macarisms is followed by another macarism, which grows into a new unit—suggests that the form exhibited by Matthew's list is rooted in the Hebrew tradition. The oft-proposed idea of the earlier date of Luke's shorter series is not obvious, as 4Q525 now provides evidence of a lengthy list written before the turn of the era.[30] Further speculation on the structural details of the series is possible. Puech, for example, has attempted to observe precise patterns by counting the number of words in the series.[31] For the purposes of this article, however, it is adequate to observe the major structural parallels and proceed to the question of identity formation.

Macarisms—Outlines of Group Prototypes

As briefly mentioned above, an aspect of exhortation is embedded in macarisms, which gives them a pedagogical flavour.[32] Building on this aspect of the macarism formula, I will next discuss how the authors of 4Q525 and Matthew sought to educate their audiences by means of macarisms.

Both series outline an ideal person, a fictitious group prototype, whose portrayal embodies a set of group norms; as such, the macarisms provide their audiences with models to follow and emulate. Such an intention is natural in the case of 4Q525, a teaching that was explicitly given in order to gain wisdom, discipline, and understanding (frag. 1.2). In a similar vein, the series in Matthew is preceded by a statement that Jesus *taught* the disciplines through the macarisms (Matt. 5.1-2), which places them in a pedagogical context in the gospels.[33]

In 4Q525, a group prototype begins to be sketched out, as the fortunate one is said not to slander with his tongue (frag. 2 ii 1). The next macarisms are

---

29. Brooke, "Wisdom of Matthew's Beatitudes," 222.
30. Puech, "Collections of Beatitudes," 359, 362.
31. Puech, "Collections of Beatitudes," 360–1.
32. The exhortative—and even warning—aspect is particularly clear in the case of 4Q525 because of the antithetical form of the macarisms, as pointed out by de Roo, "Is 4Q525 a Qumran Sectarian Document?," 342.
33. In general, the Gospel of Matthew has rich pedagogical resonances. Teaching is part of Jesus' self-understanding (Matt. 23.10; 26.18), and other people call him a teacher (Matt. 8.19; 9.11; 12.38; 17.24; 19.6; 22.16; 22.24; 22.36). The Sermon can be seen as one of Jesus' five speeches or discourses with a pedagogical flavor (Matt. 5.1–7.29; 10.1-42; 13.1-52; 18.1-35; 24.1–25.46). For Jesus as a teacher, sage, and scribe, see Craig S. Keener, *A Commentary on the Gospel of Matthew* (Grand Rapids, MI: Eerdmans, 1999), 54–5.

directed at those who hold fast to "her" statues (i.e., the statutes of wisdom and/or torah) and not to the ways of injustice (frag. 2 ii 1-2), rejoice in "her" instead of bursting forth on the paths of folly (frag. 2 ii 2), and seek "her" with pure hands and not with a deceitful heart (frag. 2 ii 2-3). The final macarism culminates the series and proclaims how the one who attains wisdom walks in torah (frag. 2 ii 3-4); this statement is the most explicit identification of wisdom and torah in the Dead Sea Scrolls (compare, for example, Sir. 24; 4Q185 frags. 1–2 ii 8-15). The next poem continues to outline the exemplary follower, who is said to establish his heart on "her" ways, not to forget "her" in difficulties, and continue to ruminate on "her" (frag. 2 ii 4-8).

This portrait of the group prototype that earnestly seeks wisdom and then attains it reflects the group norms of 4Q525's background community. By means of macarisms and the related poem, the author assures his audience about the importance of leading an honest and considerate life, or to use the phrases of his wisdom tradition, he aims to lead the audience to seek wisdom and reject folly. In the world of 4Q525, this outlook is embodied in torah-piety, which implies that the author is seeking to construct a torah-devoted self-image for the audience. The blessing accounts, which promise divine protection to the pious, concern the results of such conduct (frags. 11–12; 14 ii 6-16). Although the rather abstract language makes it difficult to say anything specific about the nature of the out-group against which the "positive distinctiveness" of 4Q525's audience is measured, it is remarkable that the author congratulates those who find their wisdom in torah, given that there were many ways to speak of revealed wisdom in the late Second Temple era.[34]

The appropriate way of life is characterized in the Matthaean macarisms as well. As explained by Ulrich Luz, rather than documenting a historical episode of Jesus' speech and embedding it in the gospel's narrative thread, the author goes beyond describing "the way things were" and directly addresses his audience, as well as inviting the community to apply Jesus' teaching to the present.[35] Happiness and divine favor are promised to those

---

34. For example, the best-preserved wisdom texts among the Dead Sea Scrolls seem to include explicitly torah-oriented instructions, Sapiential Admonitions B (4Q185) and Beatitudes (4Q525), as well as teachings that assume the importance of torah, but also invoke the revelation of *raz nihyeh*, "the mystery to come" or "the mystery of being." The latter include Instruction (1Q26; 4Q415–8, 418a, 418c, 423) and Mysteries (1Q27; 4Q299–301). In particular, Instruction has received a great deal of scholarly attention. See, e.g., Matthew J. Goff, *The Worldly and Heavenly Wisdom of 4QInstruction* (Studies on the Texts of the Desert of Judea, 50; Leiden: Brill, 2003); Grant Macaskill, *Revealed Wisdom and Inaugurated Eschatology in Ancient Judaism and Early Christianity* (Supplements to the Journal for the Study of Judaism, 115; Leiden: Brill, 2007).

35. Ulrich Luz, *The Theology of the Gospel of Matthew*, trans. J. Bradford Robinson (New Testament Theology; Cambridge: Cambridge University Press, 1995), 44–5.

poor in spirit (Matt. 5.3), the mourning ones (Matt. 5.4), the meek (Matt. 5.5), those who hunger and desire righteousness (Matt. 5.6), the merciful (Matt. 5.7), the pure in heart (Matt. 5.8), peacemakers (Matt. 5.9), and the persecuted (Matt. 5.10-11).

All of these proclamations do not embody an ideal state of affairs that should be pursued; some of them—especially the last two on persecution—rather present an unfortunate reality. Even so, the majority of the designations employed in the macarisms—those poor in spirit, the meek, those who desire righteousness, the merciful, the pure in heart, and peacemakers—mirror group norms.[36] The labels constitute a "catalogue of virtues"[37] and point to behavioral endeavors that the audience should undertake.[38] The flavor of the mentioned group norms is explicitly spiritual; the exemplary person seems to be differentiated from other people through his/her righteousness.[39] The appeal of such spiritual aspects and inner motifs seems to suit the social situation reflected in Matthew; the Jewish-Christian author of the gospel competes with his out-group opponents, named as "the scribes and the Pharisees" (esp. Matt. 23), who were actually very close to his own group.[40] It seems plausible, therefore, that the differences used to demonstrate the "positive distinctiveness" of Matthew's in-group had to be created out of fairly abstract elements.

---

36. On the role of group norms in Matthew's beatitudes, see Esler, "Group Norms and Prototypes," 168–70. As for the macarisms on persecution, it should be noted that although they do not seem to embody group norms in the first place, this does not mean that they could not serve in the construction of group identity in other ways. Suffering as the "prize" of in-group membership may indicate the value of the group and hence increase its cohesion and attractiveness. I thank Nina Nikki for pointing out this aspect of early Christian suffering discourse.

37. Luz, *Matthew 1–7*, 243.

38. Esler, "Group Norms and Prototypes," 170, remarks that instead of naming the members of the in-group, the author makes use of labels that can be regarded as "cognitive representations of group norms."

39. In light of Matt. 5.20, the notion of righteousness indeed seems to serve as a marker that differentiates the addressed community of others, as argued by Philip F. Esler, *The First Christians in Their Social Worlds: Social-Scientific Approaches to New Testament Interpretation* (London: Routledge, 1994), 8.

40. Hence, it is not surprising that the Gospel includes several sections of parenesis directed at the in-group; see Matt. 7.15-23; 13.24-30; 18.15-18; 22.114. For identity formation in Matthew, see Petri Luomanen, "Matthew's Corpus Mixtum in the Light of the Social Identity Approach," in *Voces Clamantium in Deserto: Essays in Honor of Kari Syreeni*, ed. Sven-Olav Back and Matti Kankaanniemi (Studier i exegetik och judaistik utgivna av Teologiska fakulteten vid Åbo Akademi, 11; Åbo: Åbo Akademi University, Faculty of Theology, 2012), 199–215. For Matthew and Judaism, see also Antonio J. Saldarini, *Matthew's Christian-Jewish Community* (Chicago Studies in the History of Judaism; Chicago, IL: The University of Chicago Press, 1994).

As descriptions of acceptable behavior in terms of a positive group prototype demonstrate, the macarisms in 4Q525 and Matthew indicate and crystallize the core values of the background communities, as well as teaching them to initiates. In 4Q525, they reflect such values as wisdom, prudence, torah-piety, and endurance (in addition to frag. 2 ii, see esp. frag. 5). Matthew 5, on the other hand, lists partially overlapping qualities that include spiritual poorness, meekness, mercifulness, purity of heart, peace-seeking mentality, and perseverance in times of persecution.

The virtue of hope is present in both series in one way or another: the poem that follows the macarisms in 4Q525 encourages the audience to keep "her" (i.e., wisdom and/or torah) at the time of trials and distress (frag. 2 ii 5), while Matthew's addressees are guided and encouraged to view their conflicted present situation—including troubles and even persecution—against the promise of future rewards (Matt. 5.11-12). In relation to 4Q525's torah-piety, it should be noted that the Sermon, the immediate literary context of Matthew's macarisms, also associates the aspired life with torah-devotion (Matt. 5.17-20) and promises divine care for the righteous (Matt. 6.33).

In short, the macarisms in 4Q525 and Matthew portray various exemplars that contribute to a more "abstract" prototype, a wise or righteous person respectively, who embodies norms held by the background communities. As such, they offered models to audiences and eventually played a role in character formation.[41] Drawing on research on group norms, Esler points out that the macarisms in Matthew could both describe and prescribe the behavior of the group to which they were addressed.[42] The series in 4Q525 might also depict a particular group; the most obvious example of such is the text's later sectarian audience in the Qumran movement. Yet the aspirational language primarily seems to prescribe ideal conduct. This interpretation echoes the observations made by scholars of social identity that expressions of identity not only reveal existent social categories and mature group identities, but they are visions that create a future social reality.[43]

---

41. The aspect of character formation regarding Matthew's beatitudes has also been pointed out by Charles H. Talbert, *Reading the Sermon on the Mount: Character Formation and Decision Making in Matthew 5–7* (Columbia, SC: University of South Carolina Press, 2004), 29.

42. Esler, "Group Norms and Prototypes," 165. Compare Hogg and Reid, "Social Identity," 12-3.

43. S. Alexander Haslam, Stephen D. Reicher, and Michael J. Platlow, *The New Psychology of Leadership: Identity, Influence and Power* (New York: Psychology Press, 2011), 65, 72, 188.

Macarisms—Invitations to the In-group

The social relevance of macarisms can be further illustrated by an analysis of their performative force. Since texts are rooted in real-life situations and answer questions posed by them, as set out by Carol Newsom, they do not merely reflect the world, but serve as acts that "do something in it and to it."[44] Every word has both the verbal context and the context of situation.[45] Depending on its placement, the word can either maintain or change the current order; this is evident, for example, in the case of blessings and curses that can either include or exclude the addressees.[46]

Therefore, the use of language means performing acts, as has been clarified by speech act theory.[47] Macarisms, like any other words, are intentional acts with inherent social functions.[48] As for their role in 4Q525 and Matthew, which will be addressed next, nothing in these compositions suggests that the series were employed in specific rituals. Yet they involve profoundly performative elements: they create a certain state of affairs—or at least reassert an already existing one.[49]

The macarisms do not remain abstract statements, but become performed in some context; in the cases of 4Q525 and Matthew, it is especially one of education (whether real or imaginary). Since macarisms delineate ideal and/or undesirable conduct, they can be regarded as social markers and acts that disclose who is in and who is out—that is to say, what kind of a person fulfils the criteria set for the wise or righteous person.[50] Such an active

---

44. Newsom, *Self as Symbolic Space*, 16.
45. Kenneth Burke, "What Are the Signs of What? A Theory of 'Entitlement'," in *Language as Symbolic Action: Essays on Life, Literature, and Method*, ed. K. Burke (Berkeley, CA: University of California Press, 1966), 359–79, 359.
46. For other biblical examples, note how the word of God or Jesus can control natural phenomena or heal (cf. Ps. 104.7; 107.20; 147.18; Matt. 8.8; 9.2; Mark 2.5, 9), to mention but a few explicit cases; Anthony C. Thiselton, "The Supposed Power of Words in the Biblical Writings," *Journal of Theological Studies* 25 (1974): 283–99.
47. In particular, see John L. Austin, *How to Do Things with Words: The William James Lectures Delivered at Harvard University in 1955*, ed. J. O. Urmsson and Marina Sbisà (2nd edn.; Oxford: Clarendon, 1975); John R. Searle, *Speech Acts: An Essay in the Philosophy of Language* (Cambridge: Cambridge University Press, 1969).
48. Compare Esler, "Group Norms and Prototypes," 155, who describes the macarisms of Matthew as "a meaningful configuration of language carrying a communication from their composer to his audience."
49. Performance and performative elements clearly are not something restricted to ritual alone; see Roy A. Rappaport, *Ritual and Religion in the Making of Humanity* (Cambridge: Cambridge University Press, 1999), 115.
50. Compare Esler, "Group Norms and Prototypes," 169, who similarly notes that Matthew's macarisms both characterize a social group and differentiate it from other social groups.

role of the series is closely related to their placement in the composition. Remarkably, macarisms appear at the beginning of both 4Q525 and Matthew. Based on the material reconstruction of 4Q525, the series was located in the second column out of 13, following the prologue (of which only frag. 1 remains).[51] Respectively, Matthew's list appears in chapter 5 out of a total of 28 chapters. Furthermore, it occurs at the very beginning of the Sermon, which is a self-contained literary unit.

The placements of the series within the compositions are barely coincidental considering to their significant social implications. In both 4Q525 and Matthew, macarisms congratulate the target audiences, invite them to participate in the promised blessings, and function as promises that bind the audiences to the texts' agenda already at the outset. Hence, they are directed to those who identify themselves with the description of the exemplary fortunate person (at least to some extent). Janzen's remark that the effect of macarisms was less direct than that of blessings is valid, but while they did not create a new state of "being fortunate," they confirmed an emerging or already existing state.[52] As such, the macarisms create a sense of security, contribute to the addressees' sense of belonging to an in-group, and invite them to remain within it. To use the words of self-categorization theory, the macarisms enhance the self-categorization process of the audience as they make the recipients understand themselves as part of (and identical to) the happy and blessed people; these people constitute one "class of stimuli," which is contrasted against another such class, the out-group not involved in the same state of happiness.

Admittedly, the language used to describe in-group behaviour in the macarisms of 4Q525 and Matthew is rather generalizing.[53] The intended process of identity formation is not, however, necessarily any weaker because of the nature of the language. On the contrary, studies on linguistic intergroup bias have shown that the use of generalizing language is not uncom-

---

51. For the material reconstruction of 4Q525, see Elisa Uusimäki, *Turning Proverbs towards Torah: An Analysis of 4Q525* (Studies on the Texts of the Desert of Judah, 117; Leiden: Brill, 2016), 23–46.

52. This observation is in accord with the idea that macarisms can serve as a sort of entrance liturgy. Brooke, "Wisdom of Matthew's Beatitudes," 233, associates the macarisms in 4Q525 and Matthew 5 with ancient initiation performances undertaken "when new members joined the community." Brooke draws on the observations of Hans Dieter Betz, *Essays on the Sermon on the Mount*, trans. L. L. Welborn (Philadelphia, PA: Fortress, 1985), 17–36, 26–7, who addresses, in relation to Matthew's first macarism, the function of a macarism found in the Homeric Hymn to Demeter and used in the initiation to the Eleusinian mysteries.

53. Or, in the case of 4Q525's antithetical macarisms, this may concern the description of both in- and out-groups, even though the emphasis is on the former.

mon in attempts to induce social stereotypes because vague statements are beyond verification and falsification.[54] Similarly, the fairly abstract idioms of 4Q525 fragment 2 ii and Matthew 5 enable a range of people to take part in the intended process of identity construction, rather than excluding part of the audience already at the outset.

Applied Kingship and Identity

Another shared aspect of identity created in 4Q525 and Matthew is how these texts seem to provide their audiences with "royal" self-images that draw on the Solomonic tradition.[55] In other words, King Solomon, the sage *par excellence* in the Jewish tradition (cf. 1 Kgs 4.29-34), can be seen as providing a royal prototype whom the addressees can emulate, at least to some extent. This is natural in that prototypicality, the membership in a given category, is understood as a sliding "matter of degree"; each member represents it more or less.[56]

The macarisms of 4Q525 are preceded by a prologue that probably referred to the quasi-Solomonic authorship of the text. This is suggested by the extant formula "which he spoke in the wisdom given by God to him" (frag. 1.1), since God is said to have granted great wisdom and understanding to Solomon (1 Kgs 5.9, 26). Regardless of the prologue, the prominent use of Proverbs elsewhere in the text, including the macarisms (cf. frag. 2 ii 1-2 and Prov. 3.18; frag. 2 ii 3 and Prov. 3.13), demonstrates that 4Q525 follows the Proverbs tradition associated with Solomon (Prov. 1.1).[57] Interestingly, the Sermon refers to the glory of Solomon as well, although not in the context of

---

54. Klaus Fiedler and Jeannette Schmid, "How Language Contributes to Persistence of Stereotypes as well as Other, More General, Intergroup Issues," in *Blackwell Handbook of Social Psychology: Intergroup Processes*, ed. Rupert Brown and Sam Gaertner (Oxford: Blackwell, 2001), 261–80, 267, 272.

55. For the reception history of Solomon, see Joseph Verheyden, *The Figure of Solomon in Jewish, Christian and Islamic Tradition: King, Sage and Architect* (Themes in Biblical Narrative, 16; Leiden: Brill, 2013). It should be noted that the shared scriptural resonances of the series are not exhausted by the links to Solomonic tradition; in particular, compare Ps. 24.4, 4Q525 frag. 2 ii 3-4, and Matt. 5.8. Both 4Q525 and the Sermon also seem to echo Ps. 37 (cf. 4Q525 frag. 2 ii 8 and Ps. 37.31; Matt. 5.5 and Ps. 37.11). The same sources of inspiration might point to some kind of "curriculum" of scriptural texts in early Jewish education.

56. Michael Sinding, "After Definitions: Genre, Categories, and Cognitive Science," *Genre* 35 (2002): 181–219, 186.

57. For the use of Proverbs in 4Q525, see Uusimäki, "Use of Scripture in 4QBeatitudes," 71–97.

the macarisms, but in the next chapter (Matt. 6.29; cf. 12.42).[58] Despite being more subtle and less explicit than the Gospel of John, Matthew's underlying wisdom motif, the idea of Jesus as God's wisdom (cf. Matt. 11.19, 29; 12.42), also should not be forgotten, as it is another factor that points to the continuum of the (royal) wisdom tradition in Matthew.[59]

The presence of the royal tradition connected to Solomon highlights the Hebrew roots of 4Q525 and Matthew.[60] Even though the Davidic monarchy had ceased to exist long before, the theme of kingship continued to live on in the Jewish and early Christian imaginations. The link to Solomon is also relevant in terms of target audiences and their identities, since both 4Q525 and Matthew seem to inform about a phenomenon that could be designated as the "democratization of kingship"—that (metaphorical) kingship does not belong only to the royal figure(s), but can be attained by other people as well—even though they may adapt the previous tradition with different outcomes.

The concept of "democratization of kingship" has been advanced by Judith Newman, who argues that in Wisdom of Solomon, the idiom of kingship has been adapted to serve the idea of "all human creatures as regents" (cf. Wis. 5.16; 6.20-21; 9). Wisdom no longer belonged to kings alone. The idea being that one king, a Judahite monarch, could be rejected and kingship democratized because all righteous Jews are, as it were, monarchs.[61] As Newman phrases this notion of kingship: "'Everyman' can be a king, to the degree that it is possible for all to gain wisdom."[62]

Although the kingship idiom is sparse in the extant parts of 4Q525—the series of macarisms is followed in line 2 ii 9 by a fragmentary reference to crowning and being seated with kings—the text's profound participation

---

58. For Solomon in Matthew, see Walter Brueggeman, *Solomon: Israel's Ironic Icon of Human Achievement* (Studies on Personalities of the Old Testament; Columbia, SC: University of South Carolina Press, 2005), 245–53.

59. For Jesus as God's wisdom and word, see James D. G. Dunn, *Christology in the Making: A New Testament Inquiry into the Origins of the Doctrine of the Incarnation* (2nd edn.; Grand Rapids, MI: Eerdmans, 1989), 163–250.

60. The Solomonic attribution functions similarly elsewhere in Jewish literature. As for Proverbs, the sages behind the work attempted to demonstrate "that their tradition was firmly in line with the institution of the house of David" by the means of the superscription; see Leo G. Perdue, *Proverbs* (Interpretation: A Bible Commentary for Teaching and Preaching; Louisville, KY: John Knox, 2000), 64–5.

61. Judith H. Newman, "The Democratization of Kingship in Wisdom of Solomon," in *The Idea of Biblical Interpretation: Essays in Honor of James L. Kugel*, ed. Hindy Najman and Judith H. Newman (Supplements to the Journal for the Study of Judaism, 83; Leiden: Brill, 2004), 309–28, esp. 324–8.

62. Newman, "The Democratization of Kingship," 327.

in the Proverbs tradition, associated with Solomon, similarly hints at the process of "democratizing kingship." The extant evidence makes it difficult to draw any definite conclusions, but it seems possible to read 4Q525 so that the addressee, who studies the text and follows the exemplary behavior described in the macarisms, is promised with rewards and metaphorically set in the royal court. The implied message is that all wise and torah-dedicated Jews are worthy of kingship; it does not belong only to King Solomon, the prototypical sage, but can be attained by leading a wise and pious life.

Traces of the democratization of kingship also appear in Matthew. As pointed out by Walter Brueggeman, in the Sermon, where Jesus serves as the instructor, the author seems to deconstruct the kingship of Solomon by downplaying his glory and wealth in comparison with the simple beauty of flowers (Matt. 6.28-29).[63] To this I would add that the Sermon does not reject but rather transforms the theme of kingship in line with the idea that all followers of Jesus can metaphorically become royal figures, in the sense that they are promised receipt of the heavenly kingdom.[64] The motif is repeated twice: the first macarism promises the kingdom of heaven to those poor in spirit (Matt. 5.3), whereas the eighth macarism prophesies the kingdom to those who are persecuted for the sake of righteousness (Matt. 5.10).[65] The final macarism further mentions the heavenly rewards of the righteous (Matt. 5.12).[66]

In short, while 4Q525 (like texts such as Wisdom of Solomon)[67] seems to promise metaphorical kingship to wise and devout Jews, Matthew

63. Brueggeman, *Solomon*, 246–7.

64. Regarding the "royal" content of Jesus' message, compare with the idea that Jesus' ethic could be understood as "democratised aristocratic ethic" insofar as it "makes the values and norms of the upper class accessible to all." This view has been presented by Gerd Theissen, *A Theory of Primitive Christian Religion*, trans. John Bowden (London: SCM, 1999), 82.

65. For the different dimensions of the concept of kingdom of heaven in Matthew, see, e.g., Jack Dean Kingsbury, *Matthew: Structure, Christology, Kingdom* (Philadelphia, PA: Fortress, 1975), 137–49.

66. While Matthew uses kingship as a positive honorary title, this does not apply to all kingship language in the New Testament. For example, Paul's pejorative claim in 1 Cor. 4.8 is to be understood over against the Stoic idea of sages as kings due to their capability to rule themselves. Because this notion had widespread influence and became part of popular philosophy, kingship could, broadly speaking, designate high status in the Greco-Roman society in the first century CE. In 1 Cor. 4.6-13, Paul thus juxtaposes the low status of the Christian apostles against the fictitious "kingship" of some Corinthians with high status, scolding them for their pride; Dale B. Martin, *The Corinthian Body* (New Haven, CT: Yale University Press, 1995), 65–6.

67. Compare the promise of kingship to the wise in 4 Macc. 2.21-23 and Philo's comments on philosophy as the royal road to God the King in *Post.* 101–2 (cf. Num. 20.17).

democratizes the royal wisdom tradition differently by making followers of Jesus eligible to inherit the kingdom of heaven.[68] In late Second Temple Jewish and early Christian imagination, kingship is not only a characteristic of the prototypical sage, Solomon, but it can be attained by people through their wisdom and piety.

Conclusions

In this article, I have reflected on the macarisms of 4Q525 and Matthew 5 from the viewpoint of identity formation. Points of contact between these series are not confined to structural similarities, but cover aspects related to identity formation. As enumerators of group norms, both lists sketch out positive prototypes that the audiences should emulate. The macarisms serve as social markers as they delineate in- and out-groups. The emphasis is placed on the construction of a positive in-group identity, as is suggested by the placement of the series at the beginning of the compositions. This placement suggests that the series serve as an invitation to take part in the promised blessings and are meant to bind the audience to the texts' agenda from the outset. Further light can be shed on identity formation by an analysis of how both 4Q525 and Matthew democratize kingship, although with different outcomes. In 4Q525, kingship belongs to those wise ones who are devoted to torah, while in Matthew the righteous followers of Jesus become metaphorical royal figures insofar as they are said to inherit the heavenly kingdom.

Biographical Note

Elisa Uusimäki works on the literary and cultural history of Judaism in antiquity, serving as an associate professor at Aarhus University. She also holds the title of docent at the University of Helsinki. Uusimäki has published on topics such as wisdom, ethics and exemplarity, early biblical interpretation, travel in antiquity, the Dead Sea Scrolls, and Hellenistic Judaism.

---

68. Note also that both 4Q525 and Matthew adapt the wisdom tradition into an eschatological worldview, but the matter of eschatology is more urgent in Matthew; in this regard, see Brooke, "Wisdom of Matthew's Beatitudes," 227. Moreover, for Jesus as a social marker between Matthew's group and other contemporary Jewish groups, see Petri Luomanen, "Social-Scientific Modeling in Biblical and Related Studies," *Perspectives on Science* 21 (2013): 202–20, 210–4.

Bibliography

Assavavirulhakarn, Prapod. "Blessing," 2:979–85 in *Encyclopedia of Religion*. Edited by Lindsay Jones. 15 volumes. 2nd edn. Detroit, MI: Macmillan, 2005.

Austin, John L. *How to Do Things with Words: The William James Lectures at Harvard University in 1955*. Edited by J. O. Urmsson and Marina Sbisà. 2nd edn. Oxford: Clarendon, 1975. https://doi.org/10.1093/acprof:oso/9780198245537.001.0001

Bertram, Georg. "Μακάριος in the LXX and Judaism," 4.364–7 in *Theological Dictionary of the New Testament*. Edited by Gerhard Kittel. 10 volumes. Grand Rapids, MI: Eerdmans, 1967.

Betz, Hans Dieter. *Essays on the Sermon on the Mount*. Translated by L. L. Welborn. Philadelphia, PA: Fortress, 1985.

Boon, James A. *Other Tribes, Other Scribes: Symbolic Anthropology in the Comparative Study of Cultures, Histories, Religions, and Texts*. Cambridge: Cambridge University Press, 1982.

Brooke, George J. "The Wisdom of Matthew's Beatitudes," *Scripture Bulletin* 19 (1989): 35–41.

—*The Dead Sea Scrolls and the New Testament*. Minneapolis, MN: Fortress Press, 2005.

Brueggeman, Walter. *Solomon: Israel's Ironic Icon of Human Achievement*. Studies on Personalities of the Old Testament. Columbia, SC: University of South Carolina Press, 2005.

Burke, Kenneth. "What Are the Signs of What? A Theory of 'Entitlement'," 359–79 in *Language as Symbolic Action: Essays on Life, Literature, and Method*. Edited by K. Burke. Berkeley, CA: University of California Press, 1966. https://doi.org/10.1525/9780520340664-023

Charlesworth, James H. "The Qumran Beatitudes (4Q525) and the New Testament (Mt 5:3–11; Lk 6:20–26)," *Revue d'Histoire et de Philosophie Religieuses* 80 (2000): 13–35. https://doi.org/10.3406/rhpr.2000.5590

Dodd, Charles H. "The Beatitudes," 404–5 in *Mélanges bibliques rédigés en l'honneur de André Robert*. Travaux de l'Institut catholique de Paris, 4. Paris: Bloud & Gay, 1956.

Dunn, James D. G. *Christology in the Making: A New Testament Inquiry into the Origins of the Doctrine of the Incarnation*. 2nd edn. Grand Rapids, MI: Eerdmans, 1989.

Esler, Philip F. *The First Christians in Their Social Worlds: Social-Scientific Approaches to New Testament Interpretation*. London: Routledge, 1994.

—"Group Norms and Prototypes in Matthew 5.3-12: A Social Identity Interpretation of the Matthean Beatitudes," 147–72 in Tucker and Baker, eds., *T&T Clark Handbook to Social Identity in the New Testament*, 2014.

—"An Outline of Social Identity Theory," 13–39 in Tucker and Baker, eds., *T&T Clark Handbook to Social Identity in the New Testament*, 2014.

Fabry, Heinz-Josef. "Der Makarismus – mehr als nur eine weisheitliche Lehrform: Gedanken zu dem neu-edierten Text 4Q525," 362–71 in *Alttestamentlicher Glaube und Biblische Theologie: Festschrift für Horst Dietrich Preuß zum 65 Geburtstag*. Edited by Jutta Hausmann and Hans-Jürgen Zobel. Stuttgart: Kohlhammer, 1992.

Fiedler, Klaus, and Jeannette Schmid. "How Language Contributes to Persistence of Stereotypes as Well as Other, More General, Intergroup Issues," 261–80 in *Blackwell Handbook of Social Psychology: Intergroup Processes*. Edited by Rupert Brown and Sam Gaertner. Oxford: Blackwell, 2001. https://doi.org/10.1002/9780470693421.ch13

Fitzmyer, Joseph A. "A Palestinian Collection of Beatitudes," 509–15 in Vol. 1 of *The Four Gospels 1992: Festschrift Frans Neirynck*. Edited by F. van Segbroeck, C. M. Tuckett, G. Van Belle, and J. Verheyden. Bibliotheca ephemeridum theologicarum Lovaniensium, 100. Leuven: Leuven University Press, 1992.

Goff, Matthew J. *The Worldly and Heavenly Wisdom of 4QInstruction*. Studies on the Texts of the Desert of Judah, 50. Leiden: Brill, 2003. https://doi.org/10.1163/9789004350489

—*Discerning Wisdom: The Sapiential Literature of the Dead Sea Scrolls*. Supplements to Vetus Testamentum, 116. Leiden: Brill, 2007. https://doi.org/10.1163/ej.9789004147492.i-372

Guelich, Robert A. "Matthean Beatitudes: 'Entrance-Requirements' or Eschatological Blessings?" *Journal of Biblical Literature* 95 (1976): 415–34. https://doi.org/10.2307/3265274

Hanson, K. C. "How Honourable! How Shameful! A Cultural Analysis of Matthew's Makarisms and Reproaches," *Semeia* 68 (1994): 81–111.

Haslam, S. Alexander, Stephen D. Reicher, and Michael J. Platlow. *The New Psychology of Leadership: Identity, Influence and Power*. New York: Psychology Press, 2011.

Hogg, Michael A., and Scott A. Reid. "Social Identity, Self-Categorization, and the Communication of Group Norms," *Communication Theory* 16 (2006): 7–30. https://doi.org/10.1111/j.1468-2885.2006.00003.x

Janzen, Waldemar. "'AŠRÊ in the Old Testament," *Harvard Theological Review* 58 (1965): 215–26. https://doi.org/10.1017/S0017816000031321

Kampen, John I. *Wisdom Literature*. Eerdmans Commentaries on the Dead Sea Scrolls. Grand Rapids, MI: Eerdmans, 2011.

Käser, Walter. "Beobachtungen zum alttestamentlichen Makarismus," *Zeitschrift für die alttestamentliche Wissenschaft* 82 (1970): 235–50.

Keener, Craig S. *A Commentary on the Gospel of Matthew*. Grand Rapids, MI: Eerdmans, 1999.

Kingsbury, Jack Dean. *Matthew: Structure, Christology, Kingdom*. Philadelphia, PA: Fortress, 1975.

Lichtenberger, Hermann. "Makarisms in Matthew 5:3ff. in Their Jewish Context," 40–56 in *The Sermon on the Mount and Its Jewish Setting*. Edited by H. J. Becker and S. Ruzer. Cahiers de la Revue biblique, 60. Paris: Gabalda, 2005.

Luomanen, Petri. Matthew's Corpus Mixtum in the Light of the Social Identity Approach," 199–215 in *Voces Clamantium in Deserto: Essays in Honor of Kari Syreeni*. Edited by S. O. Back and M. Kankaanniemi. Studier i exegetik och judaistik utgivna av Teologiska fakulteten vid Åbo Akademi, 11. Åbo: Åbo Akademi University, Faculty of Theology, 2012.

—"Social-Scientific Modeling in Biblical and Related Studies," *Perspectives on Science* 21 (2013): 202–20. https://doi.org/10.1162/POSC_a_00094

Luz, Ulrich. *The Theology of the Gospel of Matthew*. Translated by J. Bradford Robinson. New Testament Theology. Cambridge: Cambridge University Press, 1995.

Macaskill, Grant. *Revealed Wisdom and Inaugurated Eschatology in Ancient Judaism and Early Christianity*. Supplements to the Journal for the Study of Judaism, 115. Leiden: Brill, 2007. https://doi.org/10.1163/ej.9789004155824.i-294

Martin, Dale B. *The Corinthian Body*. New Haven, CT: Yale University Press, 1995.

Mroczek, Eva. "Thinking Digitally about the Dead Sea Scrolls: Book History before and beyond the Book," *Book History* 14 (2011): 241–69. https://doi.org/10.1353/bh.2011.0006

Newman, Judith H. "The Democratization of Kingship in Wisdom of Solomon," 309–28 in *The Idea of Biblical Interpretation: Essays in Honor of James L. Kugel*. Edited by Hindy Najman and Judith H. Newman. Supplements to the Journal for the Study of Judaism, 83. Leiden: Brill, 2004.

Oakes, Penelope J., S. Alexander Haslam, and John C. Turner. "The Role of Prototypicality in Group Influence and Cohesion: Contextual Variation in the Graded Structure of Social Categories," 75–92 in *Social Identity: International Perspectives*. Edited by Stephen Worchel, J. Francisco Morales, Dario Páez, and Jean-Claude Deschamps. London: Sage, 1998. https://doi.org/10.4135/9781446279205.n6

Parry, Donald W., and Emanuel Tov, eds. *The Dead Sea Scrolls Reader: Calendrical and Sapiential Texts*. 6 volumes. Leiden: Brill, 2004.

Perdue, Leo G. *Proverbs*. Intepretation: A Bible Commentary for Teaching and Preaching. Louisville, KY: John Knox, 2000.

Puech, Émile. "Un hymne essénien en partie retrouvé et les Béatitudes," *Revue de Qumrân* 13 (1988): 59–88.

—"4Q525 et les péricopes des Béatitudes en Ben Sira et Matthieu," *Revue biblique* 98 (1991): 80–106.

—"The Collections of Beatitudes in Hebrew and in Greek (4Q525, 1–4 and Matt 5, 3–12)," 353–68 in *Early Christianity in Context: Monuments and Documents: Essays in Honour of Emmanuel Testa*. Edited by Frédéric Manns and Eugenio Alliata. Studium Biblicum Franciscanum Collectio Maior, 38. Jerusalem: Franciscan, 1993.

—"4QBéatitudes," 115–78 in *Qumrân Grotte 4 – XVIII: Textes Hébreux (4Q521–4Q528, 4Q576–4Q579)*. Edited by Émile Puech. Discoveries in the Judean Desert, 25. Oxford: Clarendon, 1998.

Rappaport, Roy A. *Ritual and Religion in the Making of Humanity*. Cambridge Studies in Social and Cultural Anthropology, 110. Cambridge: Cambridge University Press, 1999.

de Roo, Jacqueline C. R. "Is 4Q525 a Qumran Sectarian Document?," 338–67 in *The Scrolls and the Scriptures: Qumran Fifty Years After*. Edited by Stanley E. Porter and Craig A. Evans. Journal for the Study of Pseudepigrapha Supplement Series, 26. Sheffield: Sheffield Academic Press, 1997.

Saldarini, Antonio J. *Matthew's Christian-Jewish Community*. Chicago Studies in the History of Judaism. Chicago, IL: The University of Chicago Press, 1994.

Searle, John R. *Speech Acts: An Essay in the Philosophy of Language*. Cambridge: Cambridge University Press, 1969. https://doi.org/10.1017/CBO9781139173438

Sinding, Michael. "After Definitions: Genre, Categories, and Cognitive Science," *Genre* 35 (2002): 181–219. https://doi.org/10.1215/00166928-35-2-181

Tajfel, Henri. *Human Groups and Social Categories: Studies in Social Psychology*. Cambridge: Cambridge University Press, 1981.

Talbert, Charles H. *Reading the Sermon on the Mount: Character Formation and Decision Making in Matthew 5–7*. Columbia, SC: University of South Carolina Press, 2004.

Terrien, Samuel. "Wisdom in the Psalter," 51–72 in *In Search of Wisdom: Essays in Memory of John G. Gammie*. Edited by Leo G. Perdue, William J. Wiseman, and Bernard B. Scott. Louisville, KY: Westminster John Knox, 1993.

Theissen, Gerd. *A Theory of Primitive Christian Religion*. Translated by John Bowden. London: SCM, 1999.

Thiselton, Anthony C. "The Supposed Power of Words in the Biblical Writings," *The*

Journal of Theological Studies 25 (1974): 283–99. https://doi.org/10.1093/jts/XXV.2.283

Tucker, J. Brian, and Coleman A. Baker, eds. *T&T Clark Handbook to Social Identity in the New Testament*. London: Bloomsbury/T&T Clark, 2014.

Uusimäki, Elisa. "Use of Scripture in 4QBeatitudes: A Torah-Adjustment to Proverbs 1–9," *Dead Sea Discoveries* 20 (2013): 71–97. https://doi.org/10.1163/15685179-12341245

—*Turning Proverbs towards Torah: An Analysis of 4Q525*. Studies on the Texts of the Desert of Judah, 117. Leiden: Brill, 2016. https://doi.org/10.1163/9789004313415

—"Wisdom, Scripture, and Identity Formation in 4QBeatitudes," 175–86 in *Social Memory and Social Identity in the Study of Early Judaism and Early Christianity*. Edited by Samuel Byrskog, Raimo Hakola, and Jutta Jokiranta. Novum Testamentum et Orbis Antiquus / Studien zur Umwelt des Neuen Testaments, 116. Göttingen: Vandenhoeck & Ruprecht, 2016.

Verheyden, Joseph. *The Figure of Solomon in Jewish, Christian and Islamic Tradition: King, Sage and Architect*. Themes in Biblical Narrative, 16. Leiden: Brill, 2013. https://doi.org/10.1163/9789004242913

Viviano, Benedict T. "Eight Beatitudes at Qumran and in Matthew?," *Svensk Exegetisk Årsbok* 58 (1993): 71–84.

Chapter Twelve

Remembering the Sermon in the Mountains of France

Alicia J. Batten

"Do you think all we are is what we remember?"
—Mariam Toews, *All My Puny Sorrows*

Introduction

The story of events in the Plateau Vivarais-Lignon, or "the Mountain," of France during the Second World War is now familiar to many. Books, films, and articles have been produced describing the efforts of the region's inhabitants who collaborated with persecuted people, many of them Jews who were fleeing from the French authorities and eventually from the German occupiers. The Plateau, especially the town of Le Chambon-sur-Lignon, has been celebrated, both as an example of altruism and as a prescription for nonviolent resistance. However, some works have received criticism for inaccuracies, or for contributing more to the "commemoration" and "mythologization" of events in the region, rather than to a historically accurate account. In particular, the emphasis in some of the work upon the Protestant pastor in the village of Le Chambon-sur-Lignon, André Trocmé, has provoked reactions from various quarters.[1]

---

1. One of the first accounts of events in the plateau was written by Philip Hallie, a WWII veteran and philosopher from the United States. His book, *Lest Innocent Blood Be Shed* (New York: Harper Perennial, 1994 [London: Michael Joseph, 1979]), unfortunately contained some historical errors and centered on the work of André and Magda Trocmé without sufficient attention to the many other participants in the region. There have been other contentious issues as well. Pierre Sauvage's poignant film, *Weapons of the Spirit* (Los Angeles: Le Chambon Foundation, 1989), the French version of which received a very positive reception at the Cannes Film Festival in 1987, spawned strong reaction from several people involved in the efforts to help people during the war because it suggested (but did not assert) that one of the German occupiers, Major Julius Schmäling, the commander of the German garrison in Le Puy, might have conveniently overlooked some of the illegal activities taking place. In addition, significant debates remain regarding how many Jews were actually assisted, and the roles of various individuals such as Schmäling as well as Robert Bach, the French prefect of the Haute-Loire region. Moreover, there is considerable disagreement regarding to what extent nonviolence factored in the resistance movement. These issues, and others, were discussed

Several commemorative events have occurred, including an official visit to Le Chambon in 2004 by French President Jacques Chirac accompanied by concentration camp survivor and French politician, Simone Veil. During the visit, Chirac declared that the Plateau had been the "conscience" of France. Later, in 2007 while honouring the "les justes" of France at the Pantheon in Paris, Chirac referred to Trocmé and to Le Chambon, the name of which, he said, resonates in our hearts today and forever.[2] Barack Obama also recalled Le Chambon during a 2009 Remembrance of the Holocaust event in the United States, and stated that 5000 Jews were saved in the area, "one life saved for each [of the village's] 5000 residents."[3] Indeed, hundreds of lives were saved because of the efforts of the people in the Plateau, but the actual number of people assisted remains debated.

Jews and others fleeing from the Nazis were welcomed sometimes as paying tourists[4] but also hidden away on farms, provided with false papers, and aided to escape across the border into Switzerland. Residents of the Mountain—Huguenots, Roman Catholics, Jews, members of small Christian groups such as the "darbysts"[5]—and those who did not identify with any religious tradition, welcomed people, often at great risk to themselves. Not all were committed to nonviolent resistance, and various individuals, such as members of the *maquis*, engaged in direct violence.

Some historians, however, are concerned about how the history of events in the Plateau has been told, and what purposes such "tellings" could serve. Does commemoration, in particular, simplify or distort the complexity of what actually happened, and the multiple motives for why the area's inhabitants assisted people?[6] Has the story become a kind of symbol of the French

---

at a colloquium convened in Le Chambon in 1990. See Pierre Bolle, ed., *Le Plateau Vivarais-Lignon: Accueil et Résistance 1939–1944* (Le Chambon-sur-Lignon: Société d'histoire de la Montagne, 1992).

2. For a review of the reception of the story of the plateau, see François Boulet, *Histoire de la Montagne-refuge aux limites de la Haute-Loire et de l'Ardeche. La montagne, de la Réforme protestante à la seconde guerre mondiale. Le Chambon-sur-Lignon, Tence, Fay-sur-Lignon, Saint Agrève, Le Mazet-Saint-Voy et leurs environs* (Polignac: Les Éditions du Roure, 2008), 307–14. More recently, Patrick Henry has provided a review of much of the secondary literature in his "Le Chambon-sur-Lignon," *The French Review* 89 (2016): 83–96.

3. Barack Obama "Holocaust Days of Remembrance Commemoration Address" (23 April, 2009) https://www.americanrhetoric.com/speeches/barackobama/barackobamaholocaustdaysofremembrance.htm.

4. Boulet, *Histoire de la Montagne,* 177.

5. French term for followers of the ideas of John Nelson Darby.

6. This is the concern of Marianne Ruel Robins, in "A Grey Site of Memory: Le Chambon-sur-Lignon and Protestant Exceptionalism on the Plateau Vivarais-Lignon," *Church History* 82 (2013): 317–52; and her subsequent publication in French on the

Resistance? Have the lives of these particular Protestants come to be representative of the Protestant experience more generally in France? The story is especially contentious because witnesses to some of the events are still alive and have their own memories of what occurred. Perhaps it is appropriate to describe the story as on the border between Pierre Nora's understandings of memory and history. On the one hand, it remains a memory, and as Nora has written, memory is always changing, and subject to the dialectic between remembrances and amnesia. But on the other hand, the narrative is part of the reconstruction of history and, as such, eternally problematic and incomplete.[7]

Despite these complexities, what took place in this remote area of France during the Second World War has much to tell us. French historian François Boulet states that the history of the Mountain, which includes both profound religious and moral dimensions, allows us to live better, now and in the future. It permits us to hope, he says.[8] Death, betrayal, selfishness, and conflict were part of the "life" on the Mountain, but there were also exceptional acts of solidarity, compassion, and courage, committed by a variety of persons. Although historians may disagree about the roles of specific individuals and motivations, overall the number of people who risked arrest and possible execution to assist others, regardless of what propelled them to do so, is striking. Narratives of such accounts, despite their contested and incomplete nature, enable others to live more engaged and meaningful lives because they inspire; they hold out examples of what others can aspire to be and to do. This feature accounts, in part, for why some are drawn to such stories, regardless of their religious, ethnic, or political identity.

Thus, memories or stories serve important purposes. As the authors of *Habits of the Heart* wrote in 1985, "stories ... make up a tradition [and] contain conceptions of character, of what a good person is like, and of the virtues that define such a character."[9] This is in part why stories and memories are also so contested; they matter to social groups. The ongoing

---

same theme, "Les Justes, une autre 'Histoire Périlleuse.' Histoire et Mémoire Protestantes sur le Plateau Vivarais-Lignon," *Revue d'Histoire de l'Eglise de France* 101 (2015): 95–120.

7. See Pierre Nora, *Les Lieux de mémoire*. Vol. 1 (Paris: Gallimard, 1986), 25. Nora is cited by Aziza Gril-Mariotte, "Des commémorations aux musées, la patrimonialisation d'un territoire," in *La Montagne Refuge: Accueil et Sauvetage des Juifs autour du Chambon-sur-Lignon*, ed. Patrick Cabanel, Philippe Joutard, Jacques Sémelin, and Annette Wievorka (Paris: Albin Michel, 2013), 307–21, 321.

8. Boulet, *Histoire de la Montagne-refuge*, 319.

9. Robert N. Bellah, et al., *Habits of the Heart: Commitment and Individualism in American Life* (New York: Harper & Row, 1985), 153.

disagreement about what happened in France is only one small example of contention over what and how to remember.

This brief description of the debates surrounding the Mountain underscores the need to attend to social memory. The study of social memory has emerged as a significant field within the social sciences, and is used now in a variety of disciplines, including biblical studies and early Christianity.[10] Given the task of this volume, namely, to determine how cognitive and social science methodologies can assist in understanding dimensions of the Sermon on the Mount, I will employ insights from social memory studies in the interpretation and use of the Sermon by one of the Mountain's most famous inhabitants, André Trocmé.

Philip Hallie focused on Trocmé in his well-known book, *Lest Innocent Blood be Shed*, and the pastor receives considerable attention in Pierre Sauvage's documentary, *Weapons of the Spirit*, although Sauvage broadens the discussion to include other pastors, members of the resistance, and a variety of other religious groups. As indicated above, some have challenged this emphasis upon Trocmé,[11] but the stress upon a particular individual at a dramatic historical moment is not new, and is perhaps, as Barry Schwarz has argued, a consequence of humanity's penchant for "oneness."[12] It is easier to remember particular individuals associated with historic incidents as heroes as opposed to sorting out a series of events involving multiple and relatively ordinary people. It is tempting to commemorate such individuals, and to render them as symbols of an ideal, rather than to remember an event or a movement as a complicated system of factors with many participants. As Schwartz says, to "give credence to all who deserve it … would make history less meaningful and reduce the clarity of the ideal they would represent."[13] Many studies of the Plateau Vivarais-Lignon since the pub-

---

10. See, e.g., Alan Kirk and Tom Thatcher, *Memory, Tradition, and Text: Uses of the Past in Early Christianity* (Leiden: Brill, 2005).

11. A recent challenge comes from the popular level book by Caroline Moorhead, *Village of Secrets: Defying the Nazis in Vichy France* (Toronto: Random House Canada, 2014). Unfortunately, Moorehead's book contains several factual errors and some overall inconsistencies. See reviews by Stephanie Corazza, "Review of Caroline Moorhead, *Village of Secrets: Defying the Nazis in Vichy France*," *Contemporary Church History Quarterly* 21 (2015), (available at https://contemporarychurchhistory.org), and Pierre Sauvage, "Does 'Village of Secrets' Falsify French Rescue during the Holocaust?" *Tablet Magazine* Online (31 October, 2014), https://www.tabletmag.com/jewish-arts-and-culture/books/186652/moorehead-le-chambon

12. See Barry Schwartz, "Collective Forgetting and the Symbolic Power of Oneness: The Strange Apotheosis of Rosa Parks," *Social Psychology Quarterly* 72 (2009): 123–42.

13. Schwartz, "Collective Forgetting," 140.

lication of Hallie's book have attempted to give such credence to a much broader spectrum of people, but perhaps due to this predilection for "oneness," Trocmé has become somewhat famous in the story of Le Chambon.

The purpose of this essay, however, is not to argue for or against Trocmé's importance. Memory wars aside, he remains, for many, a fascinating and important figure as does his wife, Magda.[14] Rather than entering into the discussion of the degree to which Trocmé influenced the course of events, this essay examines his interpretation of the Sermon, the presumption being that "interpretation," even of a written text, can be a type of remembering. Of course, the fact that the Sermon is in the Bible and part of Jesus' teaching are fundamental reasons for its value to Trocmé and his community. However, using social memory theory as a heuristic tool affirms that dimensions of Trocmé's identity, experience, and social frameworks are fundamental contributors to explaining why and how the Sermon was deeply significant to him.

Social Memory

Paul Ricœur, who for three years directly after the war taught at Collège Cévenol, a school in Le Chambon founded by Trocmé and his colleague Edouard Theis, reminds us that the link between consciousness and the past is memory, noting that "since Saint Augustine memory is the *present of the past*."[15] Memories are the source of stories that are told and retold, often articulating moral purposes, as mentioned above. This is why memory is so important to identity. "Who 'we' are depends upon who 'we' were, not only because we often see ourselves as continuous with previous generations, but because the substance of that continuity provides us with moral lessons (though not necessarily those intended by earlier generations)," writes sociologist Jeffrey Olick.[16] Telling stories, or remembering, whether it is in an official, ritual setting, or around the kitchen table, is not simply something that people do, it is who they are.

Central to the notion of social memory is the fact that we do not remember in isolation, but in conversation and practices with other people. Social memory is the ongoing dialectic between the past and present that shapes our

---

14. See, e.g., Richard P. Unsworth, *A Portrait of Pacifists: Le Chambon, the Holocaust, and the Lives of André & Magda Trocmé* (Syracuse, NY: Syracuse University Press, 2012).

15. Paul Ricœur, "Memory – History – Forgetting," in *Meaning and Representation in History*, ed. Jörn Rüsen (Oxford: Berghahn Books, 2006), 10.

16. Jeffrey K. Olick, "Products, Processes, and Practices: A Non-Reificatory Approach to Collective Memory," *Biblical Theology Bulletin* 36 (2006): 6.

identities through participation in communicating with others, in rituals, celebrations, and commemorative events. We remember things as individuals, but the point social memory theorists want to emphasize is that group dynamics play a vital role in individual remembering. Families, associations, villages, and many other communities of people, large and small, have memories that their individual members have articulated, creating social memories. By participating in these groups, we draw on social memory as we remember or reconstruct the past.

In addition, through social encounters, we gain access to more distant memories than we as individuals can reach. Maurice Halbwachs, a student of Durkheim who first published work on the social frameworks of memory in 1925,[17] was one of the pioneers in thinking about collective or social memory. He pointed out that individual memory relies upon the social environment; it depends upon interactions with other people. As he wrote:

> If we enumerate the number of recollections during one day that we have evoked upon the occasion of our direct and indirect relations with other people, we will see that, most frequently, we appeal to our memory only in order to answer questions which others have asked us, or that we suppose they could have asked us. We note, moreover, that in order to answer them, we place ourselves in their perspective and we consider ourselves as being part of the same group or groups as they ... It is in this sense that there exists a collective memory and social frameworks for memory; it is to the degree that our individual thought places itself in these frameworks and participates in this memory that it is capable of the act of recollection.[18]

The individual mind is part of society. By interacting with society we obtain access to much older memories—of our family, or social group, or nation—than we can as individuals. For example, we are rarely certain of any early childhood memories but rely upon others to confirm or clarify vague recollections that we may have.

In addition, as Eviatar Zerubavel puts it, the social characteristic of memory,

> presupposes the ability to experience events that had happened to groups and communities to which we belong long before we joined them as if they were part of our own past ... [s]uch *sociobiological memory* also accounts for the sense of pride, pain, or shame we sometimes experience with regard

---

17. The first person to use the term "collective memory" was Hugo von Hofmannsthal in 1902. See Jeffrey K. Olick and Joyce Robbins, "Social Memory Studies: From 'Collective Memory' to Historical Sociology of Mnemonic Practices," *Annual Review of Sociology* 24 (1998): 106.

18. Maurice Halbwachs, *On Collective Memory*, ed., trans. Lewis A. Coser (Chicago, IL: University of Chicago Press, 1992), 38.

to events that had happened to groups and communities to which we belong long before we joined them.[19]

Any number of examples of people who have such experiences may come to mind, such as those who have descended from slaves or who belong to indigenous peoples, upon whom so many atrocities were committed. Or there may be a larger memory of shame, such as the situation of those who feel a sense of guilt for the crimes of the Nazis even though they were born long after the crimes took place.[20]

Despite the emphasis upon the social dimension to memory, and as Halbwachs would concur, it is still individuals who remember. However, his point is that memory possesses a profoundly social dimension. Our conscious memories are not simply the products of our own minds, separated from engagement with others. Our consciousness is only truly isolated when we are dreaming, but in dreams, images randomly combine and lack the frameworks that are furnished by social memory.[21] Some would argue here that one can make a distinction between objective and subjective aspects of memory. The objective dimension can be found in variety of places including written records, memorials, archives, rituals, architecture, and material objects[22] while the subjective is found in people; in their subjective memories that are affected by feelings. The objective aspect of memory is largely passive because it holds knowledge while the subjective element is active, for "it experiences and recalls to consciousness."[23] Those interested in social memory therefore attempt to elucidate how the individual and social dimensions of memory interact, and the multiple social frameworks in which individual memories are located and by which they are shaped. They attend to both the autobiographical memories that people have, but which occur within social contexts, as well as the larger historical memories of groups, such as memories of wars, persecutions, or exile, which extend far beyond individuals. No particular person has any direct recollection of these latter

---

19. Eviatar Zerubavel, "Social Memories: Steps towards a Sociology of the Past," in Olick, Vinitzky-Seroussi, and Levy, eds., *Collective Memory Reader*, 221–4, 224.

20. Zerubavel, "Social Memories," 224.

21. Halbwachs, *On Collective Memory*, 42.

22. Writing on the roles of architecture, museums, and material objects for building memory, S. Brent Plate "*Zakhor*: Modern Jewish Memory Built into Architecture," in *Religion, Art, and Visual Culture: A Cross-Cultural Reader*, ed. S. Brent Plate (New York: Palgrave, 2002), 195–204, 199 observes that "[m]emory is not somehow stored *in* a material object. Rather, the object works with personal and collective minds to *reenact* memory."

23. James Fentress and Chris Wickham, *Social Memory: New Perspectives on the Past* (Oxford: Blackwell, 1992), 5.

collective memories as they occurred so far in the past, but they are crucial in forming and sustaining identities.

Attention to social memory underscores the fact that narrative forms part of the overall context for understanding identity, as mentioned earlier. And as our identities are built out of where we perceive ourselves to be within a larger narrative, our identities, like the narrative itself, are works in progress. We do not remain static in how we understand ourselves and our place in the world but situate ourselves, or are situated by others, in narratives in varying ways as we go about daily life. Part of our identity consists of shared interests with others at a particular moment, but also a sharing which "depends in large part on a sense of common fate over time."[24] This awareness of cultural memory preserves a body of information from which a community derives a sense of unity and peculiarity.[25] Identity, it seems, cannot exist without memory. If memory were not important to identity, then why is it often so contested, and so grieved when lost?

Remembering, central to the activity of understanding ourselves as part of a larger story, is a therefore a process. It is through memory that we are able to be in time, says Olick, for it is where we negotiate past and present through which we are able to articulate and understand our individual and collective selves.[26] The act of recalling the past is dynamic, depending upon where we are, and what our aims at a given time, might be. The memories that a person or group recalls at a certain point in history might be different or shift in nature depending upon the situation, and memories may become sharper in particular sets of circumstances.

Memories can therefore inspire or constrain our actions in the present. For example, a sense that an identity is threatened, especially in the case of religious, ethnic and/or political strife, can cause groups to evoke specific social memories, particularly those of trauma and persecution, in support of their contemporary interests.[27] This is not to infer that memory is fully controlled by the present, and constructed to serve only the needs of the moment, but that history and memory, past and present, are negotiated as we engage in the process of remembering. Thus memory is not simply an "authentic residue of the past" or an "entirely malleable construction of

---

24. Olick, "Products, Processes, and Practices," 6.
25. Jan Assmann, "Collective Memory and Cultural Identity," in Olick, Vinitzky-Seroussi, and Levy, eds., *Collective Memory Reader*, 209–15, 213.
26. Jeffrey K. Olick, "Introduction," in *States of Memory: Continuities, Conflicts and Transformations in National Retrospection*, ed. Jeffrey K. Olick (Durham, NC: Duke University Press, 2003), 1–16, 15.
27. See Allan Megill, "History, Memory, Identity," in Olick, Vinitzky-Seroussi, and Levy, eds., *Collective Memory Reader*, 193–7, 194.

the present," but a combination of both.[28] The present can distort our memories just as memories can inform contemporary ignorance or correct errors in historical understanding. Memory is not simply made up, but neither is it objective or neutral.

Work on social memory studies, as it has evolved and continues to develop, articulates several characteristics of memory worth repeating: (1) social memory is a process—a dynamic—that can foster or limit actions in the present; (2) it is central to the identity of both individuals and groups; (3) it manifests itself in a range of forms; (4) it is malleable in many contexts while remaining persistent in others; and (5) as noted briefly above, social memory is contested. How we remember has consequences, whether the memories are invoked within a conversation, or memorialized in a monument. Because of these consequences, we argue about memories. These arguments are important, for we need to be critical of how we remember and memorialize for otherwise an icon of remembrance can become an idol.[29]

The Sermon on the Mount is an objective memory in the sense that it has been written down—memorialized—and placed within a specific gospel narrative. But it has been interpreted in a range of ways through the centuries.[30] It is a social memory in the sense that it was recorded based upon the collective memories of members of the early Jesus movement, and forms part of the overall distant memory for those who have understood themselves to be part of this movement in subsequent eras. As such, it is a source of knowledge for those who identify with this movement. As knowledge, this memory "provides the group with material for conscious reflection ... [which means] that we must situate groups in relation to their own traditions asking how they interpret their own 'ghosts,' and how they use them as a source of knowledge."[31] How then, is the Sermon a source of knowledge for André Trocmé?

---

28. Olick, "Products, Processes, and Practices," 13.

29. In his study of Holocaust memorials, e.g., James E. Young ("The Texture of Memory: Holocaust Memorials and Meaning," in Plate, ed., *Religion, Art and Visual Culture*, 211–5, 213–4) writes that "[i]f, in its glazed exterior, we never really see the monument, I shall attempt to crack its eidetic veneer, to loosen meaning, to make visible the activity of memory in monuments. It is my hope that such a critique may save our *icons* of remembrance from hardening into *idols* of remembrance." The same could be said of stories or other memories that are shared and "immortalized" in oral, written, or visual form.

30. See, e.g., Warren S. Kissinger, *The Sermon on the Mount: A History of Interpretation and Bibliography* (American Theological Library Association Bibliography Series; Metuchen, NJ: The Scarecrow Press, 1975).

31. Fentress and Wickham, *Social Memory*, 26.

Background of André Trocmé

Trocmé was born in 1901 into an affluent Huguenot family in the northern French town of Saint-Quentin. By the early twentieth century many Huguenots, especially those who were wealthy and urban, were assimilated into French society, but they remained a small percentage of the population, with a history of persecution and exile. Some historians argue that Protestants in France often felt a certain affinity with French Jews, as both were minorities, and had experienced persecution and exile. Huguenots referred to the period after the Revocation of the Edict of Nantes (1685) as "the desert" when they were forced to worship in secret, or sent into exile, just as Jews were exiled in 1492 from Spain. Both groups had a "Babylon" which for Huguenots was Paris, recalling the St. Bartholomew massacre (1572) during the French Wars of Religion. The Calvinist emphasis upon the Old Testament, stemming from Calvin's stress on the unity and similarity between the two covenants, contributed to the popularity of Hebrew names for Huguenots, and the predilection to call their places of worship "temples" instead of "churches."[32] This background also led some of the Protestants in the Plateau to refer to their Jewish guests in code as "Old Testaments" or "books."[33] Thus, as has been argued, there are some "affinities" at least between some Huguenots and Jews in France.[34] Huguenots would commemorate their persecuted history through hymns such as "La Cévenole,"[35] and stories. Trocmé was therefore instantly part of this rich tradition of memory.

Trocmé's father, Paul, was a respected textile factory owner and had significant influence in the Protestant community of Saint-Quentin. The young

---

32. See Christophe Chalamet, *Revivalism and Social Christianity: The Prophetic Faith of Henri Nick and André Trocmé* (Eugene, OR: Pickwick Publications, 2013), 144. Chalamet writes that "Jean Calvin, much more than Martin Luther, had a deep conviction about the substantive continuity between the two covenants of Scripture: the new covenant in Jesus Christ, far from adding any new 'content' or 'substance' to the covenant between God and Israel, only differs from the older covenant in the 'mode of dispensation' or in the way God relates to his people and to the world." Despite some of the negative comments that Calvin made about Judaism, Myriam Yardeni "French Calvinism and Judaism," *Reformation and Renaissance Review* 6 (2004): 297 has suggested that the roots of the assistance of Jewish refugees in the Plateau can possibly be found in Calvin's theology and the history of the Reformed Church in France.

33. Patrick Cabanel, *Histoire des Justes en France* (Paris: Armand Colin, 2012), 178–9.

34. See Patrick Cabanel, *Juifs et Protestants en France. Les affinités électives. XVIe-XXIe Siècle* (Paris: Fayard, 2004).

35. This hymn was first sung in 1885 at the bicentennial of the Revocation of the Edict of Nantes.

Trocmé was raised with all the comforts that affluence could provide, but various experiences that he wrote about later indicate that he questioned his privilege at a young age. Traumatic events, such as the death of his mother, Paula Schwerdtmann, in a car accident when the boy was ten years old marked his childhood. Questions of identity and place in the world plagued the young Trocmé, and contributed to his spiritual development and eventual commitment to pacifism.[36]

Despite the fact that Protestants in France had exhibited fierce nationalism during World War I[37] as well as strong support for the Vichy regime during World War II, from an early age Trocmé rejected such enthusiasm for the state or for war. The Reformed Church of France was by no means pacifist, but several experiences appear to have contributed to Trocmé's position on violence. For example, he was bullied as a child but also witnessed a crippled boy suffering beatings by classmates. The latter event prompted the young Trocmé to organize a defense of the boy and contributed to his hatred of all things military.[38]

The Trocmé family was devoutly religious, and as Paul Trocmé would later admit to his son, in 1870 during the Franco-Prussian War, he had decided that he would serve as a nurse in order not to carry a weapon.[39] Paula Schwerdtmann had been his father's second wife (Paul Trocmé had nine children by his first wife, Marie Walbaum), and the daughter of a German Lutheran bishop from Hannover. Trocmé therefore had many German cousins, other relatives, and happy memories of vacations in Germany. During World War I, some of his half-brothers had to serve in the army, which meant that they may have been fighting against some of his German relations. The idea that family members should now be forced to potentially kill one another was perplexing to the young Trocmé and another reason why war made little sense to him.[40]

Although he was not in the trenches, Trocmé witnessed firsthand many aspects of World War I's horrors. One of his favourite half-brothers, Robert, nearly died of a chest wound after returning from the bloodbath that was the Battle of the Somme. Once the Germans invaded northern France and took over Saint-Quentin, Trocmé witnessed wounded German soldiers returning

---

36. As Unsworth (*A Portrait of Pacifists*, 33) writes: "[t]o understand the spiritual origins of André's pacifist convictions, the best place to start is with those questions of identity."

37. See Laurent Gambarotto, *Foi et Patrie: La prédication du protestantisme français pendant la Première Guerre mondiale* (Genève: Labor & Fides, 1996).

38. Unsworth, *Portrait of Pacifists*, 32.

39. Chalamet, *Revivalism*, 52.

40. Unsworth, *Portrait of Pacifists*, 32.

from the front. One day, he watched some of the injured walking towards the hospital. One German soldier was missing his jaw, bleeding, and had to be supported by his comrades as he staggered forward. Trocmé later wrote that he could not hate this man, and that after witnessing such suffering, he returned home despondent.[41]

One of Trocmé's most memorable experiences as a boy was his interaction with a German soldier, Kindler, a telegraph operator who was staying with other German military in the large Trocmé home because the Germans had requisitioned the house. Trocmé later wrote of a discussion he had with this man, who explained that he was a Christian pacifist, and that he would never kill another person. Trocmé was so struck by the German's words that he invited Kindler to his youth group, the *Union chrétienne de jeunes gens*, where, upon observing Kindler's sincerity of faith and commitment to nonviolence, the other French participants welcomed the soldier. Later Trocmé wrote in his memoirs that he suddenly came to see war as total chaos, and as he knelt in prayer with Kindler and the others, he realized that "[h]ere, French people and a German were opening their eyes to the tangible reality of the Kingdom of God—Kindler prayed in German. I believe it was one of the first times I expressed my thoughts, aloud and openly, to God."[42] It appears that the idea and reality of nonviolence was part of Trocmé's overall commitment to faith.

This sense of religious piety is strong throughout Trocmé's writings, and he recalls fondly the young people's groups such as the *Union*, which had a formative influence upon his spiritual life and contributed to his own emphasis upon working with young people later in his ministry. These groups stressed commitment to God, prayer, Bible study, a certain sense of revivalism (in some cases), and consistently manifested a strong social conscience, such as in Saint-Quentin when the boys risked breaking German law by assisting the Russian prisoners of war who were kept in disgusting conditions.[43]

The duty to assist those in need, whether they were prisoners, refugees, or the poor in general, became central to Trocmé's theology and identity. In 1917, the Trocmé family had to evacuate from Saint-Quentin to the rural Belgian countryside where they experienced the magnanimity of indigent farmers who sheltered them. Here Trocmé himself sensed what it might be like to be poor, and wrote of how he felt the "throbbing, multiple and

---

41. See Pierre Boismorand, *Magda et André Trocmé: Figures de résistances* (L'histoire à vif; Paris: Éditions du Cerf, 2007), 42.

42. This excerpt from Trocmé's *Mémoires: notes autobiographiques* is translated and cited by Chalamet, *Revivalism*, 55.

43. Unsworth (*Portrait of Pacifists*, 35) notes that one *Union* member was jailed for this activity and a German guard, who had turned a blind eye to the work, was replaced.

laborious life of the blue collar working class and [h]e felt like [h]e was one of them."⁴⁴ In 1925, when he studied for a year at the Union Theological Seminary in New York City, Trocmé was most influenced by Harry F. Ward, a leader in the Social Gospel movement. It was in New York, as well, that he met the Italian social work student from Florence, Magda Grilli di Cortona, a young woman who did not believe in many traditional Christian teachings but who was fully committed to working alongside the poor for the betterment of the world. After their return to Europe, Trocmé and Grilli married in 1926 and together committed themselves to ministering to the needs of poor working-class communities.

The idea that concern and care for others, as well as nonviolence, could not be separated from the proclamation of the gospel was to become a defining characteristic of Trocmé's theology and identity as a Christian. His partnership with Grilli reinforced this orientation as did some of his teachers and peers. Earlier, when he began his university studies in Paris, he was not very interested in the historical critical approaches to the Bible that were explored in his studies with the New Testament scholar, Maurice Goguel, for example.⁴⁵ A professor who did make a strong impression, however, was the Protestant Wilfred Monod, who emphasized the importance of peace, and stressed the integration of Christian revival and social reform. As far as Monod was concerned, the beatitudes were at the centre of the Christian faith; they were Jesus' creed.⁴⁶ Monod founded the "Order of Watchers," members of which continue to this day to recite the beatitudes on a daily basis. Known as a strong ecumenist and evangelist, Monod is mostly remembered for his emphasis upon "social Christianity" whereby he stressed the integration of spiritual and social care. This emphasis resonated with Trocmé's concerns, for it blended his intense personal piety with social justice.

As a student Trocmé had joined the "groupe du Nord," which consisted of theology students committed to evangelism and social Christianity, their hero being the Protestant pastor Henri Nick, a strong advocate of "Christianisme social" ("Social Christianity") who had been ministering in working-class areas of northern France since the late 1800s. Trocmé maintained his association with members of this group as a young pastor, and met more like-minded Christians who were committed to social justice and nonviolence. Although Trocmé had completed his required military service in Morocco in 1922–1923, he had refused to use a gun, and fortunately was never ordered to

---

44. This portion of Trocmé's *Mémoires: notes autobiographiques* is cited by Unsworth, *Portrait of Pacifists*, 39.
45. Chalamet, *Revivalism*, 61.
46. Chalamet, *Revivalism*, 67.

do so.[47] While studying in Paris, Trocmé became involved in the international peace movement, especially the International Fellowship of Reconciliation (IFoR), which was organized at the end of World War I. The French branch of the Fellowship was founded in 1923, and welcomed people of all faiths, philosophies and political affiliations.[48]

In his childhood, youth, and young adult life, therefore, Trocmé was emerging as a minority voice (pacifist and socialist) within a minority Christian tradition (Huguenot) in France. He was part of a long community of memory, as mentioned, but he had also emerged within a specific social framework that included, of course, his family, but also very importantly, his teachers, colleagues, and friends who shared his commitments. Many of his close associates were not French but came from international backgrounds (for example, there was an entire German wing to his family; Magda's background was Italian and Russian, IFoR was international). Trocmé thus had a diverse social framework for developing his theology. These factors are important for the consideration of how he remembers the Sermon on the Mount, or what he refers to in a 1927 homily as "le plus beau portrait de Jésus qui existe, puisqu'il est peint par lui-même" ("the most beautiful portrait of Jesus that exists because it was painted by himself").[49]

André Trocmé and the Sermon on the Mount

From 1927 to 1934 Trocmé served as a minister in Maubeuge, then in Sin-le-Noble, both working-class towns in the north of France, and he continued his involvement with the peace movement, becoming the secretary of the European Commission of IFoR. His friend, Henri Roser, was appointed secretary of the *Mouvement International de la Réconciliation* (MIR), the French branch of IFoR, and editor of the movement's journal, the *Cahiers de la Réconciliation*, in 1927. Trocmé was a contributor to *Les Cahiers*, and his early articles reveal some of the ways in which he interpreted aspects of the Sermon.

For example, in 1933, Trocmé published "Morale Chrétienne et Objection de Conscience," in which he grounds Christian morality in the second commandment, "Love your neighbour as yourself"; a commandment that he understands to be rooted in and inseparable from the command to love God with heart, soul, and mind. He stresses the parallels between the

---

47. See Georges Menut, "André Trocmé, un violent vaincu par Dieu," in Bolle, ed., *Le Plateau Vivarais-Lignon*, 381.
48. Chalamet, *Revivalism*, 80.
49. André Trocmé "Sermon" (Maubeuge, 17 July, 1927) excerpted in Boismorand, *Magda et André Trocmé*, 84.

behavior exhorted for people of faith and the behavior of God, referring to the instruction: "Be perfect as your Heavenly Father is perfect" (Matt. 5.48) as well as the prayer to forgive our "offenses" ("trespasses") as we forgive those who have trespassed against us (Matt. 6.12), which he perceives as evidence of a parallel between human daily morality and the redemptive work of God accomplished on the cross.[50] He continues by arguing that given the evidence that Jesus never took up arms, the believer is duty-bound to follow Jesus' example and love the neighbor. Such love is not embodied by violence; rather, Trocmé calls upon his readers to imitate Jesus in all circumstances, even those of war.[51]

The year before this article was published, Trocmé had been involved in collaborative activities between Germany and France through IFoR and he set up summer school for children of all faiths and national backgrounds called "Children of Peace." 1932 was also a turning point for conscientious objection in France as a conscientious objector, Camille Rombaut, was sentenced to four months for refusing military service. Subsequently Jacques Martin was imprisoned as a conscientious objector, then Philippe Vernier in 1933. These men had all been associated with Pastor Henri Nick, who had been a strong influence on Trocmé and who thought that the Sermon had to be read and practiced literally.[52] Trocmé had testified in defense of Rombaut, and he wrote about some of these trials in a letter to an American Nevin Sayre, then the associate secretary for IFoR. He points out how, despite the lack of support for conscientious objection by the leaders of the Reformed Church in France, many working-class French people, especially socialists and communists, were receptive to it.[53] He directly criticizes the leaders of the French Reformed Church, whom he calls the "Officials, living in Paris, under the influence of big Protestant capitalists."[54] He lists reasons why he thinks that these leaders are in fear of conscientious objection, one being that they think that "Protestantism, which has been historically considered in France as foreign, will lose its big influence in France if it is compromised with radical pacifism."[55] He worries in this letter that

---

50. André Trocmé, "Morale Chrétienne et Objection de Conscience," *Cahiers de la Réconciliation* (1933): 10; Swarthmore College Peace Collection, Series B, Box 4.

51. Trocmé, "Morale Chrétienne," 11.

52. Chalamet, *Revivalism*, 113. After he completed his military service in Morocco, Trocmé was never called up for army service and during WWII he was spared from conscription as he had four children; see Unsworth, *Portrait of Pacifists*, 91–8.

53. André Trocmé, "Letter to Nevin Sayre" (4 October, 1944); Swarthmore College Peace Collection, Series B, Box 1. Also cited by Chalamet, *Revivalism*, 114.

54. Trocmé, "Letter to Nevin Sayre."

55. Trocmé, "Letter to Nevin Sayre."

without support from IFoR, French conscientious objectors would become isolated as they faced opposition from both church and state. Without spiritual leadership, this pacifist stance could be co-opted by political parties for purely political ends, and its spiritual side "disregarded and discredited … This would mean, in France, a considerable loss for the Kingdom of God."[56]

Trocmé's emphasis on nonviolence, which he found rooted in the teachings and example of Jesus, emerges, as we have seen, from his own family history and experiences, his mentors, and his association with like-minded individuals who were now paying the price for their convictions. His thinking on this issue intensifies in the context of the rise of Hitler and the likelihood that war was imminent. It is significant that he articulates his nonviolent position regarding the war, and support for conscientious objection, in the midst of conflict with both the French state and the Reformed Church of France. In 1935, after Trocmé and his family had moved to Le Chambon-sur-Lignon,[57] he published an article in *Les Cahiers* which challenged those theologies that underscored Jesus' redemptive work while denying the value of his commandments for the present day. Such a theology, argues Trocmé, states that the meaning of the Sermon is eschatological while it denies the binding nature of the Sermon for people in the here and now.[58] His interpretation of the Sermon is thus emerging in the context of conflict with both church and state. Often, as observed earlier, in situations of contestation people's memories focus upon those aspects of a narrative which are most relevant to their context. Although the Sermon appears to have always been important to Trocmé's theology, we see him appealing to specific elements of it because conscientious objection and war had become realities that were scarring peoples' lives. The Sermon is applicable, maintains Trocmé, to the here and now. His sense of conviction on this point seems to be mounting precisely because he must defend the nonviolent position from its detractors and because there was so much at stake for him and his community.

This stress upon nonviolence remained central to Trocmé's theology and sense of identity as France entered into war. Prior to the German invasion of France, Trocmé produced his own statement regarding war in which he recalls his own upbringing. He writes that the notion of hating the evil in one's self was stressed over the evil in others, recalling Matthew 7.1-5. He also indicates that his deep reading of the Bible while a theological student

---

56. Trocmé, "Letter to Nevin Sayre."
57. André and Magda Trocmé were advised to move away from northern France by their doctor as their children all faced health problems and at this point historically there was no cure for tuberculosis.
58. André Trocmé, "De Quelques Erreurs," *Les Cahiers de la Réconciliation* (1935), 7; Swarthmore College Peace Collection, Series B, Box 4.

in Paris confirmed his convictions, and speaks of Jesus as "the Nonviolent" who allowed himself to be crucified rather than to obey the commands of his contemporaries.[59] This stress on nonviolence reinforces the dynamic nature of identity and memory. As people move through life, elements of identity deepen or rise to the surface based upon the events taking place. It makes sense that Trocmé would focus on nonviolence more intently given the increasingly violent context in which he was living.

On 23 June, 1940, the day after the Vichy government signed the armistice with Germany, Trocmé and his fellow pastor, Édouard Theis, preached their well-known sermon on the "weapons of the spirit" to the Reformed congregation in Le Chambon. Overall, this message exhorted listeners to challenge the violence that was being exerted on their individual consciences and to avoid collaborating with the violence which would soon be upon them, by using their weapons of the spirit. The latter is what Christians must do.[60] The address is littered with ideas found in the Sermon, especially themes from the Lord's Prayer (Matt. 6.8-15). Trocmé and Theis declare that the parishioners should rely upon their Father who is in heaven and who provides the daily bread that they must share with others whom they should love as much as they love themselves. They also state the dire need to love and forgive their adversaries (Matt. 5.44), and to avoid the "culte de Mammon" (Matt. 6.24) or comfortable lifestyle which they had all enjoyed to some extent before the war. Although the homily calls for humility, it unequivocally states that servility or slavery to current ideologies must be rejected. The congregation must remember that faith is not lost and avoid any temptation to concede to the demands made by the state if such demands violated the gospel. The address ends with more references to the Lord's Prayer, and the appeal that God's will be done on earth as in heaven.[61] Here, then, Trocmé and Theis appeal to dimensions of the Sermon in the context of conflict and pressure to conform to state demands. Dimensions of the Sermon function as sources of resistance and grounding for behavior that could conflict with that called for by the state. Jesus' teachings are memories or sources of knowledge that the community needed as it faced the prospect of increasingly difficult circumstances and the potential of engaging in not only unconventional, but subversive, activities. Trocmé's frustration with the French Reformed Church, moreover, is evident in his reaction to an official letter he had received from the leaders of the Church. This letter came with instructions to be read aloud

---

59. André Trocmé, "Mise au point concernant mon attitude en temps de guerre," in Boismorand, *Magda et André Trocmé*, 111–6.
60. André Trocmé and Édouard Theis, "Les armes de l'Esprit," in Boismorand, *Magda et André Trocmé*, 128.
61. Trocmé and Theis, "Les armes," 128–9.

in all churches and directed Protestants to be loyal to the Vichy regime. Trocmé has scrawled "Pétainism!"[62] on his copy.[63]

During the war, Trocmé organized biblical study and prayer groups, led by members of the parish, with whom he would meet regularly. It was in these meetings that parishioners would also engage questions of how to assist those who were fleeing from the authorities. These leaders, or "responsables," would then participate in similar discussions with their respective group, including members on farms in the surrounding area. These connections with rural people were crucial, as some of these very same peasants played vital roles harboring refugees during the war. Without these study and prayer groups, the farmers may not have been as receptive to offering shelter as some were suspicious of the city people. As Trocmé later wrote in his memoirs, it was in these groups that "we" conceived of nonviolent resistance and found answers to the problems of how to shelter and hide Jews during the following months.[64]

Trocmé's notes for these biblical studies sessions during 1943–1944 survive. He lays out a series of questions that the participants, both those in rural areas and those in town, had to discuss with regard to each biblical text, beginning with Matthew 5.13-16 and parallels.[65] On the one hand, he underlines the need for a careful comparative reading of the texts, while on the other hand, he asks that they think about how the texts apply to their specific situations. Regarding the "salt of the earth" and the "light of the world," for example, he asks how these teachings articulate the Christian mission in the world. He considers Matthew 7.6 ("Do not give dogs what is holy; and do not throw your pearls before swine, lest they trample them under foot and turn to attack you") under the topic of "prudence," an appropriate topic given the risks that the members of these biblical studies groups were taking. Trocmé asks in his notes if faith excludes wisdom? What is Jesus' method? He appears to encourage his parishioners to think strategically and to see that such prudent thinking is there in the gospel.

---

62. "Pétainism" means that Trocmé interpreted the letter to be advocating for loyalty to the authority of Philippe Pétain, leader of the Vichy regime.
63. "Message du Conseil Régional": Swarthmore College Peace Collection, Series C, Misc.
64. André Trocmé, *Mémoires: notes autobiographiques*, 357; Swarthmore College Peace Collection, Series A, Box 1. See also Alicia J. Batten, "Reading the Bible in Occupied France: André Trocmé and Le Chambon," *Harvard Theological Review* 103 (2010): 322; Chalamet, *Revivalism*, 146; Unsworth, *Portrait of Pacifists*, 220.
65. André Trocmé, "Plan général d'Études Bibliques, 1943–1944," Swarthmore College Peace Collection, Series B, Box 7.

I would argue that Trocmé's interpretations of the Sermon here are not simply "his own," but developed from the social framework in which he found himself. His life experience, background, and identity are all significant, but he was reading and remembering the Sermon in the context of people who were attempting to live it. These were people taking tremendous risks to assist those who needed to hide. The Sermon was not only a source of knowledge here, but a source of hope and meaning that likely inspired these people to persevere in their dangerous work.

André and Magda Trocmé remained in Le Chambon until after the war, but Trocmé became the secretary of IFoR in 1946, eventually leaving Le Chambon and establishing a House of Reconciliation in Versailles in 1950. For the next decade they would focus their efforts on peacemaking, especially in Algeria, but elsewhere in the world as well. Trocmé travelled and spoke extensively in churches and at conferences. In 1960, he became the minister at the St. Gervais Church in Geneva, where he worked until his retirement in 1970. After back surgery, in 1971, Trocmé unexpectedly died in a Geneva hospital. Magda Trocmé continued the work of speaking and educating for peace throughout the world until her death in 1996.

In 1951, Trocmé delivered the Robert Treat Paine Lectures in the United States, which were subsequently published as a book entitled *The Politics of Repentance*. Here, Trocmé discusses church-state relations arguing that the church must be willing to challenge and speak out against state actions that it considers to be unjust. References to the Sermon appear throughout the book, but Trocmé is most explicit when he makes it clear that Jesus and his teachings are at the centre of revelation. He states:

> It is a mistake to wonder if the Sermon on the Mount, preached by Jesus, is "Pauline" enough. It is rather Saint Paul who must be passed through the sieve of the Sermon on the Mount, and we must ask ourselves if his teaching is "Christian" enough.[66]

Later in the lectures he affirms the applicability of the Sermon to earth,[67] and stresses that the church must be the "light of the world" (Matt. 5.15)[68] and must continually bear witness to the State—it must surpass the State in justice—in order that the State will know repentance.[69]

---

66. André Trocmé, *The Politics of Repentance* (New York: Fellowship Publications, 1953), 44.
67. Trocmé, *Politics*, 65.
68. Trocmé, *Politics*, 90.
69. Trocmé, *Politics*, 111. That same year Trocmé preached on "Blessed are the humble" (Matt. 5.5) at St. George's Church in New York City in which he asked churches in western nations to call upon their states to repent and to be humble; see André Trocmé,

This notion, that the church should function as a kind of conscience, emerges often in Trocmé's writings. In a pamphlet published in 1948, while the Trocmés were still in Le Chambon, he writes of the church as a witness to the peace of God; as the salt of the earth and the light of the world. The church must be willing to oppose the state and never compromise in its obedience to God. This is what "salt of the earth" and "light of the world" means and Trocmé writes admiringly of small groups of Christians; non-conformists such as Quakers, Huguenots, Wesleyans, Doukhobors, and others, who listen to their conscience and stay obedient to God.[70] His examples of these minority traditions cohere with his statement that the church must always remain a minority if it desires to remain true to the demands of God. The church will face tribulation and persecution; precisely the sorts of things that it had confronted in the past. Similar ideas can be found in unpublished notes on the Sermon and in an unpublished essay, "The Church—Lamp of the Body."[71] Some of these notes may have been for use in the parish in St. Gervais.

Notes also survive that focus on the Lord's Prayer, breaking it down verse by verse and illustrating aspects of it with parables and little drawings, as Trocmé would often do in his writings and letters. These notes appear to have been used for religious instruction for the young.[72] A set of notes in English survives, titled "Cancel Our Debts as We Cancel Those of Our Debtors."[73] Here, Trocmé focuses upon social injustice, reading what some interpret as "forgive us our trespasses" not as a reference to sin but to the economic debt faced by the world's poor. Trocmé engages with what would become a significant theme for him: Jesus' proclamation of the Jubilee. He concludes his notes by stating that "God proclaims the necessity of a Jubilee

---

"Sermon Delivered at St. George's Church," New York City, 1951; Swarthmore College Peace Collection, Series B, Box 10.

70. André Trocmé, *L'Église et le Désordre International* (Le Chambon-sur-Lignon: Mouvement International de la Réconciliation, 1948), 15–16.

71. André Trocmé, "Le Sermon sur la Montagne et le Mission de l'Église" (unpublished notes, 1962); Swarthmore College Peace Collection, Series B, Box 6; "The Church—Lamp of the Body," (unpublished essay, date unknown); Swarthmore College Peace Collection, Series B, Box 7.

72. André Trocmé, "Introduction" (unpublished notes, date unknown); Swarthmore College Peace Collection, Series B, Box 7. Trocmé was very fond of writing short stories or parables for children. During the war he would tell these stories in the "temple" in front of a large Christmas tree. Many of them stress hospitality, love of the stranger, nonviolence and compassion. See André Trocmé, *L'Église de Neige* (Le Chambon-sur-Lignon: Messageries Évangeliques, 1943; repr. Éditions Ampelos, 2012).

73. André Trocmé, "Cancel Our Debts as We Cancel Those of Our Debtors" (unpublished notes, date unknown); Swarthmore College Peace Collection, Series B, Box 10.

and He is counting more upon people who are ready to share their existence with the needy of this world, than on the rich who share only their surplus."[74]

The theme of the biblical Jubilee also features in Trocmé's book, *Jesus and the Nonviolent Revolution,* which first appeared in French in 1963 and was then translated and published in English posthumously.[75] In this book Trocmé titles his last chapter, "Jesus and Gandhi, or Can the Sermon on the Mount Be Put into Practice?" Trocmé had long admired Gandhi, but here he probes some of the differences that he sees between the two figures. He begins by pointing out that Jesus' teaching about turning the other cheek has divided Christians, with the minority arguing that such instructions had to be put into practice, while the majority claim that Jesus spoke in paradoxes, which means that given the power of the wicked on earth, "the Christian must give the state a hand in order to preserve order."[76] Trocmé grants that the majority is right to say that nonviolence cannot be made into law, but it is wrong to denounce pacifists and conscientious objectors. He clearly believes that this minority view concerning the pacifist position must be dominant in the church.

Nonviolence, as manifested by both Gandhi and Jesus, finds its roots in the actions of Jesus but also, as Trocmé claims earlier in the book, in the Mosaic principle of the Jubilee which Jesus upheld (Luke 4.16-32).[77] He then explores some of the differences between Gandhi and Jesus, pointing out that Gandhi's aims were political, and successful, while Jesus' nonviolent agenda was in obedience and witness to God, in order to inaugurate the Kingdom of God on earth. Jesus failed politically, but his act was universal. For Trocmé, Gandhi's example demonstrated that the Sermon on the Mount can in many circumstances be "politically effective" and that the "demonstration of such effectiveness in the age of automation and the atomic bomb is one of the great moral victories of the twentieth century."[78] He argues that Gandhi proved that Jesus was correct when he preached the Sermon, and that the great Hindu leader must be viewed as an ally of Jesus. But ultimately, Jesus' proclamation was in preparation for the work of God and those who follow Jesus' teaching must be ready to fail in their efforts.

---

74. Trocmé, "Cancel Our Debts."
75. André Trocmé, *Jésus et la révolution non-violente* (Geneva : Labor & Fides, 1961); *Jesus and the Nonviolent Revolution,* trans. Michael H. Shank and Marlin E. Miller (Kitchener, ON: Herald Press, 1973; repr. Eugene, OR: Wipf & Stock, 1998). The book was also edited and introduced by Charles E. Moore and published by Orbis Books in 2004. I am citing from the Wipf and Stock reprint.
76. Trocmé, *Jesus and the Nonviolent Revolution,* 159.
77. Trocmé, *Jesus and the Nonviolent Revolution,* 27–40.
78. Trocmé, *Jesus and the Nonviolent Revolution,* 166.

However, Trocmé does not want to remain overly pessimistic, for he thinks that in the mind of Jesus, God will triumph when there is true faith among committed people. He thus states squarely:

> ... Jesus sees nonviolence as inseparable from small groups of men [sic] of faith who live by God's grace and whose function on earth is to be God's witnesses of the cross and redemption. These groups are the salt of the earth, the light of the world, the city on a mountaintop.[79]

With these words we recognize a pattern in Trocmé's interpretation of the Sermon and its application to the church. Christians, thinks Trocmé, must attempt to live out the Sermon, despite the fact that they will remain a minority in doing so, and will suffer persecution and failure. Trocmé cites Matthew 5.10 ("Blessed are the persecuted") as evidence that there is no promise of success other than the final coming of the Kingdom. The Sermon is not an end in itself because in the end the Kingdom is God's work, and this final victory "comes after, not before, the cross."[80] Indeed, Gandhi's work was a "premonitory" sign of the kingdom, but despite the urgency of working for greater peace and justice, human beings must place their hope in the "final victory of Christ."[81]

Conclusion

Why does the Sermon attach itself so strongly to certain people and groups? In the example of André Trocmé, we have seen that emphases upon nonviolence and love for others, especially those who are suffering, figure as important components of his moral and religious development. These emphases were upheld by the social frameworks in which he lived, including his international family members and friends, his mentors, his ministry with the poor, his efforts to assist the persecuted during the war, and his ongoing labours to seek greater peace and justice in the world. Trocmé was consistently upholding a minority perspective, having to debate and argue with the positions of the State as well as with those of the French Reformed Church. He was obliged to defend his positions on highly contested issues such as conscientious objection, and various economic and social problems, and risk his life for the sake of caring for the persecuted.[82] Therefore, it is

---

79. Trocmé, *Jesus and the Nonviolent Revolution*, 167.
80. Trocmé, *Jesus and the Nonviolent Revolution*, 166.
81. Trocmé, *Jesus and the Nonviolent Revolution*, 169.
82. For example, Trocmé was arrested and detained for four weeks in a prison camp in 1943 (with Édouard Theis and Roger Darcissac). He was also forced to go into hiding for several months in 1943–1944 because of threats upon his life. His cousin, Daniel Trocmé, head of the Maison des roches (a residence for refugee students) was arrested

not surprising that given his identity, experiences, and social frameworks, the Sermon was tremendously important; indeed, one could argue that it was central to his theology and morality. The Sermon, in his view, was a witness of God's will for the world. He appears to have resonated with this text not only because of its wisdom, but because he perceived it to be a minority voice, just as he and his associates—family, friends, co-workers— were a minority. It thus connected with his identity and would have been reinforced by his immediate social community, even though this community would shift and change as he lived his life in various places. What we see in Trocmé's life and writings is a process whereby the Sermon, remembered in the context of constant struggle, powerfully and meaningfully informed the mind and heart of Trocmé and his peers. Yet this process was dynamic, for just as the Sermon sustained these people, they appear to have sustained the Sermon by attempting to live it out in a variety of ways, and with remarkable persistence.[83]

Biographical Note

Alicia J. Batten is Professor of Religious Studies and Theological Studies at Conrad Grebel University College, University of Waterloo, in Waterloo, Ontario, Canada. Her research interests include the Letter of James, and the social history of the early Jesus movement. Among her publications is a recent book entitled *Dress in Mediterranean Antiquity* (co-edited with Kelly Olson; London: T&T Clark/Bloomsbury, 2021).

Bibliography

Assmann, Jan. "Collective Memory and Cultural Identity," 209–15 in Olick, Vinitzky-Seroussi, and Levy, eds., *Collective Memory Reader*, 2011.
Batten, Alicia J. "Reading the Bible in Occupied France: André Trocmé and Le Chambon," *Harvard Theological Review* 103 (2010): 309–28. https://doi.org/10.1017/S0017816010000659
Bellah, Robert N., Richard Madsen, William Sullivan, Ann Swidler, and Steven M. Tipton.

---

with some of the youth by the Gestapo in Le Chambon in 1943 and murdered in Majdanek concentration camp in 1944. For a recent account in English of the story of the Plateau, see Peter Grose, *A Good Place to Hide* (New York: Pegasus Books, 2015).

83. I extend many thanks to Dr Wendy Chmielewski, curator at the Swarthmore College Peace Collection, for permission to cite from various unpublished documents from the André and Magda Trocmé papers. Gratitude also goes to Nelly Trocmé Hewett and to the editors of this volume for editorial assistance. Finally, thanks to Conrad Grebel University College at the University of Waterloo for some funding to facilitate research at Swarthmore.

Habits of the Heart: Commitment and Individualism in American Life. New York: Harper & Row, 1985.

Boismorand, Pierre. Magda et André Trocmé: Figures de résistances. L'histoire à vif. Paris: Éditions du Cerf, 2007.

Bolle, Pierre, ed. Le Plateau Vivarais-Lignon: Accueil et Résistance 1939-1944. Le Chambon-sur-Lignon: Société d'histoire de la Montagne, 1992.

Boulet, François. Histoire de la Montagne-refuge aux limites de la Haute-Loire et de l'Ardeche. La montagne, de la Réforme protestante à la seconde guerre mondiale. Le Chambon-sur-Lignon, Tence, Fay-sur-Lignon, Saint Agrève, Le Mazet-Saint-Voy et leurs environs. Polignac: Les Éditions du Roure, 2008.

Cabanel, Patrick. Juifs et Protestants en France. Les affinités électives. XVIe-XXIe Siècle. Paris: Fayard, 2004.

—Histoire des Justes en France. Paris: Armand Colin, 2012.

Chalamet, Christophe. Revivalism and Social Christianity: The Prophetic Faith of Henri Nick and André Trocmé. Eugene, OR: Pickwick Publications, 2013.

Corazza, Stephanie. "Review of Caroline Moorhead, Village of Secrets: Defying the Nazis in Vichy France," Contemporary Church History Quarterly 21.1 (March 2015). https://contemporarychurchhistory.org

Fentress, James, and Chris Wickham. Social Memory: New Perspectives on the Past. Oxford: Blackwell, 1992.

Gambarotto, Laurent. Foi et Patrie: La prédication du protestantisme français pendant la Première Guerre mondiale. Genève: Labor & Fides, 1996.

Gril-Mariotte, Aziza. "Des commémorations aux musées, la patrimonialisation d'un territoire," 307–21 in La Montagne Refuge: Accueil et Sauvetage des Juifs autour du Chambon-sur-Lignon. Edited by Patrick Cabanel, Philippe Joutard, Jacques Sémelin, and Annette Wievorka. Paris: Albin Michel, 2013.

Grose, Peter. A Good Place to Hide. New York: Pegasus Books, 2015.

Halbwachs, Maurice. On Collective Memory. Edited by Lewis A. Coser. Chicago, IL: University of Chicago Press, 1992. https://doi.org/10.7208/chicago/9780226774497.001.0001

Hallie, Philip. Lest Innocent Blood Be Shed. New York: Harper Perennial, 1994. First published London: Michael Joseph, 1979.

Henry, Patrick. "Le Chambon-sur-Lignon," The French Review 89 (2016): 83–96.

Kirk, Alan, and Tom Thatcher. Memory, Tradition, and Text: Uses of the Past in Early Christianity. Semeia Studies, 52. Leiden: Brill, 2005.

Kissinger, Warren S. The Sermon on the Mount: A History of Interpretation and Bibliography. American Theological Library Association Bibliography Series. Lanham, MD: Scarecrow Press, 1998.

Megill, Allan. "History, Memory, Identity," 193–7 in Olick, Vinitzky-Seroussi, and Levy, eds., Collective Memory Reader, 2011.

Menut, Georges. "André Trocmé, un violent vaincu par Dieu," 378–400 in Bolle, ed., Le Plateau Vivarais-Lignon, 1992.

Moorhead, Caroline. Village of Secrets: Defying the Nazis in Vichy France. Toronto: Random House Canada, 2014.

Nora, Pierre. Les Lieux de mémoire. Paris: Gallimard, 1986.

Obama, Barack. "Remarks." National Rotunda of the Capitol, Washington, DC, 23 April, 2009. http://www.ushmm.org/remember/days-of-/past-days-of-remembrance/2009-days-of-remembrance/remarks-by-barack-obama-part-1

Olick, Jeffrey K. "Introduction," 1–16 in States of Memory: Continuities, Conflicts and

Transformations in National Retrospection. Edited by Jeffrey K. Olick. Durham, NC: Duke University Press, 2003. https://doi.org/10.1215/9780822384687-001
—"Products, Processes, and Practices: A Non-Reificatory Approach to Collective Memory," *Biblical Theology Bulletin* 36 (2006): 5–14. https://doi.org/10.1177/01461079060360010201
Olick, Jeffrey K., and Joyce Robbins. "Social Memory Studies: From 'Collective Memory' to Historical Sociology of Mnemonic Practices," *Annual Review of Sociology* 24 (1998): 105–40. https://doi.org/10.1146/annurev.soc.24.1.105
Olick, Jeffrey K., Vered Vinitzky-Seroussi, and Daniel Levy, eds. *The Collective Memory Reader*. Oxford: Oxford University Press, 2011.
Plate, S. Brent. "*Zakhor*: Modern Jewish Memory Built into Architecture," 195–204 in Plate, ed., *Religion, Art, and Visual Culture: A Cross-Cultural Reader*, 2002.
Plate, S. Brent, ed. *Religion, Art, and Visual Culture: A Cross-Cultural Reader*. New York: Palgrave, 2002.
Ricœur, Paul. "Memory – History – Forgetting," 9–19 in *Meaning and Representation in History*. Edited by Jörn Rüsen. Making Sense of History: Studies in Historical Cultures, 7. Oxford: Berghahn Books, 2006.
Robins, Marianne Ruel. "A Grey Site of Memory: Le Chambon-sur-Lignon and Protestant Exceptionalism on the Plateau Vivarais-Lignon," *Church History* 82 (2013): 317–52. https://doi.org/10.1017/S0009640713000103
—"Les Justes, une autre 'Histoire Périlleuse.' Histoire et Mémoire Protestantes sur le Plateau Vivarais-Lignon," *Revue d'Histoire de l'Eglise de France* 101 (2015): 95–120. https://doi.org/10.1484/J.RHEF.5.107559
Sauvage, Pierre. "Does 'Village of Secrets' Falsify French Rescue during the Holocaust?" *Tablet Magazine Online*, 31 October, 2014. https://www.tabletmag.com/jewish-arts-and-culture/books/186652/moorehead-le-chambon
Schwartz, Barry. "Collective Forgetting and the Symbolic Power of Oneness: The Strange Apotheosis of Rosa Parks," *Social Psychology Quarterly* 72 (2009): 123–42. https://doi.org/10.1177/019027250907200204
Trocmé, André. "Cancel Our Debts as We Cancel Those of Our Debtors." Unpublished notes, date unknown. Swarthmore College Peace Collection, Series B, Box 10.
—"Introduction." Unpublished notes, date unknown. Swarthmore College Peace Collection, Series B, Box 7.
—*Mémoires: Notes autobiographiques*. Date unknown. Swarthmore College Peace Collection, Series A, Box 1.
—"Message du Conseil Régional." Date unknown. Swarthmore College Peace Collection, Series C, Misc.
—"The Church – Lamp of the Body," Unpublished essay, date unknown. Swarthmore College Peace Collection, Series B, Box 7.
—"Morale Chrétienne et Objection de Conscience," *Les Cahiers de la Réconciliation* 1933. Available at Swarthmore College Peace Collection Series B, Box 4.
—"De Quelques Erreurs," *Les Cahiers de la Réconciliation* 1935. Available at Swarthmore College Peace Collection, Series B, Box 4.
—*L'Église de Neige*. Le Chambon-sur-Lignon: Messageries Évangeliques, 1943.
—"Plan général d'Études Bibliques, 1943-1944," Swarthmore College Peace Collection, Series B, Box 7.
—"Letter to Nevin Sayre." Unpublished letter, 4 October 1944. Swarthmore College Peace Collection, Series B, Box 1.

—*L'Église et le Désordre International.* Le Chambon-sur-Lignon: Mouvement International de la Réconciliation, 1948.
—"Sermon Delivered at St. George's Church," New York, 1951. Swarthmore College Peace Collection, Series B, Box 10.
—*Jésus et la révolution non-violente.* Geneva: Labor & Fides, 1961.
—"Le Sermon Sur La Montagne et Le Mission de l'Église," Unpublished notes, 1962. Swarthmore College Peace Collection, Series B, Box 6.
—*The Politics of Repentance.* New York: Fellowship Publications, 1953.
—*Jesus and the Nonviolent Revolution.* Translated by Marlin E. Miller and Michael H. Shank. Kitchener, ON: Herald Press, 1973. Repr. Eugene, OR: Wipf & Stock, 1998.
—"Mise au point concernant mon attitude en temps de guerre," 111–16 in Boismorand, *Magda et André Trocmé,* 2007.
Trocmé, André, and Édouard Theis. "Les armes de l'Esprit," 128 in Boismorand, *Magda et André Trocmé,* 2007.
Unsworth, Richard P. *A Portrait of Pacifists: Le Chambon, the Holocaust, and the Lives of André & Magda Trocmé.* Syracuse, NY: Syracuse University Press, 2012.
Yardeni, Myriam. "French Calvinism and Judaism," *Reformation and Renaissance Review* 6 (2004): 294–312. https://doi.org/10.1558/rarr.2004.6.3.294
Young, James E. "The Texture of Memory: Holocaust Memorials and Meaning," 211–5 in Plate, ed., *Religion, Art and Visual Culture,* 2002.
Zerubavel, Eviatar. "Social Memories: Steps towards a Sociology of the Past," 221–4 in Olick, Vinitzky-Seroussi, and Levy, eds., *Collective Memory Reader,* 2011.

Index of References

Hebrew Bible/Old Testament

Genesis		24.1-4	158	33.18-19	46
4.23-24	155	24.19-22	112	34.16	46
18	45	28.5-57	45	37	299
26.11	155			37.11	299
		Joshua		37.31	299
Exodus		2.19	155	104.7	297
3	119			107.20	297
21.23-25	160	Ruth		139.21-22	98
22.2	155	3.10	102	147.18	297
23.11	112				
		1 Samuel		Proverbs	
Leviticus		18.9	46	1–9	288
5.20-26	156			1.1	299
16.29	112	1 Kings		1.1-2	289
19	99	3.13	215	3.9-10	271
19.9-10	112	4.29-34	299	3.13	299
19.9-18	99	5.9	299	3.18	299
19.17-18	77, 99, 101, 160	5.26	299	5.21	46
		10.14-27	215	10.2	275
19.18	98			11.4	275
19.32-37	99	2 Chronicles		12.21	69
19.33-34	99–100	9.13-28	215	14.31	112, 271
20.9	155	16.9	46	15.3	46
23.22	112			18.16	271
24.19-22	160	Job		19	276, 281
		29.12	112	19.4-6	271
Numbers		29.16	112	19.7	272
20.17	301			19.17	112, 264, 272–3
35.27	155	Nehemiah			
		9.1	112	20.27	188
Deuteronomy				22.9	45
11.12	46	Esther		22.22-23	272
14.28-29	112	4.3	112	23.6	45
15.7-11	45			28.2	45
19.10	155	Psalms		28.27	112, 272
19.21	161	24.4	299		

Isaiah		Jeremiah		9.3	112
6	117	16.17	46	9.21	113
49.15	185				
54.10	185	Daniel		Joel	
		4	274	1.1-14	112
		6.10-11	113		

Apocrypha

Wisdom		18.10-13	100	4.7	45, 112
5.16	300	18.13	103	4.7-11	274–5
6.20-21	300	24	294	4.16	45, 112
9	300	28	101	12.8-9	112
12–14	164	28.1-4	100, 161	14.2	112
		28.4	104	14.8	112
Sirach		29.6	112	14.10	112
7.10	112	29.12-13	275		
12.3	112	35.4	112	4 Maccabees	
14.3	45			2.21-23	301
14.10	45	Tobit			
		4	276		

New Testament

Matthew		5.6	63	5.16	97, 186
2.1-18	73	5.8	299	5.17	7, 152, 216
4.1-11	73	5.9-42	62	5.17-19	253
4.17	148	5.10	72, 301	5.17-20	152, 296
4.18	224	5.10-11	13, 295	5.17-48	61
4.21	224	5.10-12	22, 60, 65–6, 69	5.18	153
4.23-25	194			5.19	154
4.24	224	5.11	148, 256	5.20	13, 24, 65, 73, 75, 154, 253, 294
5–7	6, 174, 176, 184, 241	5.11-12	60, 62–3, 75, 147, 296		
5	299, 302	5.12	256, 301	5.21	55
5.1–7.29	293	5.13	150, 176–7, 179–80, 184, 186, 192, 199, 201	5.21-22	82, 155–6, 201, 253
5.1	207, 213			5.21-26	97
5.1-2	7, 177, 293			5.21-48	155
5.1-12	24, 147	5.13-16	13, 75, 324	5.22	23, 97, 187
5.2	5	5.14	177, 179–80, 185, 199	5.22-24	156
5.3	13, 63, 72, 301			5.23-24	97, 156, 176
5.3-10	75, 256	5.14-16	55, 150–1	5.23-26	156
5.3-11	286, 295	5.15	177, 179–80, 186, 199, 201, 325	5.25	187
5.3-12	288			5.25-26	65, 157,
5.5	13, 299				

	176–80, 186, 199	6.2
6.3-4	125, 254, 274
56		229–30, 232–4
5.26	187	6.3	126	6.25-42	22
5.27	55	6.4	97, 117, 255, 274	6.26	97, 177, 178–80, 190, 199, 214–6, 218, 222, 225–6, 228
5.27-28	254				
5.27-29	201	6.5	13, 125, 254		
5.27-30	22, 60, 157	6.5-6	163, 276		
5.28-29	54	6.6	97, 117, 164, 255		
5.28-30	23			6.27	216, 218, 222, 226–7, 231
5.29-30	65, 201	6.7	13, 24, 125, 256		
5.31-32	158				
5.33	55	6.7-8	164	6.28	214–5, 222, 225–7, 300–1
5.33-37	159, 254	6.7-15	7		
5.38	55	6.8-15	323	6.28-30	177–9, 181, 191, 199, 216, 218
5.38-42	96, 160	6.8	97, 213		
5.38-48	22–3, 68–70, 75, 77, 83	6.9	97		
		6.9-15	164	6.29	215, 218, 222, 224–5, 227, 229, 231, 300–1
5.38-39	83, 96	6.12	60, 62, 97, 321		
5.39	60, 63, 65, 76, 96				
		6.14-15	60, 62, 97		
5.40	96, 162	6.15	128	6.30	165, 227–9, 231
5.40-42	60, 63, 99, 162	6.16	125, 254		
		6.16-18	163	6.31	212–6, 218–20, 222–3, 225, 230–1
5.41	83, 96–7, 162	6.16-24	66		
5.42	56, 65, 76, 96	6.17-20	60		
		6.18	97, 117, 255	6.31-32	72
5.43	55, 83, 98	6.19-21	56, 189, 274	6.31-33	215, 219
5.43-48	98, 160	6.19-24	165, 224	6.32	24, 97, 219, 222, 227–9
5.44	63, 98, 323	6.20-21	148		
5.44-48	62	6.22-23	37–9, 57, 177, 179–80, 188, 199, 201	6.33	212–3, 222, 224, 227, 296
5.45	24, 72, 97–8, 228				
				6.34	212–6, 218–20, 222–3, 227, 230
5.46	67, 98	6.23	46, 323		
5.46-47	72, 160	6.24	56, 63, 177, 179–80, 199, 224, 232		
5.47	24, 98, 256			7.1	192
5.48	72, 97–8, 321			7.1-5	56, 97, 166, 194, 322
5.53-36	159	6.24-26	60		
6	214, 275, 279, 281	6.24-34	66, 207, 211, 212–20, 22–6, 229–30, 215	7.2	177, 179, 181, 192, 199
		6.25			
6.1	75, 117, 274			7.3-5	177, 179, 181, 192, 199
6.1-4	163, 264, 275–6	6.25-30			
		6.25-33	56, 62	7.6	166, 177–81, 193, 199, 324
6.1-8	60, 66	6.25-34	60, 63, 73, 165, 206, 219, 223–4,		
6.1-18	110, 119			7.7-8	177, 180–1, 194, 199
6.1-19	26, 27				

Matthew (cont.)		10.1-39	73	24.1–25.46	
7.7-11	56, 66, 166	10.1-42	293		293
7.9-11	177–81, 194, 199	10.7	148	24.20	113
		10.16-23	75	24.34-35	152
7.11	97, 213	10.37-39	147	24.45-51	182, 200
7.12	7, 167, 192, 216	11.19	300	25.1-13	182
		11.27	178	25.14-30	182
7.13-14	60, 167, 176–81, 195, 199	11.29	300	26.18	293
		12.1-2	255	26.41	113
		12.33	196		
7.15	196, 257	12.38	293	Mark	
7.15-20	167	12.42	300	1.22	133
7.15-23	200, 295	13.1-52	292	1.27	133
7.15-28	60	13.3	201	2.5	297
7.16-20	177, 179–81, 196, 201	13.3-8	183	2.9	297
		13.18-23	183	2.18-22	122
7.19	167	13.24-30	295	4.21	150–1
7.21	60, 66	13.47-50	201	4.21-25	151
7.21-23	65, 117–8, 167, 257	14.25-27	147	4.24	177, 181, 192
		15.10-11	255	9.29	113
7.21-27	73	16.2-3	201	9.42	158
7.24	5	16.21	73	9.43-48	157
7.24-27	117, 167, 177–81, 196–7, 199–201	17.22-23	73	9.49-50	150
		17.24	293	9.50	177, 180, 184
		18.1-35	293	10.2-12	158
		18.8-9	157	10.23-27	147
7.26-20	199	18.15-18	295	11.6	128
7.27	65	19.3-9	158	11.25	156
7.28	7, 177, 184, 230	19.6	293	13.30-31	152
		19.21	275	13.18	113
7.28-29	233, 258	19.24	185	14.21	177, 180, 186
7.29	24, 65, 74	20.1-16	200–1	14.34-35	177
8	258	20.18-19	73	14.38	113
8.1-3	258	20.25-28	68		
8.8	297	21.33-46	200	Luke	
8.8-9	258	21.41	182	4.16-32	327
8.10-12	259	22.1-14	179, 200	5.33-39	113, 122
8.13	258	22.11-14	295	6.20	63
8.19	293	22.16	293	6.20-33	288
8.19-22	73	22.24	293	6.21	63
8.23-27	73	22.36	293	6.22-23	62
9.2	297	23	295	6.27-36	62, 83, 160
9.11	293	23.1-12	68, 187	6.29	162
9.14-17	113, 122	23.10	293	6.31	167
9.38	62	23.16-22	159	6.32-34	98, 160

6.38	177, 181, 192	12.33	112	Acts	
6.41-42	177, 181, 191	12.33-36	165	3.1	113
6.43-45	177, 181, 196	12.58-59	177, 180,	3.2-3	112
6.48-49	177, 181, 197	13.24-29	177, 181, 195	3.10	112
8.16	151, 177, 180, 186	14.8-14	187	10.2	112
		14.26	189	10.4	112, 276
10.2	62	14.34-35	151, 180, 184, 187	10.31	112
10.30-37	182			10.47-48	276
11.4	62	15.11-32	182	14.23	113
11.9	177, 181, 194	15.24	147	24.17	112
11.11-13	177, 181, 194	15.32	147		
11.29-33	189	16.13	165, 177, 180, 189	1 Corinthians	
11.33	151, 177, 180, 186			4.6-13	301
		16.16-17	152	4.18–7.40	205
11.34-35	177, 180, 188	16.17	153		
11.41	112	16.18	158	1 Timothy	
12	214	18.1	113	6.18-19	275
12.22-31	62	20.16	182		
12.24	177, 180, 190	22.46	113	James	
12.27	177, 181, 191			5.12	159

Other Ancient Sources

Qumran		4Q525		15	286, 288
1Q26	294	1.1	299	15–23	288
		1.2	293	24 ii	288
1Q27	294	2 ii	286, 288, 291, 296, 299	Talmuds	
4Q185		2 ii 1	293	b. Bava Mezi'a	
1–2 ii 8-15	294	2 ii 1-2	294, 299	87a	45
		2 ii 2	294		
		2 ii 2-3	294	m. B.Qam	
4Q299–301		2 ii 3	299	3	155
	294	2 ii 3-4	294		
		2 ii 5	296	m. Ned.	
4Q415–8		2 ii 9	300	1.3	159
	294	2 ii-iii	288	2.5	159
		5	288	6.9–7.5	159
4Q423	294	11–12	294		
		14 ii	288	m. Sanh.	
		14 ii 6-16	294	3.2	159

Christian Authors

Apollinaris	Augustine	Chromatius
157	6, 212, 216–7	157

Chrysostom
Homilies on St. Matthew XVI 135

Hilary 157

Jerome 157

Classical Authors

Aristotle 6, 7, 39, 87, 144, 157

Economics
I 42

Nic. Eth.
5 ch. 3 95
6.2.1–4 6

On Dreams
459b 27-32 45

Poetics
I 7
VII 7
xxi.7-15 139

Rhetoric
2.8 102–3
III.ii.13 139
III.ii.7-15 139
III.ii.10 140
III.ii.12 140
III.xi.1 139
III.xi.2-4 139
III.xi.6 140
III.xi.16 140
x.7–xi.16 139

Empedocles 39

Homer
The Illiad 44

Philo
Post.
101–2 301

Plato 39, 87, 157

Plutarch 45

Quintilian
Institutio oratoria
VII.vi.67-68 141
VII.vi.74 141
VII.vi.75-76 141

Other Writings

Counsels of Wisdom 276
57–60 272
61–65 272

The Dialogue of Pessimism 273, 276

Didache 85, 99, 169
1.3-5 162
1.4 97, 162
1.6 163
2.4 162
3.2 156
8.1 113, 121

1 Enoch
9.4 119

4 Ezra
7.77 275

Gospel of Thomas
47.1-2 190

Psalms of Solomon
9.5 275

Shamash Hymn
118–21 273
122–7 273

SyrBar
24.1 275

Index of Modern Authors

Abrams, D. 13, 29, 80
Aglioti, S. 244, 260
Albright, W. F. 217, 234
Alcorta, C. 246, 262
Alexander, R. 242–3, 259
Algazi, G. 25, 29, 269, 283
Algoe, S. B. 77, 79
Alhakami, A. 79
Allen, W. C. 217, 234
Allison, D. C. 1, 6, 29, 39, 57, 82, 98, 106, 134, 146, 148, 151–2, 154–7, 159, 163, 166, 170–1
Ambady, N. 244, 260
Aminoff, E. 260
Anderson, G. A. 272–6, 283
Arnal, W. E. 62–3, 78
Asad, T. 110, 114, 125, 128
Assavavirulhakarn, P. 289, 303
Assmann, J. 314, 329
Atkinson, Q. 250, 259
Atran, S. 249, 260
Atwood, M. 40–2, 58
Aureli, F. 94, 96, 105
Austin, J. I. 297, 303
Avenanti, A. 244, 260
Axelrod, R. 243, 260

Bacon, B. W. 4, 29, 134, 170
Balch, D. L. 12, 29, 252, 262
Banks, R. 133, 170
Barclay, P. 278, 283
Baron-Cohen, S. 48–50, 52, 58
Barr, A. 261
Barret, J. L. 115–6, 128
Barreto, E. D. 20–1, 29
Barrett, C. 261
Barrett, L. F. 21–2, 29, 261
Batten, A. J. 324, 329

Bauckham, R. 61, 78
Baumgarten, A. I 11, 29
Becker, A. H. 11–2, 30
Becker, E.-M. 11–2, 30
Becker, H.-J. 11, 30, 286, 304
Beebe, B. 47, 58
Bekoff, M. 87, 105
Bell, C. 110, 123, 125, 128
Bellah, R. N. 309, 329
Bergen, B. 146, 170
Bering, J. 249–50, 260–1
Berkowitz, L. 94, 105
Berndsen, 70, 78
Bertram, G. 289, 303
Betz, H. D. 1, 5, 7, 30, 38–9, 55–6, 58, 118–9, 128, 147–8, 160–2, 164–5, 170, 212–6, 219–21, 223–6, 228–32, 234, 298, 303
Binsted, K. 146, 170
Bloom, G. 22
Bloom, P. 245, 260
Boismorand, P. 318, 320, 323, 330, 332
Bolyanatz, A. 261
Boon, J. A. 290, 303
Boulet, F. 308–9, 330
Bouratt, P. 250, 259
Bourdieu, P. 124, 128, 267, 269–70, 283
Bovon, F. 84, 105
Bowlby, J. 46, 58
Boyarin, D. 11, 30
Boyd, R. 243, 247, 260–1
Boyer, P. 19, 30, 115, 128, 249, 260
Braeckman, J. 247, 262–3
Brala, M. M. 10, 30
Brdar, M. 146, 170
Brdar-Szabó, R. 146, 170

Bressler, E. R. 33, 257, 262
Broer, I. 134, 170
Brooke, G. J. 288, 292–3, 298, 302–3
Brosnan, S. F. 87, 94, 105, 109
Brown, H. S. 80
Bruce, V. 48
Brueggeman, W. 300–1, 303
Bulbulia, J. 245, 262
Bultmann, R. 3, 5
Burke, K. 297, 303
Burkitt, F. C. 158, 170
Byrskog, S. 134, 170

Cabanel, P. 316, 330
Caillé, A. 266, 283
Calder, A. J. 52, 58
Cameron, L. 53, 58
Cano Mora, L. 144–5, 170
Cardenas, J. C. 261
Carlston, C. E. 205, 217, 220, 225, 228, 232, 234
Carr, L. 92, 105
Carter, R. 140, 145, 172
Carter, W. 1, 11, 30
Casey, M. 9, 30, 135, 170
Catchpole, D. R. 160, 171
Chalamet, C. 316–21, 324, 330
Charlesworth, J. H. 288, 303
Chernoff, J. 53, 58
Chiao, J. Y. 244, 260
Christoffels, I. 58
Claridge, C. 136–8, 140, 145, 154, 171
Cohen, J. D. 106
Cohen, S. J. D. 252, 260
Collins, R. F. 158, 171
Colston, H. L. 139–40, 171
Corazza, S. 310, 330
Cords, M. 96, 105
Cosmides, L. 247, 262
Coulson, S. 137, 171
Craighero, L. 92, 108
Cromhout, M. 161, 171
Crossan, J. D. 42, 58

Crouch, C. L. 100, 105
Cvitanić, J. 64, 79

d'Aquili, E. G. 80, 108
Dake, K. 67, 81
Dalgleish, T. 94, 108
Damasio, A. 87, 105
Dant, T. 50, 58
Dapretto, M. 92, 107
Darley, J. M. 106
Darwin, C. 85, 88, 106
Davies, W. D. 7, 11, 30, 82, 98, 106, 134, 148, 151–2, 154–7, 159, 163, 166, 171
Dawkins, R. 85–6, 90, 106
de Oliveira, R. P. 10, 32
de Oliveira-Souza, R. 107
de Roo, J. C. R. 287, 293, 305
de Waal, F. B. M. 87, 91–6, 103, 10–6, 108–9, 244, 263
DeBruine, L. M. 245, 260
Deignan, A. 53, 58
Deines, R. 152–3, 171
deMarici, V. 80, 108
DeMaris, R. 26, 30
Derrida, J. 268, 281, 283
DeSilva, D. A. 74–5, 79
Destro, M. F. 92, 108
Di Paolo, E. 57–8
Dibelius, M. 3, 5
Dillon, R. J. 214, 228, 235
Dionigi, A. 43, 58
Dodd, C. H. 292, 303
Dolan, R. J. 262
Douglas, M. 67–9, 79
Dowling, M. B. 77, 79
Drury, J. 184, 203
Dubeau, M.-C. 105
Dugatkin, L. A. 89, 106
Dunbar, R. 242, 247, 260,
Dunbar, R. I. M. 277, 284
Dunn, J. D. G. 300, 303
Durkheim, E. 122–3, 129, 312
Dwyer, S. 21, 31, 69, 79

Index of Modern Authors 341

East, M. P. 94, 106
Eidevall, G. 265, 283
Ekeh, P. P. 265, 283
Elfenbein, H. A. 244, 260
Ellemers, N. 13, 30
Ellingsen, T. 247, 249, 260
Elliott, J. H. 44–5, 58, 68, 79
Emel, J. 80
Ensminger, J. 261
Eskritt, M. 59
Esler, P. F. 2, 13, 23, 30–1, 71–2, 286, 290, 295–7, 303

Fabry, H.-J. 288, 303
Farroni, T. 47, 58
Fauconnier, G. 137–8, 171
Fehr, E. 243, 248, 260
Fentress, J. 313, 315, 330
Ferguson, N. 23, 32
Fessler, D. M. T. 261
Fiedler, K. 299, 303
Finucane, M. L. 64, 66, 79
Firth, U. 50, 58
Fischbacher, U. 243, 248, 260
Fischer, R. 245, 262
Fiske, S. T. 244, 260
Fitzmyer, J. A. 288, 304
Fletcher, J. A. 90, 104, 109
Fludernik, M. 202–3
Foglia, L. 16, 34
Foster, B. R. 273, 283
Foster, G. M. 43, 58,
Frank, R. H. 248, 261
Frith, C. D. 262
Frye, N. 41, 58
Funk, R. W. 135, 171

Gale, A. M. 61, 79, 148, 171
Gambarotto, L. 317, 330
Gärdenfors, P. 92, 106
Geeraerts, D. 22, 31
Geertz, C. 126, 129
Gibson, J. B. 127, 129
Gintis, H. 243, 260–1
Goble, R. 80

Godbout, J. T. 266, 283
Goddard, C. 10, 31
Goff, M. J. 288, 294, 304
Gordon, H. L. 260
Gouldner, A. 267, 284
Grafman, J. 107
Greene, J. D. 86–9, 106
Greenman, J. P. 1, 31
Gregory, C. A. 266–7, 284
Grice, P. 141–2, 171
Gril-Mariotte, A. 309, 330
Griswold, C. L. 95, 106
Grootendorst, R. 182, 203, 205–11, 217, 221, 229–30, 235
Grose, P. 329–30
Gross, C. G. 39, 58
Gudme, A. K. de Hemmer, 264, 270, 284
Guelich, R. A. 147–8, 153, 171, 287, 304
Gurven, M. 261
Guthrie, S. E. 18, 31
Gwako, E. 261

Hacham, N. 113, 129
Hagner, D. 174, 184–5, 187–90, 193–8, 201, 203, 212–5, 217–20, 224–5, 235
Haidt, J. 6, 15, 31, 69, 77, 79, 86–9, 94, 106, 240, 261
Hains, S. 47, 59
Halbwachs, M. 312–3, 330
Haley, K. J. 248, 261
Hallie, P. 307, 310, 330
Hamilton, W. D. 241, 243, 260–1
Han, S. 263
Hanson, K. C. 290, 304
Harrington, D. J. 37, 58
Haslam, S. A. 13, 30, 72, 79, 290–1, 296, 304–5
Hatton, P. T. H. 271, 284
Hauser, M. 21, 31, 69, 79
Hedrick, C. W. 174, 203
Heider, F. 19, 31
Heine, B. 22, 31

Heinemann, J. 114, 129
Henkemans, F. S. 206–10, 217, 221, 229–30, 235
Henrich, J. 247, 261
Henry, P. 308, 330
Herzog, W. R. 133, 171
Hewer, A. 107
Hietanen, M. 205, 207, 235
Hilferty, J. 10, 31
Hintze, A. 276, 284
Hoffman, M. L. 91–3, 106
Hogg, M. A. 13, 29, 71, 80–1, 291, 296, 304
Holland, M. P. 104, 106
Holldobler, B. 241, 261
Hoover, R. W. 135, 171
Horden, P. 42, 59
Horn, L. 108
Horsley, R. A. 62, 79
Houtlosser, P. 206, 210–1, 235
Howell, T. D. 150, 171
Huber, L. 108
Huebner, B. 21, 31, 69, 79
Hurowitz, V. A. 273, 284

Iacoboni, M. 92, 105, 107
Iidaka, T. 260
Iredale, W. 278, 284
Irons, W. 245–6, 261
Iser, W. 175, 203

Jackson, B. S. 163, 171
Jackson, S. 206–7, 210, 235
Jaffe, J. 47, 58
Janik, A. S. 204
Janzen, W. 289, 304
Jeremias, J. 134, 171
Johannesson, M. 247, 249, 260
Johnson, D. 250, 260–1
Johnson, L. T. 99, 107, 126, 129
Johnson, M. 9, 17, 31, 58, 143, 172
Johnson, S. M. 79
Jonas, D. 177, 203
Joosten, J. 103, 107

Kahneman, D. 15–6, 31, 34, 239–40, 261
Kaiser, M. K. 16, 32
Kampen, J. I. 287–8, 304
Kanekar, S. 77, 79
Käser, W. 289, 304
Kasperson, R. E. 73, 80
Kaye, A. S. 9, 31
Kazen, T. 25, 31, 84, 86, 88–9, 94, 107, 133–4, 137, 156, 158, 160–1, 171
Keane, J. 58
Keener, C. S. 163, 172, 174, 203, 293, 304
Keith, C. 133, 172
Keller, S. B. 139–40, 171
Kingsbury, J. D. 301, 304
Kirk, A. 310, 330
Kissinger, W. S. 1, 31, 315, 330
Kloppenborg, J. S. 99, 107
Knuuttila, S. 87, 107
Kodjak, A. 9, 31
Kohlberg, L. 86, 107
Kolsawalla, M. B. 77, 79
Konstan, D. 95, 101–3, 106–7
Krebs, D. L. 94, 107
Krueger, F. 107
Krüger, O. 250, 261
Kruiger, T. 182, 203, 206–8, 211, 221, 235

Lahti, N. 182, 203, 205, 235,
Lahti, D. C. 255, 261
Laidlaw, J. 268–9, 284
Lakoff, G. 9–10, 17, 31–2, 53, 143, 172
Lambert, W. G. 273, 284
Lamoreaux, J. T. 26, 30
Langton, S. R. H. 48, 59
Larsen, T. 1, 31
Lausberg, H. 184, 200, 203
Lawrence, A. D. 58
Lawson, E. T. 27, 32, 114–7, 121, 126, 129

Lee, K. 52, 59
Lenzi, L. 105
Leslie, A. M. 50, 58
Lesorogol, C. 261
Levine, C. 107
Lewis, D. K. 141–2, 172
Lichtenberger, H. 286, 304
Lieu, J. 253, 261
Lipp, W. 76, 80
Lüdtke, U. 23, 31
Luomanen, P. 3, 5, 7, 12–3, 29, 32, 295, 302, 304
Luz, U. 1, 7, 32, 39–40, 84, 98, 107, 148, 151–3, 155–7, 159, 163–4, 172, 212–5, 217–8, 220, 224, 228, 231–2, 235, 294–5, 304

Macaskill, G. 294, 304
Madsen, R. 329
Malina, B. J. 43, 59, 75, 80, 151, 172
Malinowski, B. 266, 268, 284
Manson, T. W. 176, 203
Marlowe, F. W. 261
Marques, J. M. 71, 80
Martin, D. B.
Merz, A. 85, 99, 108
Milavec, A. 162, 172
Miller, W. I. 95, 107, 163, 172
Mirguet, F. 102–3, 107
Mitchell, N. D. 110, 114, 129
Mödritzer, H. 76, 80
Mohrlang, R. 5, 32
Moll, J. 87, 107
Moorhead, C. 310, 330
Moss, C. R. 39, 59
Mroczek, E. 288, 304
Muir, D. 26, 30, 47, 59

Naiden, F. S. 118–9, 129
Nesse, R. M. 245, 247–8, 261
Nettle, D. 277, 284
Newberg, A. B. 77, 80, 94, 108
Newberg, S. K. 108
Newman, J. H. 300, 305

Neyrey, J. H. 63, 70, 75–6, 80, 118–9, 129
Nihan, C. 100, 108, 161, 172
Nogawa, J. 260
Nora, P. 309, 330
Norenzayan, A. 24–5, 32, 24–50, 261–2, 278–80, 282, 284
Nowak, M. A. 243, 249, 262, 277, 282, 284
Nystrom, L. E. 106

O'Brien, D. T. 279, 285
O'Doherty, J. P. 262
Oakes, P. J. 72, 79, 80–1, 290–1, 305
Oakley, T. 137, 171
Obama, B. 308, 330
Obeyeskere, G. 111, 129
Olick, J. K. 311–5, 330, 332
Osborne, R. 270, 281, 284
Overman, J. A. 12, 32
Owen, A. M. 58

Páez, D. 80
Parker, R. 271, 284
Parry, J. 269
Paschke, B. 7, 32
Pelikan, J. 1, 32
Penner, J. 113, 129
Perdue, L. G. 290, 300
Perkins, P. 134, 172
Pierce, J. 87, 105
Pinker, S. 279, 284
Plate, S. B. 313, 331
Platow, M. J. 296, 304
Porter, S. E. 22, 33
Power, M. J. 94, 108
Preston, S. D. 87, 91, 108
Price, M. E. 247, 262
Prinz, J. J. 69, 80
Przybylski, B. 5, 33
Puech, E. 286–8, 292–3, 305
Pulleyn, S. 119, 129
Purcell, N. 42, 59
Pyysiäinen, I. 7, 12–3, 29, 32–3

Racine, T. P. 48, 59
Räisänen, H. 276, 284
Range, F. 94, 108
Rappaport, R. A. 26, 33, 126–7, 129, 297, 305
Ratick, S. 80
Raynolds, K. J. 13, 34
Reader, W. 21, 34
Reddish, P. 245, 262
Reddy, V. 47–9, 59
Reed, J. 42, 58
Reicher, S. D. 81, 296, 304
Reid, S. A. 291, 296, 304
Reiser, M. 76, 80
Renn, O. 80
Reynolds, K. J. 79
Rhemtulla, M. 250, 262
Richerson, P. J. 243, 260
Ricœur, P. 311, 331
Rieke, R. 204
Rizzolatti, G. 92, 108
Robbins, J. 312, 331
Robins, M. R. 308, 331
Rohrbaugh, R. I. 151, 172
Roitto, R. 23, 25, 33, 71, 80
Rosch, E. 14, 34
Roth, M. T. 157, 172

Sadato, N. 260
Sahlins, M. 266, 285
Saldarini, A. J. 12, 33, 295, 305
Sanders, E. P. 3–5, 33, 77, 81
Sauvage, P. 310, 331
Schaffer, D. M. 16
Schaffner, C. 96, 105
Schmid, J. 299, 303
Schneider, D. M. 104, 108
Schofield, M. 157, 173
Schulz, S. 4, 33
Schwartz, B. 310, 331
Schweizer, E. 3, 33, 61, 81
Scott, S. K. 58
Seaford, R. 265, 267, 285
Searle, J. R. 297, 305

Segal, E. M. 202–3
Sesma, A. 279, 285
Seymour, B. 262
Shariff, A. F. 25, 32, 250, 262, 280, 284
Shaw, T. M. 157, 173
Sigmund, K. 249, 262, 277, 282, 284
Sihvola, J. 87, 107
Simmel, M. 19, 31
Simonetti, M. 153, 157, 173
Sinding, M. 299, 305
Singer, T. 92, 244, 262
Sirigu, A. 244, 260
Sjöberg, L. 67–8, 81
Slingerland, E. 40, 59
Slovic, P. 65, 79–81
Snodgrass, K. R. 176, 181, 198, 203
Sommerville, R. B. 106
Sørensen, J. 27, 33
Sosis, R. 26, 33, 246–7, 257, 262
Spackman, J. S. 14, 33
Spencer, S. R. 1, 21, 31, 33, 85
Sperber, D. 142–4, 173
Stambaugh, J. E. 252, 262
Stanton, G. N. 7, 12, 33
Stephan, K. E. 262
Stern, D. 47, 58
Steyrer, J. 76, 81
Stowers, S. 271, 285
Sullivan, W. 329
Swidler, A. 329
Symons, L. A. 59
Syreeni, K. 5–8, 33, 97, 99, 108, 160, 173

Tajfel, H. 12–3, 291, 305
Talbert, C. H. 6, 33, 63, 73, 81, 296, 305
Taves, A. 27–8, 33, 114, 129
Teehan, J. 24, 88, 108, 251, 262, 282, 285
Terrien, S. 290, 305
Thatcher, T. 310, 330

Theis, E. 311, 323, 328, 332
Theissen, G. 2, 34, 62, 77, 81, 85, 99, 108, 301, 305
Thiselton, A. C. 297, 305
Thompson, E. 14, 34, 56–9
Thurén, L. 174, 177, 180, 182, 203
Thurnheer, S. 96, 105
Tipton, S. M. 329
Tomasello, M. 93, 108
Tooby, J. 247, 262
Toulmin, S. E. 10, 34, 182–3, 204
Tov, E. 292, 305
Tracer, D. P. 261
Trevarthen, C. 47, 59
Trivers, R. L. 90, 108, 242, 262
Trocmé, A. 307–8, 310–1, 315–9, 331–2
Tullberg, J. 265, 280–2, 285
Turner, J. C. 12–3, 34, 53, 71, 79, 81, 290–1, 305
Turner, M. 137–8, 171,
Tversky, A. 15, 34

Ullucci, D. C. 25, 34, 265, 267, 270, 285
Ulmer, R. 44–5, 59
Unsworth, R. P. 311, 317–9, 321, 324, 332
Uro, R. 13, 26, 32, 34, 62, 81
Uusimäki, E. 286, 288, 298–9, 306

Vaage, L. E. 157, 173
Vahrenhorst, M. 159, 173
Valera, F. J. 14, 34
van Aarde, A. 61–2, 81
van Baal, J. 267, 283
van der Pligt, J. 70, 78
van Eemeren, F. H. 182, 203, 205–11, 217, 221, 229–30, 235
van Hiel, A. 262
van Lange, P. A. 13, 30, 34
van Roosmalen, A. 96, 109
van Schaik, C. P. 96, 105
van Veelen, M. 277, 279, 285
van Vugt, M. 278, 284

van Wees, H. 265, 285
van Wolkenten, M. 94, 109
Vanneste, S. 247, 262–3
Verheyden, J. 299, 306
Verplaetse, J. 247, 262–3
Versnel, H. S. 118–9, 129
Vickers, B. 146, 173
Viranyi, Z. 108
Viviano, B. T. 288, 306
Vledder, E.-J. 61–2, 81
Voitila, A. 188, 204
von Hasselt, V. B. 52, 58

Wagner-Hasel, B. 266, 285
Wang, X. 263
Watt, R. J. 48, 59
Watts, F. N. 94, 106
Weber, E. U. 65, 81
Westermarck, E. 44, 59
Wetherell, M. S. 81
White, L. J. 68, 81
Whitehouse, H. 115, 117–8, 120–2, 126, 129
Wickham, C. 313, 315, 330
Wierzbicka, A. 8–10, 34
Wievorka, A. 309, 330
Wildavsky, A. 67–9, 79, 81
Wilson, D. 142–4, 173
Wilson, D. S. 89–90, 109, 279, 285
Wilson, E. O. 85, 104, 109, 241, 261
Wilson, R. A. 16, 34
Wilson, R. B. 75, 81
Windisch, H. 3, 4, 34
Workman, L. 21, 34

Xu, X. 244, 263

Yanchar, S. C. 14, 33
Yardeni, M. 316, 332
Young, A. W. 58
Young, J. E. 315, 332

Zahavi, Am. 246, 263, 278–9, 285
Zahavi, Av. 246, 263, 278, 285

Zahn, R. 107
Zapatero, F. 64, 79
Zerbe, G. M. 84, 97–9, 101, 109
Zerubavel, E. 25, 34, 312–3, 332

Ziker, J. 261
Zimmermann, R. 174, 176, 204
Zuo, X. 263
Zwick, M. 90, 104, 109

Index of Subjects

adaptation (evolution, see also *evolution*) 18, 24, 52, 83, 89–90, 94, 114, 162, 241, 243, 250
afterlife 276
agency, perception of 15–9, 45, 93, 114–7, 249, 259, 269
almsgiving (see also *charity*) 112, 125–6, 163, 168, 254, 264–5, 272, 274–7
altruism 82–3, 85, 89–91, 93, 96–101, 103–4, 242–4, 247, 249, 265, 273, 277–8, 280–2, 307
Aristotle 6–7, 9, 42, 87, 102–3, 139–40
attribution (psychology) 18–9, 115
Augustine 311

babies, cognitive development of, see *infant cognition*
beatitudes, macarisms 7–8, 13, 63, 66, 69, 71–2, 75, 147–50, 286–98, 301–2, 304–5, 319
belonging (social) 78, 91, 227, 257, 298, 312–3
blending theory (cognitive science) 10, 22, 136–9, 144, 149, 151–2, 156, 159, 168
bodily cognition, see *embodied cognition*
body-place-tool-experience (see also *embodied cognition* and *enacted cognition*) 16

challenge and riposte (see also *conflict*) 77
charisma (sociology) 76
charity (see also *almsgiving*) 100, 265, 273, 275–7

cheaters (game-theory, evolution, see also *free-riders* and *defectors*) 243, 247–50, 252, 277–8, 282
cheek, turning the other (see also *conflict*) 70, 96, 160–1, 327
childhood development (psychology) 21, 39, 47–8, 50, 115–6
Chrysostom, John 135
collectivistic cultures 77
community, the Matthean 12–4, 23–4, 26, 60–4, 67–9, 71–2, 74–5, 78, 112, 124–5, 127–8, 154, 160, 162, 164, 169, 251, 254, 257
compensation (see also *conflict*) 95, 97, 163
conflict
 -challenge and riposte 77
 -cheek, turning the other 70, 96, 160–1, 327
 -compensation 95, 97, 163
 -enemies, love of 82, 84–5, 97–101, 104, 126, 155, 160–1
 -forgiveness 83, 85, 93–7, 99–101, 112, 128, 156, 326
 -non-retaliation 20, 22, 76–7, 85, 96–8, 101
 -nonviolence 77, 307–8, 318–9, 322–4, 327–8
 -persecution 63, 66, 72, 75, 82, 148–9, 160–2, 256–7, 296, 307, 313, 316, 328
 -punishment 24–5, 45, 155–7, 247–50, 253, 255, 258
 -reconciliation 94–7, 99, 320
 -retaliation and revenge 76, 93–7, 100–1, 162
 -tit-for-tat 90, 98, 160

contagion, emotional (see also *emotions*) 91–3
cooperation 24–6, 86, 90, 96, 242–3, 247–50, 252, 254–5, 257, 265, 278–80, 282, 284
costliness (risk estimation, game-theory, commitment signaling) 18, 24–6, 33, 124, 245–8, 254–5, 257, 259
CPS-agent (see also *ritual*) 115–6
credibility (rhetoric, see also *rhetoric*) 177, 179–81, 183, 196, 198, 200, 202

Darwin, Charles 85
defectors (game-theory, see also *cheaters* and *free-riders*) 90, 243, 253
Didache, the 85, 113, 121, 162–3, 169
disability studies 20
disgust (see also *emotions*) 65, 86, 88–9, 244, 318
doctrinal mode (ritual, see also *ritual*) 120–2
dread (risk psychology, see also *risk* and *emotions*) 65
dual inheritance theory (see also *evolution*) 19, 27

egalitarian communities 68–9
embedded cognition 16–7, 37–8, 40, 44–5, 56, 116
embodied cognition 2, 9, 14, 16–7, 20, 23, 28, 37–40, 43, 45–6, 49–50, 53, 55–7, 122, 124, 127
emotions 2, 5–6, 9, 21–2, 29, 50, 64–7, 69–72, 78, 83, 85–9, 91–7, 102–5, 120, 133, 137–8, 140, 144–5, 149–51, 153, 156–7, 161, 163–4, 166, 168–9, 175, 181–2, 202, 233, 240, 245, 248
-contagion, emotional 91–3
-disgust 65, 86, 88–9, 244, 318
-dread (risk psychology) 65
-empathy 22, 49, 52, 57, 83, 86, 88–9, 91–6, 101–4, 244–6, 250
-love 22, 77, 84–5, 97–8, 100, 133, 160–1, 167, 189–90, 201, 320–1, 323
empathy (see also *emotions*) 22, 49, 52, 57, 83, 86, 88–9, 91–6, 101–4, 244–6, 250
enacted cognition 14, 16–7, 37, 49, 53, 56–7, 127
enemies, love of (see also *conflict*) 82, 84–5, 97–101, 104, 126, 155, 160–1
eschatology 73, 118, 198, 201, 286, 322
evolution 2, 18–9, 21–2, 24–5, 27, 52, 83, 85–91, 93–5, 98, 104, 114–5, 143, 239–43, 245–52, 257, 259, 264–5, 277–80
-adaptation 18, 24, 52, 83, 89–90, 94, 114, 162, 241, 243, 250
-dual inheritance theory 19, 27
-genetics 18–9, 86, 241–2, 244–5
-innateness 2, 5, 8, 13, 16, 18–22, 27, 46–7, 86, 104, 233, 244
-primates 87, 91–4, 96
exaggeration (rhetoric, see also *hyperbole* and *rhetoric*) 10, 23, 133, 136, 139, 147, 151, 155–6, 160–1, 164–5, 167–8

fasting (see also *ritual*) 26, 112–3, 117, 121–2, 125, 164, 168, 255
feelings, see *emotions*
forgiveness (see also *conflict*) 83, 85, 93–7, 99–101, 112, 128, 156, 326
free-riders (see also *cheaters* and *defectors*) 277–9
Freud, Sigmund 240

Gandhi, Mahatma 327–8
genetics (see also *evolution*) 18–9, 86, 241–2, 244–5

Gentiles 98, 160, 193, 213, 219, 221, 227–8, 256
gift-giving (see also *reciprocity*) 25, 28, 121, 163, 194–5, 199, 264–71, 273–8, 280–2
Grilli di Cortona, Magda 319
group-grid (anthropology) 68–9
group maintenance, see *belonging, conflict, forgiveness, marginalization, meta-contrast theory, self-categorization theory, outgroups, punishment*

honor (cultural value) 43, 69, 72, 75–6, 95, 155–7, 271, 289
Huguenots 308, 316, 320
humor 23, 56, 136, 144–6, 156, 158, 169
hyperactive agent-detection device (HADD, see also *theory of mind*) 115
hyperbole (rhetoric, see also *exaggeration, rhetoric* and *language*) 23, 135–61, 163–9, 218

imagistic mode (ritual, see also *ritual*) 120
infant cognition 46–9, 245
innateness (see also *evolution*) 2, 5, 8, 13, 16, 18–22, 27, 46–7, 86, 104, 233, 244
intersubjectivity (see also *theory of mind*) 47–8, 50
itinerancy 61, 268

language, function and nature of 9–10, 17, 22, 53–4, 124, 135, 140–7, 149, 153, 158, 160, 169, 245, 298
-hyperbole 23, 135–61, 163–9, 218
-metaphor 9–10, 17, 42, 53, 55, 57, 63, 105, 135–6, 139–44, 146–7, 150, 152, 167–70, 174, 176, 184–5, 188, 195, 215, 232, 300–1
-metonymy 139, 146
-relevance theory 136, 142–4, 153–4, 168–9
linguistics, see *language, function and nature of* 34
love (see also *emotions*) 22, 77, 84, 85, 97–8, 100, 133, 160–1, 167, 189–90, 201, 320–1, 323

macarisms, see *beatitudes*
marginalization, social 63, 78, 257
Matthean community, the, see *community, the Matthean*
Mediterranean culture 38, 40–3, 45, 68, 111
memory, social 25–6, 120–1, 126, 309–16, 323, 329
meta-contrast principle 23, 72
metaphor (see also *language*) 9–10, 17, 42, 53, 55, 57, 63, 105, 135–6, 139–44, 146–7, 150, 152, 167–70, 174, 176, 184–5, 188, 195, 215, 232, 300–1
metonymy (see also *language*) 139, 146
morality 6, 22, 24, 37–8, 44, 46, 69–72, 75–6, 78, 82–3, 85–9, 97–8, 104, 126, 134, 150, 152, 154, 168, 175, 243–7, 249–51, 253–5, 257, 259, 265, 267, 279, 309, 311, 320–1, 327
motivation 21, 69, 87–9, 163, 166, 168, 281

narrative 72–4, 164, 174, 176, 178–81, 183–4, 188, 198, 200, 202, 309, 314–5, 322
non-retaliation (see also *conflict*) 20, 22, 76–7, 85, 96–8, 101
nonviolence (see also *conflict*) 77, 307–8, 318–9, 322–4, 327–8

oaths 159–60
outgroups (sociology) 13, 20, 24, 72, 75, 99, 244, 253, 258, 295, 298

parables 7–8, 22, 152, 174–90, 193–4, 196–8, 200–3
persecution (see also *conflict*) 63, 66, 72, 75, 82, 148–9, 160–2, 256–7, 296, 307, 313, 316, 328
perspective-taking (cognitive psychology, see also *theory of mind*) 91–3
Plato 39, 87
pragma-dialectics (rhetoric, see also *rhetoric*) 10, 205–8, 210, 229–30, 234
prayer (see also *ritual*) 26, 112–9, 121, 123–5, 127–8, 160–1, 164, 166, 168, 318, 323–4, 326
primates (see also *evolution*) 87, 91–4, 96
prosociality 50, 82–3, 85, 88–90, 93, 98, 160–1, 278–81
proto-morality (see also *morality*) 87
punishment (see also *conflict*) 24–5, 45, 155–7, 247–50, 253, 255, 258

reciprocity (see also *gift-giving*) 25, 119, 242–3, 264–73, 275–8, 280–2
reconciliation (see also *conflict*) 94–7, 99, 320
relevance theory (see also *language*) 136, 142–4, 153–4, 168–9
remembrance, see *memory*
reputation (sociology) 248–9, 277–8, 282
retaliation and revenge (see also *conflict*) 76, 93–7, 100–1, 162
rhetoric
  -credibility 177, 179–81, 183, 196, 198, 200, 202
  -exaggeration 10, 23, 133, 136, 139, 147, 151, 155–6, 160–1, 164–5, 167–8
  -hyperbole 23, 135–61, 163–9, 218
  -pragma-dialectics 10, 205–8, 210, 229–30, 234
risk, perception of 2, 24, 60, 62–8, 70–5, 78, 197, 270, 277–8, 282, 328
ritual 2, 19, 24–9, 95, 110–2, 114–29, 163–4, 168–9, 245–6, 254–5, 268, 312–3
  -CPS-agent 115–6
  -doctrinal mode, imagistic mode 120–2
  -fasting 26, 112–3, 117, 121–2, 125, 164, 168, 255
  -prayer 26, 112–9, 121, 123–5, 127–8, 160–1, 164, 166, 168, 318, 323–4, 326

Sally-Anne test, the (see also *theory of mind*) 51
self-categorization theory 23, 290–1, 298
self-stigmatization 74, 76–7
shame 63, 69–70, 74–6, 78, 88, 94, 312–3
signaling 24, 26, 245–8, 250, 252–7, 259, 278
stereotyping 299
swearing, see *oaths*

theory of mind
  -hyperactive agent-detection device (HADD) 115
  -intersubjectivity 47–8, 50
  -perspective-taking 91–3
  -Sally-Anne test, the 51
tit-for-tat (game theory, see also *conflict*) 90, 98, 160
Trocmé, André 307–8, 310–1, 315–29
Trocmé, Magda 319, 325
trustworthiness (psychology of risk) 73–4, 78

Studies in Ancient Religion and Culture

Series Editors:
Philip L. Tite, University of Washington
Michael Ng, Seattle University
https://www.equinoxpub.com/home/studies-in-ancient-religion-and-culture/

Published:
Death's Dominion: Power, Identity, and Memory at the Fourth-Century Martyr Shrine
Nathaniel J. Morehouse

Social and Cognitive Perspectives on the Sermon on the Mount
Edited by Rikard Roitto, Colleen Shantz, and Petri Luomanen

The Complexity of Conversion: Intersectional Perspectives on Religious Change in Antiquity and Beyond
Edited by Valérie Nicolet and Marianne Bjelland Kartzow

Theorizing "Religion" in Antiquity
Edited by Nickolas P. Roubekas

Forthcoming:
Critical Theory and Early Christianity
Edited by Matthew G. Whitlock

John Cassian and the Creation of Monastic Subjectivity
Joshua Schachterle

Re-Reading the Visions in *The Shepherd of Hermas*
Angela Kim Harkins

The Material of Christian Apocrypha
Edited by Janet E. Spittler

www.ingramcontent.com/pod-product-compliance
Lightning Source LLC
Chambersburg PA
CBHW070011010526
44117CB00011B/1507